MR ATTORNEY

The Attorney General for Ontario in Court,
Cabinet, and Legislature, 1791–1899

In early Upper Canada the attorney general was little more than a skilled functionary – the Crown's chief legal counsel; by the mid-nineteenth century he had become a leading member of cabinet and generally premier. *Mr Attorney* is the story of this transformation and many other aspects of the attorney general's role in nineteenth-century Ontario.

A central figure in the attorney general's rise was John Beverley Robinson, a slippery zealot whose loathing of libertarian ideals drove him to flout the most essential duties of the office. His mishandling of the Alien Question and failure to check civil rights abuses discredited the government and spurred the first public campaign for 'responsible government.' His successors' failure to uphold the rule of law in the face of political repression and increasing pro-government violence helped to provoke the rebellion of 1837; but the discontents of the era were rooted not only in the corrupt administration of justice but in the fact that the law itself offered farmers little protection against exploitation by merchants and financiers.

Moving into the Union period, Paul Romney explains how the attorney general acquired constitutional responsibility for the administration of justice. He reviews important procedural and administrative topics relating to the attorney general's responsibility for law enforcement: the Felon's Counsel Act of 1836, the origin of the county attorney system, the controversy over the idea of a provincial police force. A chapter on the post-Confederation struggle over 'provincial rights' depicts Oliver Mowat as a legal mastermind whose victory was the fruit of intellectual subtlety and tactical ingenuity. Turning to the attorney general's role in late nineteenth-century criminal and civil law reforms, Romney describes how trial by jury was compromised by the introduction of Crown appeal against acquittal in the Criminal Code of 1892.

This important study of the office and the men who held it offers a fresh perspective on the history of nineteenth-century Ontario and illuminates the state of civil liberties in Canada today.

PAUL ROMNEY holds degrees in history from Oxford, Cornell, and Toronto. The author of several articles on nineteenth-century social, political, and legal history, he lives in Baltimore, Maryland.

Mr Attorney

The Attorney General for Ontario in Court, Cabinet, and Legislature 1791-1899

PAUL ROMNEY

Published for The Osgoode Society by
University of Toronto Press
Toronto Buffalo London

© The Osgoode Society 1986
Printed in Canada

ISBN 0-8020-3431-4

Printed on acid-free paper

Canadian Cataloguing in Publication Data

Romney, Paul Martin, 1945–
Mr. Attorney

Includes bibliographical references and index.
ISBN 0-8020-3431-4
1. Attorneys-general – Ontario – History.
2. Justice, Administration of – Ontario – History.
3. Ontario – Constitutional history.
4. Ontario – Politics and government – 19th century.*
I. Osgoode Society. II. Title.

KE0855.R65 1986   342.713'066   c86-094274-0

PICTURE CREDITS

Archives of Ontario:
John Rolph, William Henry Draper,
Sir Oliver Mowat, Sir John A. Macdonald;
The Law Society of Upper Canada:
Sir John Beverley Robinson, Robert Baldwin, ca 1840;
Metropolitan Toronto Library:
William Warren Baldwin, Robert Baldwin, ca 1855,
Henry Sherwood, Sir Allan Napier MacNab;
Public Archives of Canada:
William Lyon Mackenzie (c1993), John A. Macdonald, ca 1856 (c5331),
John Sandfield Macdonald (c10896), younger Oliver Mowat (c8361),
Sir Samuel Henry Strong (PA25835), John Wellington Gwynne (PA27242);
State Library of Victoria:
John Walpole Willis

To Sharon

Contents

PUBLICATIONS OF THE OSGOODE SOCIETY

Foreword

THE OSGOODE SOCIETY

The purpose of The Osgoode Society is to encourage research and writing in the history of Canadian law. The Society, which was incorporated in 1979 and is registered as a charity, was founded at the initiative of the Honourable R. Roy McMurtry, at that time attorney general of Ontario, and officials of The Law Society of Upper Canada. Its efforts to stimulate legal history in Canada include the sponsorship of a fellowship and an annual lectureship, reseach support programs, and work in the field of oral history and legal archives. The Society will publish (at the rate of about one a year) volumes that contribute to legal-historical scholarship in Canada and which are of interest to the Society's members. Included will be studies of the courts, the judiciary, and the legal profession, biographies, collections of documents, studies in criminology and penology, accounts of great trials, and work in the social and economic history of the law.

Current directors of The Osgoode Society are Brian Bucknall, Archie G. Campbell, Douglas Ewart, Martin Friedland, Jane Banfield Haynes, John D. Honsberger, Kenneth Jarvis, Allen M. Linden, Brendan O'Brien, and Peter Oliver. The attorney general for Ontario and the treasurer of The Law Society of Upper Canada are directors *ex officio*. The Society's honorary president is the Honourable R. Roy McMurtry. The annual report and information about membership may be obtained by writing The Osgoode Society, Osgoode Hall, 130 Queen Street West, Toronto, Ontario, Canada, M5H 2N6. Members receive the annual volumes published by the Society.

Mr Attorney originated as a bicentennial project of the Ontario Ministry of the Attorney General. The Ministry conceived the idea of commissioning its history, funded the research and writing, made files, records, and officials available to the author, and placed senior officials on an advisory committee to the author. From the beginning members of The Osgoode Society served on the advisory committee that assisted Dr Romney, and The Society is pleased that the work now appears as its 1986 volume. We thank the Ministry for a grant to help with publication.

Students of nineteenth-century Ontario history will recognize immediately that *Mr Attorney* is a major contribution to revisionist historiography. Based on extensive research in often obscure sources, it focuses on the Office of Attorney General and the administration of justice in such a way as to reinterpret several central themes of nineteenth-century constitutional and political history. Placing legal and administrative issues fully in their social context, Paul Romney argues forcefully that controversies surrounding the administration of justice outraged many Upper Canadians and shaped, often in unanticipated ways, much of Ontario's early political and constitutional development.

Dr Romney presents his thesis in sparkling, and often combative, prose and his arguments will engage and fascinate readers even where they may not always persuade. Not the least of *Mr Attorney*'s virtues is the fact that it is the first serious examination of many developments of critical importance to the administration of justice, including the campaign for the Felon's Counsel Act of 1836, the origin of the county attorney system, developments in trial by jury, and the controversy over the idea of a provincial police force.

This important book will excite considerable controversy among historians and lawyers. It rekindles several old but unresolved historical debates and breaks significant new ground in Canadian legal history.

Brendan O'Brien
President

Peter N. Oliver
Editor-in-Chief

Preface

This book was undertaken on commission from the Ministry of the Attorney General for Ontario in celebration of the provincial bicentenary. Since the project was started only in July 1983, it was unrealistic to hope for publication in the bicentennial year, 1984; still, it was desirable to publish while the reason for the exercise was within living memory.

The constraints of time have influenced the nature of the work. This book does not purport to be a definitive history of the office in nineteenth-century Ontario; that would have required a much more time-consuming use of archives and newspapers than was possible. Such a book would have dealt more fully with the routine functioning of the office as a branch of government, with its role in the shaping of provincial law, and with the administrative response to exigencies such as the rebellion of 1837 and the Fenian incursion of 1866; it would also have noticed the attorney general's ex officio status as head of the provincial bar. I have adopted instead an ecological approach, stepping outside the attorney general's office in order to show how the attorney general, in the performance of his office and the practice of his profession, impinged in different ways on the history of the province and the dominion. This is, so to speak, a *Life and Times* (and occasionally *Crimes*) *of Mr Attorney*. This approach was, it seems to me, as useful as it was inevitable. In the nineteenth century, a succession of attorneys general had a major historical impact, not only ex officio but as leaders of parties and governments. As a result, they figure prominently in historical writing that ignores most of their activities as attorney general and, to the extent that it does discuss those activities, fails to distinguish them clearly from actions taken in other capacities. I was therefore eager to define both the office's role in the major events of provincial and Canadian history and the extent to which an incumbent's role in those events was a function of his capacity as attorney general.

This partly explains my detailed treatment of John Beverley Robinson's performance of the office in the 1820s and of Oliver Mowat's part in the struggle over provincial rights, and, also in a negative sense, my shorter narrative excursion into the land titles crisis of the 1790s. The other motive was my feeling that since both the law itself and the way in which it is administered express social values, the historical importance of the office cannot be grasped without reference to the social context. This accounts for Robert Randal's starring role in chapter 3 and his periodic re-emergence thereafter.

My work on this book has occasioned many pleasant contacts, intellectual and personal, both inside and outside the ministry. At the ministry the then deputy attorney general, Archie Campbell QC, J. Douglas Ewart, and Simon Chester were exacting but sympathetic and helpful taskmasters, scrupulously respectful of my intellectual freedom, as was A. Rendall Dick QC, former deputy attorney general and now under-treasurer of the Law Society of Upper Canada. David Flaherty and Peter Oliver provided good advice and immense encouragement. I enjoyed valuable discussions on different subjects with Frank Armstrong QC, John Beattie, Kenneth Chasse, Douglas Hay, Peter Hogg, and Graham Parker, and with John Edwards, whose authoritative work on the law officers of the Crown is the necessary starting-point even for the least 'internal' study of the office of attorney general in the British commonwealth. Marlene Shore and David Aylward, who read the first draft, provided valuable comments and reassurance. Sharon Kingsland helped me find out what I thought about things.

I gratefully acknowledge the countless enjoyable and stimulating discussions of Upper Canadian history, both in general and in reference to this book, with Victor Russell and Robert Fraser. I thank Robert Fraser too for showing me his unpublished work.

Many pleasurable moments in preparing this book were spent at the Archives of Ontario, the Public Archives of Canada, and the Baldwin Room of the Metropolitan Toronto Library. I am grateful to their staff and to that of the Thomas Fisher Rare Book Library, who showed their usual impeccable understanding of the needs of scholarship.

My work could never have been completed as quickly as it was without the help of three people who were so pre-eminently the 'do' in the ministry's 'can do': Norma Pestano, the head of the word-processing centre; Meg Turner, whose work at the keyboard was accurate and savvy; and above all Mavis Gardiner, a paragon of thoughtful, energetic, and efficient attention to detail.

Robin Sundstrom's help in sifting the Upper Canada Sundries was much appreciated. Kathy Johnson's close and authoritative, yet sensitive, copy-editing was invaluable. But my largest debt is to David Sobel. It is hard to imagine how this work could have been started, let alone completed, without his assiduous, imaginative, and engaged assistance in the research.

John Beverley Robinson and His Enemies

Slippery Zealot: Sir John Beverley Robinson

Doyen of the Bar: William Warren Baldwin

John Walpole Willis in Australia   'Sleek and Wily Traitor': John Rolph

Robert Baldwin, ca 1840

Robert Baldwin and His Enemies

Aged by Grief and Duty: Robert Baldwin, ca 1855

Tribune of the People: William Lyon Mackenzie

Loyalist Scion: Henry Sherwood

'My Politics are Railroads': Sir Allan Napier MacNab

Mid-century Personages

The First Attorney General of Canada West:
William Henry Draper

The First Attorney General of Ontario:
John Sandfield Macdonald

The Last Attorney General of Upper Canada:
John A. Macdonald, ca 1856

Equity Eagle: Oliver Mowat

Combatants over Provincial Rights

Winner: Sir Oliver Mowat

Winner: Sir Samuel Henry Strong

Loser: Sir John A. Macdonald

Loser: John Wellington Gwynne

*"There are no laws demanding a more religious observance
than those which limit and define the power of individuals
forming the government over their fellow creatures."*

William Warren Baldwin, John Rolph, and Robert Baldwin
23 June 1828
John Walpole Willis
23 September 1828

*"I am rather surprised at your advice to allow
parties to be arrested on mere suspicion of Fenianism.
Now this is a country of law and order, and we
cannot go beyond the law."*

John A. Macdonald
29 September 1866

*"It is often forgotten that the hard-won civil liberties
of a free society are not maintained only for
those who are arrested but for everyone,
and when we deprive one person of this basic right
then all are threatened."*

R. Roy McMurtry
The Globe and Mail 30 October 1970

Introduction

1791. The grandest monarchy of modern times, France of the Bourbons, was in convulsion, transformed by the collapse of social order into an experimental crucible for testing the political ideas of the Enlightenment. In 1789 the representative assembly of the kingdom had destroyed at a stroke a feudal order of centuries' growth, but a new order could not be built as quickly as the old had been abolished. In April 1791 the death of Mirabeau, president of the Constituent Assembly, unleashed forces that for a time had been held in check. Later that month, when Louis XVI tried to quit his capital for the quieter ambience of Saint-Cloud, a mob held him at Versailles, confirming what had only been a suspicion: that France's gelded monarch was a prisoner. Two months later, the royal family's bid to flee the country ended in ignominious recapture at Varennes.

The repression that followed the marquis de Lafayette's massacre of a republican demonstration in July briefly subdued the Paris mob, but the late summer's calm was illusory. Already the prospect loomed of war between France and the affronted monarchies of Europe. In October the Constituent Assembly gave way to a new Legislative Assembly. In April 1792 this body would declare war on France's threatening neighbours before yielding in its turn to a National Convention, which would declare France a republic.

Across the Atlantic Ocean a more controlled experiment in republican nation-building was already under way. In 1787 the newly independent states of the cisappalachian seaboard had united under a federal constitution embodying the *philosophe* Montesquieu's theory of the separation of powers, which prescribed the mutual severance of the executive, legislative, and judicial arms of government as a safeguard against oppression. The year 1791 saw the founding of the new federal capital, Washington, and the first, ten-part emendation of the new constitution, the Bill of Rights, which was to be the foundation of individual liberty in the infant polity. These first ten amendments to the u.s. constitution guaranteed freedom of religion, freedom of expression, and freedom to assemble and petition for the redress of grievances. They forbade unreasonable search and seizure, the levying of excessive bail or fines, and cruel and unusual punishment. No prosecution for a major crime was to proceed unless the defendant was indicted by a grand jury. The taking of life, liberty, and property without due process was prohibited, as was an individual's exposure to double jeopardy for the same offence. Due process was defined to consist in the individual's right to be informed of the accusation against him, to have a speedy and public trial by grand and petit jury, and to have the assistance of legal counsel in his defence.

Although the new republic was quiet at its centre while this experiment in enlightened government was in progress, it was troubled on its periphery. One frontier insurrection, Shays' Rebellion of 1786-7, had already disturbed Massachusetts and its neighbours, and in 1791 Congress enacted the federal excise tax on home-brewed whisky that was to lead to the 'Whisky Rebellions' of 1794. In the yet unsettled Northwest Territory, November 1791 saw the defeat of a military force under General Arthur St Clair by Miami Indians on the Wabash River, not far from present-day Fort Wayne, Indiana.

In 1791, on the fringe of these diverse social laboratories, a third political experiment was also under way, an experiment conceived in London to be carried out on the hanging shreds of His Britannic Majesty's North American empire. The materials were unpromising: a detritus of dashed hopes washed up on the north shore of the St Lawrence River and the great lakes Ontario and Erie in the wake of the American revolution. In 1784 several thousand refugees from republicanism had been organized in settlements in the uncultivated western part of the province of Quebec along its border with the newly sovereign state of New York. Irked by the antique feudal tenures still prevailing in this former Bourbon apanage, they petitioned urgently that in these previously unsettled districts at least they might be granted the familiar blessings of English civil law – above all, that of holding their land in fee simple.

This third experiment, years in the making, was designed not to extend individual liberty but to confine it. It was generally agreed in London that the refugees (the United Empire Loyalists, as they proudly called themselves) could not be denied benefits to which they had been accustomed in their old homes, and which were still being enjoyed before their very eyes in the new republic to the south; but it was no easy thing to devise a political order that would embody English liberties while avoiding the anarchic excesses that had rent the old empire. The problem was complicated by the mingling of races in both halves of the colony. The French of the New World were attached to their old feudal tenures, which the abundance of land made less oppressive than in densely populated France. Their susceptibilities could be accommodated by splitting off the newly settled western half into a new province and introducing English civil law there only; but there was a substantial French settlement at its western extremity, opposite Detroit, while the eastern half contained British residents who hankered after English law. In the end the imperial legislators pragmatically decided to let the minority in each region go hang. The province of Quebec was converted into the two new colonies of Upper and Lower Canada by the Canada Act, or Constitutional Act, of 1791.[1]

The solution to the problem of creating a stable political order was a simple one – perhaps deceptively simple. Within the limits inherent in their dependent status, the colonies were to have a constitution as much like the British as possible. Each would have a bicameral legislature, with a lower House of Assembly elected on a broad suffrage and an upper house, the Legislative Council, appointed by the sovereign. Provision was made for creating a hereditary aristocracy when conditions permitted. The sovereign's representative in both provinces was to be the governor-in-chief. Since he resided permanently at Quebec, political and logistical necessity soon made the lieutenant-governor of Upper Canada the real head of government in that province; he reported directly to London and was virtually independent of his nominal superior downriver. It was he who in Upper Canada gave the royal assent to provincial legislation or reserved it at his discretion for consideration by the imperial government. Reserved legislation lapsed automatically if it was not confirmed in London within two years, and the imperial authorities could disallow any colonial legislation within two years of its passage even if it had received the lieutenant-governor's assent and gone into operation.

In each province the governor was to be assisted by an advisory body, the Executive Council, appointed by the imperial government. Its duties were left undefined by the Constitutional Act and were regulated to some extent by legislation affecting the British colonies in general; but the relationship between governor and council differed fundamentally from that between the sovereign's representative and the federal or a provincial cabinet under the modern system of responsible government. Under the modern constitution, the sovereign's representative is only formally vested with executive authority. In practice he acts on the advice of his cabinet (still known in Ontario as the Executive Council), which is composed of the political heads of the chief departments of state. Usually these are members of the legislature, and their tenure of office is dependent on their retaining, individually and collectively, the confidence of the people as represented in the legislature. Under the colonial system instituted in 1791, real executive authority lay with the governor. He was not obliged to consult the Executive Council on every matter of state (though there were things he could not do without their advice and consent). Even if he consulted them and acted on their advice, the responsibility for his actions was not theirs but his, and it was owed not to the people of the colony as represented in the House of Assembly but to the Crown and Parliament of Great Britain.

Still, the executive councillors were not ciphers. Especially after the earliest years, usually they were leading and long-resident members of the community, whose advice was badly needed by the succession of military men sent by Whitehall to govern the colony. On the rare occasions when their advice was not acted on, it was not dismissed but referred to the Colonial Office in London for authoritative decision. The councillors ordinarily were not heads of executive departments, but collectively they supervised the executive by auditing the accounts of the public officers. For this reason, one of the two public officers who usually did belong to the council, after his office was set up in 1801, was the inspector general of public accounts, whose job was to prepare the accounts for the audit committee's review. Since, under the royal instructions to the governor-in-chief, the council was to sit with the sovereign's representative as a court of appeal in civil matters, the chief justice too was a member ex officio.[2]

In Upper Canada, in contrast to the lower province, all the main executive officers had to be appointed at the colony's inception: a provincial secretary to be responsible for official paperwork, a receiver general to take charge of its treasure, a surveyor general to administer the Crown lands, and two chief clerks (the clerk of the Executive Council and the clerk of the Crown and Pleas) to handle the routine business of the council and the courts respectively. Local criminal and civil courts inherited from the province of Quebec were already in existence, but a chief justice had to be appointed to perform the higher judicial functions.[3] And to deal with the multifarious legal business of the Crown in the new colony, there was created that antiquely impressive-sounding functionary, His Majesty's Attorney General for Upper Canada.

Today the attorney general for Ontario presides over a ministry with a staff of several thousand scattered throughout the province. Under the permanent headship of the deputy attorney general, an officer appointed by the lieutenant-governor in council, this staff is charged with assisting the attorney general in the performance of the duties belonging to his office, duties that are defined in one section of a provincial statute entitled 'The Ministry of the Attorney General Act.'[4] Those duties are a mixture of high constitutional functions and routine ministerial responsibilities. The attorney general is charged with ensuring that public affairs are administered in accordance with the law and with superintending all matters connected with the administration of justice in the province. He advises the government upon all matters of law connected with legislative enactments, and generally upon all matters of a legislative nature, and upon all other matters of law referred to him by the government. He superintends the preparation of all government measures of a legislative nature, including statutory regulations, and his mandate extends to advising the head of every ministry or other agency of the provincial government upon all matters of law connected with their responsibilities. He conducts and regulates all litigation for and against the Crown or any ministry or agency of government in respect of any subject within the authority or jurisdiction of the legislature of Ontario, and superintends all matters connected with judicial offices.

In addition to these itemized functions, two 'portmanteau' subsections impose on him a host of other responsibilities. One directs him to discharge such other functions as are assigned to him by the legislature or the lieutenant-governor in council. Currently, about 140 acts are administered by the Ministry of the Attorney General, most of them touching in some way on the attorney's primary duties.[5] A large number have to do with the administration of justice; these include the Crown Attorneys Act, the Courts of Justice Act, the Juries Act, and the Justices of the Peace Act. Other statutes regulate legal and contractual relations between private parties: the Landlord and Tenant Act, the Master and Servant Act, the Vendors and Purchasers Act, the Partnerships Act, the Pawnbrokers Act, and the Statute of Frauds. Mr Attorney also has the province's morals under his aegis; his ministry administers the Disorderly Houses Act, the Gaming Act, the Hotel Registration of Guests Act, and the Lord's Day (Ontario) Act.

A particularly interesting class of acts in the charge of the ministry comprises those touching on civil rights, a field with wide ramifications. The Habeas Corpus Act asserts an individual's right not to be held in custody except in accord with due legal process; the Legal Aid Act helps to ensure an accused a fair trial; the Metropolitan Police Force Complaints Project Act, 1981, establishes a tribunal to investigate complaints of unfair treatment by the province's largest municipal police force. The Expropriations Act and the Ontario Municipal Board Act are intended, among other things, to achieve an equitable adjustment between an individual's property rights (traditionally a class of civil rights) and the public interest when the two come into conflict.

A noteworthy subclass of these statutes relating to civil rights consists of those that charge the attorney general with protecting the rights and interests of the disadvantaged – the Blind Persons' Rights Act, the Charities Accounting Act, and the Unconscionable Transactions Relief Act, to name a few. These are all extensions of the attorney general's historic role as guardian (representing the Crown) of those who cannot help themselves, one of his present duties that is not itemized in the Ministry of the Attorney General Act. It is covered, however, by the second 'portmanteau' subsection, which states that the attorney general

shall perform the duties and have the powers that belong to the Attorney General and Solicitor General of England by law or usage, so far as those duties and powers are applicable to Ontario, and also shall perform the duties and have the powers that, up to the time the *British North America Act, 1867* came into effect, belonged to the offices of the Attorney General and Solicitor General in the provinces of Canada and Upper Canada and which, under the provisions of that Act, are within the scope of the powers of the Legislature.[6]

It may be asked why the act should not have itemized these duties – why the legislature should not have had the opportunity to consider and give its sanction to each of them individually. The answer is to be found in the historical origin of the act, a story that is not the least interesting part of the modern history of the office of attorney general in Ontario. When Chief Justice J.C. McRuer commenced his inquiry into civil rights in the province in 1964, he discovered that the expansion of government and the pursuit of efficient administration had led to an erosion of the attorney general's traditional powers and responsibilities and created something of a power vacuum in the safeguarding of civil rights. He noted the proliferation of officers and agencies with power to subpoena persons and documents and to commit persons to jail for contempt. Powers of investigation had been lavished on boards 'with reckless abandon' without any statutory inhibition against the disclosure of information to unauthorized persons. The legislature was showing an increasing readiness to delegate its authority to executive agencies, including even the power to create offences and provide for penalties. These erosions of liberty were occurring partly because the various departments of government had acquired their own legal staff, who often tended to draft departmental legislation with an eye to administrative convenience rather than the preservation of constitutional liberties. The attorney general's traditional authority to oversee government legislation was vitiated by the fact that the legislation so drafted was often referred to the responsible officer of his department, the legislative counsel, only at the last minute before presentation to the legislature.

To rectify these defects, the McRuer Report recommended, among other things, that the drafting of all government legislation be done in the office of the attorney general, and that departmental legal officers henceforth be members of his staff. These changes would help him to discharge effectively his constitutional responsibility for all legal advice tendered to the government. The report also recommended that legislative sanction be given to the attorney general's role as guardian of the constitutional administration of public business, a role which, McRuer noted, required of the attorney general an independence of action that overrode a cabinet minister's ordinary duty of loyalty to party and colleagues.[7]

It was not, then, the purpose of the Ministry of the Attorney General Act to itemize each and every power and duty of the Crown's chief law officer for Ontario. Its purpose was twofold. First, it was to affirm explicitly, on behalf of the people of Ontario, that the attorney general should continue to discharge his office, within the limits of the provincial jurisdiction, in all the plenitude of its power and responsibility as it had developed in England and Canada over several centuries. Second, it was to give express sanction to those aspects of his duty that have developed and expanded since the advent of responsible government in Canada. For it was the advent of responsible government – that is, self-government under parliamentary institutions – that made the interest of the people of

Ontario constitutionally transcendent in the administration of provincial affairs, and it was this innovation that made it possible to conceive of the attorney general as an independent overseer of the legality and constitutionality of their administration. It was responsible government, too, that caused the attorney general to acquire ministerial responsibility for the machinery of justice in Ontario. How these things came about is in part the subject of this book.

The first two chapters describe the attorneyship during the early decades. The first attorney general was not a responsible minister of the Crown, as the modern Canadian officers are; he was a skilled functionary, more as the attorney general of England still is, though his practice differed from that of even his contemporary English counterpart much as a frontier doctor's would from a metropolitan specialist's. Chapter 1 describes the efforts of John White, with few books and less money, to administer English law and constitutional practice to a colonial body politic whose circumstances often demanded inventive adaptation of both. Chapter 2 explores the implications of the fact that the attorneyship, like most other provincial offices, was essentially a sort of property in the king's gift – a privileged vendorship of fee-bearing services to the government and the public. The nature of the office, and the political expectations mirrored in its nature, impeded the development of the modern doctrine that makes the attorney general responsible to the people for the constitutional administration of public business. In those days the attorney general was responsible not to the people but to the imperial government. The notion of the office as the incumbent's property precluded the expectation that he should expiate by resignation any failure to discharge its functions.

Chapter 3 recounts the crucial role of the office and its incumbents in the political events leading to the rebellions of 1837. No one did more than John Beverley Robinson and Henry John Boulton to destroy public confidence in the integrity of the government and the impartiality of the administration of justice. Robinson was not personally corrupt as Boulton was, but his loathing of egalitarian – even libertarian – political ideals and his zeal to preserve the existing authoritarian oligarchy led him to flout the most essential duties of his office. The resulting abuses of civil liberties and due process led directly to the inauguration of the movement for internal self-government – responsible government – in 1828. The imperial authorities responded with important concessions, but persistent abuse of reformers' civil liberties by the provincial government and its supporters nurtured a climate of violent discord which was a principal cause of the rebellions.

Chapter 4 reviews the constitutional and political developments of Upper Canadian history from the perspective of the attorneyship. The politicization of public life in the 1820s promoted the attorney general's rise to political pre-eminence, since he was usually the only leading official in the House of Assembly and was also ex officio head of the province's social élite, the legal profession. When the concession of responsible government in the 1840s transferred real executive authority from the governor, the sovereign's representative, to the provincial cabinet, the attorney general ordinarily became the political leader of the province. Responsible government also turned him into a cabinet minister with general responsibility for the administration of justice.

The combined burdens of political leadership and administrative responsibility compelled successive incumbents to neglect the traditional duties of the office and made it an object of political controversy. While mainly expressing a pragmatic concern with administrative economy and efficiency, criticism was also focused on the apparent incompatibility of cabinet membership with the attorney general's duty to give the executive legal advice untainted by political considerations. Chapter 4 therefore confronts an anomaly. The advent of responsible government was essential to the growth of the doctrine that the attorney general has a special responsibility to the people for the constitutional administration of public affairs, yet it turned him into a member (and normally the leader) of the executive he was supposed to police. Although in the twentieth century the attorney general has hardly ever been premier, concern with this anomaly has persisted, and the chapter ends by posing a question that is as relevant today as it was in 1850.

One of the traditional duties the attorney general began to neglect under the press of political and administrative obligations was the conduct of prosecutions at the assizes. The need to appoint ad hoc substitutes gave political force to an old proposal to set up a province-wide bureaucracy to administer criminal prosecutions. Chapter 5 is devoted to the origin of the County Attorneys Act of 1857 and to other matters bearing on the attorney general's responsibility to preserve the public peace. This aspect of his duty was always much more pronounced in Upper Canada than in England, since even before responsible government the attorney general was active in that cause (together with the solicitor general, the subordinate law officer of the Crown) as Crown prosecutor at the assizes. In England, by contrast, public prosecution was normally confined to crimes against the state, and ordinary criminal proceedings were left for the complainant to conduct at his own expense. Since the attorney general and the solicitor general also made freer use than their English counterparts of the law officers' ancient procedural privilege of addressing the jury last, their involvement in the prosecution of ordinary (as opposed to state) crimes gave extra urgency to the movement in Upper Canada to afford persons accused of felony the advantage (traditionally denied them by English law, though guaranteed by the Bill of Rights in the United States) of a full defence by counsel.

The advent of responsible government strengthened the attorney general's identification with the maintenance of law and order, since it became part of his general responsibility for the administration of justice. Chapter 5 closes, therefore, with a review of nineteenth-century legislative proposals on the police. In contrast to England, public opinion in nineteenth-century Ontario neither resisted public control of criminal prosecutions nor evinced a concern to limit the law officers' right to the last word, but Upper Canadians shared the long-standing English fear of a centralized police as potentially repressive.

In 1867 Upper Canada, as the province of Ontario, became a part of the Dominion of Canada. The delicate and uncertain legal relationship between province, dominion, and empire vastly enhanced the importance of the attorney general's duty to advise the executive and the legislature on the legal aspects of the province's relations with other polities. As attorney general and premier from 1872 to 1896, Oliver Mowat exerted an extraordinary influence in the province's interest on the interpretation of the British North America Act, the charter of the new confederation. An unassuming mastermind, a veritable Bismarck in his combination of long vision with deft opportunism, he comprehensively out-manoeuvred Canadian Prime Minister John A. Macdonald both in politics and in the courts, although the imperial government sympathized with Macdonald and the language of the act seemed at first glance to favour Macdonald's centralist interpretation. Mowat's campaign for 'provincial rights' is the subject of chapter 6.

After Confederation the administration of criminal and civil justice underwent thorough reform in the interests of economy and efficiency. Chapter 7 describes the process. One feature of the reform was a significant reduction in the role of the petit jury in civil justice and of both the grand and the petit jury in the criminal sphere. Like the reforms discussed in chapter 5, the attack on the jury reflected a concern to achieve greater certainty of enforcement by professionalizing the administration of justice more completely. Underlying this concern was an apparent conviction that in the age of responsible government institutional safeguards that had been considered as essential to the preservation of individual liberty under a less liberal regime could safely be discarded if they were a source of inefficiency. The Conclusion ponders this basic change in Ontario's political culture in the light of ideas proposed in earlier chapters.

1

King Lear's Fool

To the Englishman who became the first attorney general for Upper Canada, nothing would have been more surprising about the Ministry of the Attorney General Act than its title. The king had ministers to oversee the different departments of his government, and these were collectively known as 'the ministry'; but none of them individually was called 'the minister of' anything. The king had several secretaries of state: one for foreign affairs, one for the Home Department (who was responsible, generally speaking, for the internal affairs of the kingdom, including its colonies until 1801), and one for war and the colonies (a united responsibility, from 1801 on, for reasons that need no explanation). He had a chancellor of the exchequer and assorted boards of lords (of the admiralty, of the treasury, and of trade), the first of whom was in each case a figure of consequence (the first lord of the treasury was prime minister). But not until the mid-nineteenth century were any of the king's (or queen's) ministers called 'minister of' this or that, and not until the twentieth did any of the individual departments of state begin to be called ministries.

THE NATURE OF THE OFFICE

Even if the king's ministers had been called minister of this or that and their individual departments ministries, there still could have been no Ministry of the Attorney General; for the attorney general was not a minister. He did perform certain routine 'ministerial' (or, as we say today, administrative) functions, but he did not grandly supervise a horde of underlings – clerks, ambassadors, colonial governors, tide-waiters, excisemen. He was an expert functionary who did things himself: the king's chief legal adviser and his principal representative in the courts in criminal and civil matters. Both the attorney general for England and the solicitor general (who may be thought of as partly his deputy, partly his understudy) worked out of their private professional offices, or chambers, in the Inns of Court almost until the end of the nineteenth century, when the Law Officers' Department was set up with a staff of two clerks in a few rooms in the Royal Courts of Justice. They received no salary, taking fees for the tasks performed by them (or in their name) as law officers of the Crown as if from a private client. Indeed, the Crown was merely the first among their clients, and one of the more lucrative aspects of each office was the prestige it conferred and the consequent boost to the holder's private practice (until incumbents were barred from private practice in 1894).[1]

Nevertheless, in his capacity as the king's chief law officer, the attorney general in particular had important constitutional duties and privileges. He normally led for the Crown in the prosecution of criminal offences against the state, such as treason and sedition. In all such offences except the most serious, he might if he wished expedite the prosecution by a proceeding, the information ex officio, which circumvented the ordinary criminal procedure of indictment by a grand jury (a deviation expressly forbidden by the American Bill of Rights). He could demand that a state prosecution be tried 'at bar' before the entire bench of whatever competent court he chose. Both he and the solicitor general could claim the final word to the jury in trials where the defendant, having called no witnesses, would normally be entitled to it. He had sole and absolute discretion to discontinue any criminal proceedings in progress before a judge and jury either before or after the jury had reached its verdict, and to decide whether a criminal cause might be appealed to the House of Lords, the court of final appeal. These were his rights and duties in relation to criminal prosecutions.

Both law officers conducted civil litigation on behalf of the Crown, but this was more a matter of contractual service than of constitutional obligation. Nevertheless, the attorney general did have constitutional duties beyond those relating to criminal prosecutions. One was the responsibility to enforce the proper execution of charitable trusts. Perhaps as an outgrowth of this, he also acquired a general discretion to uphold the law in the public interest, either on his own initiative or upon application by an aggrieved party in certain cases where no private person had a right to act. Only with his consent could the Crown itself, as opposed to its individual officers, be sued. Both the attorney general and the solicitor general ordinarily were members of Parliament, and they had an obligation to lend their expertise to the legislative process and to advise either House concerning its privileges. They were often applied to for opinions by the cabinet or by individual ministers, and it is in this capacity, advising the colonial secretary on some contentious question that had cropped up in Upper Canada, that we shall meet them from time to time in these pages.

The English criminal law prevailed in Upper Canada by virtue of the Quebec Act of 1774. From 1792 on, by the first act of the Upper Canadian legislature, the English civil law too prevailed.[2] Under these authorities the attorney general of Upper Canada arguably bore all the responsibilities and enjoyed all the privileges of his English counterpart in so far as they were applicable to the province. This is not as self-evident as it might seem, however. The constitutional history of Canada is scattered with instances of controversial assumptions based on questionable analogies between a provincial office or institution and its English counterpart or namesake. The most important example is probably the claim, made in both Upper and Lower Canada, that the colonial legislature necessarily enjoyed the same rights and privileges as the imperial Parliament – in particular, sovereignty in the colony's internal affairs and the right to impeach and try officers of the colonial executive. In 1828, the year in which the administration of justice in Upper Canada was perhaps subjected to stronger condemnation than ever before or since, controversy centred on two questions of this nature. One was how closely the constitution of the provincial Court of King's Bench resembled that of the English court. The other was whether the rights of the attorney general and the solicitor general for Upper Canada with respect to criminal prosecutions were the same as those of their English counterparts. If the king's attorney general for Upper Canada did possess the same duties and privileges as his attorney general in England, then, it was not because they bore the same title but because they stood in the same relationship to the Crown as its chief law officer.[3] In any case, the scope of the attorney general's duties, privileges, and rewards was more than once a subject of controversy during the early decades.

The record offers no very enlightening official statement of the provincial attorney general's duties at this time. The commissions issued to the early holders of the office are singularly uninformative. The mandamus (royal authorization to the provincial government) to issue a patent of office to the first attorney general, John White, specified merely that he was 'to have, hold, exercise and enjoy the said office ... for and during our pleasure, together with all and singular the Rights, Fees, Profits, Privileges and Advantages thereunto belonging or appertaining, in as full and ample a manner as any Attorney General of our Province of Lower Canada hath held and enjoyed, or of right ought to have held and enjoyed the same.'[4] Since both Lower and Upper Canada had been created by the same act, there had been no attorney general of Lower Canada to stand as a model; but no doubt His Majesty's secretary of state for the Home Department had the defunct province of Quebec in mind. White's actual patent was even less informative: it authorized him to hold his office 'together with all and singular the powers and authorities, profits, benefits, privileges and emoluments which unto the said office of Attorney General belong and appertain.' The mandamuses and patents drawn for his successors varied slightly in language but were equally vague.[5]

From time to time the office-holders were called on to state their own duties, but none of them tried to be comprehensive. William Firth in 1808 was terse to the point of evasion: his duties were 'the usual Duties of the King's Attorney General, together with those of the Land Granting Department' (what those were we shall see later). In 1817, D'Arcy Boulton was professedly 'conducting public prosecutions on the part of the Crown, advising his Majesty's Representative generally and inspecting and countersigning all Instruments made under the Great Seal of the Province.' John Beverley Robinson defined his duties in 1821 as 'conducting all criminal prosecutions on behalf of the Crown; Drafting all Public Instruments under the Seals; Giving legal advice to the Lieut. Governor upon all matters referred to him [the attorney general] for that purpose; and discharging generally all the Duties appertaining to the office of Attorney General.' Ten years later, in a report on the civil establishment of the province, Lieutenant-Governor Sir John Colborne stated that 'the Attorney General conducts all criminal prosecutions on behalf of the Crown, and is held responsible for drafting all public Instruments under the Seals. The Solicitor General may be called on to perform similar duties.'[6]

Admittedly, there is in these statements if not elaboration at least a certain unanimity. Oddly enough, though, we shall see later that both of the duties most insisted on, the conduct of prosecutions and the responsibility for drafting instruments under the seals (which included what Firth called the duties of the Land Granting Department), had to be fought for more than once during the province's first forty years. We shall see in this chapter that even the duty of giving legal advice to the lieutenant-governor as required (which only Attorney General Robinson specified) was at first confined within quite narrow limits.

A BOOT IN OFFICE

The first attorney general, John White, has left us a dull diary and some rather more interesting letters. These supplement the official archives in documenting his activities. In the early years, they show him handling all of the Crown prosecutions at assize and all of its civil litigation, drafting parliamentary bills, deeds of grant, and other official instruments under seal, and advising the government on matters of law referred to him for his opinion.[7] As a member of the first House of Assembly, he was made responsible for preparing authentic copies of legislation originating in the lower House for transmission to the Colonial Office (the chief justice, a member of the Legislative Council, did the same for acts originating in the upper House). In 1797, though, this responsibility was shifted entirely to the chief justice, who was also to report the reasons for those enactments that had originated in the upper House, while either the attorney general or the solicitor general reported on those originating in the Assembly. Since White had not been re-elected to the Assembly in 1796, this duty devolved upon Solicitor General Robert Gray.[8]

More interesting than what the first attorney general did is what he did not do. He may have been chief legal counsel to the Crown, but he was far from being its chief law adviser. That role fell to the chief justice, William Osgoode. Lieutenant-Governor Simcoe's official correspondence is full of Osgoode's opinion on this and that, and it was Osgoode and his successor, John Elmsley, who were responsible for nearly all of the important measures respecting legal policy and legal institutions during the first decade. Osgoode drafted the Judicature Act of 1794, which abolished the four district civil courts of common pleas inherited from the province of Quebec and set up a single superior Court of King's Bench with both criminal and civil jurisdiction. He framed the province's jury laws, also enacted in 1794, which lasted, with minor modification, until 1850.[9] Even mundane business that one might expect to see referred to the attorney general as a matter of course was put to the chief justice. Simcoe cited Osgoode's opinion on the proper number of executive councillors to constitute a quorum and whether a new nominee to the council might serve before the mandamus to appoint him had arrived from England, and it seems to have been Osgoode who drew the first form of patent for the freehold grant of Crown lands.[10]

Partly this pattern mirrored the rough-and-ready style of administration to be expected in a large frontier colony with a tiny population, and partly the attorney general's inferiority to the chief justice in the official hierarchy. The latter was ex officio Speaker of the Legislative Council and president of the Executive Council, but the attorney general belonged to neither body and might have no political importance beyond what he could claim as a member of the Assembly. White, indeed, owed his very appointment to Osgoode, whom the Colonial Office had asked to find a man for the job. When recommended by the chief justice-designate, a friend of his brother-in-law Samuel Shepherd (later attorney general of England), he was a failed barrister studying to take holy orders.[11] One of White's letters to Shepherd nicely illustrates the relationship between the three men. Assuring his brother-in-law that he is getting on well with 'the Chief,' he adds: 'Upon this subject, don't let your letters to be *too urgent*. A man in my situation must appear to depend a little on himself. Or, a boot will hold the office as well as I can.'[12] From time to time White found it hard to avoid becoming a doormat.

This became especially evident after Osgoode left Upper Canada in 1794 to become chief justice of Lower Canada. White had relied on him to hold the lieutenant-governor to proper legal form in governing the province, and without a lawyer in the Executive Council Simcoe's impetuosity was uncontrolled. 'A Military man from his earliest years, altho' a member of the House of Commons, he has not the desire to be a civilian,' lamented White. 'Questions of the most serious import he will put to you in conversation – and if you desire time and a case stated, tho' it may be promised, you never receive it – but whatever falls from you in conversation, is adopted, if convenient. And, what is actually no more than common conversation, will sometimes be made the basis of the most serious transactions.'[13] White feared that Simcoe might not merely act on some tentative, unofficial opinion of his but might also quote it to the colonial secretary as authority for the act.

Even the two-year hiatus between Osgoode's departure and Elmsley's arrival occasioned little increase in White's influence as legal adviser to the executive. Two crises of those years merit scrutiny for the light they shed on the nature of the attorneyship and the social milieu in which it then functioned.

THE LAND TITLES CRISIS

With the defeat of the loyalist cause in the rebellious southern colonies, the government had granted land to the soldiers and refugees anxious to settle in western Quebec by means of a provisional instrument called a certificate of occupation. This document promised the person named in it a permanent grant under seigneurial tenure upon the completion of specified improvements. Because the introduction of freehold land tenure according to English civil law was expected in the territory, the holders of these certificates made no effort to turn them in for a permanent title under the old French law; instead, the habit quickly grew of treating the certificates themselves as conveying a freehold, and many commercial bargains were made on that assumption.

Simcoe's first plan for dealing with this problem was to institute tenure in fee simple by means of a provincial statute converting the certificates into freehold patents. Yet this turned out to be impracticable. So many certificates had been traded away by the persons named in them that to convert them into instruments conferring legal ownership on the nominee would undo several years of commercial activity in the colony. Simcoe therefore decided to take executive instead of legislative action. A proclamation was issued calling on all persons wishing to be confirmed in the freehold tenure of the lands they claimed to submit the documents supporting their claim for adjudication by the government.[14]

Simcoe's new scheme alarmed the colony's few wealthy merchants. These men had built up a dominant position in the tiny, dispersed frontier society at the expense of the old loyalist officers who might have been expected to emerge as its natural leaders. This ascendancy had developed partly through their control of the economy but also because of their good relations with the army, whose trusted provisioners they were; their good contacts with the distant provincial capital of Quebec through constant commercial intercourse with the lower St Lawrence; and, it is fair to say, their superior talent and education. When Simcoe arrived in the new colony he met two of them, the business partners Robert Hamilton of Niagara and Richard Cartwright of Kingston, as members of his small Legislative Council. He met them also as the dominant judges of the court of common pleas in their respective districts. And in the vicinity of the village of Newark (now Niagara-on-the-Lake), his new capital at the mouth of the Niagara River, he met Hamilton as the dominant figure in the commission of the peace – the bench of magistrates who formed the local government and court of petty criminal and civil jurisdiction in each district.[15]

Along with their dominance, Simcoe discovered their unpopularity. 'The fact is,' wrote Attorney General White in 1793, 'that those who have had power, have lorded it with a rod of iron ... The people fly to me as a protector. And it was told the Governor publicly the other day that many people (*naming them*) would have gone into the States but for the succour that they have received from me.' Simcoe himself had fought in the American War. He was deeply committed to the loyal ex-defenders of the United Empire, whom the new colony had been created to shelter, and he thought it unfair that their harbour had fallen under the control of merchants who seemed to place their own mercenary interests above those of the empire that nurtured and protected them.[16]

One of the main motives for the Judicature Act of 1794 was Simcoe's wish to unseat the merchant judges, who had abused their office by rendering decisions that were unduly favourable to the merchant interest. The act abolished the courts of common pleas and set up a single central superior Court of King's Bench composed of professional judges. A second act set up district courts under a single part-time local judge to render justice in disputes of debt and simple contract up to fifteen pounds' value (petty debts of up to two pounds' value had been assigned by an act of 1792 to a new local tribunal called the court of requests, which consisted of two or more justices of the peace). Chief Justice Osgoode was responsible for the Judicature Act, but White framed the district court bill. After its passage, while remaining attorney general, he became judge of the Home District Court, which sat at Niagara.[17]

Cartwright and Hamilton vainly opposed the judicature bill in the Legislative Council. They stressed the inconvenience, in a large and sparsely peopled territory, of concentrating in a single central court all jurisdiction in matters above fifteen pounds' value and in all matters of whatever value that did not take the form of debt or simple contract. To be sure, the actual trial would take place at the annual court of assize in the district where the action originated; but all preliminary process would have to be administered in the office of the clerk of the Crown at the seat of government (where the Court of King's Bench was to be located), involving great loss of time to the litigants (or great expense to any who employed an attorney). Indeed, the complexity of the newly imported English civil law would make the help of a professional attorney indispensable; it entailed a multiplicity of forms of action and a very complex procedure, and a merely technical mistake of form or procedure could thwart the most justifiable proceedings. The system would result in delay and expense, and only the province's fledgling legal profession would profit by it.[18]

Time would justify these forebodings, but the House of Assembly embraced the reform eagerly, so anxious were they to be rid of merchant judges. Cartwright complained to a mercantile associate in London that the 'bill was hurried through in a manner not very decent,' without even being printed; but Simcoe told the secretary of state that it was only with the greatest difficulty that the Assembly had been restrained from passing it in a single day.[19]

Like Simcoe's judicial reform, his decision to solve the land titles problem by executive rather than legislative action was aimed at the merchants. One way in which the merchant judges had abused their office was in treating certificates of occupation – which they themselves had acquired in great clusters in the course of business – as freehold titles. They would have suffered seriously from Simcoe's first scheme of converting each certificate by statute into a freehold title vested in the nominee, but such a general measure would also have harmed others who did not deserve it. An examination of each claim by the Executive Council would enable the government to reject only those that had been acquired by the unconscionable use of economic power.[20]

The merchants met the threat with finesse. Cartwright sent Simcoe a memorandum stressing the danger of invalidating even unconscionable transactions in land certificates. Such land might later have been fairly disposed of to a party who was guiltless of the impugned bargain, and reversing that bargain might lead to his ejectment from land in which he had invested much labour and capital. Cartwright defended treating land certificates as freehold titles by pointing out that the Constitutional Act seemed to consider them such. Section 44 implied it by stating that on surrendering his certificate the holder might 'receive a *fresh* grant'; section 45 envisaged that lands held by certificate might be subject to certain rights that could not exist unless the certificate conveyed a freehold title.

This was true enough, but the solution Cartwright proposed was rather disingenuous. He advocated legislation which, according to him, would protect 'fair and honest alienations' only; but the criteria he proposed for adjudging a transaction as bona fide were unlikely to exclude all those concluded under undue influence. One was endorsement by the land boards that had been set up in 1789 to guard against the acquisition of certificates by speculators, in part by undue influence over the poorer inhabitants. It was notorious that these boards had been negligent, if not at times dishonest (Hamilton had belonged to the board for the Nassau District and had dominated it to his own benefit just as he dominated the court of common pleas). Another standard was confirmation by two witnesses; but the cause célèbre of *Randal* v *Phelps* more than twenty-five years later would show how little two witnesses could command the trust of a jury when the subject at issue was large enough.[21]

Cartwright and Hamilton got nowhere with Simcoe, but they had already taken another route to their goal. Hamilton went to England and consulted an eminent counsel, William Grant, a former attorney general of Quebec and now a friend of the prime minister, William Pitt. Grant concluded that in the absence of an express declaration in the Constitutional Act (which he had helped to shape), certificates of occupation could not be taken as conveying a freehold.[22]

Grant's opinion contradicted one of the premises of Cartwright's memorandum, but it helped the merchants by throwing doubt upon all titles to property that had been alienated by bargain. If the certificates had possessed the force of a freehold grant, as Cartwright contended, anyone who held land by their transfer might expect a patent under Simcoe's proclamation as long as the transfer had not been unconscionable. This offered no security to the merchants, though, who could not expect Simcoe to be indulgent towards their claims. If the certificates did not grant a freehold, though, the rights they did convey still rested in the original holder, or his heirs, who might legally claim the promised freehold patent and proceed to eject the present occupier of the land, no matter how honestly he had come by it. This created an emergency that could be rectified only by legislation, which was exactly what the merchants wanted.

In reporting Grant's opinion to the provincial executive, Hamilton enlarged on its implications with sombre glee. The transfer of land by sale had been so widespread that if such transactions were declared void 'such a scene of confusion of Injury and of ruin would ensue as can neither be described nor easily conceived.' There was no way out but by adopting his and Cartwright's scheme: an act must be passed validating all bona fide transfers and authorizing the issue of freehold patents to the present possessor.[23] The previous year, in opposing the judicature bill, the two men had adopted a populist stance in vain, since their rhetoric was so obviously self-serving. In this crisis they could more plausibly claim to be speaking for the typical settler. Hamilton was soon boasting that he could carry an act through both houses of the legislature, whether Simcoe wanted it or not, making the certificates themselves valid title deeds not for the original nominees but for their current holders.

Grant's opinion forced Simcoe to refer the question to his attorney general prior to placing it before the imperial government. White expounded the executive's case ably enough. Grant's opinion undoubtedly conformed to the letter of the law of England, 'but nothing in England since it has been a Kingdom, can be adduced similar to the condition of this Province.' If the certificates of occupation did not convey a freehold, then tenure under them pending the issue of the promised patent could only be as a tenant-at-will of the Crown. But the certificates clearly purported to convey a more substantial estate than that of a mere tenancy-at-will. A tenant-at-will could not alienate, but the certificates expressly empowered the possessor to alienate with the consent of the land board. Section 45 of the Constitutional Act recognized a similar power to alienate in envisaging that lands held under certificate might be subject to rights in remainder or reversion, which presupposed alienation. Section 44 also implied that the certificates conveyed a freehold. To avoid the confusion that must follow (as Hamilton rightly observed) from Grant's opinion, the certificates must be construed as having conferred an 'imagined fee.' 'I am aware that I am using language unknown among Lawyers,' White added, knowing that his reasoning would ultimately be judged by the law officers of England, 'but the situation of this Country is without precedent.'[24]

The English law officers forbore to comment on White's argument and responded to the case by drafting a provincial act to meet it. Their reply did not imply disagreement with White so much as a feeling that the problem was better resolved by express legislation than by niceties of academic analysis. Their bill was well calculated to undermine the merchants. It provided that any claimant could apply to the government for letters of declaration that the original title to the lot in question had the legal status of a freehold grant made by the Crown at the moment of the introduction of English civil law (and hence of freehold tenure) by the statute of 1792; but the validity of each claim was to be decided by the lieutenant-governor in council. By this means the bill sought to reassure bona fide claimants of the security of their titles while leaving questionable claims open to executive scrutiny as Simcoe had intended.[25]

Unfortunately, the bill contained a serious lacuna – or at any rate one serious enough to be exploited by someone seeking to discard it. Under English law a wife was entitled at her husband's death to a life interest in one-third of all the real estate he had owned at any time since their marriage. Land could be sold free of this burden, the so-called right of dower, only if the seller's wife voluntarily renounced her right in open court at the time of sale. This had never been done in selling land held on certificates, either before or since the introduction of English law, but the law officers' bill made no provision for this omission.[26]

The bill arrived too late to be presented to the legislature during its session of 1796. Before the next session, the new chief justice, Osgoode's successor, had also arrived. John Elmsley was a man of enough intelligence, energy, and sympathy with the aspirations of the leading officials (which were chiefly to make their fortunes and lord it in their frontier fish-pond) to dominate the provincial executive in the absence of Simcoe, who had left the province in 1796. Elmsley discarded the bill in favour of a bold scheme of his own. This was the creation of a peripatetic commission to adjudicate all claims, subject to appeal from its decision to the Executive Council. Each adjudicating panel, consisting of two lay notables and a judge of the Court of King's Bench, was empowered to authenticate not only ownership claims but also mortgages and judgments for debt that were binding on land. This Heir and Devisee Commission was the forerunner of the quasi-judicial tribunals that are familiar to Canadians today.[27]

Obviously, Elmsley's plan differed from the law officers' draft much more than the flaw in their bill could justify, so he explained his reasons in a lengthy report for transmission to London. The investigation of a host of land transactions, often concluded without written agreement, was better undertaken by a peripatetic tribunal with exceptional powers than by the Executive Council at York. As for the right of dower, it was currently worthless in Upper Canada because land was so abundant that a widow could neither derive rental profit from her right nor hire labour to cultivate the land. The creation of the Heir and Devisee Commission represented 'one great effort ... to restore the Province to the usual routine and current of human affairs.' The voiding of dower in respect of transactions upon certificates was a wise and temporary remission of the full force of English law which would help to preserve the institution for a later time when it would have real value. 'Tho' we have made the Laws & Customs of our mother Country our own,' Elmsley concluded, 'yet I must be allowed to think that we mistake both our situation and our Interest if we think that a precipitate introduction & indiscriminate application of every part of them can be made with impunity ... While we keep inviolate the spirit and principle of every institution we adopt, we must be careful so to mould & modify the form of it, as to adopt [sic] it to our own circumstances.'[28]

Elmsley's scheme is perhaps one of the more daring to have been implemented in the history of the administration of justice in Canada. It boldly did away with the normal standards of evidence, recognizing that the anarchic informality of land transactions in the dozen years since the first settlement made them impossible to apply. The commissioners were given substantial discretion in deciding whether a claim was valid.

The commissioners' terms of reference also made up for an important deficiency in the province's legal establishment under the Judicature Act of 1794. The Court of King's Bench had been given the entire jurisdiction of the three English superior courts of common law – King's Bench, Common Pleas, and Exchequer. The English system of civil law also included a supplementary jurisdiction called equity, which was administered by the Court of Chancery. Equity had been developed in order to make up for the deficiencies of the common law, which was so rigid in its form and procedures that it often failed to resolve disputes justly. For instance, had the land titles crisis been resolved as Simcoe first intended, by a statute converting certificates of occupation into freehold titles, a person who had bought a lot honestly would have had no remedy at law had the original recipient of the certificate enforced his new freehold title by ejecting the settler. The settler might theoretically have sought redress in equity, but since the Judicature Act had provided no equity jurisdiction he could not actually do so. This omission was to cause repeated controversy over the next forty years: a whole area of the English civil law, adopted with due pomp by the parliament of Upper Canada as its first act of legislation, could not be enforced for lack of machinery.[29] The defect did not hamper the Heir and Devisee Commission, though, because its founding statute authorized the commissioners to take equitable considerations into account in adjudicating claims.

Elmsley's act was bitterly criticized by his fellow judge of the Court of King's Bench, the sarcastic and self-assertive Bostonian William Dummer Powell. This was an ironic twist of events, since it was Powell who had sparked the initial crisis by encouraging Hamilton to seek the opinion of Grant (a personal friend whose advice to Powell, then a refugee in England, had led him to emigrate to Quebec). When the division of the old colony was first proposed, the governor-in-chief, Lord Dorchester, had recommended Powell as chief justice of the upper province. Osgoode's appointment had reduced his expectations to a mere associate or puisne judgeship, which he received in 1794 when the Judicature Act set up the Court of King's Bench. Osgoode's departure soon afterwards meant that the forty-year-old Powell was the first judge actually to preside in the new superior court, of which he was the sole member for more than two years. By this time, though, he had fallen afoul of Simcoe, partly because he was favoured by Dorchester, with whom the lieutenant-governor was soon at loggerheads; partly because, to the chauvinistic lieutenant-governor, Powell's speech, views, and demeanour bore a Yankee taint; and partly

because of his own quarrelsome nature. This rift ruined any hopes he might have nurtured of succeeding Osgoode.[30]

Pending Osgoode's replacement, Powell demanded and received Simcoe's recognition of his status above Attorney General White as 'the Senior Law Officer of the Crown.' It was a hollow triumph, conferring no actual power. Later he sarcastically acknowledged to Simcoe that, 'of course, as the only channel of legal opinion to your Excellency, I conceive [White's] sentiments should weigh against the meer [sic] suggestions of a Volunteer' (Powell himself). Twice kept out of the chief justiceship by English interlopers, Powell concluded that, since he would hardly have been left alone on the King's Bench for two years had his judicial capacities been in doubt, his exclusion must obviously flow from Simcoe's belief in his unfitness as an executive councillor. He proposed to Whitehall that he be promoted, but without a seat in the council as long as Simcoe remained in command.[31]

Powell had only himself to blame for his exclusion from power. The reservations that prompted him to advise Hamilton to consult Grant about the land certificates were doubtless genuine, but Simcoe and his attorney general can hardly be blamed for thinking that he should have confided in them rather than in a London barrister with close ties to the imperial government. Powell's excuses for doing so were certainly specious: solely responsible for the administration of justice in the absence of a chief justice, he wrote, yet deprived by his exclusion from the council of opportunities to suggest measures for the colony's welfare, he had applied directly to London, 'doubting the quality of any advice to be obtained this side the water' (another gibe at White).[32] Yet he could constitutionally have made his views known to Simcoe, and the lieutenant-governor could hardly have avoided referring the matter to London once he had done so.

The crabbed chorus of dissent, studded with obsequious self-vindication, that Powell directed to London in these years reveals his ability and his devotion to Upper Canada's welfare as a British colony as fully as it exposes his prickly nature. His criticism of Elmsley's Heir and Devisee Act is no exception. He would have preferred to see the commissioners bound by strict statutory guidelines in their adjudication of claims and aided by a jury in their determination of facts. Under Elmsley's scheme, 'a power, greater than that of the Chancellor of England' (the presiding judge of the Court of Chancery) was 'vested in a Commission, without a single principle for their Government, or any known Precedent to guide their discretion, and this in ascertaining facts, as well as in the adjudication upon them, without the aid of a Jury, or even the retention of Testimonies, on which their adjudication might be revised.'[33]

Powell's approach perhaps reflected the bias of an American common lawyer, since the courts of common law were geared to the resolution of fixed forms of question according to the letter of the law with the aid of a jury in deciding the facts, while the Court of Chancery, the very raison d'être of which was to make up for the law's defects, operated without a jury and often applied principles contrary to those of law. His dislike of Elmsley's imaginative measure might therefore be dismissed as crabbed conservatism but for the fact that it was fully justified by the way the commission proceeded to execute its mandate. The leading mercantile land speculators – Cartwright and Hamilton and their Detroit associate, John Askin – were appointed as commissioners and empowered to decide matters to the advantage of their friends, unhampered by the help of twelve good men and true, just as in the old days in the courts of common pleas. Those judges who tried to redress the balance – Powell and his fellow puisne, Henry Allcock, who arrived in 1799 – were outvoted by their lay coadjutors. Elmsley himself was sympathetic to the speculator interest, seeing in the creation of inequalities of wealth a stimulus to the colony's economic growth. When the commission's authority was extended in 1802, the rules of evidence were relaxed still further in order to vitiate the standards of proof that Powell and Allcock had tried to impose.[34]

While Powell's criticism of the Heir and Devisee Commission was sound, the commission's shortcomings were due less to the underlying theory than to the prevailing attitude in ruling circles after Simcoe's departure in 1796. The lieutenant-governor left no one behind him to promote his vision of the colony, or at least no one who felt that it entailed keeping the merchant speculators in their place, as opposed to allowing them and anyone else who might to engross as much wealth as they could at the expense of the rank-and-file farmer.[35] Receiver General Peter Russell, administrator of the province from 1796 to 1799 while Simcoe was absent on leave, was loyal to his chief's more easily comprehensible ideas, but he was an elderly fusspot and easily intimidated by the young and forceful Elmsley, who dominated the executive until the arrival of Lieutenant-Governor Peter Hunter. Russell tried to reserve the Heir and Devisee Act for consideration by the imperial government, but Elmsley and White joined forces to persuade him that it must be put into effect at once.[36]

Even after Hunter's advent no effort was made to appoint commissioners who would adjudicate claims in the spirit of Simcoe's proclamation of 1795. Though personally sympathetic to the merchants and their spokesmen in the Executive Council, the new lieutenant-governor proved in legal questions to be as open to the anti-mercantile views of Allcock as to those of Elmsley. But his residence downriver at Quebec, which was required by his duties as military commander-in-chief, deterred him from taking a strong interest in any non-military subject but the efficient working of the land-granting system, from which he derived substantial fees.[37] The mercantile interest was able to sway the third Upper Canadian parliament not only in respect of the Heir and Devisee Act of 1802, but also in securing legislation to facilitate the alienation of real estate by married women and the sale of land in execution of judgments of debt. At Allcock's urging, Hunter reserved the last two matters for consideration by the king in council, but in due course both provisions became law.[38]

But what of the curious incident of the dog in the night?

'The dog did nothing in the night.'
'That was the curious incident,' said Sherlock Holmes.

Unlike the dog in the tale of Silver Blaze, John White was not entirely supine during the land titles crisis; but from our point of view nothing is more curious about the crisis than his minor part in it. After 1820 it would be unlikely, and after 1840 inconceivable, that the attorney general could take so subordinate a role in the determination of a major question of legal policy by the government he served. In the second half of the nineteenth century, the reform of the law and its institutions to meet the exigencies of economic and social change was to be pre-eminently his responsibility. Yet in these early years, when English property law – recently received into the colony on the promise that it would make every settler's home his castle – was undergoing extraordinary modification in the interests of merchant capital, the relative unimportance of the attorneyship and its incumbent limited the office to a minor advisory role. The same was to be true of the other big domestic alarm of the decade, the dispute between the government and the Iroquois nations over the nature of their tenure of their reserve on the Grand River.

THE INDIAN TITLE CRISIS

The Grand River reserve had been set aside at the end of the American War of Independence to accommodate the six Iroquois nations of upstate

New York, who desired a refuge from the power of the newly sovereign United States. To Governor Sir Frederick Haldimand at Quebec the reserve, curving in a broad band along the river just west of the head of Lake Ontario, must have seemed a distant and desolate tract, but within a dozen years it was bordered by white settlement and stood as an obstacle to the westward extension of settlement north of Lake Erie. For their part, the five nations that eventually sought sanctuary there began to suffer from a decline in the game stocks on their reserve and to receive approaches from land speculators wishing to buy large blocks of it. The Indians' spokesman, the Mohawk war chief Joseph Brant, was willing to oblige, since the decline of hunting meant that the Indians would have to switch to farming, for which they needed much less land than the reserve comprised.[39]

The Indians occupied the reserve by a licence of occupation in perpetuity, a sort of perpetual tenancy. At first both Simcoe and Lord Dorchester, Haldimand's successor, resisted Brant's demand for a title that would permit them to sell the reserve. It had long been government policy that none but the government could buy land from the Indians, a restriction designed to protect the Indians from fraud. This consideration was reinforced in Simcoe's mind by his wish to prevent the merchant speculators from acquiring huge tracts of fertile land. Dorchester, however, saw the force of the Indians' argument that they were morally entitled to the same absolute control over their lands in Canada as they had possessed over those in New York, which they had lost in the service of the king. He forwarded a deed drawn by the attorney general of Lower Canada (Jonathan Sewell), which conveyed the power to sell or to lease land provided that it was first offered to the Crown for pre-emption.[40]

Simcoe was less ready to concede. The local officers of the Indian Department reported not to him but to Dorchester, and consequently Simcoe was anxious to assert his will in Indian affairs. He told the governor that he would execute the deed if it was approved of by the law officers of Upper Canada, and proceeded to refer it to White. It is hard to tell if he really hoped, or had reason to suppose, that White might uncover some insuperable objection to it, or if he was merely making a formal assertion of his authority as opposed to Dorchester's.[41]

White did indeed propose an objection to the deed founded on the fact that the Five Nations claimed to be not subjects of the king but his sovereign allies. As such they were aliens, and under English common law aliens could not be freeholders. The question was partly academic, since Brant rejected Sewell's deed because of the pre-emption clause, but

White made his own proposal to meet the Indians' demands: they should surrender to the Crown any lands they wished to sell, and the Crown would then deed them to the intended purchasers. Simcoe apparently approved of this scheme, but an obstacle appeared in the form of general instructions from the imperial government prohibiting the provincial authorities from making grants in excess of 1,200 acres, with a few specified exceptions.[42]

This was how things stood when Simcoe went on leave. His deputy, Russell, tried to put Brant off as long as possible, hoping to receive instructions from England. The months passed and Brant's discontent grew. He talked of going to London himself but went instead to Philadelphia, the u.s. capital, where he complained to the British ambassador and consorted ostentatiously with the pro-French party. By June 1797 Russell was grasping at excuses to put Brant off from day to day, and in this extremity he claimed that he must consult the Executive Council about the scope of his legal power to satisfy the Five Nations' demands. As rumours swirled of a Franco-Spanish invasion from the Mississippi Valley, the council decided that Russell possessed the authority to give the Indians what they wanted. Even now he temporized, making Brant an offer short of what the council had said he might and one that was unsatisfactory to the Mohawk statesman.

While the two men bickered over these details, orders at last arrived from London forbidding compliance with the Indians' demands but authorizing Russell to offer them the same terms they had agreed on with the speculators, in return for the surrender of the lands in question to the Crown. This was simply a revival of the pre-emption proposal Brant had rejected when it appeared in Sewell's draft deed. Russell asked the Executive Council whether these instructions relieved him of the obligation to negotiate further with the Indians; but Chief Justice Elmsley, who had earlier advised him to wait for the instructions, now led the council in pressing him to give in to Brant. Eventually Russell agreed to confirm the land sales the Five Nations had already contracted for, but he succeeded in withholding carte blanche for future sales without government approval. Six blocks of land, ranging in extent from 19,000 to 94,000 acres, passed into the hands of white speculators, and the chequered story of the settlement of the Grand Valley ended its first chapter.[43]

A SKILLED FUNCTIONARY

In both of these crises, as throughout his eight years as attorney general,

White appears as the skilled functionary, carrying out his allotted duties and supplying his expertise to the government on demand. In neither case does he seem to have tried to influence official policy; even in the land titles crisis, which was fundamentally a question of legal policy, he was ready to second both Simcoe and Elmsley in their very different approaches. Unlike Powell, if he had any views on policy he kept them to himself.

This abstinence is strikingly illustrated by White's performance when Russell was instructed by the secretary of state in 1797 to consult the Executive Council, the judges, and the law officers of the Crown on the best means of using Crown lands to form a fund for the payment of grammar-school teachers. The officials named by the minister met in committee under the chairmanship of Elmsley, who posed five questions to each of them: what sum should be raised; how many acres should be appropriated; how many schools should eventually be founded, and where; how many were required at once; and what was the best way of fostering education in the province, if not by founding grammar schools. All but White, including Robert Gray, the young solicitor general, addressed the policy issues put to them, but the attorney general limited himself to a statement of the different legal means of disposing of Crown lands. This abstention was deliberate, as he made clear: 'This is the *manner* in which I presume the waste lands of the Crown may be appropriated, and rendered productive. As to the *extent* I apprehend it wholly depends upon the plan of the intended Establishments upon which I do not presume to offer my opinion: conceiving it not to be the purport of your Honor's letter to call on me to that effect.'[44] It was entirely in keeping with the nature of his office: the attorney general of England at that time would have been quite surprised to find himself bidden to attend the cabinet to advise on a question not of law but of education policy, and so probably would his successor today. White's main duties as attorney general of Upper Canada were, first, to expedite the government's legal business (including assize prosecutions); second, to advise it on matters of law when called upon to do so; and third, to draft legislative bills at the government's behest.

The advisory role was one for which White had several competitors. We have seen Judge Powell's attempt to assert his primacy over White as a law adviser to the Crown in 1795. Elmsley behaved similarly two years later. Simcoe had left Russell to carry out his intention of shifting the seat of government from Newark (Niagara) to York (Toronto), which was then a huddle of huts in the middle of nowhere, separated from Newark by forty miles of lake or seventy miles of what was mostly Indian country. Elmsley, immediately on his arrival, had plunged £1,500 into a house at Newark. At once he conceived a necessity to keep the capital there, since the Judicature Act required both the Court of King's Bench and the Home District Assizes to be held at the seat of government, and he doubted that enough grand and petit jurors for an assize could be assembled in the middle of the wilderness. After failing to carry the Executive Council with him, the chief justice did gain the council's and Russell's agreement to an enactment allowing the governor to retain the Court of King's Bench at Newark for up to two years, as might be found expedient. He then exceeded his authority by pushing bills through to keep both the Court of King's Bench and the assizes there for the whole two years.

Russell did not discover Elmsley's manoeuvre until he was preparing to give royal assent to the session's legislation. When he did, he told Simcoe, 'I immediately informed the Chief Justice that I should take the opinion of the Executive Council upon the propriety of passing or rejecting these two bills, and that I had sent for the Attorney General to advise me on the subject. He was pleased to be greatly offended with me on this occasion, as he could not see the necessity, he said, of my consulting the Attorney General, while he was present to advise me.'[45] On this occasion, Russell wrote to his sister, 'The Attorney General was of infinite use to me in bringing an impetuous indiscreet man to reason.'[46] But had he not needed White's opinion to counteract Elmsley, he might well have gone no further than the chief justice in this case, just as a few days earlier he had consulted the Executive Council but not White on the extent of his authority to treat with the Five Nations.

Upper Canada in the 1790s was a difficult country to govern. Its few thousand souls were scattered in tiny clusters across a great forested wilderness. They were as diverse as they were scattered: Roman Catholic clansmen from the Scottish highlands; German mercenaries recruited to suppress rebellion in the old colonies; American farmers and American Indians who had chosen, or found themselves aligned with, the losing side in that struggle; French settlers clustered about the fur-trading entrepôt of Detroit; Scottish and American merchants scattered along the great aquatic artery that linked the continental interior with the warehouses and counting-houses of Glasgow, Liverpool, and London; aboriginal peoples, settled along the lakes and streams of what had just become the Upper Canadian interior. Each of these little communities, each of the individuals who composed them, had their special values and purposes. The ties of common value and purpose that might bind them into a larger community were frail: a more or less developed sense of alienation from the new American republic – a menace from which they were insulated only by the still unsettled expanses of northern New York and Pennsylvania – and a slight feeling of obligation, uncertainly compounded of interest and sentiment, towards the English Crown and its local representatives.

The handful of officials charged with governing this territory were by and large slenderly equipped with talent and resources. Communications were poor within the colony and poorer still between the colony and imperial headquarters; military support was exiguous. There was a lively sense of being perched on a low-lying, narrow, windswept islet of civilization amid stormy seas of chaos. To keep the upper lip stiff there was only personal ambition, pride in representing the widest empire the world had known, and brandy.

To hold back the ocean there was a sandbag rampart of English institutions. In return for obedience, Simcoe proffered the forms and ideology of ordered liberty – parliamentary government and the rule of law. His promised 'image and transcript of the English constitution' was a guarantee of consensual government; the common law, impartially administered by professional lawyers, a guarantee that every man's home was his castle; the Church of England an assurance of divine sanction for this earthly order. The structure was makeshift, and its materials, much like the orderly forward march of red-coated infantry, needed substantial modification to be useful in the North American forest – often more substantial than the local administrators could easily devise or the imperial authorities allow. Simcoe, Russell, and their legal advisers more than once found themselves virtually having to make up law as they went along.

Under such circumstances, John White's duty as watchdog over the constitutionality of public administration was both difficult and thankless, and there is no reason to suppose that he performed it with special alacrity. Yet one can hear a pre-echo of the McRuer Report in his anxiety, expressed to his brother-in-law in England, to keep a runaway governor within the confines of legality. Not that White's duty in this respect was identical with his modern successor's; but the difference is a subtle one that lies less in the substance of the duty than in the consequences that might be expected to follow from his failure to perform it effectively.

The modern attorney general, like any other cabinet minister, assumes two kinds of responsibility to the people of Ontario: a collective responsibility for all cabinet decisions, and an individual responsibility for the conscientious and effective performance of his departmental duties. Should he find himself in conscientious disagreement with his cabinet colleagues on a matter of policy, or if he should fail in a serious way to execute the duties especially pertaining to his office, it is constitutionally requisite that he express that responsibility by resigning his office. The first attorney general was in a very different position. He owed his appointment not to the people of Upper Canada but to the imperial authorities. Consequently, although his was an office of trust, the responsibility it imposed was owed not to the people of the colony but to the Crown and Parliament of the empire. This meant that once John White had warned Lieutenant-Governor Simcoe of the danger of transgression, he was off the hook (or at least that all he had to worry about was the possibility that Simcoe might erroneously cite his advice in endeavouring to justify some ultra vires action to the secretary of state).

In a sense, White's position was like that of King Lear's Fool: he was the keeper of the king's conscience, but the king's failure to heed his rebukes did not impose on him any requirement to resign. Thus in 1795, when Simcoe rejected his claim to draft all the land-granting deeds, a claim advanced on the ground that they were instruments issuing under the great seal of the province, White could write: 'I do hereby absolve myself of all responsibility to the King and Parliament for any Lands that may be granted, the deed of Conveyance of which has not been examined by me, previously to the affixing of the Seal of the Province.'[47] He had done his duty in representing the proper course of action; the responsibility for its neglect belonged not to him but to the head of the colonial executive. He could view the results of that neglect with a clear conscience.

2

The Rewards of Office

The law officers and judges of Upper Canada devoted a lot of ink, and no doubt a lot of breath, to asking for higher pay – or, as they would have put it, an augmentation of their emoluments. This was partly because the comforts of life were costly in the tiny frontier colony, and partly because appointment to public office was sought after and awarded as an opportunity of making one's fortune. To an official from Great Britain, the initial investment entailed in accepting office in Upper Canada was considerable, since he had to pay his own way out. When the return failed to measure up to expectation the skirl of lamentation was prolonged.

Public office was, in fact, a sort of property: an incorporeal hereditament, as it was classed by the mid-eighteenth-century English jurist, William Blackstone.[1] Traditionally, offices might be granted for life, for a term of years, in reversion (which meant a promise of succeeding the current holder on his death or retirement), or during pleasure (the pleasure of the grantor, the Crown). They might even be inherited: that is what 'hereditament' means. During the first fifty years or so of Upper Canada's history no major office was awarded except during pleasure, but some at least of the lesser offices were life appointments, and an appointment during pleasure conveyed an expectation that it was for life, barring the greatest incompetence or misconduct. Officials tried hard to pass their offices on to their sons.

This proprietary nature constitutes an important difference between the office of attorney general in 1791 and that office today. The incumbent did receive an annual salary of £300 from the imperial government as a sort of retainer, but for the extra money that made the difference between comfort and hardship he had to rely on fees for services. These fees were derived from private practice, from the government, and from private individuals for services performed to their benefit in his official capacity. With respect to the two latter sources the attorney general was, like most of his colleagues in the government service, a privileged vendor of services to the government and the public. This is an important point to remember when we run into complaints that the official clique – the Family Compact, as they became known – 'monopolized' public office: they were not only a collective monopoly, or oligarchy, but the offices they monopolized were themselves monopolies.

A FIGHT FOR FEES

John White's commission authorized him 'to have, hold, exercise and enjoy' his office, 'together with all and singular the Rights, Fees, Profits, Privileges and Advantages thereunto belonging or appertaining.'[2] He soon found that it entailed too much exercise and all too little to enjoy. Especially arduous were the annual assize circuits, when a judge holding commissions of oyer and terminer and general gaol delivery from the lieutenant-governor toured the province to hold a court in each district.

The assizes tried all cases of crime too grave to be dealt with by the district magistrates at the quarterly general sessions of the peace ('quarter sessions'), as well as lesser cases if the accused was in prison pending trial; any complaint made at the assizes and certified by the grand jury could also be tried. Under the Judicature Act of 1794, the judge also held a court of civil jurisdiction, or nisi prius, for the trial of actions instituted in the Court of King's Bench. The importance of the occasion and the number of the participants made the assizes the great public event of the year, at least when there was no parliamentary election. The members of the grand jury, who reviewed the criminal cases to decide if the evidence warranted proceeding to trial, numbered nearly two dozen; a pool of petit jurors selected by the sheriff attended, from which twelve-man juries were formed for both criminal and civil trials; counsel, court officials, and witnesses swelled the throng.[3]

It was White's duty and privilege as attorney general to travel the circuit along with the judge in order to conduct the criminal prosecutions on behalf of the Crown. In the early years especially, when there were only four districts and very few settlements, the distances were long, it was often necessary to camp overnight, and the business to be done was not worth the effort. On one such occasion White complained to his brother-in-law that he was about to go to Detroit at a cost of thirty pounds in order to conduct a single prosecution.[4] Lieutenant-Governor Simcoe alleviated White's plight by instituting an allowance, which became known as circuit money, to defray the expenses of the officers (the judge, the Crown prosecutor, and the clerk of assize) engaged in the annual assize circuits. The yield from prosecutions at assize also rose, but even in the last year of White's tenure it never exceeded seventy pounds;[5] and after the appointment of Robert Gray, a young loyalist, as solicitor general in 1796, not all of it went to him.

Gray's appointment led to a row over the privileges of the two offices in 1798, when the province was divided into eight districts and two assize circuits – an eastern and a western – were set up. Gray claimed the right to travel the circuit the attorney general did not choose for himself. White denied the solicitor's right to take the circuit as a matter of course, though he admitted that the lieutenant-governor might order its assignment to him. Citing the leading case of *R.* v *Wilkes* in a letter to the English attorney general (Sir John Scott, known to posterity as the eminent Lord Chancellor Eldon), White contended that the solicitor might exercise all the duties and privileges of the attorneyship when that office was vacant or its incumbent out of the province, but that otherwise the solicitor enjoyed no official privilege that trenched on the emoluments of the attorneyship.[6]

Still, once two simultaneous circuits were in operation someone had to substitute for the attorney general on the second circuit (or so it was assumed at the time), and it became normal for the solicitor general to do so. The resulting loss of emoluments compounded the damage White had sustained in 1797 by the removal of the seat of government from the commercial entrepôt of Niagara to the campsite capital of York, which cost him what little private practice he had enjoyed. In November 1798 he complained to the under-secretary of state that he was so poor that he had to dig his own potatoes and cut his own firewood. If he died his family would be dependent on the bounty of mankind. As it happened, the attorney's death in a duel just over a year later left his family dependent on a wealthy brother-in-law; it was his mistress and their two children who were thrown on the bounty of mankind.[7]

The meagre return from his legal duties made White eager to augment his income from routine administrative functions. With the help of Chief Justice Osgoode, he tried to carve a slice out of the revenues belonging to the provincial secretary, William Jarvis – another testy colonial who, like Judge Powell, was somewhat out of sympathy with the British interlopers who lorded over the colony during Simcoe's administration.[8] Osgoode persuaded Simcoe that it ought to be the attorney general's duty to draft land grant deeds, although in other colonies that was done by the provincial secretary on receipt of the attorney general's fiat, or order, to do so.

After Osgoode left the province, Simcoe began to question the need for the attorney general's interference in the land-granting procedure, and White had to defend his newly acquired territory. He argued that his commission required him to transact all of the king's legal business in the colony, and it was therefore his duty to see that land-granting instruments were legally made and executed. If the provincial secretary drew these instruments, it would be necessary for that officer to show them to White in order to ascertain their legality. This procedure might suffice in other colonies, but the state of land tenure in Upper Canada was so muddled that it would be almost impossible for Jarvis to draw a deed without first stating a case for the attorney general's opinion. That would entail delay and expense all around, and especially to the secretary himself, who would have to pay White a fee for each opinion. It would be better for everyone if the attorney general drew the deed in the first place.[9]

White's reasoning did not commend itself to Jarvis, who insisted on what he called 'the inalienable prerogatives of my Office consistent with the established Precedents of all other British American Provinces.' The very language betrays Jarvis's conception of his office as a species of property, a monopoly of certain services which a fellow official was trying to muscle in on. He saw no reason why the practice in Upper Canada should differ from that in the lower province, especially since White's mandamus stated that he was to hold office on the same terms as his counterpart at Quebec. It was this riposte that provoked White formally to absolve himself from all responsibility for improvident land grants made under the system Jarvis preferred.[10] About this time, however, Simcoe heard that the imperial authorities intended the attorney general to have a fee for issuing his fiat for land grants, and the Executive Council decided that he should receive half of the fee that went in other colonies to the provincial secretary for drawing the deed.

White had won the political battle, but his expectations of reward were to prove too sanguine. In 1794 he predicted that the land-granting process would make his office more remunerative than its Lower Canadian counterpart, but the delay in setting up a procedure for authenticating land grants put a stop to the business for years. When at last the Heir and Devisee Commission began its work, White found that the half-fee charged on grants to loyalists was too small to yield a profit, the more so since his spoliation of Jarvis made Jarvis's part in the land-granting procedure a losing proposition and gave the secretary no incentive to work quickly.[11]

White's successor, Thomas Scott, did better financially. As the population rose, the yield from prosecutions at assize rose with it; and though it varied widely from year to year, it reached an unprecedented £235 in 1804. Under the resolute administration of Peter Hunter, the kinks were ironed out of the land-granting procedure (much to the chagrin of Secretary Jarvis, who was forced to speed up his output but not allowed to economize by substituting paper for parchment). But Scott did not leave the increase of his emoluments to chance and the exertions of others. In 1802 he persuaded the government to adopt the table of fees that had been fixed for the attorney general of Lower Canada a year earlier. This enabled him to claim fees for certain services that had not until now been remunerated at a fixed rate, and also to claim payment in sterling for services that had previously been paid for in local (Halifax) currency, then worth about seven-eighths of sterling. He also benefited from an annual allowance for office rent and a clerk's salary, which the Executive Council had authorized in 1797 but which White for some reason had never accepted.[12]

Most important of all, the elderly Scot saw eye to eye with his fellow Caledonians who now dominated the colony commercially and politically. Although he seconded Judge Allcock's anti-mercantile stand against Elmsley's married women's property and sheriff's bills of 1801,[13] he got on well with the network, stretching from the Atlantic seaboard to the Detroit River, of merchants who controlled the trade of British North America, and served them in his private practice. He also gained the approval of Hunter, another Scot, who nominated him to the Executive Council in 1804. There, in Hunter's absence, he formed a quadrumvirate with Allcock, Inspector General John McGill, and the Scottish merchant Aeneas Shaw. When Allcock moved on to Lower Canada in 1805, like Osgoode and Elmsley before him, these credentials sufficed to secure Scott's succession as chief justice of the upper province, despite Hunter's coincident death and the rivalry of the newly arrived puisne justice Robert Thorpe, an old acquaintance of the then secretary of state, Lord Castlereagh.[14]

Scott was followed as attorney general by a very different character. William Firth, a scholarly Englishman from Norwich, was a friend of William Windham, secretary of state for war and the colonies, in the short-lived 'Ministry of All the Talents' (a florid term for an all-party coalition), which took office on William Pitt's death in 1806. During his tenure of office, the attorney general's fees became the subject of a controversy that did not wane until the most essential functions of the office had been questioned.[15] Hardly a crisis, the Firth Fees Fuss reveals a good deal about the nature of the office, and of the administration of the colony in general, on the eve of the war of 1812. It also gave rise to the first controversy over the execution of the prosecutorial function in the province.

THE FIRTH FEES FUSS

Firth's concern for his emoluments was evident almost from the moment he arrived in Upper Canada in November 1807. Barely three months later he was writing to the Colonial Office to claim the attorney general's salary for the whole period from June 1806, when Scott had become chief justice, to the time of his appointment as Scott's successor in March 1807. He alleged that prior to his arrival fiats for land grants had been issued with 'an unusual precipitation,' thereby depriving him of fees that he might otherwise have earned. The imperial authorities evidently saw nothing to blame in the solicitor general, D'Arcy Boulton, making the most of his chance at the attorney's trough; in fact, they rewarded his zeal by granting him the attorney general's salary for the whole period between Scott's promotion and Firth's advent. Since Boulton had been doing the job, this was only fair; but it was undoubtedly a blow to Firth, who had pleaded that it had cost him £600 to travel to Upper Canada – more than two years' salary, once the wartime income tax of 10 per cent was deducted.[16]

Firth's resentment of his colleagues was sharpened when the Executive Council audited his first half-yearly account. Complaining to Lieutenant-Governor Francis Gore that the Board of Audit had trimmed the account by more than forty pounds, he expostulated:

They appear to me to have done this at their arbitrary pleasure, subject to no control, allowing no Appeal, calling for no Explanation, & not even abiding by the Rules they themselves have either laid down or affect to adopt. With submission, Sir, ye King's Attorney General will not brook having a righteous Account with

Government disallowed by a fluctuating arbitrary decision without investigation, depending on no known Rules ... other than those suggested by the imperative will of the moment.

That his remonstrance emanated from no merely sordid love of gain Firth, a Cambridge man, made quite clear:

To any person of Honor and Education brought up to ye English bar, it must needs be painful to descend to the making of a charge at all, much more to have the Items of a just Account rudely scrutinized as if it were a common tradesman's Bill. I have only to add that the present Account, in England will be found to be far below ye compensation chearfully [sic] allowed by a private Client in any [sic] the meanest of circumstances.[17]

Though Firth did not itemize the cuts, they seem to have included the attorney general's £100-a-year allowance for a clerk and office rent, and fees for pardons under the Great Seal of the province.[18]

Both of these charges were eventually restored by order of the lieutenant-governor, who pointedly asked Inspector General McGill (according to Firth, at any rate) why he saw fit to challenge an item that he had authorized annually since 1800. One other item remained in dispute, however, and raised a wider issue. Firth had put in a claim for twenty-two guineas (£23 2s) for the same number of warrants issued to sheriffs under the lieutenant-governor's seal-at-arms to hold elections in the various parliamentary constituencies of the province. The board of audit disallowed all but £1 1s of this claim on the ground that Firth was entitled to a fee only for the draft of such an instrument, not for every copy. Firth maintained that he was entitled to be paid for such instruments on exactly the same basis as for instruments under the great seal, each of which brought him a fee whether he had prepared a special draft for it or not. But Firth's contention only raised the question of whether he was entitled to be paid on such a basis for instruments under the great seal.[19]

The administration of the province required a constant stream of such instruments. The assize judges could not go on circuit without commissions of assize and nisi prius, and of oyer and terminer and general gaol delivery, for each separate district of their circuits. A general election necessitated one proclamation to dissolve the existing parliament and another to elect a new one. No one could be appointed to public office without a commission, be he judge, magistrate, sheriff, or inspector of flour and pot and pearl ashes. All these proclamations and commissions had to be prepared, or engrossed, by the provincial secretary, according to a form drafted by the attorney general, upon receiving the latter's fiat.[20] For each fiat the attorney general received a fee from the individual benefited by the instrument, if it was (say) a land grant deed, a ferry lease, or a commission of appointment to an office of profit (one that brought the holder fees or a salary), and from the government in other cases. As the population grew and the form of administration became more settled, the secretary was preparing more and more of such instruments; but a much larger proportion of them was based not on a special draft by the attorney general but on a standard form. The Board of Audit now began to object to the attorney general's claim to a fee from the government for instruments prepared from these standard forms.

The issue was complicated by rivalry within the Executive Council between William Dummer Powell, who had just been nominated to it by the newly arrived Gore after years of exclusion, and the other councillors – especially Chief Justice Scott, whose office made him the caustic puisne's special target. Powell had persuaded Gore to authorize the attorney general's allowance for a clerk and office rent when it was challenged by McGill. In the matter of payment for instruments under the seals, it was Scott who defended Firth's claim and Powell who persistently opposed it.

The quarrel was embarrassing to the chief justice because Firth based his claim on the fact that Scott had received such payments as his predecessor. In arguing that they were unjustified according to the Lower Canadian fee table that Scott had persuaded the government to adopt in 1802, Powell was all but accusing the chief justice of knowingly demanding fees under false pretences. Scott insisted that he had asked the council to adopt only the fees relating to legal services, not those for routine ministerial functions like those now in question; to these the previous practice, under which the attorney general had claimed a fee for every instrument, remained applicable. In refuting Scott, Powell pointed to the wording both of Scott's petition and of the council minute adopting the new table.

When the quarrel came to a head in March 1810, Scott withdrew from the discussion on the ground of conflict of interest. His colleagues reported their view that Firth was not entitled to the disputed fees, but admitted that Scott's receipt of them made the question debatable. According to Powell's later account, Gore forwarded the report to London in May 1810 in a dispatch, drafted for him by Scott, in which he espoused the chief justice's view of the government's intention in adopting the tariff of 1802. But as Powell put it, in characteristic style, 'The delusion practised upon Lieut. Governor Gore on this occasion was dissipated shortly afterwards and he was able to distinguish which of his Advisors was moved by self interest, and which by a higher principle.'[21] The probable cause of Gore's turnabout was a dispatch from London on a political cause célèbre of the previous year that had caused him serious embarrassment.

On arriving in Upper Canada in 1806, Gore had found the colony in turmoil. The discontents that had been building up for six years, during the administration of his high-handed predecessor Hunter, had erupted into a constitutional crisis when the House of Assembly remonstrated against the government's unauthorized expenditure of surplus revenues from previous years. The crisis was inflamed by the agitation of a trio of Irish office-holders who were at odds with the dominant clique: a lawyer and MPP, William Weekes, a district sheriff, Joseph Willcocks, and a newly arrived judge of the Court of King's Bench, Robert Thorpe. Thorpe, a devious and hysterically irresponsible man, had been a fellow law student of the secretary of state, Lord Castlereagh. He sent one shrill screed after another back to London blaming the crisis on the misgovernment of the Hunter clique and representing himself as attempting – with great success, of course – to calm things down. In fact he was attending the sittings of the House in order to direct its tactics. When Weekes was killed in a duel in October 1806, Thorpe secured his own election to the Assembly at the ensuing by-election.[22]

Gore handled the crisis with a judicious mixture of soft soap and vigour. He mollified the House by admitting that the government had acted unconstitutionally, and he suspended from office Thorpe, Willcocks, and another newly arrived official malcontent, Surveyor General C.B. Wyatt. But while the political situation was calmed, an articulate opposition persisted under the leadership of Willcocks, who started a newspaper and was elected to the House of Assembly at a by-election. In a further attempt to discipline the opposition, Gore took two steps, one at Firth's urging and the other upon his advice. The first was to authorize Firth to prosecute Willcocks for seditious libel. The second was to dismiss a supporter of Willcocks in the Assembly, a prominent United Empire Loyalist called David McGregor Rogers, from his office as registrar of deeds for the Northumberland District.

Firth failed in his prosecution of Willcocks, which had been mounted against the judgment of Gore's more experienced advisers. Rogers resisted his dismissal by refusing to hand over the official records of the district to his nominated successor. When the government moved in the Court of King's Bench for a mandamus to compel his compliance, the application was turned down by no less a personage than William Dummer Powell. The judge accepted his fellow loyalist's contention that although his patent appointed him during pleasure, it was overruled by the provincial statute that had created his office, which provided that it be filled *during good behaviour* – a life appointment, terminable only because of the holder's incapacity or misconduct in office.[23]

As we noted, Gore had dismissed Rogers principally on Firth's advice that to do so was within the scope of the royal prerogative. Although he had nominated Powell for the Executive Council soon after assuming the governorship, he seems at first to have viewed Powell's elevation of the statute over the prerogative as yet more evidence of the Yankee levelling tendencies imputed to the dour Bostonian by earlier governors. As soon as he had sent off the Audit Board's report on Firth's fees, accompanied by his own recommendation in the attorney general's favour, he was surprised to receive the English law officers' opinion that Powell had been correct. At once Gore saw both men in a clearer light, vastly to Firth's disadvantage: on the one hand the ageing loyalist, who in 1806 had urged the Executive Council to adopt the same frank and conciliatory approach to the House of Assembly that Gore had later applied with success – a man with twenty years' service on the bench and an understanding of the needs and desires of the Upper Canadian settler; on the other a fussy, conceited Englishman, with a head full of antiquarian legal scholarship but no idea of how to apply it to the circumstances of a North American frontier colony.[24]

At this very moment, Firth was foolish enough to take a political stand that was both hostile to Powell and critical of Gore, and which exposed his preoccupation with his fees in the worst possible light. In October 1809, on returning from his assize circuit, Powell had reported widespread discontent at the high cost of lawsuits in the Court of King's Bench and had recommended that lawyers be prevented from inflating their fees by pursuing in that tribunal causes that were within the jurisdiction of the much cheaper district courts.[25] At its next session, the legislature responded to this discontent by assuming the power, previously exercised by the judges of the court, to regulate the fees payable to lawyers for services in the Court of King's Bench and instituting a somewhat lower tariff.[26] Firth and his fellow law officer, D'Arcy Boulton, denounced the measure as one that lessened the respectability of the bar by making it 'completely subject to the casual and oscillating mandate of a Popular

Assembly' and establishing a table of fees 'incapable of supporting any professional character as a Gentleman.' It flowed, they averred, from 'an invidious spirit of republicanism, which seeks to reduce all orders of Men to a level, and to put the man of Science on a footing with the labourer, a spirit which the Inhabitants of this Colony from their perpetual inter- course and connection with a neighbouring Country are but too apt to imbibe.' Worst of all, and 'a paramount and decisive objection to the Bill,' it appeared to be 'a species of innovation (borrowed from the popular institutions of a neighbouring State) directly levelling the King's preroga- tive by curtailing the Power, authority and rightful Jurisdiction of his Supreme Courts.' Powell and his colleague, Chief Justice Scott, had been remiss in not protesting against it, and Gore in not reserving it for consideration by the imperial government.[27]

Firth had played these particular tunes once too often. The remon- strance reached Gore just after the English law officers' opinion on the Rogers case; why should he believe Firth's trumpetings about the royal prerogative this time? The last legislative measure that Firth, then only newly arrived in the province, had denounced as a republican assault on the prerogative had been a bill of 1808 designed to remove litigation from the Court of King's Bench to the inferior courts. On that occasion too he had publicly challenged the right of the legislature to interfere with the judicial system, an assertion the House of Assembly had rejected with contempt.[28] All in all, the attorney general's understanding of what the king's honour demanded and what the law directed seemed too much influenced by his personal interests to be trusted. Referring a legal question to the Colonial Office in August 1810 with a request to take the opinion of the English law officers, Gore remarked: 'I have been so misled in one important act of Government by the Advice of the Attorney and Solicitor General of this Province, that I no longer have confidence to act upon their opinions in a matter of such weight.'[29]

According to Firth, it was about this time that Gore and Powell determined to encompass his ruin. If so, the first stroke came when, with the annual assize courts about to commence, Gore ordered Firth to take the western circuit, which was far less lucrative than the eastern. The attorney general protested against this unprecedented infringement of his rights. 'When I accepted ye Office of Atty Genl I well knew that (amongst other Privileges) it was always considered his right to choose his own Circuit in preference to ye Solicitor General *as such*, and knowing all the *accustomed* sources of his Income, I received the appointment of His Majesty, judging naturally I should enjoy ye like Emoluments of ye

Office.' The prosecutions pending on the eastern circuit exceeded those on the less populous western by tenfold, and Gore's order would subject him to a loss of over £200.[30] Now the lieutenant-governor, who had hitherto supported Firth against the depredations of the Board of Audit, had struck a blow against his emoluments.

The skirmishing between Firth and the board continued throughout the next few months, and in March 1811 the embattled attorney played into his enemies' hands. He applied for Gore's authority to issue his fiat retrospectively for any commission under the great seal that might have been uttered by the provincial secretary without it. His fiat, he explained (following White in 1795), was the government's assurance that an instrument was legal and the king had not been misled in making it. According to English usage, any instrument under the great seal that did not 'pass thro' ye ancient accustomed Offices' was subsequently voidable by the Crown as improvident.[31]

Gore referred Firth's claims to the Executive Council, who recommended that the matter be referred to London. In the meantime, Gore ordered the provincial secretary not to affix the great seal to any instrument without the attorney general's fiat and forbade Firth, while this rule remained in force, to quit the capital without the lieutenant-governor's special permission. What this meant was brought home to Firth that summer. He applied for permission to travel the eastern assize circuit and was told that Gore considered his absence incompatible with the public service as long as he remained an indispensable party to every act of government requiring the great seal.[32]

In 1808 Firth had loftily described his official responsibilities as 'the usual Duties of the King's Attorney General.' Now he was forced for the second time in six months into crass particularities. 'The first, highest and most important Branch of the official Duty of the Attorney General, both as it respects the King and the Country, Consists in his Conducting in person, the Crown Prosecutions against Criminal Offenders and the violators of the Law of the Land. It is the chief end of the Institution of his high Office to prosecute in the name of the King, altho' he may have also other subordinate Duties to perform, which of course must give way to the higher and Superior Functions.' Although his duty required him to authenticate with his fiat every instrument under the great seal, most of these were land grants and leases in which a few months' delay was immaterial. Proclamations could be prepared in advance if necessary, as had always been done up to now. The assize circuit now produced at least three-quarters of the attorney general's emoluments, and Firth expressed confidence that the 'strict sense of justice' of Gore and the council would ensure to him 'all the rights, fees, privileges, profits advantages and Emoluments of the Office of Attorney General in as full and ample a manner as my Predecessor enjoyed them, which I believe are the words of the King's Warrant under the Sign Manual.'[33]

One might expect that at least this unequivocal statement of the attorney general's chief duty would command general assent, but it did not. The Executive Council advised Gore that there was no need for a Crown counsel to appear at the assizes 'unless matters especially regarding the King's Interest are to be there agitated.' The attorney general's wish to do so seemed incompatible with his pretension to be an indispensable party to every act of government requiring the great seal, and the council could advise the lieutenant-governor to accede to it only 'as an Indulgence subject to Your Excellency's Judgement of its Expediency.' It was on this basis that Gore granted Firth permission to go, stating his agreement with the council but 'apprehending that the Public may not at present be prepared for the change.'

Faced with what he termed the virtual abolition of his office by the denial of its most important function, Firth fled back to England without Gore's permission in order to plead his case at the foot of the throne. Solicitor General Boulton was already absent on leave, with no prospect of an early return. No law officer remained in Upper Canada to perform the duties that Firth maintained were vital.[34]

A LEAGUE OF SHARKS

Firth was a greedy, conceited bungler, who seems on the face of it to have merited all the harassment the Executive Council and the lieutenant-governor meted out to him. During the three-hundred-year history of the British empire, similar incompetents were sent out by the dozen to plague and misgovern one colony or another. They would gain office through their own or a patron's influence with the responsible minister of the Crown, often with little attention given to their suitability for the job; and a small, poor colony like Upper Canada could not expect the pick of the crop. Often, when they reached their destination, their dreams of profit or glory were dashed. The appointment was unrewarding, the climate burdensome, the natives horrible. Their fellow officials were venal, vulgar, and determinedly oblivious to, or else envious of, the newcomer's dazzling merit. Owing to the proprietary nature of office, once appointed the malcontents were hard to get rid of, unless (as often happened) they defied the governor's authority or got mixed up in politics. If they did neither of these things, the process of expelling them could be arduous and grinding. So it was with Firth.

The attorney knew quite well what they had done to him. He was fussy and hypersensitive, and consequently prone to magnifying his wrongs, but he was far from dense; his tale of suffering merits attention, highly coloured though it was. In his memorial of complaint to the secretary of state, Lord Liverpool, he characterized Gore as boisterous, unruly, capricious, violent in his resentments, and quite uncontrollable when pursuing the object of his displeasure: in short, a man cast in the same mould as Simcoe and Hunter. 'He possessed in an ardent degree that cardinal and fatal error to all placed in ye like Station, a restless curiosity to hear tales, & know ye private history of every Individual; he was most eager to hear every thing said of himself. To obtain this gratification a complete establishmt of espionage was organized, a system on ye effects of which it is unnecessary to dwell: Slander & calumny must frequently be called in to fill up Chasms.'

At first the lieutenant-governor had sympathized with Firth; but once the attorney general had the bad luck to incur his displeasure, Gore and Powell jointly resolved upon his ruin.

From this period to ye day of my departure from ye Province, these two with their unworthy Hirelings pursued me to ruin, & myself & family dragged on our solitary existence in misery. I was visited with all sorts of oppression & persecution; every engine of Power was put in requisition, & every ingenious invention, to contribute to my discomfort & annoyance; & every possible indignity was offered me to excite me to some expression or act of violence which might be laid hold of to furnish some ostensible ground of suspending me from my office.[35]

Nor was this persecution directed solely at Firth: it was part of a 'grand system of terror & oppression,' which proceeded in a 'general, established & systematic routine.'

The sanctuary of ye Post Office was violated; letters were intercepted & opened; some wholly stopped; others, ye contents being read, suffered to proceed to their destination, to observe in secret ye workings of their known contents ... False accusations were daily sent abroad to destroy ye best Characters, which had no other origin or foundation than their being brooded & hatched in ye malignant mind of ye Spies of Mr. Gore.[36]

Firth himself had been stigmatized as an associate of the dismissed officials, Thorpe and Wyatt, although he was unacquainted with either man, both of whom had left the colony before his arrival. Yet even while denying any link with them, he recognized that his complaints only echoed theirs, not to mention the constant refrain of Willcocks's weekly newspaper and the burden of a pamphlet on Upper Canadian politics published in London in 1809 by a well-connected Englishman, John Mills Jackson.[37] Firth suggested to Liverpool that the very prevalence of such complaints created a prima facie presumption that they were justified.

Firth's diatribes, though self-serving, were not wholly groundless. By 1805, the little world of York officialdom had developed the traits of an in-group with a proprietorial attitude to the government they administered. They resented the imperial government's habit of appointing outsiders to the chief offices of profit and were predisposed to be hostile to the newcomers. If the latter were out of sympathy with the dominant faction, as Thorpe proved to be, and scorned the manners of the province's 'shopkeeper aristocracy,' as Thorpe and Firth both did, they were in for trouble. Hunter and Gore were army men like Simcoe, but neither of them shared the first governor's hostility to the merchants and their official friends, who by 1806 had acquired a patina of authority which predisposed Gore on his arrival to accept theirs as the voice of 'respectable' opinion and ignore the complaints of the Thorpe faction against their self-serving and repressive administration. The personal foibles of Thorpe and Weekes make Gore's predilection understandable; but Thorpe's basic theme of a mainly Scottish merchant network, stretching from Halifax (or Newfoundland) to Detroit (or the Mississippi), and dominating the colonial executive and judiciary with the help of influential friends in London, was far from fantastic.[38] Gore did not at first share their animus against Firth, a fellow Englishman of genteel antecedents who had no truck with the spokesmen of dissent; but once Firth had made an enemy of him, the attorney general's goose was cooked.

Gore, of course, was alienated by Firth's incompetence; but it is arguable that what offended the dominant officials was not his incompetence so much as the amount of money he was making. By the time of his arrival, the attorney general's office had ceased to be the meagre provider that White had found it and was yielding a very nice return indeed. An official return of 1808 stated the gross yield for ex officio services as more than £1,000 sterling and the net at more than £800, while in 1807 Gore had stated the income from private practice to be about £400 Halifax currency (about £350 sterling).[39] The official clique did not mind Scott's making money, because he was their sort of man; but Firth was something else. He started off on the wrong foot by complaining of the fees he had lost to the too briskly zealous administration of the land-granting procedure before his arrival, and as well as alienating his colleagues he had the bad luck to get squashed between William Dummer Powell's rapidly ascending elevator and the side of the shaft. Although Firth's mandamus of appointment specified that he was to hold and enjoy his office with 'all and singular the Rights, Fees, profits, Privileges and advantages thereunto belonging or appertaining in as full and ample a manner as the said Thomas Scott held and enjoyed the same,' the Executive Council began to challenge first one and then another of the perquisites that Scott had enjoyed – and they did so despite the fact that the ex-attorney general, as chief justice, was one of their number and well aware of the justice of Firth's claims.[40]

The fate of D'Arcy Boulton offers an illuminating contrast. He was an Englishman who had emigrated to the United States about 1797 to retrieve his fortunes after going bankrupt in a business venture. Three years later he moved to Upper Canada and was called to the bar in 1803, at the age of forty-four, under a provincial statute that authorized the lieutenant-governor to admit six competent persons without their having served under articles. Only two years after that, following Robert Gray's death by drowning in 1804, he was appointed solicitor general by Lieutenant-Governor Hunter.[41]

Boulton was a man of less learning and no greater professional competence than Firth. He seconded Firth's opinion in the Rogers case, and he joined him in protesting against the King's Bench fee tariff of 1810. Before Firth ever arrived in Upper Canada, in fact, Boulton had caused Gore political embarrassment in a manner comparable to Firth by instituting an ill-advised libel prosecution against Thorpe after the judge complained to the postmaster at York about the government's interference with his mail.[42] Yet he exhibited conspicuous loyalty in resisting the blandishments of the Thorpe faction and in due course received his reward. Although neither Gore nor Powell liked him, he succeeded to the attorneyship in 1814, with all the perquisites that the Executive Council had tried to deny Firth, and in due course became a puisne justice of the Court of King's Bench. Of course, as solicitor general, Boulton was entitled to only £100 a year in salary, a modest slice of the prosecution pie, and a clear run at the attorney's fee trough in the latter's absence; but the real secret of his survival and eventual success is that he managed not to offend the dominant clique at York.

Not that being innocuous was always enough, as John Small found to his cost. Small arrived in Upper Canada in 1792 and the next year became clerk of the Executive Council. His career survived his killing Attorney General White in a duel in 1800, and six years later he received the additional office of clerk of the Crown and Pleas (the chief administrative officer of the Court of King's Bench) over the head of the deputy clerk, William Warren Baldwin, an Irish physician and lawyer who was tainted by his friendship with his countrymen of the Thorpe circle. During the next few years, however, Small's new prize was progressively curtailed by Lieutenant-Governor Gore under the influence of Judge Powell.

At issue was the clerk of the Crown's right to the emoluments of the clerks of assize. Small's predecessor had always travelled one assize circuit himself and nominated a deputy to administer the other, paying him part of the circuit money but keeping all the fees. In 1808 Powell disputed Small's right to name the clerk of assize who was to travel his circuit and persuaded Gore to appoint a protégé of Powell's, the future attorney general John Macdonell. Gore ordered Small to pay Macdonell all of the travel allowance for the circuit and its entire yield of nisi prius fees (that is, those produced by civil litigation). Next year Powell had his own son appointed to travel with him and tried to deprive Small of part of the fees for criminal prosecutions by withholding the circuit records. When balked in this attempt, he got the Board of Audit (to which he belonged) to suspend Small's fees for that circuit on the ground that Small had not administered it personally.[43]

In 1810 Gore went further still. He deprived Small of his choice of circuit (like Firth in the same year) by issuing separate commissions to John Powell as clerk on the eastern circuit and Small on the western. Small appealed to the Colonial Office for protection, pointing out that if Gore could do this he could as easily appoint Small to neither circuit. In 1816 this actually happened, and Small continued to protest in vain against the loss of the 'ancient and accustomed fees' of his office. After a decade of lamentation, he elicited opinions from the provincial law officers which offer an interesting contrast in approaches to the task of applying English law and legal institutions to colonial conditions.[44]

Solicitor General Boulton (D'Arcy's son, Henry John) thought Small's grievance justified because his patent of office as clerk of the Crown allowed him all the fees and emoluments attached to it during the time of his predecessor. The judges' claim (first voiced by Powell) that they had the same right as English judges to appoint their own clerks of assize was based on a false analogy, since clerks of assize in England and Upper

Canada had little in common but the name. The English clerk of assize was a senior officer, appointed for life, with power to choose his subordinates. Usually a barrister, he was subject to severe statutory penalties for dereliction of duty. The Upper Canadian officer performed trivial duties and was often a mere law student, not even of legal age. He did not hold office by the same tenure, being newly appointed for each assize circuit; nor (despite the judges' claim) was he appointed by the same person, being commissioned by the lieutenant-governor – albeit at the assize judge's suggestion.[45]

The attorney general, John Beverley Robinson, vindicated the judges' analogy. The Upper Canadian legal system so resembled the English that no definition of the offices of clerk of the Crown and clerk of assize in the colony had been thought necessary; the names said it all. In both countries the offices pertained to different courts, the one to the Court of King's Bench and the other to the courts of assize. Small's predecessor, and Small himself, might have exercised the latter office in the past, but they had not done so by virtue of being clerk of the Crown. Small's patent, therefore, in granting him the emoluments enjoyed by his predecessor as clerk of the Crown, could not extend to those of the clerkships of assize. Robinson went on to dismiss Small's appeal to usage, remarking that the colony's courts were all of recent institution and the appointment of their earliest officers within living memory. A practice of such brief duration could not bear against a strictly legal decision of Small's claim; but in any case, a contrary practice had been successfully asserted for some years.[46]

Boulton's analysis of the case was influenced by what he perceived to be its implications for other provincial offices, that of attorney general above all. While the clerk of assize in Upper Canada performed much narrower functions than the English clerk, other provincial officials had much broader responsibilities than their English namesakes. This applied with particular force to the clerk of the Crown, who performed the duties of so many different officers of the English Court of King's Bench that unless his patent protected him he 'might be stripped of 9/10th of his emoluments on the same grounds that he has been deprived of the appointment of Deputies to go the Circuits.' This was equally true of other officers, several of whom performed not only the duties of their English namesakes but others which in England might occupy a whole department.

In England the Clerk of the Crown would no more think of performing 9/10th of the service rendered by that officer here than the Attorney General of England would of attending him in person to perform them as is often done in this and other colonies by the Crown officers, and therefore if we begin to assign duties here solely by analogy to the names of our offices in England we should few of us have any thing to do, and offices would be so multiplied that few of them would be worth the expense of the Commission.[47]

This prospect did not worry Robinson, who did not agree that the argument from analogy bore this implication. Small would not be deprived of every duty that the clerk of the Crown in England did not perform, only of those that were not 'within the competence of the office'; that is, the clerkships of assize. He might still perform by right any ministerial duty pertaining to the Court of King's Bench. As for the attorney general, he performed no duty that was not 'within the competence of the office' and stood to lose nothing.

Robinson might have sung a different song had he thought back to Firth's travails. Small may well have suffered from Firth's vendetta with the Executive Council, for it was in the same year, 1810, that Gore challenged both men's right to choose their assize circuit – probably on the advice of Powell. Each man defended his territory with the same arguments: an appeal to his patent, which granted him the same emoluments as his predecessor, and an appeal to usage (a ground also adopted by Secretary Jarvis in 1795 in his dispute with White). True, Firth was not claiming, as Small was, to exercise an office distinct or distinguishable from that to which he was appointed, but he was claiming to perform functions that were not inherent in his office. This was established by the imperial law officers' opinion of 1811 contradicting his contention that instruments under the great seal must be uttered on his fiat or be voidable. Yet, even while confuting Firth on the point of law, they advised that the prevailing usage be adhered to unless it could clearly be shown to be erroneous.[48] The usage they upheld was twelve years shorter in duration than that which Robinson dismissed in Small's case in 1826.

It was not law that queered Small's pitch so much as simple weakness. He was an Englishman of good family and modest talent, who performed his duties with average incompetence and made no enemies. Even the duel with White was forced on him by White's slighting reference to Mrs Small, with whom he had had an affair. As a known cuckold, however, with no special force of personality, and married to a social pariah, he was easy meat in the shark-infested fish-pond called Upper Canada, and grounds of appeal that might avail others could not defend him against more powerful rivals.

The emoluments of the clerk of assize were valuable. The travelling allowance of £120 was proportionally greater than that awarded to the Crown counsel, who received £150 but had to take a clerk with him; the fees on prosecutions were also greater for mere ministerial duties than those received by the counsel. Solicitor General Boulton did not mind these moneys going to the clerk of the Crown, but he thought it absurd that emoluments of £200 per circuit should go to youths 'with no families to support or dignity to maintain.'[49] In 1808 Judge Powell had seen it differently. He had sons and protégés to advance; newly in power, he had a decade and a half of exclusion to make up for. It was an old colonial's revenge on the British interlopers who had lorded over Upper Canada during the administrations of Simcoe and Hunter.

The explanation of why Boulton argued so vehemently in Small's favour is best left until later, when we shall find the law officers' role in prosecutions at assize under challenge not from the magnates of the Executive Council in the chambers of power, but from the spokesmen of a popular opposition in the halls of the legislature. For the moment, it is enough to notice Robinson's insistence on a strict analogy between the Upper Canadian legal system and the English. In its implied claim to perform all the duties and exercise all the powers of the attorney general in England ('by law or usage, so far as those duties and powers are applicable' to the province, as today's Ministry of the Attorney General Act puts it), it constituted the strongest statement we have from this period of the scope of the attorney general's duties. The analogy of 1826 was stated with a generality Robinson would find expedient to modify only two years later, when a judge of the Court of King's Bench would argue on similar grounds against the court's legality as it had normally been constituted since its founding in 1794.

THE LADDER OF PREFERMENT

In England appointment as a law officer of the Crown was prized not only for the emoluments but for the further promotion it promised. It was understood that the solicitor general might expect the attorneyship and that the attorney general might expect any judicial post of sufficient eminence that fell vacant while he was in office.[50] Their namesakes in Upper Canada nourished similar aspirations. These for the most part were gratified, though not inevitably, nor always easily.

Among the attorneys general, the big losers were White and Firth. White claimed to have received on taking office a 'reasonable expectation,' though not an actual promise, of succeeding Osgoode as chief justice, but in 1794 he was passed over in favour of Elmsley. It has been suggested that he was denied promotion because the government wished to avoid the invidious choice between him and Powell, but two other explanations are possible: either he was deemed not to be Executive Council material, or the attorneyship was so unremunerative that the government despaired of replacing him with a competent British barrister. As for Firth, his tenure of office ended in dismissal for quitting the province without the lieutenant-governor's permission.[51]

The other two attorneys general who were not promoted to the Upper Canadian bench were John Macdonell and Henry John Boulton. The twenty-six-year-old Macdonell, a protégé of William Dummer Powell's, was appointed acting attorney general on Firth's departure, but Gore asked for a permanent replacement from Britain because (he declared) no lawyer in either Upper or Lower Canada was fit for the post. The American war broke out in 1812 before his request could be answered, and it was twenty-one years before Upper Canada again received an attorney general from outside. In August Major-General Sir Isaac Brock, administrator of the colony in Gore's absence on leave, asked for Macdonell to be confirmed as attorney general. He said nothing about professional talent but stressed Macdonell's service as his aide-de-camp during the capture of Detroit. London obliged; but before the dispatch was sent Macdonell was dead, slain with his general at Queenston Heights.[52]

When next the province received an attorney general from outside, the cause was Boulton's misconduct in office. In 1833 he and the solicitor general, Christopher Hagerman, were simultaneously dismissed for persisting, against the colonial secretary's express order, in an unconstitutional line of conduct in the House of Assembly. Months later they persuaded a new minister that they had been treated unfairly, but meanwhile the attorneyship had been filled by an English barrister, Robert Jameson. Hagerman was reinstated as solicitor general and Boulton was appointed chief justice of Newfoundland, where he at once commenced the unpopular conduct that was to get him dismissed once more in 1837.[53]

All of Upper Canada's solicitors general succeeded to the attorneyship except the first. Gray was denied promotion on White's death in 1800; Lieutenant-Governor Hunter requisitioned a replacement from London on the same ground as Gore was to do in 1811. Four years later Gray was drowned when Hunter sent him and a newly arrived King's Bench justice, Thomas Cochrane, in an unseaworthy vessel to conduct a trial at Newcastle.[54] But while Gray's successors were luckier than this, their translation to the attorneyship was by no means always smooth. D'Arcy Boulton, appointed to replace Gray in 1805, did not succeed Thomas Scott when the latter was promoted to chief justice in 1806. By 1810 Boulton obviously doubted his chances of succeeding Firth; in that year he set off to London to seek a place on the provincial bench, evidently counting on the difficulty of finding a competent British barrister to fill a puisne judgeship for a mere £750 a year. Gore and Powell both warned the Colonial Office against the appointment; Gore averred that Boulton was 'not qualified, by sufficient legal information, or weight of personal Character, for that situation.' They need not have worried, for Boulton's ambition had led him astray. His ship was captured by an enemy privateer and he spent the next two years as a guest of the French.[55]

Nevertheless, in the long run Boulton's pertinacity placed him where he had not expected to be – in the attorneyship. Upon Macdonell's death in 1812 another of Powell's protégés was appointed acting attorney general in his turn: the twenty-one-year-old John Beverley Robinson, who had not even been called to the bar.[56] Robinson's service was prolonged when Edward Bowen, the Lower Canadian lawyer appointed to succeed Macdonell, became a justice of the Quebec Court of King's Bench instead.[57] The young man did well, and before the war's end in 1814 Powell and Chief Justice Scott had pleaded for his confirmation in office; but D'Arcy Boulton, released from captivity, meanwhile had been pressing his own claims in London and had even secured admission to the English bar. Robinson had to be content with appointment as solicitor general and an extended leave in London during which he read for his own admission to the English bar. He was well placed there to block Boulton's bid to appropriate half of the fees he had earned as acting attorney general in the twelve months after the issue of Boulton's mandamus in January 1814.[58]

Robinson did not have long to wait. Boulton had soon proved his incompetence even to his own satisfaction and applied once more to be made a judge. Gore supported the application: not that he now thought Boulton fit for the bench, but he supposed he could do less harm as one of three judges than as attorney general. Boulton became the first attorney general to be kicked upstairs, and Robinson succeeded him in 1818 at the age of twenty-six.[59]

Even in resigning the attorneyship, though, Boulton remained true to the principles of Upper Canadian ladder-climbing: calculating that Gore would do almost anything to be rid of him, he tried to make his move to the bench conditional on his son's appointment as solicitor general in place of Robinson. Henry John Boulton was perhaps the most ambitious man in Upper Canada. He had offered himself as attorney general (not merely 'acting') on Macdonell's death in 1812, and at different times in the 1820s he would actually petition for appointment to both the Executive Council and the Legislative Council. Neither Gore nor the colonial secretary would traffick with his father in 1818, however. Henry John spent the next two years as acting solicitor general only, while Gore, back in London once more, did his best to prevent his confirmation, though ultimately in vain.[60] Boulton became attorney general on Robinson's promotion to chief justice in 1829.

Boulton's successor as solicitor general had an even rougher road to the attorneyship. In 1828 Christopher Hagerman provisionally was made a puisne justice of the Court of King's Bench, under exceptional circumstances which are related in chapter 3. He was assured at the time (he later claimed) by both Robinson and the lieutenant-governor, Sir Peregrine Maitland, that the appointment would be confirmed, and to accept it he gave up offices worth more than £500 a year, as well as a lucrative practice in Kingston. A year later he was suddenly stripped of his robes and reduced to the position of solicitor general, which was worth only £350 a year in salary and fees – far below the £900 of a puisne judgeship. True, he could expect a substantial private practice, but he would have to start from scratch in a new city.[61] In 1833, after his dismissal along with Boulton, he would find himself scrambling to retain the post he had accepted so grudgingly four years earlier; but he succeeded and in 1837 followed Jameson in the attorneyship.

One danger to the ambitious climber was recalcitrance higher up the ladder of preferment, which might block his progress and allow someone to be promoted above him. The first three chief justices of the province (Osgoode, Elmsley, and Allcock) had all succeeded to the chief justiceship of Lower Canada. When Thomas Scott refused promotion in turn in 1808, William Firth claimed the vacancy. 'I believe it has been customary on these occasions to promote ye Chief Justice of Upper Canada to ye Chiefship of ye Lower Province, & ye Atty. Genl. to ye vacated Ch. Justiceship: also invariably to give ye Chiefships of both ye Canadas to regularly bred English Barristers, & not to Provincial ones, or to Gentlemen educated in ye United States,' he explained. He based his claim not only on this seventeen-year chain of precedent but on the fact that he had taken the attorneyship only on the promise of promotion in the usual course; indeed, no lesser prospect could tempt a respectable English lawyer to quit the most polished society in the world for the 'very limited circle of his *Pares* in rank & literary acquirements' that Upper Canada could offer.[62] Firth's claim was perhaps out of order, since he had been in Upper Canada only a few months and Scott had not succeeded Elmsley after longer service as attorney general in 1802. But Scott had been guaranteed a place behind Allcock in the queue for the chief justiceship on taking office.[63]

In 1825 H.J. Boulton faced a similar obstacle when Robinson refused to succeed William Dummer Powell as chief justice, probably because of the loss of income it would entail. Boulton applied not for the chief justiceship but for the vacancy created by the promotion of a puisne justice, William Campbell. In his petition he stressed that the pay was of no consequence, since his professional duties and private practice together earned him far more than any judge, but his seniority to Robinson in age meant that he could not count on succeeding to the attorneyship unless Robinson vacated it, and he was 'anxious to maintain that professional precedence he at present enjoys in this Province.'[64] Boulton contended, like Firth before him, that his present office gave him a preference for the vacancy; but Lieutenant-Governor Maitland opposed Boulton's promotion as inexpedient,[65] and it remained the rule that the solicitorship gave a preference only for the attorneyship and the attorneyship only for the Upper Canadian bench.

Indeed, it is testimony to the strength of this expectation, based on English example, that Boulton was promoted to attorney general in succession to Robinson; in the previous decade no one had done more than he to disgrace the legal profession and the administration of justice in the public mind. 'Mr. H. Boulton ... is *very* unpopular,' noted Sir John Colborne, Maitland's successor, 'and I regret to add, that his conduct in many instances, as a professional man appears not free from blame. The local Government will therefore be rather embarrassed by his promotion.'[66] Yet there is no evidence that any other candidate was considered, although the only precedents in Upper Canada for the succession from solicitor general to attorney general were the promotion of Boulton père and Robinson.

The 1840s opened a new era in the history of the law officerships. Upper and Lower Canada were politically reunited in 1841 as the province of Canada, with a semi-federal structure under which each section retained its old judicial establishment. The advent of responsible government in this decade produced fundamental changes in the Upper

Canadian law officerships, the chief being that the attorney general normally, though not invariably, became the leading Upper Canadian member of the government and often the province's prime minister. The politicization of both law officerships, which is discussed in chapter 4, precluded automatic succession from solicitor general to attorney general from then until the solicitorship was abolished in 1867. Only four out of fifteen solicitors general during the Union became attorney general, and only one was promoted directly to the attorneyship; this was John Ross, one of the few attorneys general not to be the leading Upper Canadian minister. Three solicitors general were appointed directly to the bench.[67]

Even so, the tradition of succession that the Boultons had laboured to establish died hard. When William Henry Draper resigned the attorneyship in 1847, Governor General Lord Elgin offered it to the solicitor general, John Hillyard Cameron, as a matter of course. It is not clear whether the premiership was attached to the offer, although Cameron for several years was in the running for the leadership of the Upper Canadian conservatives. On this occasion he thanked Elgin for 'the recognition of the claims to advancement which the office of Solicitor General confers upon me' but declined the promotion; the governor general then turned to Cameron's predecessor as solicitor general, Henry Sherwood, who did form a short-lived government.[68] When Sherwood's successor, Robert Baldwin, resigned in 1851, it was said that the solicitor general, John Sandfield Macdonald, should have succeeded him.[69]

The attorneyship was first affected by modern political considerations in 1840, when Hagerman was kicked upstairs to a puisne judgeship in order to make way for a man (Solicitor General Draper) who would support the imperial plan to reunite the Canadas. Draper became the first Upper Canadian attorney general-premier, serving twice before scrambling to the safety of the bench from the wreck of his second political mission – resisting responsible government – in 1847.[70] Henry Sherwood, who succeeded him briefly, was undoubtedly disqualified for the bench in the eyes of his own successor by his links with the Orange Order, which Baldwin detested. Baldwin himself retired from the attorneyship into private life. His successor, William Buell Richards, was the last nineteenth-century attorney general to resign the office for the bench – the last, indeed, to become a judge at all. In 1872 Oliver Mowat would reverse the old trend by quitting the Chancery bench to become attorney general (and premier) of Ontario.[71]

This discussion has taken us ahead of our story, and its details are less important than its general bearing on the way the law officerships were perceived. For most of the first half of the nineteenth century they were seen as a sort of property, entailing not only a privileged vendorship of services to the government and the public but also the promise of promotion when a suitable vacancy arose. It was this idea that led William Firth in 1808 and H.J. Boulton in 1825 to apply for promotion when the men ahead of them declined it; Boulton was anxious, as he put it, 'to maintain his professional precedence' – that is, his place in the queue.

The constitutional implications of this notion of the attorneyship were important. While the position was obviously one of trust, the trust was of a sort that was fulfilled by conscientiously serving the interest of the grantor, the Crown. The proprietorial conception of the attorneyship was incompatible with the notion of a trust that might require the incumbent in certain circumstances to resign his office without compensation. Only under responsible government could that idea become feasible.

3

A Question of Confidence

Between about 1830 and 1850, the system of government in Upper Canada was transformed. The old authoritarian system of rule came to an end, and with it the conception of high executive office as a species of property in the royal gift, tenable for life at the king's pleasure. It was superseded by the system of political democracy called responsible government, in which tenure of the chief executive offices depends on an individual (and his party) possessing the confidence of the people as represented in the legislature (or, in a bicameral legislature, its lower chamber). The chief executive officers of state were converted from appointed trustees of the monarch into elected trustees of the people. The judges ceased to be appointed 'during pleasure' and achieved the greater independence of tenure 'during good behaviour.'

These important changes were achieved without a revolution, but not until a good deal of social strife, climaxing in rebellions in both Upper and Lower Canada, had convinced the imperial authorities that a new approach to governing the North American colonies was needed. In Upper Canada, this social strife arose from several causes. One was antipathy between the farmers, who formed the bulk of the population and produced most of the colony's wealth, and the merchants and government officials, whom they tended to see as parasites growing fat on the fruits of their labour. This antipathy was a product not simply of conflicting material interests but of incompatible values: a contrast of attitudes between those whose aim in life was to make a fortune and those whose aim was to make a living. A second cause of friction was ethnic tension, arising from the fact that the officials and leading merchants, but for a few loyalists, were of English or Scottish origin, while most of the farmers (at least until the 1830s) were non-loyalist Americans who had been lured to the province by the availability of land, not by any preference for monarchical over republican political institutions.

These social fissures caused the majority increasingly to resent, and the minority zealously to defend, the authoritarian political structure that buttressed the existing order. The Legislative Council, the appointed upper House of the provincial legislature, became a particular target of discontent by rejecting bill after bill which the elected lower chamber, the House of Assembly, passed in order to make Upper Canadian society more equal. The Council was all too obviously a coterie of successful fortune-hunters, totally committed to the established order which had served them so well but which seemed to so many of the rank and file a perpetuation of injustice. Another affront was the government's access to funds – the so-called prerogative revenues established by the Quebec Revenue Act of 1774 – that were beyond the House of Assembly's control. By providing an inviolable resource out of which official salaries could be paid, these revenues deprived the Assembly of any prospect of using 'the power of the purse' to influence policy.

One aspect of the province's constitution aroused particular resentment because it touched ordinary people. This was the preferred position given to the Church of England under the Constitutional Act of 1791. Under the act, up to one-seventh of the colony's land was reserved for the support of 'a Protestant clergy,' a term which the official élite insisted meant only the English church, thereby offending many loyal Scottish inhabitants who claimed it embraced their national church as well. This sectarian inequality was enhanced by the application of English law to the colony in 1792. Even as subsequently amended by the provincial legislature, the law restricted the right to celebrate marriages to ministers of the English, Scottish, and Lutheran churches, thereby discriminating against the dissenting sects and their many and zealous adherents.[1]

The political discontents of the period fell especially heavily on the law officers of the Crown, and on the attorney general above all. This was partly owing to coincidence. The incumbent from 1818 to 1829, John Beverley Robinson, was one of Lieutenant-Governor Maitland's closest advisers. This was enough to make enemies; but to the role of éminence grise he added that of official apologist. During the 1820s, as the only high officer of the provincial executive in the Assembly, it fell to him to defend one unpopular policy after another. But the attorney general's unpopularity also arose from causes that were not accidental to his office but inherent in it. Of all the injustices perceived in the Upper Canadian political system, none aroused louder complaint than the inequitable administration of justice itself. The attorney general's central role in this made him a particular target of criticism.

Historians of this period have presented these alleged inequities in the administration of justice in terms of specific 'outrages': abuses of civil rights and due process inflicted by a frightened government on its leading critics in a vain effort to suppress opposition. The current standard authority tends to play down not only these celebrated 'outrages' but the whole subject. General discussion of it is limited to one page. The chief cause célèbre of the period, the dismissal of Judge Willis in June 1828, is dispatched in half that space. Other important cases of victimization, one a rank denial of due process, are dismissed as 'a number of rather petty instances of the exercise of executive authority which were blown up ... until they appeared as cruel and heartless "outrages."' The role of the Crown law officers, which that same denial of due process brought under unprecedented (though inconclusive) public scrutiny, is totally ignored.[2] So far have we come from the first major study of the period, published one hundred years ago, which narrated the antecedents of the rebellion of 1837 almost entirely in terms of such abuses, virtually ignoring the economic, ethnic, and religious frictions that were equally important.[3]

It is suggested in this chapter that the pendulum has swung too far. 'Petty' most of these abuses were, if set beside the chronicle of massacre, torture, and repression that now confronts us daily in the news. By the same standard, the whole history of a colony that even in 1841 comprised fewer than half a million inhabitants may seem petty. Yet there are some far from petty reasons for studying the history of that small colony. One is that its petty political struggles led to the conception of Canada's present form of democratic government and contributed to the forging of its distinctive social consensus. It was the accumulation of such abuses, climaxing (though not terminating) in the dismissal of Judge Willis in 1828, that led directly to the inauguration of the movement for responsible government less than a month later.

Yet to tell the history of civil rights and the administration of justice during these years only in terms of such 'outrages' encourages the reader to underestimate the problem. It is all too easy even for a historian to forget that, at a distance of 150 years, a surviving fact may project from the lost past as merely the tip of an iceberg. Taken out of context, a few abuses recounted serially may not seem to amount to much. Historians of Upper Canada have done little to expose the submerged mass that might reveal them as merely the visible sign of a social milieu that was perhaps more repressive than is at first apparent. Moreover, the emphasis on 'outrages' makes it appear that the unpopularity of the administration of justice at this time had mainly to do with its repeated perversion to the repressive purposes of the provincial government and its partisans. This was not so. What most offended ordinary people was the fact that the justice system seemed to offer the poor man little or no protection against the oppressions of the rich. The promise of 1794 – the promise that English civil law administered by professional judges would secure the ordinary colonist in his property – had not been fulfilled.

This chapter attempts to explain why the administration of justice in general, and the conduct of the attorney general in particular, became the target of so much criticism in the 1820s and 1830s. It starts with the story of Robert Randal, whose extraordinary career illustrates so many of the ways in which the justice system seemed to be biased against the ordinary colonist and in favour of the rich. It moves on to the Alien Question, one of the most important legislative issues to confront the province in the two hundred years of its history. The attorney general played a central role in this affair, which imbued a large part of the people with an unappeasable suspicion of his and the government's political integrity. From there it proceeds to the abuses of civil rights and due process which further aroused popular hostility toward the administration, but it focuses on lesser-known events outside the capital rather than on the celebrated episodes that are usually stressed. It ends by showing how all these grievances were brought to a head by the dismissal of Judge Willis, which provoked the opposition to commit itself firmly to the reform of the political system. In this chapter we see in broad outline the social milieu and the judicial system within which the attorney general operated in the first fifty years of the province's history, and we see the officer himself in many different roles: as private practitioner, legislative draftsman, legal adviser to both the government and the legislature, and, finally, as the chief criminal prosecutor for the Crown.

THE TRIALS OF ROBERT RANDAL

Robert Randal came from the iron-making country of northeastern Maryland, about sixty miles from Philadelphia, where the Susquehanna

River spills into the top of Chesapeake Bay. He is remembered for his part in one startling episode in the political history of Upper Canada which is recounted below; but his début on the stage of history had occurred more than thirty years earlier, and it was no modest one. In 1795 he became the first person ever to be cited for contempt by the United States House of Representatives for trying to bribe its members.

Randal's ignominy flowed from events on two continents. In 1794, by Jay's Treaty, Britain had agreed to evacuate the frontier posts in u.s. territory, including Fort Niagara, Detroit, and Michilimackinac, that it had continued to occupy in defiance of the treaty of Paris, by which the war of American independence had been ended eleven years before. In August 1795, General 'Mad Anthony' Wayne's defeat of the Miami Indians at the battle of the Fallen Timbers had reversed the setback suffered four years previously on the Wabash by General St Clair. The battle shattered the hopes, shared among others by Lieutenant-Governor Simcoe and the British Indian-traders of Detroit, that American power might be contained by setting up an Indian state in the Ohio and Mississippi valleys which the British empire could dominate commercially.

Desperate but ever resourceful, the leading Detroit merchants schemed to recoup their losses by persuading the u.s. government to sell them the entire southern peninsula of Michigan, from the Miami village on the Wabash (now Fort Wayne, Indiana) northward to Michilimackinac, westward to Chicago, and eastward to modern Toledo, Ohio, on Lake Erie. Their plan was to warn the u.s. government that Wayne's victory had not effectually pacified the Indians and that only by their influence could the hostile nations be persuaded to surrender their territory to white settlement. As a further inducement they empowered their American agents, of whom Randal was one, to allow any federal legislator who supported the scheme in Congress to join in the speculation. This aspect of the plan incensed one or two of the more scrupulous congressmen and led to Randal's arrest.

Randal pleaded that he had not thought the proposal improper. The scheme would benefit the public, and complaisant legislators were not to receive any special consideration but merely to be let in on the purchase on the same terms as the present partners. He was defended by his local congressman, who claimed to have known him as a respectable character for years and ascribed his lapse to the corrupting influence of the British traders who had made him their dupe. Although Randal was said to have told one congressman that anyone who disliked land speculation could take his cut in cash, the House let him off with a reprimand and a few days in custody.[4]

While in Canada, Randal had had other business dealings. Lieutenant-Governor Simcoe had recently granted John McGill (the future executive councillor) and Benjamin Canby, a local land speculator, a prime four-acre mill seat on the Niagara River, just above the falls, on which they had proceeded to build a grist-mill and a sawmill. In October 1795 Randal had concluded a provisional agreement to buy a one-third share in this concern. He had recently been insolvent (though he probably kept this to himself), but no doubt the Detroit scheme gave him hope that he would soon be able to afford this investment and others besides. At any rate, his Detroit associates were of enough stature to gain a man consideration anywhere along the Laurentian trade route. They included William Robertson, the only merchant appointed to the Executive Council of Upper Canada in 1791, and John Askin, whom we met in chapter 1 as a land speculator and member of the Heir and Devisee Commission.[5]

Randal's purchase agreement with McGill and Canby lapsed in the wake of his reverse in Philadelphia, the u.s. capital, but Randal's interest in the site did not. In November 1798 he reappeared in Upper Canada and petitioned to the government for a 999-year lease of a riverside tract, immediately north of the McGill-Canby grant, on which to erect an iron foundry. He presented a letter of introduction from a Philadelphia merchant and ex-congressman and one from Robert Hamilton, the Queenston merchant and legislative councillor, who was a business associate of his old Detroit principals, Robertson and Askin. Hamilton stated that Randal had 'very respectable recommendations' from friends of Hamilton's in New York. After some hesitation, the Executive Council authorized Randal to go ahead on the understanding that he would receive the lease he wanted once he had started to manufacture iron on the site. Randal at once contracted to buy the adjoining mills from McGill's and Canby's successors in the mill-seat lease, Elijah Phelps and David Ramsay. The combined property, which Randal renamed the Bridgewater Works (or Mills), was to figure as the subject of an epic legal and political battle that would symbolize to many Upper Canadians the inequities of the colony's judicial system, compromise the reputation of John Beverley Robinson, and irretrievably besmirch the reputation of Henry John Boulton.

Randal embarked enthusiastically upon his milling and iron-founding enterprise but soon ran short of money. In June 1800 he signed two-thirds of the concern over to his Montreal suppliers, Burton and McCulloch, in liquidation of a debt of £1,600. Two years later they went bankrupt and disposed of their interest in the enterprise to their English creditors, who sent out their agent, James Durand (the future radical MPP), to assume control of the property. A subsequent series of transactions in October 1802 left Randal a one-third partner in the concern, with Durand holding the major share on behalf of his English principals.[6]

The following summer Randal moved to the Cornwall area, leaving the business in the hands of Durand and their clerk, Samuel Street Jr. During the next three years Randal undertook a variety of petty enterprises on both sides of the St Lawrence. By 1806 he was heavily in debt to several Montreal merchants. He spent the second half of 1807 dodging their writs and nagging them to grant him an amnesty that would allow him to go about his business without fear of arrest.

Randal's scheme to recoup his fortunes entailed building an iron works on a superb hydraulic site he had discovered at the Chaudière Falls on the Ottawa River. These works were to be supplied from an equally abundant supply of ore, which he had acquired by grant from the Crown across the river in Lower Canada. In February 1809 he at last obtained a grant of the Chaudière site from the Executive Council at York, but his hopes were dashed upon his return downriver, when he was arrested for debt in Montreal. He spent the next six-and-a-half years in prison at the mercy of his prosecutor.[7]

Randal's protracted imprisonment represented an attempt by ruthless men to wrest the Bridgewater Works from his grasp. From the moment he left the Niagara area, he had encountered difficulty in obtaining the payments due him from Durand, who bought out his English principals in 1804 and took Street into partnership. In 1806 Randal suffered a serious blow when Elijah Phelps, who (unlike David Ramsay) had never surrendered the legal title to his half of the property according to his contract with Randal, recovered possession by means of an action of ejectment. Durand failed to inform Randal of the action, thereby preventing him from resisting it. He may not have been the chief villain of the piece, though, since Phelps sublet the property to Street, who exploited the situation in order to exact better terms of partnership from Durand. These manoeuvres are made yet more obscure by the fact that the principal lease seems to have been back in Durand's hands in 1810 when Street and the Scottish merchant Thomas Clark coerced him into selling them his interest in the property.[8]

Then they went after Randal. Clark visited him in prison in 1812 to try to force him to dispose of his share. When Randal refused, Clark obtained a judgment against him in Montreal for a debt owed to the concern. Randal always maintained that this was no real debt but merely an accounting transaction between himself and the business, of which he had been whole owner at the time; but as an imprisoned debtor he was unable to defend himself against Clark's action. The adamant Marylander languished in jail until October 1815, by which time Clark had found another, better means of dispossessing him. The financier had gone to England and, representing himself to the government to be the lawful tenant of the coveted site (which was held from the Crown under licence of occupation), had obtained a royal order to the colonial administration to grant him the freehold.[9]

Randal returned to the Niagara area bent on asserting his right to the Bridgewater property.[10] In addition to the site itself, £4,000 was at stake – expected compensation from the government for damage sustained during the recent war with the United States. Randal's first step was to institute an action against Phelps for failing to transfer the legal title to his half of the property according to their contract of 1799. He possessed a deed of title to Ramsay's half and may have hoped that a successful action against Phelps, affirming his equitable title, as it was called, to the other half, would sustain a petition to the government to void the freehold grant to Clark as improvident on the ground that Clark had obtained it by falsely pretending to be the lawful tenant.

Four years in a row, *Randal* v *Phelps* came on at the Niagara District assizes. The chief evidence for the defence was a supposed instrument of June 1801, by which Phelps and Ramsay had conveyed the lease of the property to Randal's Montreal suppliers and partners, Burton and McCulloch. According to Phelps they had done so with Randal's consent in fulfilment of his articles of partnership with Burton and McCulloch in June 1800. If valid, this instrument constituted ground for arguing that Randal had renounced all title to the premises in 1801, and that the one-third share he claimed under his agreement with Durand in October 1802 was a new interest which he had later forfeited by failing to fulfil that agreement.

Randal denounced the supposed conveyance of June 1801 as spurious. It was in any case nugatory as far as Ramsay was concerned, since Ramsay had already transferred the legal title to Randal in 1799 and only Randal himself could have transferred it to Burton and McCulloch (had he wanted to do so) in 1801. Randal also produced the evidence of McCulloch's father-in-law, a prominent local storekeeper, that McCulloch had orally denied before leaving Canada that he and Burton had ever possessed legal title to the property. Against Randal's evidence, Phelps produced the testimony of two local notables (William Dickson, a legislative councillor, and Robert Nichol, MPP) that Randal had been present and consenting at the alleged conveyance in June 1801.

The testimony for the defence failed to sway two successive juries. In 1816 Randal was awarded nominal damages, the actual damages to be decided by arbitration; but his opponents refused to negotiate in good faith and the matter came to trial again the following year. This time the jury specified damages of £10,000 – the full amount of Randal's claim – but the verdict was set aside by the Court of King's Bench as excessive.

So far, Randal's advocate had been Attorney General D'Arcy Boulton, whom he had employed on and off for a decade or more. Upon Boulton's elevation to the bench in 1818, his son Henry John took over Randal's cause. By now the Boultons had a substantial unpaid bill against their client, who was penniless until he could successfully assert his claim to the disputed property. At the 1818 assizes the younger Boulton, now acting solicitor general, refused to act until Randal gave him a note of hand, or IOU, for twenty-five pounds as advance payment, as well as security for the hundred pounds Randal already owed him and his father. After Randal had given him the note and a mortgage on a lot he owned, Boulton went into court; but the presiding judge was his father, who refused to hear the case on the ground that he had earlier acted for Randal. The trial was held over for another year. Randal and his friends always maintained that young Boulton must have known, or at least guessed, that his father would refuse to hear the case, though the solicitor general denied it.

Then followed the events that earned Boulton lasting infamy. Before the assizes of 1819, Randal's debt fell due. When Randal did not pay it, Boulton instituted proceedings against him in the Court of King's Bench. After the initial summons Randal heard nothing more and assumed, he later claimed, that Boulton had not proceeded to trial. In fact, Boulton had done so and obtained judgment without Randal's knowledge. In doing so, his critics later charged, he broke at least three rules of the court and unfairly exploited another – which Randal and his many sympathizers alleged was ultra vires of the court – that allowed a creditor to proceed to judgment without notifying the debtor when the latter lived (as Randal did) outside the district in which the action was brought. After the statutory year's delay, the whole of Randal's Chaudière property was auctioned at a sheriff's sale in execution of this dubiously obtained judgment. The price was £449 – far more than the amount of the debt, but only a small fraction of the property's value, which was becoming known as a result of settlement in the Ottawa Valley. Randal claimed to have been ignorant of any of these proceedings until he heard of the sale in January 1821; but when he sought to have them set aside, the Court of King's Bench rejected his application on the ground of excessive delay.

Long before that, the breach with Boulton had brought about the ruin of all Randal's hopes. After the 1817 trial the Niagara plutocrats had dropped their local attorney in favour of John Beverley Robinson. When *Randal v Phelps* came on for the fourth time, in August 1819, the plaintiff, devoid of counsel, faced the pre-eminent lawyer in the province. The evidence that had favoured Randal in 1817 now produced a verdict against him. His strategy for recovering his property – that of using legal confirmation of his title to the lease as ground for an appeal to the Crown to void the freehold grant to Clark – was ruined.

Given the unequal forces involved in the contest, such an outcome might be considered as a foregone conclusion. According to Randal himself, though, it was not achieved without an extraordinary act of oppression by the judge, William Dummer Powell. In a letter written shortly afterwards, he recounted that the chief justice had threatened the jury, if they found for the plaintiff, with 'a taint' – that is, the issue of a writ of attaint. This was a way of disciplining a jury that was believed to have deliberately rendered a verdict against the evidence without the justification of private knowledge that contradicted it. The matter was put to a specially summoned jury of twenty-four freeholders. If they reversed the verdict, the members of the trial jury were liable to punishment and the loss of civil rights.

There is one earlier report of an Upper Canadian jury being threatened with attaint. That was in 1792, when Attorney General White is said to have made the threat in defending an army officer prosecuted for an alleged trespass committed in the course of his duty in entering land that the government claimed as a military reserve. The threat was outrageous, since the legal status of the writ of attaint was dubious at best. The medieval statutes that had established the proceeding were unrepealed (it was not abolished in England until 1825); yet Blackstone concluded in the mid-eighteenth century that it had long since been made obsolete by the practice of granting a new trial to the aggrieved party.[11]

It is hard to imagine how Powell can have broached the subject in his charge to the jury in *Randal v Phelps* without transgressing the canons of judicial equity, and one's doubts are reinforced by the opinion of three lawyers that the verdict of 1819 was rendered against the evidence. These were Barnabas Bidwell (a former attorney general of Massachusetts, now settled in Upper Canada), whom Randal consulted a few weeks after the trial, an English solicitor he consulted in London in 1827, and a Canadian practitioner consulted by his son-in-law in 1844.[12] But equity was evidently a term with a special meaning in Upper Canada. When Randal asked the Court of King's Bench for a new trial, the judges acknowledged that there were good legal grounds for his request but refused it on the ground that they doubted the equity of his claim against Phelps.[13] Thus inequity was piled upon inequity in the name of equity.

The key evidence against Randal was his supposed consent to the conveyance of the Bridgewater lease by Phelps and Ramsay to Burton and McCulloch in June 1801. That consent was supposed to have voided his own prior claim to the lease by virtue of his contracts of 1799 with Phelps and Ramsay. The evidence for Randal's consent was the testimony of two witnesses, William Dickson and Robert Nichol. It had been found insufficient by two juries of their neighbours at successive trials in 1816 and 1817. That the matter should ever have gone to a third trial was on the face of it unjust, since it went against Blackstone's dictum (which was known to Randal) that 'if two juries agree in the same or a similar verdict, a third trial is seldom awarded: for the law will not readily suppose, that the verdict of any one subsequent jury can countervail the oaths of the two preceding ones.' The contrary verdict of the third jury, rendered under admitted judicial misdirection and the other peculiar circumstances of the 1819 trial, can hardly justify the departure from that rule in *Randal v Phelps*. Still less can it excuse the Court of King's Bench for ignoring the first two juries' doubts about the crucial evidence of Dickson and Nichol and relying on it as a reason for denying Randal the new trial to which the judge's oppression and the desertion of Randal's counsel entitled him.[14]

It was, moreover, an injustice fraught with class discrimination. Like Thomas Clark (the real defendant in the case), Dickson and Nichol were members of a tightly knit local élite with close ties to the official oligarchy at York. Clark and Dickson were cousins from the lowland Scots county of Dumfries. Both men were kinsmen and protégés of Robert Hamilton, who had brought them from Scotland in the 1790s to help him dominate the commerce of western Upper Canada. Each had followed Hamilton into the Legislative Council, while Nichol, an old friend of theirs from Dumfries, became the Niagara mafia's spokesman in the House of Assembly. Nichol had been John Askin's clerk at the time of the Michigan land scandal of 1795, when Askin had been one of Randal's principals.[15]

The ancient origin of the jury lay in the need of itinerant royal judges for the sworn witness of men of the neighbourhood, who might be expected to know best the truth of the matter at issue.[16] The rule against granting a third trial when two juries had concurred in a verdict reflected the same principle: a jury drawn from the locality might best be expected to know the truth of the matter. It was impossible that the King's Bench could reject two such juries' opinion of the evidence of Dickson and Nichol without the appearance of injustice. Whether they did so out of a corrupt preference for their fellow grandees or from a sincere belief in their veracity is immaterial. The system of justice they administered was founded on the assumption that all men were equal before the law. Even a sincere preference for Dickson's and Nichol's evidence over the two verdicts represented an implicit denial of that assumption.

There is, as it happens, evidence of the justice of Randal's cause which was not available to him at the time, but which is relevant because it confirms the probability that the slighted verdicts were founded on local knowledge of the truth. It consists in a mortgage deed drawn up in July 1804, when James Durand bought the major share of the Bridgewater Works from his London principals. The transaction was made in England and never registered in Upper Canada, which is why the evidence of this deed was unavailable to Randal at the time of the trials. After recording the transactions between Randal and Durand in October 1802, the deed states 'that at or previous to the time of the said several indentures being so made and executed the said Robert Randal was in reality entitled to 1/3 part or share of and in all the said [property], and that in consequence thereof the said James Durand became bound to the said Robert Randal for such his 3d part or share of or in the said [property].' This statement undermines the contention that Randal had relinquished all claim to the Bridgewater property in June 1801, and that the transactions between him and Durand in October 1802 constituted his acquisition of a new interest in it.[17]

These circumstances explain why Randal's misfortunes confirmed the Upper Canadian farmers' worst impressions of provincial justice as a system run by the rich for the rich. Randal was not, of course, a farmer like them, and he does not quite belong to the class of those who aspired to make a living, not a fortune. Yet he was not a hard-boiled plutocrat like his Scottish adversaries. Even if we dismiss as jaundiced his characterization by John Strachan (archdeacon of York and a major power in provincial politics) as 'so stupid as to be utterly impenetrable,'[18] the fact is that he projects himself across the years to us as rather naïve, even simple: very much a man who might be duped by crafty Scots traders like his Detroit principals in 1795. He dreamed grand dreams; but he was only an adventurer, skilled in iron-making, with an eye for a good mill seat – a prospector, not a businessman. His disastrous manufacturing and mercantile enterprises on the St Lawrence are a case in point. By his own account they were undertaken on a whim, because he had some spare cash and nothing to do. His free spirit, American nationality and sad destiny all combined to endear him to farmers who felt themselves oppressed by an alien élite.

The impression the Bridgewater case made on contemporaries is epitomized in a letter written sixteen years later by one of Randal's neighbours near Niagara Falls. The United Empire Loyalist Joseph Pell had also lost a valuable estate to Clark and Street, who had brought in a shiftless nephew of Pell's from the United States and bankrolled his proceedings against his uncle on the understanding that they would split the proceeds. Pell lamented:

We are sacrificed one by one. No man of property, and whose fair possessions a legislative councillor or man of political influence may covet (as Ahab did Naboth's vineyard) is safe under the present system, or can tell that his turn may not be next. The law and the courts instead of protecting him join to plunder him, and who can say that he may not be the next victim!!! The choosing of councillors, of judges, of governors, of juries, of sheriffs, of every thing, is a party-job – and as Mr. Randal proved, and I have since found to my cost, the verdict of a jury given, again and again, in the face of the country, is no safeguard against the partizanship of the hired advocates of the legal vultures of the colony when they are transferred to 'the Court above.'[19]

The analogy of Naboth's vineyard is illuminating. Naboth refused to surrender his patrimony to King Ahab either for money or for a better vineyard elsewhere, whereupon Queen Jezebel had him falsely accused of blasphemy by the elders and nobles of his city, convicted, and stoned to death. She brought about his downfall by a perversion of legal process. Clark's holding Randal in jail year after year in an effort to force him to give up the Bridgewater estate was seen in the same light, and it was not a unique occurrence. Pell claimed to have been victimized by Clark and Street in the same manner, and William Dickson used similar tactics to acquire the land that was to figure in the 'Niagara Falls Outrage' of 1827.[20] Attorney General Robinson's part as counsel in the Randal and Pell cases evoked the role of the elders and nobles, and so did the decisions of the judges of the King's Bench.

Randal too, of course, had the help of an attorney general and a solicitor general, but this was palpably the exception that proved the rule. If a poor man had the help of such notables, verdicts gained at the assizes were overturned in the court above and his counsel abandoned him in mid-course to join the ranks of his despoilers. H.J. Boulton's excuse for prosecuting Randal for debt in the spring of 1819 was that he knew that other creditors intended to do so and he wanted to obtain priority over them in attaching Randal's estates. Was this professional integrity? During his quarrel with Randal that spring, he rashly told his client: 'Any further than my duty to my client prompts me I do not care a farthing about you.' Was this a commitment to the cause of justice? The man Boulton wished to beat to the plunder was none other than Thomas Clark, who was due to prosecute Randal at the coming Niagara assizes on the judgment for debt he had procured against him in Lower Canada in 1812.[21]

Between them, the Bridgewater scandal and the Chaudière affair dramatized virtually every important way in which the law itself and the administration of justice were seen by ordinary Upper Canadians to be unduly favourable to the rich. In the Bridgewater case, the chief engine of oppression was simply the high cost of justice. Randal's enemies had sought to outlast their penniless opponent by delay: for example, by refusing to arbitrate in good faith in 1816 (a proceeding which alone cost Randal more than forty pounds). They succeeded spectacularly when his attorney went on strike and left him in the lurch. The radical journalist William Lyon Mackenzie, who is said to have taken up politics under the influence of Randal's misfortune, played up this aspect of Boulton's villainy in reporting an attempt to revise the proceedings in *Boulton v Randal* in 1825. He published Boulton's bill for the abortive arbitration of 1816 and noted of another account: 'Those that dabble in justice may receive amusement, and obtain instruction by perusing the many heads into which this industrious man of law divides a charge of £5 9s. for writing an affidavit and petition and presenting the same to Gov. Gore.' As to the Chaudière scandal, Mackenzie observed that the young attorney had undertaken Randal's cause not from any idealistic love of justice but because Randal's affairs, 'from their pleasing perplexity and evident intricacy, promised to the legal reaper a rich and luxuriant harvest.' He stressed Boulton's confessed indifference to Randal's cause 'otherwise than as a professional man.'

We must remember that Upper Canada was a frontier colony, in which ways of making a secure living were scarce. Together with public office, the legal profession was the provincial élite's preferred way of setting its sons up in life. If the ordinary colonist disliked litigation, he did so partly because it entailed paying out large amounts of scarce, hard-earned cash to an already prosperous practitioner. We saw in chapter 2 the discontent aroused by lawyers' preference for pursuing a case in the Court of King's Bench rather than the district courts for the sake of the higher fees. Mackenzie reported Boulton's argument that if *Boulton* v *Randal* were ordered to be retried many other cases must, and commented: 'At these words, the faces of the lawyers present appeared to us to wear a very agreeable pleasant smile.'[22]

A second means of oppression in the Bridgewater case was the law that allowed a defaulting debtor to be kept in prison by his creditor. This has long since been abolished, but even if it still existed, the modern development of the doctrine of undue influence might nowadays nullify as unconscionable a bargain like that into which Clark and Street tried to coerce Randal. But even had this doctrine been fully developed in Randal's day it still could not have helped him. It belongs to the branch of law called equity, which had grown up through the centuries to mitigate the rigour of the common law in cases where its literal application was manifestly unjust. In Randal's day, equity was administered in England by a separate court, the Court of Chancery. No such court had been set up in Upper Canada, and the Court of King's Bench, the province's only superior court, was confined by its founding statute to a common-law jurisdiction.[23]

The resulting anomaly occasioned much concern in the colony's early years. The civil law of England had been received into the province, but an important part of it could not be enforced for lack of machinery. There was no way of foreclosing on a mortgage. Contracts could not be enforced, since the only common-law remedy for breach was monetary damages. Trusts were also unenforceable; the property rights of minors were unprotected; there was no means of moderating the harshness of the common law in the interests of justice. Henry Allcock mentioned unjust ejectments as a particularly frequent case of injustice that could not be corrected for lack of an equitable remedy.

Although the absurdity of the situation was acknowledged both in Upper Canada and England, nothing was done about it. Attorney General White drew up a bill in 1798, but for some reason it was never presented to the legislature. Allcock made repeated efforts to set up a Court of Chancery during his residence in the province from 1799 to 1805.

Thorpe in 1806, and Powell in 1807, urged the court's erection, and each offered himself as its judge. The situation remained unresolved, partly owing to uncertainty whether the court could be set up by proclamation of the lieutenant-governor (who was chancellor of the province, and thus the court's presumptive head, by virtue of being custodian of the great seal) or whether a law must be passed. At last it was decided in London that the lieutenant-governor should erect the court by exercise of the royal prerogative, but Gore never did so. By the time the question arose again, in 1822, indecision prevailed once more.[24]

The lack of a Court of Chancery was a serious handicap to Randal. He could have asked it to reverse the ejectment that Phelps had obtained against him (perhaps collusively, certainly unjustly) in 1806. He could have sued Phelps for specific performance of the contract for the transfer of the Bridgewater lease instead of merely seeking damages for Phelp's failure to do so. He could have directly challenged the freehold grant to Clark as improvident instead of pursuing the roundabout course imposed on him by the common law (this particular function of the Court of Chancery was related to its common-law rather than its equitable jurisdiction, but the matter was no less irremediable for lack of such a court).[25] Chancery would also have afforded a better means of reversing the judgment and subsequent process in the Chaudière case. Twice, in 1828 and 1830, the House of Assembly passed bills to set up an equity tribunal for the special purpose of inquiring into that affair, but each bill was thrown out by the Legislative Council.[26]

The sudden lapse of interest in erecting a Court of Chancery that occurred in governing circles after 1807 was itself part of the broader pattern of inequity dramatized by Randal's misfortunes. The major interest behind the move to set up the court was the merchants, who owned many debts secured by mortgage. In cases of default, the lack of a court of equity prevented them from acquiring absolute title to the mortgaged lands by foreclosure, and their right to seize land for debt under common law was questionable because it was illegal in England. An imperial statute of 1732 had authorized such seizure in the colonies, but the reception of the whole system of English civil law into Upper Canada in 1792 raised doubts whether the statute still had force there.

In 1799 the Court of King's Bench decided that the statute did still apply, and two years later Chief Justice Elmsley carried his Sheriff's Bill, which set up procedures for its enforcement. Elmsley's bill took several years to come into force, however. The decision of Lieutenant-Governor Hunter, under Judge Allcock's influence, to reserve it for imperial consideration delayed the royal assent until 1803, by which time Elmsley's departure for Lower Canada had shifted the balance of the court against the interpretation of the law that the statute was designed to enforce. Only after the removal of Thorpe and the ascendancy of Powell, in 1807-8, did the court begin to act on the bill. Then the pressing need for a court of equity suddenly vanished.[27]

In criticizing the bill of 1801, Allcock had stated two main objections. First of all, the sale of land in execution of judgments for debt was calculated to deprive the farmer of his best means of paying off his debt – the produce of his land. Second, since the scarcity of specie and abundance of land made land prices very low, the vindictive creditor would be able to strip a debtor of his land in order to buy it himself at auction for a song (virtually for nothing, in fact, since he might get back the whole purchase price, less costs, in payment – or part payment – of the debt).[28] Randal's spoliation showed the force of both objections. To many Upper Canadians, the seizure of property for debt was a deprivation of civil rights ('the total loss of property is the loss of a man's rights and privilliges [sic],' as Randal himself put it),[29] and the Chaudière affair in particular seemed to be just such an abuse of the practice as Allcock had predicted twenty years earlier. It was now a common grievance that sheriff's sales of land or chattels seized for debt were not adequately advertised, and that sheriffs held such sales secretly in order to relieve persons with whom they were in collusion from competition in the bidding. People were scandalized to find a valuable property like the Chaudière sold so far below its value. Why had so much more land been seized and sold than was necessary to satisfy the judgment? Much was made of the fact that the sheriff who seized and sold the land at Boulton's behest was a brother-in-law of both Boulton and one of the co-purchasers, Levius Sherwood of Brockville (a future justice of the King's Bench).[30]

Further scandal arose from the fact that the system had apparently allowed Boulton to carry through his proceedings against Randal without the defendant discovering them until it was too late. Boulton had broken several rules of the court, but attention was concentrated on one promulgated in 1814. The Judicature Act of 1794 had provided that when a defendant residing outside the district in which the court was held did not appear to plead his cause, he must be served with a demand of plea and given eight days to respond to it before the judgment was made absolute. The rule of 1814 ordered that the demand of plea need not be served on him at all. Instead, it could be entered in the Crown office in the district in which the court was held, accompanied by the affidavit of the plaintiff or his attorney that the defendant's place of abode within the district was not known to them. Judgment could be made absolute in four days.

Reporting on the scandal in 1828, a select committee of the House of Assembly noted that this rule of court arbitrarily halved the statutory period of grace allowed to defendants living at a distance from the court and deprived them of any possibility of being notified of the proceedings. In the case in question, Boulton had taken advantage of it by having his attorney file the requisite oath that he did not know 'the defendant's place of abode within the district,' although he knew Randal's address perfectly well and knew that it was not within the district at all. This allegedly ultra vires rule of court, Boulton's dishonest exploitation of it, and his breach of other rules, had deprived Randal of the opportunity of discovering the proceedings against him and had contributed to the delay in trying to reverse them that the Court of King's Bench had deemed excessive. Boulton had been allowed 'to shelter himself under his own wrong.'[31]

Now, in respect of both these inequities the system was as much to blame as the man. Boulton had not uniquely perverted or ignored the rules of the court to his own advantage; he had done for himself in this case what he and every lawyer habitually did in all such cases. Moreover, we happen to know by Randal's own private admission that Randal knew of the judgment against him within five months of its delivery, and that his failure to contest it before hearing of the subsequent sale was not due (as he always maintained in public) to his being unaware of it until then.[32] These facts do not exonerate Boulton. They do emphasize that his wickedness towards his client was facilitated by a system that tended to deny equitable protection to the poor man for the convenience of the rich. After all, that Randal had happened to discover the judgment against him did not make it any less true that the proceedings by which it was obtained were singularly devoid of safeguards to ensure that he did so.

The same is true of the sheriff's sale. There is no doubt that abuses like that alleged in the Chaudière case did occur. A particularly flagrant example flowed from the judgment Thomas Clark obtained against Randal in August 1819 on the basis of the Montreal judgment of 1812. That judgment led to the sale of 1,200 acres of Randal's land in the Niagara peninsula to Clark himself for the derisory price of forty pounds – which, when the court paid it back to Clark as the beneficiary of the judgment, left £400 of the debt still unpaid, for which he was able to harry his victim further.[33] But in the Chaudière case there was no collusion between Boulton and the other brothers-in-law to lower the price of the property. Sherwood had not heard of the sale from them, but from another man who happened to know the value of the property and was looking for a rich partner to finance the purchase. The sale itself was as well advertised as such sales usually were; this happened not to be well enough to reach the neighbouring proprietors, who also knew the property's value and would have been most interested in bidding high for it. And so a thousand-acre estate was sold for less than the fair value of its single most desirable acre.[34] At least in this case the price exceeded the amount of the judgment. It was no doubt to ensure this that Boulton had caused such a valuable property to be seized and sold.

To sum up: the story of Robert Randal impressed ordinary Upper Canadians with the inequity of the province's legal system in several distinct ways. The cost of justice, the imperfections of the court structure, the apparent partiality of the judges and the very substance of the laws had all operated to deprive Randal more or less unjustly of his property. Richard Cartwright's worst forebodings about the Judicature Act of 1794 had if anything been exceeded by reality; although, ironically enough, it was not merchants like Cartwright who suffered by it so much as the farmers whose representatives had then embraced the new judicial order. For all these reasons, the Randal case would provide a rallying-point for politicians who wished in the 1820s and 1830s to persuade Upper Canadians of the need for a new political order.

The teens were the decade of Randal's spoliation, the twenties that of his revenge. It was a hard-fought, grinding revenge, less often composed of triumphs than of a refusal to lie quietly in the corner into which he had been kicked. Yet triumphs there were, and the greatest was devastating.

In July 1820 Randal stood for election in the Fourth Riding of the county of Lincoln. The record of his life shows little prior interest in politics, but his resistance to the Niagara plutocracy had made him a popular hero and its outcome had filled him with an unappeasable rage. 'It is private injuries that produce public grievances,' he told the electors from the hustings. 'My private grievances, and the public rights, are so blended, that a doubt cannot be entertained of my integrity.' He inveighed against 'that influence that strengthens the strong arm of aristocracy, by favouritism and patronage, and that seeks to suppress the general prosperity of the province, that makes a monopoly of all places of profit or honour, that marks every patriotic man, in his country's cause, with a stigmatized disgrace.' He did not call, like radicals of a later era, for an equal distribution of wealth but for 'an equal distribution of justice' and 'a liberal dispensation of rights.'[35] The impoverished Marylander was elected in place of Isaac Swayze, who two years earlier had made himself the tool of Thomas Clark and William Dickson in another sensational episode of that time – the hounding from the province of the tribune Robert Gourlay.[36]

Randal also continued his quest for personal justice, this time with the help of the brilliant young advocate and physician, John Rolph. An action against Clark for ejectment failed because Randal could show legal title only to Ramsay's half of the property, but Randal drew satisfaction from Clark's astonishment at his 'silly efforts in attempting to renew a contest with a man of his artillery' and from the general pleasure that greeted his action throughout the district. This episode gave rise to new scandal when Lieutenant-Governor Maitland asked Attorney General Robinson to report on the merits of Clark's and Randal's rival claims to the £4,000 awarded to the righful possessor of the Bridgewater property in compensation for war losses. Robinson was Clark's counsel in the ejectment action then pending, and when he asked to see the evidence on which Randal founded his claim, both Rolph and his client protested against the impropriety of the demand. Robinson reported in favour of his client.[37] Eventually Randal's petition for the voiding of the freehold grant reached the Colonial Office, but the result of a clash so much closer to the mouths of Clark's artillery than of Randal's Niagara District musketry was a foregone conclusion. The counsel to the Colonial Office, James Stephen, reported in Clark's favour on the basis of the same dubious evidence that had swayed the King's Bench (that is, the testimony of Dickson and Nichol).[38]

Meanwhile, Randal continued his war of attrition on the Chaudière front. A second attempt to reopen *Boulton* v *Randal* foundered on a rule of the Court of King's Bench which precluded the court from rehearing a question it had once decided. A third attempt to do so, by means of a writ of error, remained inconclusive because it was impossible to obtain a decision of the full court on the matter, both D'Arcy Boulton and his successor on the bench – Levius Sherwood of Brockville – being interested in it.[39] Here too Randal's petitions were unavailing, despite the sympathy expressed by the governor-in-chief at Quebec, the Earl of Dalhousie, who believed that Sherwood's co-purchaser had bid for the property knowing that the Lower Canadian government intended to buy part of it for public purposes. Still, it was several years before Sherwood nerved himself to test his title by moving to evict Randal's tenants.[40]

Randal's persistence provoked his enemies to make another and this time ill-conceived effort to crush him. In standing for re-election in 1824, Randal, like every other candidate, had to swear that he met the property qualification. The oath had to name the property on which the claim rested, and Randal's cited all the properties of which he had been despoiled. On the information of Samuel Street (or of Thomas Clark – the sources differ), Attorney General Robinson drew up an indictment charging Randal with perjury. The case came to trial at the Niagara District assizes of 1825, where it would normally have been prosecuted as part of the criminal business of the western circuit by Solicitor General Boulton; but Boulton stood down, 'owing to some private misunderstanding' between Randal and himself. The Crown counsel in his stead was the rising young advocate and executive councillor James Buchanan Macaulay. Six years earlier, as Boulton's clerk, Macaulay had acted as the solicitor general's attorney in procuring the uncontested judgment in *Boulton v Randal*.

It was a day of resounding humiliation for the mighty of Niagara and York. When Thomas Clark took the stand to swear to his freehold patent for the Bridgewater property, John Rolph, for the defence, forced him to confess in open court how he had visited Randal in the Montreal jail in 1812 in order to coerce him into surrendering his interest in the lease. This was the prelude to a speech in which Rolph, combining ingenious argument with magnificent forensic rhetoric, contrived to present the prosecution as a plot by the entire provincial establishment to crush a political enemy. 'Methinks there is already rendered an almost impossible verdict – I hear from the few the screams of inordinate triumph – "Up with Randall to the pillory! – Nail his ears to it! – Jam his head between its pillars! – Pelt him with rotten eggs, and filth, and mire, and dirt! – Load him with reproaches! – Behold Randall! – The friend of the people! – The choice of the people! – lately at the head of the Lincoln Poll, and now elevated to the pillory!"'[41]

The defence blocked Macaulay's claim, as the solicitor general's substitute, to the law officers' privilege of the last word to the jury. The twelve sworn neighbours of Randal and Clark took only five minutes to reach their verdict.[42] Despite Chief Justice Campbell's hostile summing-up, Randal left the court that day in October 1825 a free man. A month later, the political storm burst which was to vouchsafe him his tremendous triumph over the mighty of Upper Canada.

JOHN BEVERLEY ROBINSON AND THE ALIEN QUESTION

Robert Randal's story has dramatized some of the ways in which both the administration of justice and the law itself seemed to be biased against the poor man. The law officers of the Crown have not always taken centre stage, but we have observed them in professional or official conduct which was all too likely to confirm that impression. In the Alien Question, the attorney general occupies the limelight in the roles of legislative draftsman and legal adviser to the government and the House of Assembly. The question itself is one of the most important legislative issues to have confronted the province in the two centuries of its history. It concerned the title of most of the population to civil rights they had exercised unchallenged since the colony's first founding, including the capacity to own real estate, to serve on juries, to vote at elections, and to serve in either house of the provincial parliament. While Randal's story stands for an unknown number of individual experiences that sapped public confidence in the fairness of the colony's legal institutions, the Alien Question was a single crisis which destroyed, in a matter of weeks, the confidence of a large part of the Upper Canadian people in the political integrity of the provincial government and the character of its chief law adviser as guardian of the people's civil rights. Nothing did more to unite Upper Canada's aggrieved special interests into a single movement of political opposition.

The question arose out of the war of 1812 with the United States. Perhaps three-quarters of the colony's eighty or ninety thousand inhabitants were non-loyalist Americans. Few of them took part against the empire, but enough did so to justify a mass trial at Ancaster in 1814, which resulted in eight men being hanged for high treason.[43] Afterwards, both the imperial and the provincial government felt that so large an American population constituted a security risk. The secretary of state decided to discourage American immigration by banning the granting of Crown lands to such immigrants, but Lieutenant-Governor Gore exceeded his instructions and tried to block the flow entirely by forbidding the oath of allegiance to be administered to them.[44]

Gore's action irked the land speculators of the Niagara peninsula. They had no objection to the imperial policy, since the denial of Crown lands to American immigrants would tend to raise the price of land in private hands. A total ban on American immigration, by contrast, could only send the price of land plummeting. William Dickson refused point-blank to withhold the oath of allegiance as Gore directed, and Robert Nichol staged an attack on the lieutenant-governor's policy in the House of Assembly that panicked Gore into proroguing the legislature prematurely.[45]

The response of the Colonial Office to these events was hardly calculated to soothe the situation. Nichol's resolutions in the House of Assembly had been based on two imperial statutes, one of 1740 for the naturalization of foreigners settled or settling in Britain's North American colonies and one of 1790 entitled 'An Act for encouraging new settlers in his Majesty's colonies and plantations in America.'[46] Nichol contended that both acts had been passed for the express purpose of encouraging settlement in His Majesty's American dominions, both were still in force, and both entitled Americans, upon complying with the acts themselves and with the laws of the province, to enter and settle in Upper Canada, hold lands there, and enjoy all the privileges and immunities of natural-born subjects. The secretary of state concluded that while Gore's endeavour to bar American immigrants from taking the oath of allegiance was illegal under the act of 1790, his critics were wrong in contending that either statute allowed foreign immigrants to hold lands in the province before they had resided there for seven years. It was by the enforcement of this rule, which was contained in the statute of 1740, that the imperial government had intended to discourage American settlement. Now, in November 1817, Lord Bathurst required it to be proclaimed throughout Upper Canada 'that no Foreigner will be permitted to hold Lands in the Province unless he "shall inhabit or reside for the space of seven years or more in any of His Majesty's Colonies in America and shall not have been absent out of some of the said Colonies for a longer space than two Months at any one time during the said seven years" and shall have complied with the other conditions prescribed in the said Act.' He further instructed Samuel Smith, administrator of the colony in Gore's renewed absence, to take the necessary legal measures for dispossessing any foreigners who had acquired lands illegally since the war.[47]

Smith referred these instructions to the province's new attorney general, whose duty it was to draw up official proclamations. John Beverley Robinson duly prepared a draft, but he urged Smith to think twice before publishing it. He warned that it would almost certainly be construed as a threat that not only newcomers but even long-resident aliens would be dispossessed of their lands. Worse still, there was a legal complication that the Colonial Office seemed to have overlooked. Many of the province's land-owners were persons whose nationality had never been officially decided. Some of them (called antenati) were persons born in the United States before Britain had recognized their independence by the treaty of Paris in 1783. Others were their children born in the United States after independence. The antenati had been born British subjects. If the treaty of Paris had not deprived them of their natural allegiance, there was nothing to worry about, since the children of British males, though themselves born outside the empire, were entitled to British nationality. This question had never been settled, however, and if it should be decided that the treaty had deprived them of their natural allegiance, the situation was delicate indeed. Not only were they and their foreign-born children aliens, but – worse still – there was no way whereby the antenati could reclaim their lost nationality. The statute of 1740 provided for the naturalization only of persons born outside the king's allegiance, but they had been born within it.[48]

There was a particular reason in April 1818 why the Upper Canadian government might wish to ignore this quandary. A few months before, the province had witnessed the début of the agitator Robert Gourlay. Gourlay's wife was a niece of Robert Hamilton and a cousin of William Dickson and Thomas Clark, both of whom had encouraged him to emigrate to the colony. A few months after his arrival in 1817, he had obtained the administrator's permission to publish in the official gazette an address to the resident land-owners of Upper Canada, to which was appended a questionnaire on the provincial economy. He proposed that township meetings be held to prepare answers to his questions.[49]

Although Gourlay's plan of research had generally been well received at York, it aroused alarm in John Strachan. Strachan, a member of both the Executive Council and the Legislative Council, liked neither the idea of the township meetings nor the tenor of Gourlay's final question, which invited general expressions of opinion on what most retarded the progress of the province; they seemed to him to add up to an invitation to insult the government. Strachan's opposition provoked Gourlay in February 1818 into openly denouncing the provincial establishment.[50] Immediately there followed a second successive turbulent session of the legislature, which again had to be prorogued prematurely. This time the cause was a quarrel between the two chambers over the Legislative Council's claim to be able to amend money bills.[51] Gourlay reacted to the prorogation with a circular calling on the inhabitants to elect representatives to a convention – an ominous name, duplicating that of the French revolutionary legislature that had presided over the Reign of Terror. This convention would meet at York to petition the imperial government for the redress of grievances. It was under this shadow that Robinson urged delay in the implementation of Bathurst's new policy on American immigration.[52]

Gourlay's convention, held in July 1818, was a tame affair, sparsely attended and inconclusive. The agitator continued his career, however, and in August was acquitted of seditious libel at two trials at assizes on the eastern circuit, even though both were in districts that had been quite unresponsive to his addresses.[53] Finally he was checked by his own kinsmen, in a manner that was to prove embarrassing to the provincial government.

Dickson and Clark had at first encouraged Gourlay's exercise in political economy in the hope that it would prove the folly of restricting American immigration; but they had publicly repudiated him when he called his convention. The new lieutenant-governor, Sir Peregrine Maitland, who arrived in August, soon showed himself determined to put down Gourlay. Under his influence the legislature passed an act banning meetings like the July convention (which was supposed to reconvene imminently) as seditious, while the Assembly called for its author's prosecution. Clark and Dickson recognized the importance of impressing the new governor with their loyalty, and they resolved to suppress Gourlay themselves. When he published an intemperate response to the Seditious Meetings Act in a newspaper, they had the editor, Bartemus Ferguson, arrested for seditious libel. Then they moved against Gourlay himself under the Sedition Act, a repressive provincial statute of 1804.[54]

The Sedition Act had been passed to meet an apprehended danger from French and Irish revolutionaries during the wars with France. It permitted the deportation of anyone who had not been 'an inhabitant' of the province for six months immediately preceding the initiation of proceedings under the act, or who had not taken the oath of allegiance, if that person 'by words, actions, or other behaviour or conduct' had 'given just cause to suspect that he [was] about to endeavour to alienate the minds of His Majesty's Subjects of this Province from his person or Government, or in any wise with a seditious intent to disturb the tranquillity thereof.' The head of government, any judge of the King's Bench, or any executive or legislative councillor might order the arrest of such a person and require him to prove that the suspicion he had evoked was groundless. If he could not do so, the officer who had had him arrested might order him to leave the province. The failure to obey such an order was itself made an offence for which the accused might be held for trial without bail. The accused also bore the onus of proof that he did not come within the terms of the statute.[55]

Dickson set up Isaac Swayze, MPP, the man who had informed against Bartemus Ferguson, to inform against Gourlay. When Gourlay was arrested in December 1818, he stood on his rights as a loyal Briton and indignantly refused to leave the province as ordered. He soon found that under the Sedition Act a loyal Briton had no rights. By the time he came to trial for failing to leave the province, eight months of imprisonment under disgraceful conditions had unhinged an already unstable mind; he was incapable of defending himself. His conviction and banishment were a matter of course. This travesty of justice was administered by Chief Justice Powell at the same assizes, in August 1819, that saw the downfall of Robert Randal.[56]

Even as early as February 1818, the provincial government had been alarmed by Gourlay's conduct. In April, with Gourlay's convention looming, Samuel Smith had readily acceded to Robinson's advice, confirmed by the Executive Council, not to implement the new imperial policy of dispossessing illegal settlers.[57] The Alien Question remained a matter of whether or not it was desirable to discourage American immigration. The problem of whether the antenati and their children were entitled to the civil rights they had always exercised was allowed to sleep.

All too soon, the monster was aroused. The cause was Barnabas Bidwell's election in 1821 as MPP for the county of Lennox and Addington, just west of Kingston. Bidwell was one of the province's most distinguished inhabitants, having been Thomas Jefferson's House leader in Congress and then attorney general of Massachusetts. He was under consideration for appointment to the U.S. Supreme Court in 1810 when his failure to balance his books as treasurer of Berkshire County sent him scurrying for the border.[58] Legally speaking, his position was no different from that of any other antenatus who, having fulfilled the seven-year residential qualification imposed by a provincial statute of 1795, now sought to exercise his political rights to the full. But Bidwell's radical politics and shady reputation made him anathema to the provincial political establishment. Writing to a Kingston friend in 1821 to propose that they share the expense of digging up dirt on Bidwell in the United States which might sustain a challenge to the victor's return, John Beverley Robinson declared his squeamishness at having to sit in the same room as 'rascals' such as Bidwell and Robert Randal.[59]

The petition Robinson presented against Bidwell's return was grounded on allegations of moral turpitude; but as soon as it began to be debated in the Assembly the question of nationality arose. Robinson now showed little of the reticence he had advised three-and-a-half years previously under the shadow of Gourlay's convention. In fact, he at once asked his Kingston friend, John Macaulay, to procure evidence that Aaron Burr, the former vice-president of the United States, had been deported from England as an alien in 1807 or 1808 (actually, the date was 1809). This precedent was important, because it offered a way of exploiting the nationality issue to get rid of Bidwell without having to assert the alienage of all antenati and their children. It could be argued instead that Bidwell's alienage, like Burr's, stemmed from the conspicuous part each man had played in the politics of the republic, and the oaths each had sworn on taking high public office. But although Robinson was discreet enough to stress the exceptional nature of the case, the Assembly was too wary of the implications to go along with him even on this carefully circumscribed basis. It voided Bidwell's election by a majority of one on the ground of moral turpitude, but only after voting down a motion to expel him as an alien.[60]

Robinson's pursuit of Bidwell as even an exceptional alien quickly proved to have been rash. Bidwell's son Marshall stood at the ensuing by-election; the returning officer rejected him as an alien; a petition of his outraged supporters brought the question again before the Assembly. Jonas Jones of Brockville had shown no disposition to compromise on the nationality question in the case of Barnabas Bidwell. With the attorney general absent in London and unable to exert a moderating influence, Jones now placed it squarely before the House by moving 'That Marshall S. Bidwell, Esq. ... *having been born in the United States of America since the independence of those States*, is by Common Law an Alien, and ... therefore incapable of being elected to serve in the Parliament of this Province.'[61] This language expressly disfranchised and dispossessed every postnatus in the colony, but it implicitly threatened the antenati too; if the latter had retained their natural allegiance, the u.s.-born children of male antenati could have claimed British allegiance (as we have seen) by virtue of their father's nationality.

Most of the MPPs were no more inclined to compromise than Jones. They defeated both his motion and an amendment by William Warren Baldwin that would have declared Marshall Bidwell ineligible as an alien but without ascribing his incapacity to the time and place of his birth. This was a recasting of Robinson's approach of 1822 to apply to the younger Bidwell, since it permitted the inference that the latter's disqualification stemmed from his being the son of a father whose alienage was the result of exceptional circumstances.[62]

Even so, the majority tacitly accepted that they were fighting a rearguard action. In February 1823, while affirming Marshall Bidwell's incapacity to sit among them, they also passed resolutions acknowledging that many inhabitants of the province, although not essentially disqualified, had not observed the legal formalities required to qualify them as British subjects and had thereby incurred a disability that could be removed only by an act of the imperial Parliament. They asked the lieutenant-governor to solicit the British government's early attention to the problem.[63]

Little did they know that Maitland had already done so, and in terms that were not in the least calculated to reassure them. Immediately after the second Lennox and Addington by-election, in April 1822, in which Marshall Bidwell's candidature had been rejected by the returning officer, the lieutenant-governor had written to Lord Bathurst of the need for imperial action. He referred to Bathurst's own instructions of November 1817 as evidence of the alienage of many post-loyalist American immigrants, but he also cited Attorney General Robinson's report of 1818, written in response to those instructions, to illustrate 'how dangerous it would be to act up to the spirit of the British statutes [of 1740 and 1790] at this period' without prior legislation at Westminster to protect the interests of long-resident aliens.

What would have terrified the imperilled class was the limited nature of the protection that Maitland envisaged. He proposed that the imperial enactment should secure them in the ownership of their property, but that it should disqualify them from membership in the House of Assembly. About voting he said nothing; but it is reasonable to assume, in the absence of a positive recommendation to secure the aliens in their voting as well as their property rights, that he intended their complete exclusion from the political rights they had exercised since the colony's founding.[64]

As it happened, even as Maitland was framing this dispatch, John Beverley Robinson was on his way to London. He had been appointed as provincial commissioner to look after the colony's interests in the redistribution of customs revenues between Upper and Lower Canada. When he arrived, he found that the British government, influenced by the powerful Lower Canadian merchants' lobby, had committed itself to a scheme to reunite the colony that had been sundered in 1791. This complication was to keep him in England for more than a year, and he had several discussions there on the Alien Question. He also found time to meet the Home Office official who had dealt with Aaron Burr and get copies of the proceedings in the case.[65]

Robinson found the imperial authorities reluctant to commit themselves on the question. He himself drew up two clauses for inclusion in the Union Bill; only one of them was approved by the attorney general of

England, Sir Robert Gifford, and even this was finally dropped for fear of introducing further controversy into an already contentious measure (which was eventually abandoned). Gifford was quite ready to agree privately that Barnabas (and, by extension, Marshall) Bidwell was disqualified by alienage from sitting in the Assembly; but Robinson noted that the English law officers had never given an official opinion on his statement of April 1818, and he feared that Bathurst would not compel them to do so in this instance.[66]

His forebodings were justified. The subject was left in suspense until November 1824, when a judicial decision was rendered in England which the law officers held to apply to Upper Canada. Then they wrote to Bathurst that 'after very elaborate argument it has been decided that a person in the situation of Mr. [Barnabas] Bidwell is not a natural born subject of His Majesty but an Alien and that the son of such a person born in the United States after the treaty of 1783 is also an Alien. This question therefore which has been so long and so frequently agitated may at length be considered as fully determined.'[67] So little did His Majesty's attorney and solicitor general for England know of politics in Upper Canada!

The decision in *Thomas* v *Acklam*[68] went far beyond the Bidwells' status. As we saw, both Robinson in 1822 and Baldwin in 1823 had argued that the Bidwells were aliens by virtue of the father's active part in American politics, which had included the tenure of offices that could be assumed only upon abjuring allegiance to the English crown. Such an argument could not affect the farmers who formed most of the imperilled class. But *Thomas* v *Acklam* held that every American-born person who had continued to reside in the United States after the treaty of Paris had thereby relinquished British allegiance, and that the children of such a person born in the United States after that date were necessarily also aliens. The net of proscription could not have been more widely cast.

The decision made actual the crisis that had been imminent. Maitland sent Robinson to England again to confer with the Colonial Office. This time the lieutenant-governor ignored the question of political rights completely and raised only that of property rights.[69] The latter issue reached far beyond the aliens in its effects, since any proprietor of realty that had once been owned by an alien might now find his title impeached on the ground that the alien had not been its lawful proprietor and that his disposition of it therefore had necessarily been unlawful. In this respect, the Alien Question threatened to revive on a much larger scale the land titles crisis of the 1790s.

In England, Robinson found Lord Bathurst 'exceedingly condescending and kind ... I trust I shall be able to take out satisfactory answers on most points,' he wrote back to Maitland's civil secretary. 'The desire to comply with every wish of Sir Peregrine's is as strong as you found it on a similar occasion.'[70] On the Alien Question, the secretary of state opined that it was advisable to enact legislation conferring 'the civil rights and privileges of British subjects' on those colonists declared to be aliens by *Thomas* v *Acklam*, but Maitland's communication had arrived too late in the session for Parliament to act that year. Lord Bathurst therefore left it to Maitland's discretion whether or not 'to submit to the Legislature of the Province at its next session a bill for the relief of such persons as are now in the Province.' With respect to the future, Bathurst invited Maitland's suggestions concerning 'such enactments as would in his judgment place the naturalization of emigrants resorting to Upper Canada on a footing the most convenient, and the most likely to conduce to the security and welfare of the Colony.'[71]

On the basis of this dispatch Robinson drew up a bill, which he entitled 'An Act to confirm and quiet in the possession of their estates, and to admit to the civil rights of subjects, certain classes of persons therein mentioned.' It was introduced into the Legislative Council, who passed it and sent it down to the House of Assembly at the end of November 1825. At once a storm burst which was to rage for more than two years and alter for ever the shape of Upper Canadian politics.

From the moment two weeks earlier when Maitland informed the provincial parliament of the need to legislate, doubts had been growing as to the expediency of such action. *Thomas* v *Acklam* concerned a u.s. resident's claim to property in England. It had no reference to Upper Canadian conditions. Spokesmen for the imperilled class resented the idea that an English judgment in such a case could deprive them of rights that had been held out to them by the government as an inducement to settle in Upper Canada; rights that were implicitly acknowledged in several provincial statutes; rights that they had enjoyed unmolested for thirty-five years. As Marshall Bidwell put it, they acknowledged the supremacy of Parliament, but not of a court.[72]

In any case, there was one crucial area of civil rights in which it seemed doubtful that the legislature had the power to act. The right to elect and be elected to the House of Assembly was defined by section 22 of the Constitutional Act of 1791, which denied it to anyone who was not 'a natural-born Subject of His Majesty, or a Subject of His Majesty naturalized by Act of the *British* Parliament, or a Subject of His Majesty, having become such by the Conquest and Cession of the Province of Canada.' Surely the provincial legislature could not alter this enactment, and clearly it could not, by any act of naturalization, confer rights where this enactment denied them. Several MPPs expressed the fear that if they passed any bill but one declaring that the imperilled class was and always had been entitled to all the rights and privileges of British subjects, they would not be remedying their disfranchisement but confirming it.[73]

The text of the bill intensified fear into hysteria. The preamble declared it expedient that the colonists affected by *Thomas* v *Acklam* 'should be confirmed and quieted in the possession of their Estates, and should be admitted to the Civil Rights of Subjects, with such exceptions as have been from time to time provided by the Legislature of this Province with respect to persons having been resident in the United States of America or having taken the oath of allegiance to their Government.'[74] This was fair enough, but the three enacting clauses seemed to speak a subtly different language.

The first clause stated that all residents of Upper Canada were henceforth to be taken within the province to be natural-born subjects, 'so that no Estates of what nature or kind soever' to which they had or should in any manner become entitled should be jeopardized by their being aliens at the time of acquisition. The second extended the same protection to former residents of the province, 'so that' estates they still possessed there, and those held by others in succession to them, should not be endangered. These clauses were acceptable as far as they went, but how far did they go? Despite the general reference to civil rights in the preamble and the pretence of both clauses to naturalize resident aliens in all respects, did not the words *so that* restrict their effect to what was subsequently specified – the protection of property rights? And even if their effect was as general as could be, and they conferred not only property rights but other incidents of British allegiance such as the right to hold public office and to sit on a jury, what about the problem of political rights posed by the Constitutional Act?

Even if the provincial legislature could undo section 22 of the Constitutional Act, the final clause of Robinson's bill seemed calculated rather to confirm it. It provided 'that nothing in this act contained shall extend, or be construed to extend to repeal or make void or in any manner interfere with any law of this Province respecting the qualification of persons entitled to vote in the Election of members to be returned to the House of Assembly, or to be returned, as members of the said Assembly.' This language diverged significantly from that of the preamble, which preserved the force only of any law of 'the Legislature of this Province' affecting the imperilled class. The phrase in the preamble referred only to the provincial legislation defining the terms on which the immigrants from the United States might exercise political rights: in particular, the statute of 1795 that imposed a seven-year residential qualification. The proviso preserved the force of 'any law *of this province,*' a more general phrase that surely encompassed British laws applicable to the province, including the Constitutional Act.[75]

On 5 December the House went into committee of the whole – the critical stage in the legislative process when the provisions of a proposed measure were discussed in detail. It was the occasion for the attorney general to perform his constitutional duty as legal adviser to the House. In general, our knowledge of these crucial days of debate is weak; but we know exactly what Attorney General Robinson said on this occasion, because his speech was published as a pamphlet.[76]

Robinson first took the House through the history of the settlement of Upper Canada. He noted the encouragement held out to American loyalists to move there and the influx of many other Americans who were, if not actually hostile, at least indifferent to monarchical government. He acknowledged that the latter as well as the former had been given reason to expect the enjoyment of political rights, and that they too had therefore 'the strongest and most equitable claim' on the government to confirm them in those rights at the present crisis.[77]

He went on to prove that such confirmation was now necessary and that a merely declaratory act, such as the opposition proposed, would be a futile gesture which merely stated that to be law which was not law. The imperial statute passed in 1790 to encourage American settlement in British North America was not in any sense an act of naturalization, and very few immigrants had complied with it anyway. Equally few had complied with the act of 1740, under which postnati (though not antenati) might have become naturalized. The provincial act of 1795 was one that expressly imposed a seven-year residential qualification on natural-born subjects coming from the United States, not one that purported to naturalize aliens. Even before *Thomas* v *Acklam* had destroyed the claim resting on the assumption that antenati still retained their natural allegiance, the House of Assembly had acknowledged by its resolutions of February 1823 that many of the colony's inhabitants needed legislative relief because of their failure to comply with the relevant statutes. Robinson fully expounded the terms of the decision in *Thomas* v *Acklam* to show how it left the need for such relief in no doubt.[78]

At last, Robinson turned to the questions that had aroused such suspicion in the minds of the opposition. If a positive enactment was needed to relieve the imperilled colonists, could the provincial legislature pass such an act, and was the bill now before it couched in terms that could afford the necessary relief? Taking the second question first, he answered yes. Despite an inaccuracy in the first clause, which might have crept in through a clerical error or because the Legislative Council had wrongly supposed at one point that it could grant only property rights, it was clear to him 'that the Legislative Council intended their bill to include the grant of every civil right of British subjects; otherwise the preamble of the bill and the title of it, and the proviso it contains for preserving our own Statutes respecting sitting and voting in the Assembly, would be altogether inconsistent with the enactments.'[79] Thus did he blandly glide over the charge that the inconsistency had been intentional.

As to the larger question, Robinson admitted that in his own view the legislature could not confer political rights where the Constitutional Act denied them. Nevertheless, he urged that the bill be passed. The legislature had frequently passed bills repugnant to the act and had seen them first confirmed in London and later acknowledged in imperial enactments. The Assembly had passed one earlier that day, a bill enabling dissenters to hold public office although their religion barred them from swearing an oath. The sanction of Bathurst's dispatch provided the best reason to suppose that the present, of all such bills, would be acceptable in London. To pass it could not at any rate throw greater doubt on the rights of the imperilled class than *Thomas* v *Acklam* had done already. If the imperial government did disallow it, they were in honour bound to promote an act of Parliament to the same effect.[80]

Robinson's blandishments were in vain. The next speaker denounced the bill as a plot to strip Americans of their rights and frighten them out of the country. When the attorney general again took the floor, it was not to reason but to warn. Suppose there should be a general election before the crisis was resolved; suppose some person coveted an American's lands. The House would do well to think on the consequences of protracted lawsuits. Robinson's warnings also were in vain. The Assembly amended the bill into a form which, as they stressed in an address to the king, merely declared what had hitherto been the uniform construction of the law in Upper Canada. Their address stated that Robinson's 'new and alarming construction of the law' must 'tend to destroy all confidence in the security of civil rights, and in the certainty of the laws in general,' and asked for an imperial enactment to prevent the law 'from being enforced to the terror, prejudice and disfranchisement [of persons] who have quietly and loyally confided in the security and certainty of the Laws as uniformly construed and administered for more than thirty years.' They added insult to injury by passing a second address, which extolled the benefits of American immigration.[81]

The uproar continued for more than two years. In the spring of 1826 John Rolph went to London to represent the threatened colonists at the Colonial Office. The imperial government had already learned of the need for imperial legislation on political rights from Solicitor General Boulton, who was in London on behalf of the Welland Canal Company (an enterprise formed to build a navigable waterway between Lake Erie and Lake Ontario). In May 1826 Parliament passed an act conferring full political rights on persons naturalized by the provincial legislature.[82]

Rolph returned to Canada and introduced a naturalization bill into the Assembly. At this point instructions arrived regarding the contents of the bill which the Colonial Office had formulated only after he had left England. Two of the provisions now belatedly insisted on were very unpopular: in order to benefit by the bill, persons must register individually and abjure allegiance to the United States. It fell to Attorney General Robinson to amend Rolph's bill to include these provisions. The Assembly first rejected the amended bill, and eventually adopted it only from fear of the consequences if a general election should be held before an enfranchising measure was passed.[83]

At this point, in February 1827, the matter seemed finally settled; but the most extraordinary episode in the whole affair was now to unfold. With the aid of two anti-government journalists, Francis Collins of the *Canadian Freeman* and William Lyon Mackenzie of the *Colonial Advocate*, a petition against the bill was distributed throughout the province, signed by thousands and (instead of being submitted to the lieutenant-governor, as was customary, for forwarding to the Colonial Office) sent off to England in the care of none other than Robert Randal, MPP.[84] The petition was not merely informally forwarded: it was unprecedentedly addressed not to the king but to Parliament.

Members of the provincial élite imagined with glee the brisk dismissal that such a petition, with such an advocate, must meet in London; but they were in for a shock.[85] It was a time of political uncertainty in Britain. The government was anxious to conciliate the radical press and the provincial opposition's friends at Westminster, chief among them the Scottish radical Joseph Hume. The naturalization bill met more conservative detractors than Hume, including George Stanley, who in six years' time would become colonial secretary himself. In any case, the Colonial Office had remembered that the British government did not admit that an individual could abjure his natural allegiance without the consent of the government to which it was owed. The abjuration provision of the naturalization bill, which had been included at Bathurst's insistence, was therefore unacceptable on the ground of high policy.[86] A stunned Archdeacon Strachan, who was in London to promote the interests of the Church of England in the colony, reported to York how the under-secretary of state, Robert Wilmot Horton, had found Randal 'so stupid as to be utterly impenetrable,' yet the Colonial Office had acceded to the petitioners' every wish.[87] Randal returned to Canada with a promise that the provincial government would be ordered to introduce an acceptable bill at the next legislative session and that, if it was not passed at York, such a bill would be enacted at Westminster.[88]

The British government's apparent capitulation to Randal infuriated the Upper Canadian élite. Relations between Wilmot Horton and John Beverley Robinson had already been soured by the suspicion that Robinson had duped Lord Bathurst into recommending that the provincial parliament legislate in terms that Robinson knew were ultra vires. Now Robinson addressed such a hostile letter to the under-secretary that Wilmot Horton preferred to reply through Robinson's brother Peter, lest he 'embarrass himself in answering such an attack.' Responding to a passage that expressed Robinson's habitual denigration of Randal, he declared: 'However contemptible in Mr. Robinson's eyes Mr. Randal may be, I shall never, in whatever situation I may be during my public life, receive any man who is the Representative of any class of Petitioners whatever ... as numerous as the Petitioners whom Mr. Randal represent-ed, with other than personal civility & official courtesy.'[89] Here was a lesson in noblesse oblige for the leading scion of Upper Canada's aspiring élite!

Attorney General Robinson had nothing to do with the bill that became law in May 1828, except to pass sour comments on the defects in its drafting (the work of Marshall Bidwell, MPP) when the lieutenant-governor referred it to him pro forma for his report.[90] Within six months Maitland had left the colony to become lieutenant-governor of Nova Scotia. Within twelve months Robinson had found refuge in the chief justiceship from a House of Assembly over which he had lost all influence.

It is easy enough to see why the naturalization bill of 1825 aroused such distrust among the people it purported to benefit. Before the war they had been encouraged to settle in Upper Canada. Since the war they had been treated more and more like unwelcome guests. Bathurst's decision in 1815 to discourage American immigration; Gore's illegal attempt to block it completely; the increasing credibility, and finally the official espousal, of a new legal doctrine that adjudged them to be aliens – all these things predisposed them to believe that Robinson's bill was the final step in a plan to uproot them from the soil of Upper Canada. If the story of Robert Randal reminded people of Naboth's vineyard, the remorseless unfolding of the Alien Question must have turned their thoughts to the fate of Israel in Egypt.

But how far were their suspicions justified? Could the lieutenant-governor and attorney general of Upper Canada really have been partners in a conspiracy to delude the provincial legislature in one of the most important questions to come before it in the whole two centuries of the province's history? Or was it all, as Maitland and Robinson insisted, a concoction by disloyal agitators who sought to estrange the inhabitants from His Majesty's government in the colony?

The notion of conspiracy is so unlikely at first glance that it seems sensible to approach the problem in terms of its improbabilities. In retrospect, the first of these must be that Maitland ever imagined he could get away with depriving the aliens of their political rights; yet the omission of political rights from his proposals to the imperial government in both 1822 and 1825 suggests that he did.[91] It becomes a little more comprehensible when we recall exactly what the omission entailed. It was only the antenati, the youngest of whom in 1825 was over 40, who would have been permanently alienated, since they did not come within the terms of the colonial naturalization act of 1740. Those of their sons who were postnati might become naturalized under that act, while those who were Canadian-born were ipso facto British. Maitland's plan did not amount to the permanent disfranchisement of an entire community but to its partial political neutralization during a period within which British immigration might swamp it by numbers.

The next conundrum is this: surely there was *too much* wrong with Robinson's bill of November 1825 for it to have been a deliberately deceptive draft. If Maitland and Robinson had wished to deceive the Assembly, why did they not present a bill that simply purported to confer 'the civil rights and privileges of British subjects,' as recommended by Lord Bathurst, in the most general terms possible, without the 'so thats' and the final proviso which aroused such fatal suspicions in the opposition? To this it may be answered that, if deception was intended, success depended not only on the bill's being passed by the legislature but on its being accepted in London. The bill must become law in order to safeguard property titles, and therefore its promise of political rights must be framed in language ambiguous enough not to cause its disallowance as inconsistent with section 22 of the Constitutional Act. Hence the specification of property rights in the first two clauses and the ambiguity of the final proviso, which might be explained as referring to provincial legislation when actually it had far wider reference. If deception was intended, then, the 'so thats' and the ambiguity of the final proviso were both essential. There was not *too much* wrong with the bill, but just enough.

This becomes clearer when we see *how little* was wrong with the bill. The ambiguous effect of the first two clauses depended on a single word. Past and present non-loyalist American inhabitants were to be taken as natural-born subjects '*so* that' the title to property they currently owned, or had once owned, should not be questionable by virtue of their alienage. If, instead of 'so that,' the text said '*and* that,' there was no ambiguity at all: the person was naturalized *and* the property title confirmed! This was diabolically ingenious. The 'so thats' could be explained away if necessary as a slip, while the ambiguity of the final proviso was not in itself strong evidence of bad faith. If rectified, one had a bill that was quite unambiguous – a bill with nothing to be said against it except that it was utterly futile because it contravened section 22 of the Constitutional Act.

But this brings us to a third puzzle. The existence of section 22 was no secret in 1825, either in England or in Upper Canada. It had been brought to the forefront of provincial politics four years earlier by the Bidwell affair. Why did the secretary of state recommend that the provincial legislature pass a measure which section 22 must render nugatory? How could he, and Maitland, and Robinson, expect the legislature to take such a measure seriously?

The second question is relatively easy to answer. The bill that came down from the Legislative Council on 28 November 1825 had all the force of an imperial mandate behind it. The colonial secretary himself had authorized and enjoined the enactment of a measure to confer, without exception, all the civil rights and liberties of British subjects on the Upper Canadian colonists adjudged aliens by *Thomas* v *Acklam*. Such an injunction from such an authority must surely be proof in itself that such legislation could not be ultra vires. And it was precisely in these terms that the proposal to pass such a measure, and later the actual measure itself, were defended in the Assembly in 1825. Even John Rolph, who became one of the leading whistle-blowers on the bill itself, first defended in these terms the feasibility of such legislation: 'The King's Attorney General in England had advised this measure; and shall we say that his Majesty, in all the wisdom of his counsel, had not the power to sanction this great question?'[92] But how did His Majesty, through his secretary of state for the colonies, come to sanction such a measure? Why did Bathurst encourage the legislature to act ultra vires?

It is conceivable that the Colonial Office was involved in our hypothetical scam, and that Lord Bathurst's dispatch of July 1825 was a dodge of the same order as sending someone a cheque but omitting to sign it. All the positive evidence suggests, however, that Bathurst and his undersecretary, Robert Wilmot Horton, simply overlooked the existence of section 22. After all, they had a huge empire to administer and Upper Canada was only one small province.

According to H.J. Boulton (who was in London at the time), Wilmot Horton had consulted him on the question, 'which, from papers received from Canada, then appeared to cause considerable irritation in the Colonial Legislature.' Boulton explained that the legislature could not effect Bathurst's recommendation of July 1825 because of section 22.[93] The next day, at Wilmot Horton's request, he transmitted the draft of a comprehensive settlement of the Alien Question for enactment by Parliament, recommending that it be brought in at once so as to seem a voluntary concession and not a capitulation to public pressure. This draft included the proviso

that nothing herein contained shall extend or be construed to alter or in any manner vary or repeal any of the laws passed by the Parliament of Upper Canada respecting the qualifications of persons to be returned as Members of the House of Assembly in the said Province or of persons entitled to vote at the Election of such persons, or any of the Laws relating to the Forfeiture of the Estates of persons declared Aliens by Act of the Provincial Legislature.

Boulton's crystal-clear language highlights by contrast the ambiguity of the proviso in Robinson's bill.[94]

The imperial authorities ignored Boulton's injunction to act quickly. The reason was the same as that which Robinson had run into a year previously: it was too late in the parliamentary session to introduce such an important measure, which must have cabinet approval. It was at this stage that Boulton (by his own account) proposed the enabling act, which was passed at his and Rolph's joint recommendation, extending the provincial legislature's powers of naturalization to the conferment of political as well as other civil rights.[95]

Amid these deliberations Wilmot Horton addressed a letter to Robinson. It was elaborate and deceptively casual in style but ridged with ice. He understood from Boulton, he wrote, that the power of the provincial legislature to confer political rights was questionable. 'I must presume, however, that at the time when this Bill was brought in, the framers of it were not aware of the deficiency of their own powers, as it is impossible to suppose that it was intended that this Bill should be considered by the Assembly as an entire remedy for alienage, but that when passed it should be found remedial only in the case of holding lands & not in the case of voting at Elections or of being elected to seats in the Assembly.' After reporting the current intention to do nothing until the next session of Parliament, the letter ended with a small but very sharp hook. 'I believe that at the time when this subject was discussed previously to your going to Canada Lord Bathurst was induced to suppose that a Bill brought into the Provincial Legislature would be remedial to the extent of qualifying a person not only to hold lands but also to sit in the House of Assembly. Am I correct in this view?'[96]

Four thousand miles across the ocean, Attorney General Robinson delayed answering the barbed query as long as he could. When, ten months later, he did reply, he laboured to convince Wilmot Horton that he had never tried to conceal the existence of section 22 either in Upper Canada or England. He began by claiming to have alerted the Assembly 'many years ago' to the need to petition for imperial legislation to counteract its effects. When he went to England in 1822 he was particularly charged by Maitland to urge such a measure on Lord Bathurst, 'and before my return to Canada,' he reminded Wilmot Horton, 'you may remember that circumstances arose [the Bidwell case] which induced Sir P. Maitland to address a strong dispatch to Ld. B. in the hope that an act might be passed before I left England.' Robinson had drafted clauses on the subject for inclusion in the Union Bill, but Bathurst had objected to adding matter to it that would only make it more controversial than it was already.

In 1825 Robinson had been 'instructed strongly to urge the passing of an act of naturalization' by Parliament, but he had reached London late in the session and met the same reluctance to legislate on the subject that he had encountered three years earlier. At last Bathurst suggested that the provincial legislature should pass an act to deal with 'the past,' and that the provincial government should propose an imperial enactment 'for regulating the matter in future.'

I stated several reasons why if it could be avoided it would be better not to agitate the question in the Colony but I dare say that as my thoughts naturally dwelt more upon the question *as it would affect the past,* which could only be in regard to confirmation of estates, than in the exercise in future of [illegible] civil rights, I may have failed either to speak or to think of the latter – if it had been otherwise of course I must have stated and Ld. B. must have been reminded that the particular rights spoken of could only be bestowed on aliens by a British act.

After his discussions with Bathurst were completed, Robinson and a senior clerk set about framing dispatches to Maitland on the basis of his notes. Robinson himself had written the dispatch on the Alien Question. 'I was struck at my return when I came to look at the dispatch as Crown Officer in order to reduce its recommendations to practice at the too general language in which it was expressed; but I pointed in the draft of the bill which was introduced in the Council to the effect of the [Constitutional Act] in circumscribing our power so far as respected one of the objects desired and when the bill came down and was moved by me in the Assembly I was the first to call attention in the most explicit terms to the true state of the case.' Robinson enclosed a copy of his speech on that occasion, 'in which you will find I trust the most satisfactory answer to a question not put quite duly in your letter – whether it could possibly have been intended to make a shew of granting an effectual remedy when it was known that the power did not exist. I am sure you did not wish or expect me to answer this question seriously – or I must construe too literally the terms in which it is put.'[97]

Now, if this was the best Robinson could do by way of a cover-up more than a year after the event, it can scarcely be considered watertight. It is ornately circumstantial, to be sure; but at every point where Robinson's story comes up against independent documentary evidence that might confirm or contradict it, the result is contradiction. First of all, we know that Maitland's dispatch of 1822, evoked by the Bidwell affair, did not urge imperial legislation to protect the political rights of the imperilled class; it mentioned only property rights, ignored the franchise, and urged that aliens be barred from sitting in the legislature. Likewise, Maitland's instructions of 1825 specified the need to protect property rights and ignored political rights entirely.

Robinson's explanation of Bathurst's misunderstanding in 1825, although ingenious, also clashes with what we know. Robinson suggested that when Bathurst proposed that the province should legislate to deal with 'the past,' while Westminster might subsequently do so for 'the future,' the secretary of state had forgotten that the province could not confer political rights and had meant that the province should act to relieve past immigrants. Robinson, for his part, had somehow interpreted 'the past' as referring to past deeds that needed confirmation – that is, land transactions, on which the province could legislate – and had therefore not thought to remind Bathurst that the province could not act on political rights. This interpretation is all very well, except for its failure to explain how Bathurst's slip became enshrined by Robinson himself in a dispatch couched in 'too general language,' or how Robinson, having been struck by that 'too general language' when he came to translate his own dispatch into legislation, nevertheless incorporated all that excessive vagueness and generality into his bill. The very idea of the province's official legal draftsman, the chief tool of whose trade was legal precision, drafting such an important document as 'Lord Bathurst's dispatch' in too general language strikes a false note.

This leads us, finally, to Robinson's account of what happened in the legislature in 1825. His claim to have been 'the first to have called attention in the most explicit terms to the true state of the case' was quite untrue, since the efficacy of the proposed legislation had been questioned from the moment Maitland sent down his message. Robinson's candour in committee of the whole may have reflected his belated recognition that the legislature was not to be fooled. His speech on that occasion, with its specious references to 'Lord Bathurst's dispatch' and 'the Legislative Council's bill,' did not (as he represented it to Wilmot Horton) offer a satisfactory answer to the suspicions of the opposition. As we have seen, it brazenly skated over the inconsistencies between the preamble and the enacting clauses. It ignored completely the ambiguity of the final proviso.[98] The text of his bill contains no reference to the 'circumscribing' effects of section 22 of the Constitutional Act.

None of the evidence we have reviewed is conclusive of the Colonial Office's innocence. Robinson himself testified to Bathurst's desire in July 1825 to meet Maitland's every wish. There is no evidence that the provincial government's apparent lack of concern to protect the American settlers' political rights was the subject of any argument. Wilmot Horton's apparent anxiety to get information on the effect of section 22 from H.J. Boulton in March 1826 may have been a blind. His subsequent reference of the matter to Stephen may have been a way of playing for time until it was certain that the game was up in Upper Canada. Robinson's letter to Wilmot Horton in March 1827 could have been a put-up job to get Wilmot Horton, or Bathurst, or both of them, off the hook as well as himself.

To believe all this would be convenient, since it would save us from one final, difficult riddle. If Robinson's bill of 1825 was an attempt to deceive the House of Assembly, and if neither Bathurst nor Wilmot Horton was privy to the plot, it must have been an attempt to hoodwink them too. How can Maitland and Robinson have intended to carry this off, and what could their purpose have been?

To try to suggest some elaborate strategy would be redundant. It is enough that the notion that they might have hatched some scheme to manipulate the Colonial Office is not inherently unlikely. The provincial government was the imperial authorities' only regular source of information on the affairs of the colony, and it was the colonists' only source of information on the intentions of the imperial authorities. This intermediary position was a powerful one. We have seen how Francis Gore in 1815 exceeded Bathurst's instructions on discouraging American immigration, and how, three years later, Samuel Smith suppressed them on Robinson's advice. The colonists had no way of finding out what the lieutenant-governor and the Colonial Office were saying to each other, and their only way of getting a message through to London was by an address of the House of Assembly, which the governor would send on to Whitehall with his own comments.

Whenever Maitland had to transmit an address critical of his administration, he never failed to abuse its instigators as a few factious, even seditious, trouble-makers who had somehow managed to delude the honest but ignorant majority. In the case of the Alien Question, his remarks reached extremes of deviousness and dishonesty unparalleled in the province's history. In February 1826 he embarked on a carefully planned tour of the eastern, more docile half of the colony, receiving pre-arranged loyal addresses which he forwarded to London as spontaneous effusions of support. The much larger Randal petition of 1827, by contrast, he dismissed as totally unrepresentative of public opinion.[99] Time after time he spoke of the bill that became law in 1828 as essentially identical in its provisions to that of 1825. Perhaps so, but while the terms of the two bills may have been similar, their effect was made quite different by the imperial enabling statute of 1826. When at last he made the mistake of talking in this vein not to the Colonial Office but to the Assembly, the latter took care to record the truth in an address to the king.[100]

The provincial government, then, occupied a strategic position, which it was accustomed to exploit boldly. In the early months of 1825, just before Maitland sent Robinson off to London to confer with the Colonial Office, the two men had just made the nasty discovery that the general election of 1824 had produced an Assembly unprecedentedly hostile to the administration. Under this stimulus they may well have concocted some scheme of manipulating the Colonial Office on the one hand and the legislature on the other in order to ensure that the next general election turned out differently. Proof of the matter one way or another may lurk somewhere in the archives. For the moment we must be content with raising the question and affirming that the events of November 1825 gave sceptical MPPs every reason to suspect a scam.

Never again did the Upper Canadian opposition allow the lieutenant-governor to be Whitehall's sole interpreter of provincial affairs. In 1826 the opposition sent Rolph to England, and in 1827 Randal. In 1832 William Lyon Mackenzie crossed the ocean, and four years later Robert Baldwin did so. They also discovered a way of getting at the government's correspondence with the Colonial Office. In 1833, after the Colonial Office had responded to a call for information from the House of Commons by publishing its correspondence with him on another subject of controversy five years earlier, Maitland bitterly observed: 'It has of late years grown into a practice to submit the official correspondence had with the Colonial Office to the legislature of the colonies, if called for by them, unreservedly. The Lieutenant-Governor of a colony must therefore necessarily exercise a greater degree of restraint than formerly, in addressing the Secretary of State.'[101]

THE LAW OFFICERS AND THE RULE OF LAW

The uproar over the Alien Question in 1825 heightened political tension to an unprecedented degree. One result was a rash of those 'outrages' that received so much attention in early histories of the period. It was suggested at the beginning of the chapter that this traditional emphasis may have provoked, in the last twenty years or so, a sceptical reaction. If so, it is quite understandable. The events were small in scale and are hard to take seriously alongside the gigantic atrocities of our own age. They have been invested with symbolic value as emblems of a tyranny from which Canadians escaped by their own valour into the haven of Responsible Government. Having survived while memory of the social context that engendered them has faded, these symbolic events have suffered the indignity of coming to seem trivial. We must try to see them in context again.

Some of these celebrated outrages certainly have a serio-comic tinge. The destruction of William Lyon Mackenzie's printing-office, in June 1826, by a dozen or more young 'members and friends' of the York oligarchy may have scandalized the small but very politicized village of York, but in short order a jury punished it with heavy damages. Hardly had the liberty of the press been menaced when it was vindicated.

Captain John Matthews's loss of his military pension has a similar flavour. It was his punishment (so the story goes) for being in a party of anti-government MPPs who, having enjoyed a convivial New Year's Eve dinner, called on the musicians of a visiting American theatrical company to follow up 'God Save the King' with the American anthem 'Hail, Columbia,' and on the rest of the small audience to rise and doff hats when the band played 'Yankee Doodle' instead. It was, to be sure, a heavy blow to an ageing, unhealthy man with a large family to lose the greater part of his income in a colony where cash was so scarce; but after two years he got it back and the circumstances of his discomfiture are an inducement to levity – if one overlooks the attempt to make him return to England to answer for his conduct, and the attempt to hold him under arrest at Quebec for several months while the Upper Canadian legislature was in session, and the spies and lies that led to all this, and that Matthews's ostensible offence was committed on the day the Assembly passed its resolutions condemning Robinson's naturalization bill, and that his real crimes were to have supported those resolutions and to have aroused his area of the province against the prevailing misrule.[102]

This leaves two other particularly celebrated outrages. Robert Gourlay's treatment in 1819 scandalized the majority of the House of Assembly, which passed bills eight years in a row aimed at repealing the Sedition Act; but the resistance of the Legislative Council kept the act on the statute books until 1829, when the Colonial Office authorized its repeal.[103] Gourlay was so obviously unstable, however, that it is easy to conclude at 150 years' distance that he 'brought his troubles on himself,' or that had he been a little more unstable he might have suffered a good deal more at the hands of mental doctors. The draconian punishment inflicted on Bartemus Ferguson, the newspaper editor who published his final attack on the government, is ignored.

The second celebrated outrage was the fining and imprisonment of another editor, Francis Collins. It will be noticed in due course, because it was bound up with the Willis affair. The purpose of this section, though, is not to re-examine these old stories but to recapture the context that gave them meaning. To do this fully would involve much digging in newspapers and court records, but some idea of it may be obtained by reviewing other, less well-known episodes. One of these led in 1828 to a parliamentary inquiry into the role of the law officers of the Crown in the administration of justice, while the other two formed items (along with the wrecking of Mackenzie's printing-shop) in a contemporary critique of the law officers' role by the doyen of the Law Society of Upper Canada. Underlying all of them was the fear that the judicial system in general, and the law officers in particular, could not be counted on to protect the civil rights and liberties of those who dared to raise their voices against the existing order.

In the early 1820s, Upper Canada still consisted of discrete communities separated by wide stretches of unsettled country. Despite the American war and the Gourlay fuss, the average settler's political awareness was mainly focused on his local community, not on provincial matters. The anti-government majority elected to the House of Assembly in 1824 did not constitute a single political party, with a common platform, that had defeated another such party with a different platform. It was a disparate collection of individuals, most of whom had been elected as an expression of discontents that were primarily local in focus.

This is not to say that these local grievances had nothing in common; economic, ethnic, and sectarian discontents were widespread. It means that the grievances of each locality tended to be associated in the minds of the inhabitants with powerful men in the locality rather than with the central administration at York. In the Niagara District, votes were influenced by the local élite's vendetta against Robert Randal, and in the Kingston area by the campaign of that region's élite against the Bidwells; but neither Randal nor the Bidwells were yet figures of province-wide notoriety. It took the political turmoil of the middle and late 1820s, and the founding of newspapers such as the *Colonial Advocate* and the *Canadian Freeman*, to imbue most Upper Canadian voters with a province-wide political consciousness.

In the district of London, midway along the Lake Erie shore, power was centred not in the lieutenant-governor and his leading officials as at York, nor in merchants like Thomas Clark and William Dickson as at Niagara, but in the person of Thomas Talbot, an Anglo-Irish aristocrat. In 1803 Talbot had struck a deal with the imperial authorities to settle British immigrants in the part of the province where the loyalist presence was least pronounced. For every family he settled on a fifty-acre allotment he was permitted to claim 150 acres for himself. This was land speculation on a splendid scale. Talbot ran things pretty much as he liked in the Lake Erie settlements through assistants whom he recommended to the lieutenant-governor for appointment as magistrates.[104]

In the county of Middlesex, settlers aggrieved by the way Talbot and his lieutenants ran things found a barrack-room lawyer in the person of Singleton Gardiner, an innkeeper who had served in the Napoleonic War as a sergeant in the royal marines. In 1822 two magistrates summarily convicted Gardiner in his absence, and allegedly without summoning him to appear, for not paying a local tax which he denied any obligation to pay. To recover a fine and costs amounting to 7s 6d, a constable under the magistrates' orders seized Gardiner's wagon, which the constable sold to himself for sixpence and then resold for a shilling to a friend of Gardiner's, who restored it to its owner. Since seven shillings remained to be recovered, the constable seized a valuable saddle, which he sold to himself for far less than its real value. When Gardiner heard of this he complained to the magistrates and made, he claimed, a bargain with them to get his saddle back. He went to the constable's house and repossessed his property, whereupon the constable entered an information against him for larceny. He was arrested on the magistrates' authority and sent fifty miles to the district jail before being released on bail.

Later Gardiner had to attend the district assizes for a whole week while waiting to be tried on this charge, but he was never brought to trial, the implication being that the charge was spurious. He was tried later, though, at the quarter sessions for a minor assault on one of the magistrates, Mahlon Burwell, at the time of his arrest. On this charge the magistrates imposed the outrageous sentence of three months in prison and a fine of twenty-five pounds, with his release conditional on payment of the fine and another twenty pounds in costs. These were large sums to a country innkeeper, and Gardiner might have stayed in jail indefinitely had not Lieutenant-Governor Maitland ordered his release, upon the advice of Chief Justice Powell, at the end of his three-month prison term.[105]

Gardiner fought back. He prosecuted for perjury the constable who had complained of his larceny, only to find that when the grand jury of the district quarter sessions approved the indictment the magistrates transferred the case to the assizes, for which the grand jury was chosen according to a much higher property qualification. There a panel predominantly composed of the magistrates themselves dismissed the charge.[106]

Still Gardiner resisted. What the justices had done with his criminal prosecution they could not do with a civil one. Retaining William Warren Baldwin as counsel, the old soldier instituted an action for trespass against Burwell and the other magistrate and had the good luck to come before Chief Justice Powell at trial. Powell and Talbot had a long-standing feud, dating from the days when York officialdom had tended to resent the colonel's ties with imperial ruling circles; Powell, as the leading power at York, had led the resistance to his pretensions. The chief justice also had a grudge against Burwell, relating to John Beverley Robinson's mission to London as provincial commissioner in 1822. Powell had assumed that his official pre-eminence would lead to his own appointment, and Maitland had encouraged him in that belief. But the new lieutenant-governor had formed a greater affinity for Robinson and Robinson's former schoolteacher, John Strachan, than for the old judge. A move was set afoot in the legislature for a joint address of both houses requesting Maitland to name Robinson as commissioner, which Maitland did. Strachan and Robinson did not share Powell's antipathy for Talbot, and Mahlon Burwell, as MPP for Middlesex, was a member of the committee of conference that drafted the joint address.

Powell's eclipse ignited in him an unappeasable enmity towards all who he felt had contributed to it. Whether or not he deliberately directed the jury against the evidence, as an anonymous critic later charged, he certainly had no incentive to connive at the maladministration of justice by Talbot's minions. The anonymous libeller (who was probably Burwell's brother Adam) alleged that Powell had expressed doubt whether an action lay against the magistrates but had nevertheless directed a verdict against them so that they would have to suffer the expense of an appeal. In the Court of King's Bench the verdict was overturned on a technical point concerning the plaintiff's failure to prove that the magistrates had known when they authorized his arrest for larceny that the constable's complaint against him was false.[107]

Whether or not Powell's summing-up amounted to a failure of judicial impartiality, he enraged the Middlesex élite by his strictures on the magistrates' conduct. He had given aid and comfort to the enemies of the London District establishment, much as Judge Thorpe had to the provincial government's enemies two decades earlier and as Judge Willis would a few years hence. *Gardiner* v *Burwell* lingered in the Court of King's Bench long enough to permit an anniversary gathering of Gardiner and fifty of his friends, at which songs were sung and toasts drunk in celebration of his victory at the assizes the year before. By the time of that jubilee Burwell had been ousted as MPP for Middlesex, after twelve years' service, by John Rolph and Captain Matthews at the general election of 1824.[108]

But while the political victory was sweet, the episode left a sour taste (as we shall see) in the mouth of those, such as William Warren Baldwin, who were committed to the cause of impartial justice. It was part of the attorney general's duty, they thought, to protect the civil rights of the people against oppressive magistrates. In Gardiner's case, Robinson had done nothing to correct the errant officers, one of whom was his political supporter, but instead had defended the magistrates against Gardiner's action and helped them escape punishment on a technicality immaterial to the main point at issue.

In the Gore District too the magistrates grew bold in oppression. The district was centred on the villages of Ancaster, Dundas, and Hamilton at the head of Lake Ontario. It had been carved out of the Home and Niagara districts (based on York and the Niagara River settlements respectively) only in 1816. Strategically placed to be an entrepôt for settlement of the sparsely peopled country north of Lake Erie, the three villages, and Hamilton in particular, were on their way by the mid-1820s to becoming the Calgary of Upper Canada: a place to which ambitious men unable to find a niche in older centres such as Niagara, Kingston, and York, which were already dominated by established local élites, repaired in order to make or mend their fortunes. Hamilton itself had been named after one of Robert Hamilton's sons, who had settled there to restore a severely depleted patrimony.

Loyalty was good business everywhere in Upper Canada, but nowhere more so than at the Head of the Lake, where strident devotion to king and country might mark a man out at once for appointment to the magistracy or a local office of profit. The advent of a noisy gaggle of professional jingoists was resented by the farmers, mainly American in origin, who formed the bulk of the population, and it injected exceptional animosity into local politics. The new men threatened the influence of old leaders such as 'Squire' John Willson of Saltfleet, MPP and Speaker of the Assembly from 1824 to 1828 – threatened it not with the electorate but with the government. Particularly exposed to their hostility, however, was the district's clerk of the peace since 1816, the paid official who was responsible under the magistrates for the administration of local government and petty justice. He happened to be the brother of John Rolph.

About midnight of the third and fourth of June 1826, a gang of men with blackened faces, garbed in sheets, descended on the home of George Rolph. They seized him in his nightshirt, gagged and blindfolded him, and abducted him to a nearby field, where they stripped him naked and daubed him all over with tar and feathers, uttering all the while, in disguised voices, blood-curdling threats of dismemberment. Owing to the circumstances of the crime, the victim could not name his attackers. It was months before he began to obtain reliable evidence of their identity, but in November 1826 he sent the lieutenant-governor an affidavit implicating a district magistrate, Dr James Hamilton. Rolph asked Maitland to look into the matter in order to 'determine the necessity of my meeting as Clerk of the Peace a man upon the Bench who has committed a wrong most painful to my feelings and most degrading to the Commission [of the Peace].' On Attorney General Robinson's advice, however, Maitland replied that if Rolph had reliable testimony he should prosecute Hamilton and any other suspects himself; the government could take no steps against anyone before he was found guilty by a jury.[109]

In due course Rolph did prosecute three of his attackers, but in a civil action. At the Gore District assizes of August 1827, he proceeded against Hamilton and two other men, Titus G. Simons and Alexander Robertson. Simons, a magistrate like Hamilton, was also the district sheriff; Robertson, a merchant, was Simons's son-in-law. The case against Robertson was dismissed for lack of evidence and damages of twenty pounds each awarded against the others. Maitland called for a report from the presiding judge, James B. Macaulay. Macaulay reported that the defendants claimed they had attacked Rolph because they suspected him of adultery with a woman who had left her husband and was living with him. 'As I did not think such conduct – however immoral or reprehensible if true – could either justify or mitigate so gross a violation of his person,' commented the judge, 'I refused to receive any Evidence designed either to establish or rebut the criminal conversation suggested.' Maitland informed Simons and Hamilton that they would not be reappointed to the bench when a new commission of the peace issued for their district.[110]

Simons responded by sending the lieutenant-governor two affidavits exonerating himself from the outrage. He explained that he had not called the deponents as witnesses because it would have given John Rolph, as counsel for the plaintiff, the opportunity of having the last word to the jury and perhaps making a telling appeal to their sympathy. 'I had no wish to see a number of my friends saddled with heavy damages for a transaction which appeared to give general satisfaction throughout the District.' His not calling a witness, after Rolph had been led to expect him to do so, had disrupted the plaintiff's tactics and resulted in a very light award of damages.[111]

Indeed, despite the verdict in their favour, the Rolphs were dissatisfied with the outcome of the trial and applied to the King's Bench for a new hearing. Their grounds of appeal were twofold. First, although Macaulay claimed to have allowed no evidence respecting the supposed adultery (which George Rolph always denied, claiming that he was merely sheltering the woman from her husband), he had permitted counsel for the defence, Solicitor General Boulton, to allude to it both in cross-examination and in his closing address, while the plaintiff had been denied the right to rebut. Second, four witnesses for the plaintiff had refused to be sworn on the ground that the evidence they must give would either tend to incriminate them or entail a breach of professional confidence. Three of them, it was true, had not been previously subpoenaed by the plaintiff, but their testimony had been rendered necessary only because two of the plaintiff's subpoenaed witnesses had been induced to abscond by the defendants' attorneys. The Rolphs claimed that Macaulay had wrongly denied them this testimony, under the influence of Boulton (under whom Macaulay had articled), by refusing to commit the non-jurors for contempt; and although he had done so on the solicitor general's advice that the plaintiff could find a remedy in the Court of King's Bench, Boulton now opposed as irregular the remedy he himself had proposed. They further complained that no action had been taken against the attorneys who had induced the witnesses to abscond, although Macaulay had ordered Boulton to do so. Despite these irregularities, which the Rolphs saw as amounting to a denial of due process, the court refused them a new trial in a split decision of the judges present (Sherwood and Willis).[112]

A month earlier, a remarkable scene had been played out at the Gore District quarter sessions of April 1828. The grand jury had returned criminal indictments in the tar-and-feather outrage against Simons, Hamilton, Robertson, and seven others. The new accused included some striking names. Allan MacNab and Alexander Chewett were the attorneys who had induced the witnesses at the civil trial to abscond. They had themselves refused to be sworn for the plaintiff on the grounds both of self-incrimination and breach of professional confidence. Andrew Stevens, who had also refused to be sworn though previously subpoenaed, was deputy clerk of the Crown for the Gore District (that is, the man who ran the local office of the Court of King's Bench, which administered routine process in civil actions originating in the district). A fourth defendant was the clerk of the district court and a fifth, George Gurnett, was the editor of the local newspaper, the *Gore Gazette*. The other two were described as 'gentlemen.'[113]

The circumstances surrounding the return of the indictments were both irregular and sensational. It is unclear how the information implicating the accused had come before the grand jury, but it was almost certainly with George Rolph's knowledge and consent. As a result of receiving it, the jury had come into court with what it called a 'Representation,' which named the ten men and added

that from the atrocity of the crime and the danger justly to be apprehended from the influence of so disgraceful an Example by persons filling professional stations and Public offices in the said District, and considering the perplexing questions which embarrassed the trial at the late assizes for the civil injury and other matters in the knowledge and [illegible] of the said Grand Jurors, they deem it expedient and request that their representation of the said crime, may be transmitted to the Court of King's Bench and the Attorney General, being convinced that the said offence will under all circumstances be more properly proceeded upon and punished by that Superior Court.[114]

An extraordinary contest ensued between the accused men and the magistrates on the one hand and the Rolph brothers and the grand jury on the other. The former tried to force the grand jury to return indictments so that the trial could be held there and then. The Rolphs insisted on George Rolph's right as prosecutor not to go to trial immediately, and on the jurors' right to make their representation and have it acted on without being exposed to extraordinary pressure from the bench to act against their consciences. Twice the jurors retired at the order of the court. The first time they returned to present their 'Representation' once more; the second time they presented a 'Remonstrance' against the court's refusal to transmit their representation. They reported that two indictments had been laid before them in the matter, but that they did not think it expedient at the moment to prefer them.[115]

At this point the court allowed one of the accused, MacNab, to begin a bullying cross-examination of George Rolph and the grand jury. MacNab repeatedly declared his disbelief that indictments had been laid before the jury and assailed Rolph with epithets such as 'fool,' 'liar,' 'ass,' 'scoundrel,' and (allegedly) worse, without check from the bench. When Rolph refused to answer questions from an accused party, the court itself put the questions at MacNab's prompting. At last, finding himself plagued with repetitious questions designed to entrap him in some insignificant inconsistency that might be inflated by his tormentors, Rolph demanded that the questions be put in writing and that he be allowed to give written answers with his brother's counsel. When the court still insisted on the grand jury preferring the indictments, John Rolph played his final trick: he produced a writ of certiorari, signed by Judge Willis, commanding the court to stay proceedings in the matter and transfer the indictments to the Court of King's Bench.[116]

During this episode, the magistrates had suspended George Rolph as their clerk. They now appealed to the lieutenant-governor for Rolph's dismissal. Apart from vague assertions that his conduct had been unsatisfactory for some time, the only specific charges referred to the events of the April quarter sessions. Rolph responded with a comprehensive defence backed up by several affidavits, and Maitland did not act on the magistrates' appeal. In April 1829 they dismissed Rolph themselves, without either attempting to prove their charges or allowing a defence, under a provincial statute which the law officers of the Crown held to justify the action.[117]

Rolph did not appear at the Gore assizes in September 1828 to prosecute the ten men indicted for the crime against him. It is easy to think of reasons why he did not. MacNab had alleged at the April quarter sessions that the affair was a publicity stunt, staged to make the attack on Rolph look like 'an official riot.'[118] If that is so, the Rolphs may have felt that they had achieved their purpose by George Rolph's victory in Halton County at the summer general election. But this is unlikely. In a private letter to William Warren Baldwin, one of his counsel, George Rolph linked his desire to pursue his attackers to the occurrence of an appalling gang-rape in the neighbourhood, with aggravated brutality, in which the victim had also been tarred and feathered. His avowed wish to re-establish the rule of law in a locality where it had been violated by the leading inhabitants forbids us to dismiss his motives cynically. By his own account, Rolph took no initiative in September because he considered it the attorney general's duty to act.[119] He may also have feared that an assize grand jury mainly composed (as always) of the district magistrates would reject any bill presented at his initiative in order to prevent the evidence against the accused men from being made public and the case from coming before a trial jury made up mainly of farmers. This was what had happened to Singleton Gardiner's perjury prosecution in the London District six years earlier, and such a fear may have underlain Rolph's initial decision to proceed by means of a civil action.

The tar-and-feather outrage and its protracted aftermath were an effect of the fierce political antagonisms of post-war Upper Canada, exacerbated by the social tensions of a district where a settled farming population, mainly American in origin, found itself imposed upon by an alien élite. It was probably no coincidence that it occurred so soon after the furor over Robinson's naturalization bill and only a fortnight or so before another similar episode, the wrecking of Mackenzie's printing-shop. The affair is strewn with evidence of underlying social and ethnic tensions. There is a hint of it in John Rolph's remark at the civil trial that if the accused were 'gentlemen,' the jurors were to be congratulated on being yeomen.[120] A more substantial sign is the confrontation between the district magistrates and the grand jury at the quarter sessions (a jury undoubtedly composed mainly of farmers) in April 1828. When Rolph was dismissed as clerk of the peace a year later, Lieutenant-Governor Sir John Colborne received an address of protest from his supporters ascribing the political dissensions of the district to the recent 'noxious accession of some individuals to our society, aided by the circulation of a paper from a prostituted local press [Gurnett's *Gore Gazette*], and the assimilation of the magistracy to persons whose habits of life are destructive of the good order of any community.' It complained of the fact that the assize grand jury was invariably dominated by the magistrates and called for the replacement of the present bench by one made up of 'wealthy and intelligent farmers.'[121]

George Rolph's assailants and their friends justified the tar-and-feather outrage as retribution for his supposed adultery, but this was almost certainly untrue. To be sure, their attack did mimic a kind of rough justice, sometimes called a *charivari*, traditionally resorted to by the common people of many lands to punish a breach of popular morality such as adultery; yet in Upper Canada this sort of informal retribution was not the habitual recourse of magistrates, of sheriffs, or of court officials.[122] It is probable that in blacking their faces and donning sheets, and in going on from Rolph's house to abduct and taunt the supposedly cuckolded husband, the miscreants meant to divert suspicion from themselves by mimicking the conduct of a lower social rank. After they were exposed, they could only cling to their spurious motive – which their counsel the solicitor general did, even to the extent of suggesting that they merited praise rather than punishment.[123]

Yet the incident was a charivari. Rolph may not have been punished for a breach of popular morality but he had certainly been punished, and in vigilante fashion, for his breach of official propriety in being John Rolph's brother and maintaining no social relations with the Gore District's parvenu élite; William Warren Baldwin suggested as much at the civil trial. It was this vigilante aspect of the affair, and of the attack on Mackenzie's printing-shop, which helped to earn both episodes a place alongside the Gardiner case in Dr Baldwin's critique of the Crown lawyers' official conduct in 1828. Official law, and the canons of due process, had premeditatedly, conspiratorially been flouted by members of the province's social élite; yet the law officers of the Crown had failed to prosecute the culprits and on one occasion had even publicly applauded the abuse of the victim's civil rights.

Unlike the first two cases recounted here, the 'outrage' that actually placed the question of the law officers' official conduct on the public agenda has found its way into the standard histories of these critical years.[124] Yet even this episode has never been presented in enough detail to explain why it caused such a scandal. William Forsyth, a United Empire Loyalist, owned an inn on land overlooking Niagara Falls. Greedy to monopolize the tourist dollar, he fenced in his land so that no one could get a view of the falls from the Canadian side without entering his premises. Fortunately for the outraged public, a strip of land one chain (sixty-six feet) wide along the river bank had been set aside as a military reserve, and in due course an officer of the royal engineers appeared to demand that Forsyth remove his fence from the Crown property. Forsyth refused, maintaining that the land in question was his.

Instead of referring the matter to a court of law, Sir Peregrine Maitland himself ordered direct action. The officer returned with a few soldiers, who proceeded to demolish the fence. They also threw into the gorge an outbuilding that had stood on the now disputed land for several years. Forsyth rebuilt his fence; the army returned and tore it down again. Subsequently, the attorney general vindicated the Crown's claim to the disputed land by filing an information of intrusion against Forsyth, who also lost two actions for trespass and damages against the officer, Captain George Philpotts, and the sheriff of the Niagara District, who had joined in one of Philpotts's expeditions.

The episode became controversial when Forsyth petitioned to the House of Assembly for redress against what he considered a military abuse of his civil rights. The committee set up to investigate his complaint demanded the attendance of two colonels (one the adjutant-general of the provincial militia, the other the deputy superintendent of the Indian Department) without, as was customary, requesting the lieutenant-governor's acquiescence beforehand. The colonels refused to attend without the lieutenant-governor's permission; the lieutenant-governor ordered them to stay away. The House of Assembly committed the colonels to prison for contempt, and there they stayed until Maitland prorogued the legislature three days later. Thus what at first had been solely a scandal over the abuse of civil rights became also a quarrel over the boundaries of executive and parliamentary privilege.

In his petition Forsyth postulated that in such a case of disputed right between a private individual and the Crown 'the substitution of a military force to decide the question of right, and remove by force of arms the peaceable possessor, in defiance of, and unknown to the civil authority, would have been a high breach of the rights of the freeholders of the Province.'[125] In this case the outrage was compounded by the fact that the civil authority, in the person of Sheriff Leonard, had lent itself to the abuse; but Leonard was also a colonel of militia. Forsyth stressed that the soldiers had so acted 'in a country not under martial law' at the express order of Sir Peregrine Maitland, a serving major-general.

The select committee on Forsyth's position strongly supported the petitioner. 'It is clear,' they reported,

that a person long in possession of land, like the petitioner, ought to have been ejected by the law of the land, which is ample, when impartially administered, for securing the rights of property; but the interference of the military by such acts of violence for maintaining supposed or contested rights, is justly regarded with jealousy, in all free countries, and ought to be seriously regarded in a colony where the most unprecedented outrages have been perpetrated without prosecution, and even followed by the patronage of the local government upon the wrongdoers.[126]

Thus the committee linked the 'Niagara Falls Outrage' with other recent abuses of the traditional liberties of Englishmen such as the tar-and-feather case and the attack on Mackenzie's printing-shop.

The committee's support for Forsyth is hardly surprising. Its chairman was John Rolph, who was the innkeeper's counsel in the matter, and the other members were Captain Matthews of Middlesex, Robert Randal, and another Niagara District radical, the United Empire Loyalist Dr John Johnson Lefferty. This makes it the more remarkable that the Colonial Office sustained the House of Assembly in every particular. The Colonial Office counsel, James Stephen, observed:

From the statement of the Lieutenant Governor, himself, I should infer that there were very serious and adequate grounds for the complaint made by the House of

Assembly. It seems to be admitted that Forsyth was dispossessed by a Military Force, acting under the express command of the Lieutenant Governor, of a piece of land of which he was in the actual occupation, to which he asserted a legal title, and of which he had obtained possession without any violence or breach of the Peace. It is no subject of wonder that this kind of Military ejectment should excite great discontent and clamour, nor did the presence of the Sheriff, in my judgment, render the measure less objectionable. On the contrary, as the civil power was at hand, it may with justice be said that there was the less reason for resorting to Military authority.[127]

The secretary of state, Sir George Murray, made this verdict official in a dispatch to Maitland's successor, Sir John Colborne.[128]

Attorney General Robinson had not known of Maitland's orders in advance, but more than five years later he was offered an opportunity to comment officially on the affair. When William Lyon Mackenzie went to England in 1832 to present the grievances of his Upper Canadian supporters, he got Joseph Hume to raise the matter in Parliament. The House of Commons called for information. In due course Colborne dispatched it together with a report from Robinson, now chief justice, which the lieutenant-governor explained was essential to a true understanding of the affair.[129]

Robinson took pains to belittle the matter. It had long since been forgotten in Upper Canada, he remarked. The reservation of a chain along the bank of the Niagara River had been 'a matter perfectly notorious and well understood, and no doubt or difficulty that I ever heard of ever arose upon the subject for nearly forty years,' until Forsyth had put up his fence. 'The public' had been annoyed by it, and a petition for its removal signed by 'the most respectable inhabitants of the country' had been presented to the lieutenant-governor. 'In three several actions or cases, the opportunity was afforded of trying the question by juries of the country,' and all three had gone against Forsyth. 'With respect to the reasonableness of the complaint as to military interference, I think it would be difficult to find in His Majesty's service an officer less open to the imputation of arbitrary conduct, and a disregard of civil rights, than Sir Peregrine Maitland.' The lieutenant-governor could have taken the easy course and allowed the public to remain inconvenienced while the matter was decided by the leisurely processes of law. Instead, though fully aware 'how easy it is, in a certain temper of men's minds, to make a trifling matter the cause of an unjust excitement,' he had acted promptly for the public good. 'Without pretending to decide the matter in its strictly legal point of view,' concluded the chief justice, 'I must say I have not much doubt that if, in any part of England or in the United States of America, an intruder were to insist on encumbering a barrack square with his waggon, or were to plant posts and rails in a parade ground, the nuisance would be removed under the direction of an officer on the spot.'[130]

A more disingenuous presentation than this can hardly be imagined. Forsyth had never denied the reservation of a chain's width along the river bank. It so happened that the topography of the area made it highly disputable whether the land in question (which was not twenty but 100 yards from the water's edge) was part of that reserve, and Forsyth's right to the land (on which his blacksmith's shop had stood for years) had never been challenged until Philpotts turned up in May 1827. The three lawsuits may ultimately have been decided against Forsyth, but not by three juries; at least one jury had awarded him £200 in damages only to see its verdict set aside in the Court of King's Bench.[131] The attempted analogy to the obstruction of a barrack square or parade ground was a piece of scandalous dishonesty, since the land in question had been under the evident occupation not of the army but of the innkeeper.

It is hard to interpret Robinson's report as anything but a conscious attempt to deceive, and this impression is strengthened by reviewing other remarks of his that were relevant to the affair. Earlier in 1832 he had described Forsyth's two actions against Captain Philpotts, in which he had acted for the defence by order of the lieutenant-governor, as 'two very difficult causes, before Special Juries' – not exactly what one would expect in the cut-and-dried affair he described in his report to Colborne.[132] Another revealing document is his official opinion given in November 1827, when the legality of the action against Forsyth was still undecided, concerning the legal means of dispossessing unauthorized occupants of another military reserve. At this time Robinson opined that summary eviction would probably be considered illegal, and added: 'Individuals sometimes incur the responsibility of such a step rather than meet the delay and expense of an action against an indigent litigant. It is prudent, however, to consider that in the case of a public Officer, and more especially a Military Officer proceeding in this summary manner without resorting to the aid of the law, a Jury would probably be inclined to award high damages to the party suing him in an action of trespass.'[133] Compare the language in his report of 1832: 'An individual whose property had been thus trespassed upon would have had a clear right by law to abate the nuisance, and it seemed no unreasonable expectation that the

Government should protect its rights as firmly and promptly as individuals may.'[134] Although Robinson had quit the bar for the bench, it is the later statement that bears the stamp of advocacy.

Of course, in five years a man may change his mind; and in the meantime two lawsuits had decided the point that had been doubtful in 1827, notwithstanding at least one jury's inclination to award high damages against Captain Philpotts. J.C. Dent, writing 100 years ago, noted the 'very general belief throughout the Niagara District at the time' that Sheriff Leonard had packed the juries in the government's favour.[135] The degree of latitude that sheriffs enjoyed in selecting juries was a common complaint against the administration of justice in these years, and Leonard certainly had every incentive to exercise that latitude to the full in a group of related cases, in one of which he was a co-defendant. There is, moreover, one fact about the juries in the two actions for trespass that is highly relevant to the outcome of the affair, and for which we have Robinson's own authority: they were 'special juries' – that is, juries chosen not from the whole pool of petit jurors, but from the richest inhabitants of the district.[136] This fact takes on particular significance when we discover that those 'most respectable inhabitants of the country,' who had so urgently petitioned for Forsyth's ouster – the 'public' to whose repeated complaints Lieutenant-Governor Maitland had so energetically responded – were none other than Robinson's old clients, Messrs Thomas Clark and Samuel Street.

In 1818 Forsyth had erected a covered stairway on the chain reserved for military purposes in front of his property in order to make it easier for visitors to get a good view of the falls. He had provided a boat to ferry tourists and travellers across the river directly below the cataract. Two years later he wrote to the government of a rumour that someone had petitioned for a licence to occupy the reserve at that spot and for a monopoly of ferry privileges there. He asked that these benefits be given to him instead, or, alternatively, that they be left ungranted for general enjoyment.[137]

The privileges in question were left ungranted, to Forsyth or anyone else. But in 1825 Clark and Street asked for and received a monopoly of ferry privileges for twenty-one years upon their undertaking to build a carriageway from the verge of the gorge down to the ferry dock. By now tourism was big business at the falls. Forsyth was running a daily coach from Buffalo which visited 'the celebrated battle grounds of Fort Erie' before proceeding downriver to the cataract. Faced with this challenge to his livelihood, he embarked on a guerrilla war against the privileged usurpers, during which the latter's stairway into the gorge was wrecked and three of their ferry boats in succession either cut to pieces or set adrift down the rapids. Meanwhile, the innkeeper continued to operate his unauthorized ferry. Clark told the government that he would feel safe only if he received a licence to occupy the reserve, whereupon he could put Forsyth and his boats off by force; but he hesitated, he said, to ask for this, 'as it might in me have a grasping or monopolizing appearance.'[138]

A year later, his scruples gone, Clark was Captain Philpotts's companion when the engineer officer entered on what until then had been Forsyth's unchallenged property to redefine the boundary of the military reserve to the innkeeper's injury. A few days after Forsyth's fence had gone down and his blacksmith's shop been flung into the gorge, Clark made a formal application for the licence of occupation, which he duly received. Soon afterwards, notice of the grant issued from the Niagara plutocrats to the innkeeper, along with a warning to stay off the land which he had always thought his but which the government now certified to be theirs.[139]

To Thomas Clark, Forsyth was 'a man I must say the most perverse in our district.'[140] Yet Forsyth cannot fairly be ranked above Robert Randal in perversity, since he did what Randal had not done, even under the coercion of protracted imprisonment: he sold to Clark and Street at what he maintained was far less than the former value of his property. This action set up an amusing sequel.

In his report of 1832, Robinson had observed that Forsyth no longer owned the property at the falls, 'having sold it to persons who, I am convinced, will never pretend that they have a right to inclose the public reservation to which he asserted a claim.'[141] Within months of his writing these words, Robinson's old clients had done exactly that. When Captain Richard Bonnycastle of the royal engineers moved to assert the Crown's claim, Clark and Street won a verdict for trespass and £100 damages at the Niagara assizes of 1833. This verdict was set aside in the Court of King's Bench as being against the evidence, but Street was in undisputed legal possession of the land in 1839 (Clark having died) when the Executive Council turned down Forsyth's petition to be compensated for the losses he had suffered twelve years earlier. Refusing to make any distinction between the innkeeper and his assignees (Clark and Street), the council noted that 'the damages suffered by Mr. Forsyth or his assignee, had been considered and allowed by a jury' – that is, the damages Clark and Street had recovered in the 1830s were to be considered as compensation for Forsyth's loss in 1827! The original decision against him had been 'the act of a judge and jury, and not of the Government, and it took place without any improper influence or interference with their proper functions.' His personal losses were 'nothing but what was the natural consequence of protracted litigation.'[142] Thus Clark and Street took all the gain and Forsyth all the pain.

It is no coincidence that our historical tour of the province has brought us back to the scene of Robert Randal's spoliation. Justice was probably even more unequal in the Niagara District than elsewhere. In the early decades it was by far the most commercialized part of the province. By the 1830s it was the site of the grandest capital project in the colony, the Welland Canal. Land values were high and money was mighty. Part of Forsyth's land at the falls had been bought from Thomas Clark's cousin and fellow legislative councillor, William Dickson. Dickson had acquired it, as Clark had tried to acquire the Bridgewater property from Randal, by keeping the indebted proprietor in prison till he cracked. It had taken only a year to break Francis Ellesworth's will in the jail that had brought Robert Gourlay to the verge of insanity in less than nine months.[143] The 'Niagara Falls Outrage' was one more reason that Robert Randal's call for 'an equal distribution of justice' won him four successive elections between 1820 and his death in 1834.

Episodes such as the harassment of Singleton Gardiner, the attack on George Rolph, and the military chastisement of William Forsyth can easily be trivialized: a tug-of-war over the tourist dollar at Niagara Falls; another over a saddle in darkest Middlesex; the scragging of a bounder by the true-blue hearties of Gore. Taken together, however, these incidents and others like them created the impression of a province ruled by men who were ready to punish any sort of opposition by violence and coercion. The 'types rioters' who attacked Mackenzie's printing-shop were nearly all closely connected to the government; the district magistrates were its sworn representatives, commissioned to administer local government and petty justice.

Only by some resolute act of disavowal could the government have avoided the appearance of condoning these excesses, yet no such action was taken. True, the lieutenant-governor had dismissed his private secretary, one of the types rioters, but he had soon afterwards made him registrar of the Niagara District. Another soon became clerk of the peace in the same district, while the leader of the band, Samuel Peters Jarvis, was appointed deputy provincial secretary.[144] Maitland had also declared his intention to dismiss Titus Simons and James Hamilton from their offices in the Gore District after the verdict against them at the assizes of 1827; but Hamilton's dismissal did not take effect for several months and Simons's seems to have been rescinded, for he was included in the new commission of the peace that issued in April 1828. That commission also included two men who, like Hamilton and Simons, were then under criminal indictment for the tar-and-feather outrage. One was the deputy clerk of the Crown, Andrew Stevens, who had refused to testify at the assizes, though subpoenaed by the plaintiff, from fear of self-incrimination.[145] No – Sir Peregrine Maitland did not normally chastise his over-zealous minions, he rewarded and promoted them, and his own unconstitutional action in the Forsyth affair proved his personal predilection for their methods.

It was this pattern of official misbehaviour between June 1826 and May 1827 that turned the parliamentary investigation of the Forsyth affair into an inquiry into the official conduct of the law officers of the Crown. Forsyth told the select committee that he thought the aggression against him a proper subject for criminal prosecution but was deterred by the fact that both the attorney general and the solicitor general, whose duty it was to conduct criminal prosecutions at the assizes, had been retained for the defence in his civil actions against Captain Philpotts and Sheriff Leonard. He would still prosecute if he could employ other counsel, but he understood that the law officers claimed the sole right of conducting such prosecutions.[146] The committee's report, as quoted above, spoke of Upper Canada as 'a colony where the most unprecedented outrages have been perpetrated without prosecution, and even followed by the patronage of the local government upon the wrong doers.' A second select committee was set up to look into the law officers' role in the administration of criminal justice.

The question was not a new one in the province. It had first arisen in 1811, when Lieutenant-Governor Gore had confined Attorney General Firth to the capital after Firth claimed the right to authorize every instrument of government issued under the great seal. Alarmed at the prospect of losing the large revenue he derived from the assizes, Firth had insisted that the conducting of criminal prosecutions in person was 'the first, highest and most important Branch of the Official Duty of the Attorney General, both as it respects the King and the Country.' The Executive Council had contradicted his claim, asserting that there was no need for either the attorney general or a substitute to attend at the assizes 'unless matters especially regarding the King's Interest are to be there agitated.' In another report, the council explained that the custom of the attorney general travelling the assize circuit had begun when the English criminal law was first introduced into the old province of Quebec, and the attorney general, as the only English lawyer in the colony, had alone possessed the expertise to conduct prosecutions. When Quebec had been split in 1791, the practice had continued in Upper Canada for the same reason. Now, the council implied, there were other lawyers competent to conduct such proceedings.[147]

With Firth's departure and the accession of more acceptable men to the attorneyship, the question had been allowed to lapse; but it is worth noticing that the two sides were to some extent arguing at cross-purposes. Firth's claim, it will be recalled, was based on the idea that his office was a species of property consisting of certain revenue-producing functions that were his to perform by right. The council ignored the question of right and addressed only that of expediency.

In 1818 the question arose again as a result of the murder and mayhem that had taken place on the Red River two years earlier. The Scottish philanthropist, the Earl of Selkirk, had sought to establish a colony of Scottish emigrants near modern Winnipeg. The powerful Montreal-based fur-trading organization, the North-West Company, had objected to this settlement as a threat to its operations and aroused the local Métis population against it, inciting them to an attack that resulted in the massacre of some twenty settlers and the dispersion of the rest. On the orders of the imperial government, the governor-in-chief at Quebec had appointed two special commissioners to restore order in the region, which lay far beyond the borders of Canada.

The anglophones of Lower Canada were almost all sympathetic to the North-West Company, the richest commercial organization in the colony. The commissioners proved to be less interested in pursuing the instigators and perpetrators of the massacre than in proceeding against Selkirk for his own vigorous countermeasure in seizing the company's base at Fort William (Thunder Bay) on Lake Superior. The official élite at York was also prejudiced against Selkirk, partly out of sympathy with the Montreal merchant community (to which John Strachan was connected by marriage), and partly because they disliked people encouraging precious British emigrants to settle anywhere but in Upper Canada. Selkirk found himself involved in a series of harassing and expensive legal proceedings, both criminal and civil, in both colonies (the Lower Canadian criminal proceedings were transferred to the upper province from fear that juries below would be biased against the North-West Company).[148] The whole affair was in several ways an outrage of civil rights comparable to the contemporary case of Robert Gourlay; yet, although it occupies fifty times the space in the Colonial Office papers, it has never been noticed as such by historians, chiefly because it did not affect Upper Canadian politics and therefore failed to enter the mythology of official misrule that began to be formed in the mid-1820s. It is illuminating to the historian of Upper Canada, however, since it shows both Robinson and Maitland employing against Selkirk the same weapons of specious argument and character assassination they were later to use against their Upper Canadian critics.

The question of the attorney general's claim to conduct criminal prosecutions at the assizes came up indirectly. Selkirk complained about John Beverley Robinson's refusal to prosecute one of the special commissioners, Major John Fletcher, for his outrageous treatment of a party of Selkirk's people near Fort William (which, though hundreds of miles from the nearest settled region, formed part of the Western District of Upper Canada). In defending his refusal, Robinson observed that it by no means precluded Selkirk from pursuing a criminal prosecution against Fletcher by his private counsel; the attorney general's refusal to act meant only that the Crown would not bear the expense of such proceedings. Thus in 1818 Robinson expressly admitted that others than officially appointed Crown counsel could conduct criminal prosecutions at the assizes. But this statement, like that of the Executive Council seven years earlier, remained submerged in the official archives. [149]

In the mid-1820s the question surfaced again, under circumstances that are obscure and can only be recovered in part. In 1823 the House of Assembly was anxious to introduce semi-annual instead of annual assizes in each district while incurring the smallest possible increase in the cost of the administration of justice. The extra expense would consist largely in the travel allowance, or circuit money, granted to the judges, Crown prosecutors, and clerks of assize. The select committee set up to consider the matter proposed to meet this extra cost by abolishing the allowance to the Crown prosecutors and clerks of assize entirely and by paying the judges only what they actually laid out on their travels instead of the fixed sum they now received. They justified their recommendation by the fact that the income of these officials was much larger than when circuit money had been introduced, and the continuance of that subsidy was therefore unnecessary. Going more deeply into the cost of the administration of justice, the committee proposed a reduction in the official fees received at assizes and the abolition of the attorney general's annual grant of ninety pounds for office rent and a clerk's salary. They complained that many criminal cases that were tried at public expense at the assizes which should properly be tried at the complainant's expense at quarter sessions. Their labours were fruitless, though, because Lieutenant-Governor Maitland refused to countenance any fee reductions. A second assize was set up in the most populous districts, but a year later it was abolished at the Assembly's request because of its excessive cost.[150]

Another of the committee's recommendations is especially relevant to the present topic, though frustratingly obscure in its details. The committee introduced a bill to authorize the appointment of district attorneys, which was passed by the Assembly but scotched in the Legislative Council. It must have occasioned much debate, for the form in which it emerged from the Assembly was adopted only by the Speaker's casting vote. Unfortunately, no report of the debate survives, nor any discussion that might reveal the details of the bill.[151]

This was not the first time the institution of district attorneys had been proposed in the province. William Dummer Powell had suggested it about twenty years earlier. The gist of Powell's scheme was this. Too many prosecutions at assize were failing because the Crown prosecutor had to go into court with an inadequate case. This was the fault of the district magistrates, who were responsible for preparing cases for trial. The administration of criminal justice would be much more efficient, Powell asserted, 'if some young Gentleman of the Bar was retained as King's Counsel in each district, whose duty it would be to represent the Attorney General at the quarter and general sessions of the peace, have communication of all Indictments and Informations, assist the Magistrates in matters of form, point their attention to the objects of police which want regulation and hold a hand to the execution of the laws in those respects.' This system had been found necessary in the United States, and something like it had existed in Quebec under the French regime.[152]

Powell did not suggest outright that the district attorneys might actually conduct prosecutions at assize, and in a second paper in 1811 he proposed that the preparation of such prosecutions should be the duty not of a special officer but of the clerk of the peace.[153] Still, the idea of appointing a 'King's Counsel' in each district, entitled (as Powell specified) to wear the silk gown that distinguished the rank in England, was capable of such extension, and it is significant that both of Powell's memoranda are today to be found attached to the Executive Council report on Firth's claim as attorney general to conduct all Crown prosecutions at assize. Likewise, whether or not the bill of 1823 went so far, its introduction in the context of an attempt to reduce the cost of the administration of criminal justice may well have evoked the suggestion that district attorneys should assume the conduct of such prosecutions, thereby making the law officers' expensive peregrinations redundant. The point was certainly hinted at during the next session, when the cost of the administration of justice was debated again. James Crooks of Halton remarked: 'Altho' they had a 2d Circuit in England, the crown officers never travelled on circuit; they had proper and fit persons to do their duty in every District or County, but in this Province, the crown officers went the whole round, to the great injury of the young practitioners in country parts; because the persons who are concerned in suits of any consequence, instead of giving them to those of the profession in their own vicinity, generally wait for the Crown Officer to come round, and give him the preference, and they had too much in his opinion without that support.'[154] Crooks was specifically complaining about the amount of civil business the law officers derived from the circuit; but it was only a small step from this to the notion that the criminal business might also be beneficially shared among 'the young country practitioners.'

The year after the parliamentary rumblings about the law officers' monopoly of prosecutions at assize, their control of criminal proceedings in that court sustained a setback in the Court of King's Bench. In R. v Elrod, for bigamy, the defendant failed to appear in answer to the indictment and Dr Baldwin moved for a writ of outlawry to compel his appearance. This was a matter of instituting process rather than conducting a prosecution, but the court asked the Crown officers if they consented to Baldwin's right of motion. The attorney general raised a doubt on the ground that bigamy was a capital crime, all such prosecutions in Upper Canada being conducted by the Crown lawyers. As Robert Baldwin, the doctor's son, recalled four years later,

On a subsequent day, upon the motion being renewed, the Attorney General ... informed the Court that he had looked into the authorities, and could find no authority against the right to make the motion claimed by Mr. Baldwin. I was at the time a student at law only, but I distinctly recollect it was conceded as a matter of right, and not of courtesy. The Solicitor General certainly did, at the time, in a low tone of voice, suggest to the Attorney General not to give up the right.[155]

As reported, the decision rested on the fact that the provincial statute regulating outlawry did not expressly restrict the institution of proceedings to the Crown officers.[156]

These various threats to the law officers' control of criminal proceedings at assize no doubt explain why, in 1825, Solicitor General Boulton imported the subject into his discussion of John Small's claim, as clerk of the Crown, to the emoluments of the clerks of assize. Small based his claim on the same ground Firth had chosen in 1810 and 1811: that his predecessor had enjoyed the right in question and his own patent of office expressly endowed him with all the benefits enjoyed by his predecessor. The judges contested it on the ground that in England clerks of assize were nominated by the judge of the court in which they served. In supporting Small, Boulton argued in general that an Upper Canadian office could not necessarily be taken as identical in constitution and function with its English namesake. If every provincial official were confined to the duties performed by his English synonym, few would have enough work to make a living.

That Boulton's concern was related to the law officers of the Crown in particular is clear from two ostensibly extraneous elements in his discourse. First, he contradicted the Executive Council's argument in 1811 – which he ascribed to Powell in particular – against the necessity of the Crown officers' attendance at the assizes. The idea that they had first 'gone the circuit' because they alone had the expertise to conduct criminal prosecutions was 'quite gratuitous, and unsupported by any fact.' The practice instituted in the province of Quebec, and continued in Upper Canada, was one common to the North American colonies and one that still existed in the former colonies to the south. In all these jurisdictions, the institution and conduct of criminal proceedings was the exclusive duty of the public prosecutors.

Next, Boulton veered even further off course to challenge the contention – which he also ascribed to Powell – that the increase in the law officers' income from prosecutions at assize constituted grounds for abolishing their circuit money. The Crown officers' account for criminal prosecutions, he argued, consisted of fees for services actually performed. 'I do not think that His Majesty's Government expects its Law Officers to abate their charges as their duties increase, as Contractors with the Commissariat may be expected to do when large supplies of Beef are to be furnished.'[157] His basic point, though left unstated, was this. If usage and prescriptive right, as enshrined in his patent of office, gave an Upper Canadian official no protection against being stripped of any of his functions that were not performed by his English namesake, the law officers had no security in their monopoly of criminal prosecutions at assize, since no such monopoly was exercised by the attorney general and solicitor general of England.

Robinson denied that the rejection of Small's claim had to go so far. The

Upper Canadian judicial system and the English were indeed strictly analogous; however, the analogy did not deprive a provincial official of all the functions not performed by his English namesake but only of those that were not within the competence of his office. Applying this doctrine to the provincial law officers, he admitted that their English counterparts did not normally conduct criminal prosecutions at the assizes, but maintained: 'It is clear that these duties tendered by the Attorney General are only such as he, or indeed any other Barrister whom the Crown may please to employ, is unquestionably competent to perform in his capacity of Barrister – and the only difference between this Country and England in that respect is that the Government here chooses to employ its Law Officers more frequently than in England to perform a duty unquestionably within their Competency to discharge.'[158] Thus Robinson set the law officers' monopoly on a different footing from Boulton's. Whereas the solicitor general based it on the unvarying practice in the North American colonies, his senior colleague founded it on a supposed right of the attorney general in England, as the king's counsel, to assume the conduct of any prosecution.

The evidence taken by the select committee of 1828 reveals no consensus that such a right existed. None of the witnesses denied that the Upper Canadian bar enjoyed exactly the same rights with respect to the conduct of criminal prosecutions as the English bar – but what were those rights? According to Judge Willis, recently arrived from England,

In all matters of revenue, treason, and personal rights of the crown, and those under its immediate protection, as the affairs of lunatics and charities, the crown officers were bound to protect the public rights, in the same way as any counsel generally retained by his client is bound to protect his rights. But in all other matters, in which the crown was not so immediately concerned, as in felonies, and in those misdemeanours which are not prosecuted in the crown office, or by ex-officio information, I have always understood the right of being employed by prosecutors to be open to the Bar.[159]

So spoke Willis; but the other witnesses (except for Judge Sherwood, who refused to elaborate), could only point to the fact that in Upper Canada the Crown officers had always tried to monopolize criminal prosecutions at assize and had received the support of the court in resisting the pretensions of other barristers to conduct them. Bartholomew Beardsley, the Niagara District MPP who chaired the committee, understood the monopoly 'to be claimed, and scarcely contested, being considered as sanctioned by the court of King's Bench; and therefore I should consider the assertion of the right as hopeless.' Archibald McLean, a future Speaker of the Assembly and chief justice of Upper Canada, remembered one solitary instance during Firth's tenure of office when John Macdonell had tried to assert his right to conduct such a prosecution but had desisted 'from some objection then made to it by the Court.' Otherwise the law officers' monopoly had gone unchallenged, although he did not know the ground on which it was claimed. Robert Baldwin had 'always understood that the Attorney and Solicitor General have claimed the exclusive right of conducting criminal prosecutions in this province,' although the case of R. v Elrod led him to 'infer a doubt of that exclusive right countenanced by the Court, and conceded by the Attorney General.'[160]

In its report, the committee swept by these uncertainties in a masterly evasion. 'It appears,' they declared,

that the Crown Officers, who exercise an exclusive right to conduct criminal prosecutions at the courts of oyer and terminer, and general gaol delivery, are in the habit, even in the first instance, of being retained, and taking an active part in the defence of the civil action for the wrong; by which it is inevitable that prosecutors will be discouraged to apply to them for professional aid, and justice therefore, in many cases, fail, unless the rights of prosecutors, and of the bar, are asserted and upheld as in England.

From the testimony given, your Committee do not hesitate to come to that conclusion, in which they are supported by the testimony of the honourable Mr. Justice Willis, and nearly all the witnesses examined.[161]

Had the committee called the attorney general to testify, he might have told them that R. v Elrod was not the first case in which he had disclaimed an exclusive right to conduct criminal proceedings in the province. He might have cited his willingness to let Selkirk proceed by private counsel against Major Fletcher in 1818. And he might have gone on to state that all this made no difference whatever to his present position. Within a few months he would be afforded an opportunity to explain all this by courtesy of Judge Willis and Francis Collins.

John Walpole Willis had arrived from England only in September 1827. He had been appointed to replace D'Arcy Boulton on the Court of King's Bench, but he was a specialist in equity. The chief reason for his selection was the Colonial Office decision that the province should at last have a Court of Chancery over which Willis should also preside.

As soon as he arrived, Willis fell out with Maitland. The judge's wife was an earl's eldest daughter; the lieutenant-governor's was a duke's daughter, but not his eldest. This led to a spat over social precedence in which the husbands inevitably became entangled. To make things worse, the Crown officers in England decided at this point to reverse the orthodoxy of decades in voicing the opinion that the Crown could not as an act of prerogative set up any but a common-law court. This made the erection of a Court of Chancery in Upper Canada dependent on provincial legislation, which it became Attorney General Robinson's duty to introduce at the session of 1828. The legislation stalled – according to Willis because of Robinson's lethargy, according to Maitland because Willis had deliberately encouraged the opposition to delay it, having formed a desire to be appointed chief justice in succession to Campbell, whose death or retirement was thought to be imminent.[162]

Immediately after the session, in April 1828, Willis presided over the Home District spring assizes (the Home District, centred in the capital, had two assizes a year). Several months previously William Lyon Mackenzie had published a pamphlet, provocatively entitled *The History of the Destruction of the Colonial Advocate Press by Officers of the Provincial Government of Upper Canada and Law Students of the Attorney and Solicitor General*, about the attack on his printing-shop in 1826. In discussing the subject in February 1828, Francis Collins, the pugnacious young Catholic Irishman who edited the *Canadian Freeman*, branded the leader of the rioters, Samuel Jarvis, as a murderer because of his part in a duel a decade earlier. In this affair of 1817, the son of the late provincial secretary had gunned down his eighteen-year-old opponent after the latter's pistol had fired prematurely. Jarvis, who had been acquitted of murder at the time, published a reply that included statements of exoneration from the two seconds on that occasion, H.J. Boulton and James Small (a son of the clerk of the Crown).[163] Collins responded in terms that led both Jarvis and Boulton to request Attorney General Robinson to prosecute him for libel. Robinson brought these libels before the grand jury at the April assizes, along with a libel against the government. The grand jury returned indictments, including one of their own for a libel on themselves uttered in the *Canadian Freeman*'s latest number.[164]

When Collins was brought before the court for arraignment, he denounced the attorney general for partiality in prosecuting him for libel when Robinson had never prosecuted either the types rioters of 1826, who had close ties with the government, or Solicitor General Boulton (now a confessed accessory) for his part in the murder of John Ridout in

1817. He announced his own intention to prosecute the persons concerned in both crimes in order to compel Robinson to do his duty by conducting the proceedings against them. When Willis directed him to lay his evidence before the grand jury, Collins voiced the fear that they would not deal with his accusations impartially. Jarvis was one of their number, as were the solicitor general's brother and others who were either involved in the crimes or intimate with those who were. He also expressed doubt whether the Crown officers could be trusted to exert themselves wholeheartedly in the prosecution of either crime. Willis encouraged Collins to proceed with the assurance that he himself would see that everyone did his duty.[165]

The normal preliminary process now ensued in both cases. The attorney general drew up indictments against the accused and presented them to the jury, along with the sworn testimony of Collins and any witnesses whose testimony may have been available and relevant. In due course the grand jury returned indictments against Boulton and Small for murder and against the known wreckers of Mackenzie's printing-shop for riot. When the murder case came up for trial, however, Collins applied for permission to have the proceedings conducted not by the attorney general but by his own private counsel, Robert Baldwin. Thus the question of the law officers' monopoly of criminal prosecutions at the assizes was formally brought before the court. It had already provoked a first-class row between Willis and Robinson at the time of Collins's initial complaint, and now it sparked off another. Contemporary newspaper reports and the subsequent written statements of both parties allow us to reconstruct the terms of the dispute.[166]

Robinson addressed two questions: should he have preferred an indictment against the types rioters, and was his view of the rights of the Crown officers in Upper Canada with respect to criminal proceedings correct? On the first question he noted that the offence of riot was a petty misdemeanour, usually cognizable by the district quarter sessions rather than the higher court where the Crown officers prosecuted. Such petty offences were generally prosecuted at the assizes only to empty the jails of persons awaiting trial there for want of bail. Had Robinson instituted an assize prosecution in respect of the types riot, he would have exposed himself to the charge of inflating his account for criminal prosecutions by proceeding in a case that lay within the jurisdiction of a lower court.

Moreover, in cases such as riot or assault and battery, where the perpetrators were open to both criminal and civil proceedings, it was normal to allow the victim to choose his mode of action; Mackenzie had chosen civil proceedings. Had Robinson instituted criminal proceedings prior to the civil trial, he could have been accused of trying to inflict a criminal penalty on the culprits in order to lessen the damages that Mackenzie was likely to obtain. In fact, he revealed, friends of the types rioters had asked him to institute criminal proceedings with just that end in view, but he had refused. After the civil trial he had urged the grand jury to call Mackenzie before them to find out if he wished to press a criminal prosecution as well, and Mackenzie had declined to do so. He had taken this exceptional step, he explained, in order to protect the grand jury against subsequent calumny as being biased in favour of the rioters. In England, though, when an individual punished by heavy damages found himself subjected to criminal proceedings for the act that had incurred the civil penalty, it was usual for him to apply to the attorney general to exercise the discretionary power of the office under common law to stay criminal proceedings by entering a nolle prosequi.[167]

The general question – that of the Crown officers' rights with respect to criminal prosecutions – fell into two parts. One was the right to institute proceedings or not as they saw fit; the other the right to conduct any criminal proceedings they chose. It had always been the custom in Upper Canada, as in England, for the law officers to institute prosecutions only in matters immediately affecting the rights of the Crown or its traditional wards. In 'all cases of Felony, or other Offences against the Peace, or against the Person or Property of Individuals,' they proceeded only upon an information taken by a magistrate, or the presentment of a grand jury, or the personal complaint of the injured party. There had been no such initiative in either of the cases in which Collins had alleged a dereliction of duty.

But while the decision to proceed or not was a matter within the Crown officers' absolute discretion, the decision not to do so did not preclude an aggrieved party from proceeding independently. To be sure, in almost every European country but England and Ireland criminal prosecutions were invariably conducted by a public officer. It was so in Scotland, and it was so in the British colonies. It was a practice the United States had been careful to preserve since attaining independence, and even in England, where it did not prevail, it was widely acclaimed as tending to prevent the vexatious prosecutions that abounded where private individuals had unfettered initiative. In Upper Canada, however, as in England, the law officers claimed no exclusive right to prosecute, even at the assizes. It was open to any individual, if the law officer declined to act on his complaint, to pursue it independently by his private counsel – though of course the

Crown would not defray the expenses of a prosecution which its officers did not sanction. This had been his position ten years earlier, Robinson recalled, when confronted by the complaint of Lord Selkirk.

Yet although Robinson conceded the right of an individual to pursue privately a prosecution that the Crown officers refused to countenance, he did not admit the right to dispense with their aid in cases where they were inclined to give it. Any individual might institute criminal proceedings at the assizes without first applying to the Crown officers; but the Crown officers were the public prosecutors 'whose Duty and whose Right it was to conduct all Criminal Prosecutions for which they thought there was Ground.' On this basis Robinson stood aside to let Robert Baldwin prosecute Boulton and Small for murder; but when, after their acquittal, Collins applied for Baldwin to conduct the prosecution of the types rioters, the attorney general intervened to assert his right, since the offence was one in which he had had no objection to conducting proceedings eighteen months previously. Willis upheld his position on the ground that the subject had been referred to the imperial authorities and it would be improper to anticipate their decision. Robinson then proceeded to prosecute the defendants, who were convicted and fined five shillings each.

Soon after the April assizes, George Rolph's application for a new hearing in the tar-and-feather case came before Justices Sherwood and Willis in the Court of King's Bench. The question again arose of the Crown officers' duty to prosecute gross breaches of the peace, whether or not the victim had laid a complaint. Like Robinson a few weeks earlier, Boulton cited the risk of appearing to pad his account if he instituted criminal proceedings in such a case.[168] (Assault and battery, like common-law riot, was an offence normally cognizable at the quarter sessions.) Immediately afterwards, the attorney general sent a circular to every member of the Law Society of Upper Canada, quoting the strictures of the Assembly select committee and asking what 'instances of daring outrages' had, within their knowledge, passed unprosecuted, and whether they attributed the failure to his dereliction of duty. He also wished to know of any cases in which he had acted for the defence in a civil action for a wrong which ought to have been subjected to criminal prosecution, but which had not been prosecuted because of his professional association with the wrongdoers.[169]

To this circular Dr Baldwin, a senior member of the provincial bar and several times treasurer of the Law Society, returned a long and thoughtful reply.[170] He cited three major cases of fault on both Robinson's and

Boulton's part: the types riot, the tar-and-feather outrage, and the Gardiner case. Of the types riot he observed that Robinson should at least have prosecuted the culprits promptly, but in Baldwin's view he should also have done more. Several of the rioters had been law students, some of them clerks in Robinson's own office. As ex officio head of the provincial bar, Robinson should have reproved his clerks 'in some public and impressive manner' – perhaps in the presence of the Law Society – and reminded them of the barrister's oath to uphold the constitution and defend the rights of his fellow citizens. He should also have advised against the public subscription instituted by one of the York magistrates to pay the damages – a proceeding showing 'a degree of boldness and disregard for the Laws of the Country in my mind highly reprehensible.' Robinson's failure to do these things had brought discredit upon the Law Society and the profession.

The other two episodes were both examples of the Crown officers acting for the defence in a civil action arising from a wrong that merited criminal prosecution. The tar-and-feather outrage constituted 'a violation of law, of decency, of individual safety and public peace so gross, so devoid of all reasonable or honest provocation, so coward-like, so mean – nay so impious in its details, that the Crown officers, the Attorney General, the Solicitor General, the Governor himself, can never escape the public censure for not promptly and vigorously pursuing the Law against the perpetrators.' The delay in dismissing Dr Hamilton from the bench, the inclusion of Andrew Stevens in the new commission, and Boulton's conduct as counsel for the defence in the civil action must all tend to bring the administration of justice into disrepute. How could George Rolph confide in the solicitor general as prosecutor after Boulton had urged the plaintiff's witnesses not to be sworn and had congratulated the defendants in court on the salutary moral lesson they had administered? About this time two men who had committed a brutal rape had been allowed by the district magistrates to escape punishment because they had taken part in the attack on Rolph, yet the magistrates responsible had been included in the new commission of the peace and subjected to no reproof for their gross dereliction of duty (so much for morality).

The Gardiner case, too, involved abuses that had been allowed to pass unchastised. Perhaps the technical ground on which *Gardiner* v *Burwell* had been decided in the magistrates' favour might be said to preclude a subsequent criminal prosecution for their misconduct, but Baldwin did not think so. 'I thought the defendants fit subjects' for a criminal information at the instance of the Attorney General or at least they should have been omitted in the Commission of the Peace. I felt the whole matter highly discreditable to the jurisprudence of the Country; whether you knew all the facts I will not say; but sufficient must have come to your knowledge to have made your official interference both proper and necessary.' Yet Robinson had figured in the affair only as counsel for the defence in the civil action.

By 1828, what had begun as a debate about the extent of the law officers' official privileges had turned into a controversy over the rule of law in the province. In its new guise, the dispute had become a central event in the progressive confrontation between the provincial government and its critics. It turned on three linked questions: the law officers' claim to monopolize the conduct of criminal prosecutions at the assizes; their alleged duty to institute criminal proceedings against breakers of the public peace should the public interest demand it, even if the victim of the breach chose not to do so; and their claim to the right, in their private capacity as barrister and attorney, to defend the perpetrators of such outrages in civil actions arising from the wrong.

In England the Crown officers instituted and conducted criminal prosecutions only in matters immediately concerning the Crown and its traditional wards. In all others, proceedings had to be instituted by a private person, who might retain any attorney and counsel he pleased to conduct them. Robinson's critics contended that this practice reflected an absolute right on the part of the individual both to institute prosecutions and to conduct them by counsel of his choice. Robinson admitted the right to institute proceedings, but he maintained that the Crown enjoyed the prerogative of nominating counsel to conduct them if it thought fit and that the individual's right to do so was contingent on the waiving of that prerogative. In England the Crown almost invariably did waive. Yet the prerogative existed, and the only difference between England and Upper Canada was (to quote his opinion in Small's case) that the government in the colony chose to employ its law officers more frequently than in England.

Robinson's reasoning was probably accurate as far as it went. No one doubted the attorney general's right to stay criminal proceedings at his discretion by a nolle prosequi, and that was a more drastic intervention than merely taking over their conduct. As Robert Phillimore, the mid-nineteenth-century English law reformer, member of Parliament, and later judge, was to put it in 1856: 'According to the theory of English law, the Crown is the fountain of justice. The powers vested in the Attorney-general enable the Crown to undertake, control and terminate any criminal prosecution.'[171] To Robinson's critics, however, it seemed that he was trying to have it both ways. The Crown's prerogative of nominating counsel to conduct any prosecution, if it existed, could rest only on a general obligation to protect society from civil disorder. The law officers ought not therefore to defend the perpetrators of such disorder in civil actions arising from their misdeeds. They ought, however, to be prepared to defend the public by instituting criminal proceedings against such miscreants if the victim of the crime omitted to do so. A private citizen might dispense with satisfaction for an injury, noted Willis, but he could not remove the necessity of a public example.[172]

On one level the argument still concerned the Crown officers' use of their property; for we have seen that public office was conceived of at this time as a species of property, which in this case included the right to perform certain public functions for pay and the ancillary benefit of an extended private practice. If the English law officers did have the right to assume the conduct of criminal prosecutions, they had no incentive to exercise it since they had more than enough work and income without doing so. In any case, no two men could have monopolized prosecutions at the assizes, because the number of circuits and quantity of business was so great. In the colony, with its two annual circuits, the law officers could easily attend every assizes and assert 'their right and duty to conduct all criminal prosecutions for which they thought there was ground.' And of course they did so – not only beause the work itself yielded a substantial income (by this time about £800 or £900 a year between the two of them),[173] but because travelling the circuits at the public expense made it easy for them to acquire in their private capacity a significant share of the civil litigation undertaken at the assizes.

But in a polarized society with authoritarian political institutions, a special duty rested on officers possessing such a monopoly to exert moral leadership in vindication of the rule of law. It was the failure of Robinson and Boulton to give such leadership that evoked the challenge to their monopoly in 1828. When, in the face of outrages such as the types riot and the tar-and-feather case, the law officers presumed to combine a monopoly of criminal prosecutions with an insistence, on the one hand, on the right to defend the perpetrators of such outrages in civil actions arising from the wrong and a denial, on the other hand, of any duty to take the initiative in instituting criminal proceedings against them, the whole system of criminal justice began to look like an apparatus of oppression.

No one who tried to rebut these criticisms did so convincingly. When

Judge Willis castigated Boulton in the Court of King's Bench for defending miscreants in *Rolph* v *Simons* who were fit objects for criminal prosecution, his colleague Sherwood remarked that their victim could have complained to the assize grand jury, the assize judge, or a magistrate. Had the solicitor general, influenced by his professional connection with the accused, refused to do his duty and prosecute them on an indictment approved by the grand jury, the court would have instituted the prosecution itself.[174] But the events at the Gore quarter sessions only a few weeks earlier showed how unlikely it was that an assize grand jury that was dominated (as they generally were) by the district magistrates would have returned an indictment on a complaint by George Rolph in the tar-and-feather outrage unless he had gone before them with the full moral backing of the solicitor general. In any case, Sherwood was missing the point. What Willis and Dr Baldwin and the Assembly select committee complained of was not even that the Crown officer might refuse to prosecute his clients, but that his professional association with them created a presumption that his zeal in prosecuting them would be impaired, a prospect that was bound to deter their victim from seeking his aid.

John Beverley Robinson's remarks on the matter were typically specious. It was no defence of his failure to prosecute the types rioters to say that riot was an offence normally cognizable at the quarter sessions. This was no ordinary riot; it was an outrage committed by a band of the best-connected people in the province, including Chief Justice Powell's son-in-law and Judge Sherwood's son (future Attorney General Henry Sherwood). Magistrates had looked on without intervening, and one of them had later launched a subscription among the town's élite to defray the civil damages. Indeed, the victim later maintained that had he known that his assailants were to be let off in this way, and rewarded with lucrative offices into the bargain, he would never have declined to prosecute when Robinson invited him to do so – thus William Lyon Mackenzie disposed in advance of Robinson's contention that the types rioters had not been prosecuted only because Mackenzie chose not to do so.[175] Robinson's defence of public control of prosecutions as a safeguard against malicious proceedings also rang hollow; for he had done nothing about the malicious prosecution of Singleton Gardiner except defend the guilty magistrates in the resulting civil action.

The victimization of Gardiner, the types riot, and the tar-and-feather outrage were all acts of violence by members of a local élite against a political enemy. The attorney general's failure to punish what were, in a minor way, acts of terrorism inevitably looked like acquiescence in them – that he had not received a complaint from the victims was irrelevant. It was this political context that made the events of the April assizes so significant. The prosecution of Ridout's and Jarvis's seconds for murder a decade after the surviving principal had been acquitted of the crime was superficially an absurdity. But in both this case and that of the types riot, the fact that the attorney general had been compelled to administer the law of the land without fear or favour was an event of deep symbolic importance. It was a blow against the whole structure of monopoly and privilege that the official élite of Upper Canada had built on the basis of the province's authoritarian political institutions.

Inspired by political passion, the debate on the law officers' duty with respect to criminal prosecutions achieved in 1828 a seriousness of principle beyond anything it had achieved in the past or would in future. Even so, a crucial aspect of that duty remained unexplored: the question of how far the attorney general was subject to government direction.

The case might have been different had Robinson more fully revealed the position he had taken a decade earlier in refusing Lord Selkirk's demand that he prosecute Major John Fletcher. Robinson had declared that the offences alleged against Fletcher were such as would normally cry out for both criminal and civil prosecution, but Fletcher's official capacity as special commissioner created a presumption that his conduct represented a justifiable exercise of 'that discretion on which his government relied for preventing the recurrence of disorders' like those that had led to his appointment. 'Peculiar circumstances [such as] the special appointment of Mr. Fletcher may place the Attorney General, who is not supposed to act without the sanction, much less against the wishes of his Government, in that situation that he will conceive it his duty to await their directions, before he involves them in a responsibility which his Acts in some measure impose upon them.'[176]

Robinson's assumption that he must not act contrary to the wishes of the government is significantly at variance with the modern doctrine concerning the attorney general's responsibility with respect to criminal prosecutions. That doctrine holds that the attorney general may seek advice as to the policy of a particular course of action, and may even be offered such advice by others at their initiative, but that he is not subject to direction in the matter because his reponsibility is owed not to the government but to the public.[177] It is noteworthy that this doctrine, though reasserted for our time by the 'Campbell Case' of 1924, has eighteenth-century antecedents. Sir Charles Pratt (later Lord Chancellor

Camden), who became attorney general in 1757, always insisted that he was responsible to the public as well as to the government and must be guided by his own judgment in matters respecting criminal proceedings; in 1793 Sir John Scott (later Lord Chancellor Eldon) rejected the idea 'that the Attorney-General of England is bound to prosecute, because some other set of men choose to recommend it to him to prosecute, he disapproving of that prosecution.'[178]

In 1818 Robinson obviously had no wish to act against Fletcher and was merely seizing on the attorney general's supposed duty to the government as a pretext for not doing so. Nevertheless, his contradiction of the doctrine expounded by Camden and Eldon is significant. They maintained that the attorney general must do as he saw fit; Robinson held that the attorney general must advise the government as he saw fit, but having done so he must act according to the government's decision. Robinson's view of the office left it still in the subordinate status it had occupied in John White's time.

Robinson's critics condemned him in 1828 for failing to uphold law and order impartially. Had Robinson fully revealed his views as expressed in 1818, he must have raised the question of whether the attorney general owed a duty to the public that transcended his duty to the government. He was able to avoid the question because the matter at issue was not his refusal to prosecute on demand a government officer for acts done in an official capacity, but his failure to prosecute such officers (in the case of Burwell, whose oppression of Singleton Gardiner was ex officio) without such a demand. The persistence of the status quo was illustrated in 1838 when the provincial government laid down by order in council the basis on which the attorney general was to decide whether or not to prosecute men involved in the previous year's rebellion.[179]

Francis Collins paid dearly for his part in the events of April 1828. After the acquittal of Boulton and Small, his counsel John Rolph suggested with Willis's approval that it would be proper to drop the libel charges against Collins: they had been by-products of the tragic affair, and their prosecution could only prolong the bitterness it had caused. But Robinson was not in a forgiving mood. He discontinued proceedings in two of the cases, but in the other two he only deferred proceedings until the next assizes, saying that Collins's public conduct in the meantime would determine whether he went ahead with them. Collins protested that this was an attempt to muzzle the press and insisted on being tried now or never, but the attorney general had his way.

When the autumn assizes opened, it transpired that Collins had not merited clemency. This can have come as no surprise, considering his pointed comments during the summer about Robinson's latest conflict of interest. A dispute had arisen between the contractor for the Burlington Bay canal and harbour and the commissioners established by statute to supervise the work. As attorney general, Robinson had drawn up a bill providing for arbitration; as an MPP, he had urged it on the legislature. The commissioners refused to abide by the arbitrators' report, and when the contractor sued them they retained Robinson as counsel to negate the intention of his own bill! Collins commented that the attorney general's role 'appear[ed] to be most infamous, and to argue a total want of common principle. As the adviser of the Executive, he recommended a bill ... brought in the bill himself – and after it passed into a law, took a fee from the Commissioners to prevent it from taking effect! This is vile, unprincipled, shameful!'[180]

Indeed it was, but saying so was not calculated to coax Robinson into leniency. The attorney general went ahead with one of the libel cases and Collins claimed the right to traverse – that is, to postpone his trial until the next assizes. Robinson resisted on the ground that Collins had been arraigned and had traversed at the previous assizes, but on examining the record it turned out that he was wrong; amid the chaos of the April assizes Collins had never been formally arraigned. Robinson still resisted on the ground that Collins's indictment in the spring deprived him of the right to traverse now. When the court upheld Collins, Robinson demanded such heavy security for his good behaviour in the meantime that Collins elected to be tried at once. He was acquitted, and Robinson was denied his revenge.[181]

Collins now did a foolish thing. In reporting these events in the *Freeman* he dwelt astringently on the attorney general's conduct, accusing him of uttering 'an open and palpable falsehood in Court' and remarking on his 'native malignancy.' He added some further reflections on Robinson's part in the Burlington Bay scandal. As soon as Robinson read this billet-doux he complained to the assize grand jury, which approved a new indictment for libel. The editor was tried before Judge Sherwood, convicted, and sentenced to twelve months in prison and a fine of fifty pounds, a very severe punishment. Worst of all, he was to remain in jail until he provided security in the sum of £600 for his future good behaviour. It was potentially a sentence of life imprisonment; but six months previously, Sherwood had seen his son tried for riot and his brother-in-law Boulton for murder at Collins's instigation, and he was not in a forgiving mood either.[182]

The House of Assembly passed a series of resolutions criticizing the attorney general and the judges, and eventually the propriety of the sentence was referred to the law officers in England. They reported that both sentence and recognizances were at least twice as heavy as they would have been in England and recommended that they be halved (since money was scarcer in the colony than in England, even this underestimated the severity of the sentence).[183] Collins's fine was paid by public subscription, but the slow communications between Canada and England condemned him to serve his full prison term before being released without recognizance as an act of 'clemency.'

THE KING'S BENCH AND THE RULE OF LAW

Months before Collins's chastisement, Judge Willis had paid for his own part in the effort to enforce an impartial administration of justice. His dismissal led directly to the first popular demand for responsible government in the province and gave point to the reformers' demand for an independent judiciary. Although the imperial authorities withheld colonial self-government for another two decades, they moved at once to sever the ties between the judiciary and the executive by making future judicial appointments tenable 'during good behaviour' instead of 'during pleasure' and barring the chief justice from membership in the Executive Council. In short, the storm over the dismissal of Judge Willis was no short-lived controversy but an event of historic importance.

The man at the centre of the struggle was no knight in shining armour; he was a self-seeking, insensitive snob, who was as much to blame as his official enemies for the rift between them. Vanity gleams in his efforts before leaving England to get the colonial secretary to present him to the king ('Answer No,' Goderich jotted tersely on his second plea),[184] and in a dozen snubs offered in Upper Canada to his official colleagues and York society in general.

Goderich's successor, William Huskisson, had ordered Lieutenant-Governor Maitland to consult the provincial law officers and the judges on the best way of instituting an equitable jurisdiction and, in particular, whether it was preferable to annex it to the Court of King's Bench or to set up a completely independent tribunal. Willis chose not to subscribe to his colleagues' thoughtful joint report but penned a brief and shallow response of his own, which paid no attention to Upper Canadian conditions and merely parroted the self-serving views of the current English equity judges.[185] He pressed Robert Peel's brand-new criminal law reforms on Attorney General Robinson as the last word in metropolitan wisdom; he intervened officiously in the affairs of the York Grammar School, the Anglican Sunday school, and the Society for Promoting Christian Knowledge (to the special chagrin, no doubt, of Archdeacon Strachan); he tried to mediate between John Galt of the Canada Company (a British corporation formed to speculate in Upper Canadian land) and the provincial establishment, with whom Galt had quarrelled. Worst of all, perhaps, he canvassed the idea of setting up a savings bank for immigrants and establishing a branch of the Bank of England in the colony. This challenged the monopoly of the Bank of Upper Canada, the colony's only chartered bank, which was dominated by the official clique at the capital and served as an important instrument of their collective and individual self-aggrandizement.[186]

Willis showed similar insensitivity with respect to the province's politics. He subscribed to all four newspapers published at York, radical and conservative alike, out of a reluctance to 'take sides,' all heedless of the fact that in Upper Canada such ostentatious neutrality on the part of a high official was itself a partisan act. He cultivated the acquaintance of John Rolph and the Baldwins, correctly perceiving them to be three of the best-bred and best-educated men in the colony, oblivious to the fact that in Sir Peregrine Maitland's eyes they were arch-seditionists.[187]

Two manifestations of political neutrality above all incensed Willis's colleagues. In 1828 the start of work on the Rideau Canal, and the consequent founding of Bytown (Ottawa), at last nerved Judge Sherwood to test his title to the Chaudière property (which lay just west of today's downtown Ottawa, where the Chaudière and Portage bridges sweep across the river to Hull) by instituting an action to eject Robert Randal's tenants. Since the action was to be heard at Brockville, Sherwood himself had to choose the western assize circuit and leave the eastern to Willis. Ordinarily Sherwood would have taken his son Henry with him as clerk of assize; but, wishing Henry to be at Brockville to give evidence, he asked Willis to take Henry along as his clerk so that the young man would not lose the profits of that lucrative sinecure.

At first Willis assented, but soon he changed his mind. He had seen Randal's petition to the Assembly about the Chaudière scandal, he explained, and feared that if he took Henry with him as his clerk he might be suspected of favouring his fellow judge 'in a business which has already excited *so much suspicion* that Justice would not be impartially administered.' Willis's excuse was impeccable – the more so since Governor General Dalhousie at Quebec, still fuming over the circumstances in which Sherwood had purchased the property eight years earlier, had made a government case of it and ordered Attorney General Robinson himself to defend the action (in the event, Robinson made an excuse and assigned the case to a local attorney).[188] Willis's parade of impartiality was unlikely to sit well with Maitland, who execrated Randal and had been at loggerheads with Dalhousie for years. Willis's relations with the Sherwoods had deteriorated by June to the point where he and Henry had a public row in the street and he accused the types rioter of threatening his life.[189]

Willis's other obnoxious show of neutrality took place about the same time. When the question of establishing a Court of Chancery came before the legislature in February 1828, Willis discussed the matter with Rolph and Marshall Bidwell, two leaders of the opposition whose education and professional status gave them a special claim to be consulted. This action might seem innocuous; but this was the very moment when the merits of 'responsible government' were beginning to be touted in Upper Canada. As advocated by the Baldwins, Bidwell, and Rolph, this policy meant superseding the province's authoritarian political institutions by something closer to the modern form of parliamentary government, in which the executive is headed by ministers whose tenure of office depends on the confidence of the representative assembly. This system was just coming to maturity in Britain, but in treating the leaders of the Upper Canadian opposition as though their position were analogous to that of the leaders of 'His Majesty's Loyal Opposition' at home, Willis was giving credence to political views which Maitland and his advisers execrated. The offender claimed to see no harm in discussing with Rolph and Bidwell something 'which could not possibly be considered a political Question,' but his doing so was inevitably a political act.[190]

Lieutenant-Governor Maitland saw (or professed to see) these discussions as evidence of Willis's wish to scuttle the Chancery scheme in order to create a case for his appointment as chief justice in succession to William Campbell. Since the chief was ex officio Speaker of the Legislative Council and a member of the Executive Council, this would enable him to co-operate more effectively with the opposition. For his part, Willis ascribed the bill's failure to Robinson's dilatory promotion of it. He claimed to have had no interest in the chief justiceship but merely, after it transpired that the imperial authorities would not set up an equity court by royal fiat, to have observed to Robinson and others 'that I was sure, from the Consideration I had received [at the Colonial Office], that I should not be permitted to be a Loser, in case any thing should occur to prevent my Commission being speedily perfected; but that I should get the Chief Justiceship, or something equivalent to my Court of Equity, until it was created; at the same Time expressing my comparative Dislike to Common Law, having always been accustomed to practice in Courts of Equity.'[191]

By his very appointment to the Court of King's Bench, Willis had already disappointed expectations that J.B. Macaulay, who had been acting in a temporary capacity, would permanently succeed D'Arcy Boulton on the bench.[192] For this interloper to expect the chief justiceship, the summit of Robinson's ambition, as temporary relief for the loss of the 'equity' half of his salary, while at the same time disparaging the attorney general's second religion, the common law, was the height of tactlessness. By the time Willis publicly criticized the administration of criminal justice in Upper Canada in his remarks to the select committee on the petition of William Forsyth in February 1828, he was completely estranged from the provincial establishment. His subsequent strictures from the bench in April and May merely broadened a rift that was already unbridgeable. It is hard to believe that his dismissal had not been decided upon weeks before he provided the excuse for it.

The incident that led to Willis's 'amoval' occurred in June 1828. Chief Justice Campbell had been given leave to go to Britain for the sake of his health. In his absence, Judges Sherwood and Willis had differed in several cases in the court of King's Bench, one being George Rolph's application for a new trial in the tar-and-feather case. About a fortnight before the beginning of Trinity term, Willis wrote letters to the secretary of state and to James Stephen, the Colonial Office counsel, announcing that in his opinion the court was not legally constituted unless all three judges were present. The Judicature Act of 1794, by which the court had been founded, specified that 'His Majesty's Chief Justice of this Province together with two Puisne Justices shall preside in the said Court.' Willis based his opinion on the use of the words 'together with' instead of 'and,' and on the rule that courts set up by statute must always operate strictly according to the word of the founding instrument.[193] He thought it his duty, he told Stephen, to state his views publicly when the court reopened, although he feared they would provoke great excitement.

It took less than that to excite Sir Peregrine Maitland. Willis informed the lieutenant-governor of his opinion and intention by the insultingly casual method of leaving his letters to the Colonial Office unsealed when he sent them to Government House to be forwarded. Maitland dashed off a letter of his own to the secretary of state, fuming at Willis's insolence. 'I have been ten Years in this Government,' he proclaimed, 'and as I have received no representations against either the Laws or the manner in which they have been administered, I must conclude that the people are content with both.' Maitland's secretary warned Willis that 'if those circumstances occur to which you call the attention not of this Government but of the Secretary of State, it will remain for his Excellency [Maitland] to pursue whatever course such circumstances may appear to him to require.'[194]

When the court opened on the sixteenth of June, Willis rose and delivered a long statement of his opinion. He also declared that the chief justice had taken leave illegally, since his departure had been sanctioned by the lieutenant-governor alone and not by the lieutenant-governor in council as required by an imperial statute of 1814. Under that statute the chief had forfeited his office; and since the practice he had followed was the norm in Upper Canada, so had every other serving officer who had taken leave under it. Willis named no one, but the attorney general and the solicitor general both fell under his ban.[195]

The government reacted swiftly. The law officers and Judge Sherwood each submitted refutations of Willis's opinions to the lieutenant-governor. The law officers also reported jointly on the lieutenant-governor's power to remove a judge.[196] These documents were referred to the Executive Council. In recommending Willis's dismissal the council recognized 'that unless corrupt Conduct can be imputed to a Judge in the legitimate discharge of his Official duties, the independence of the Bench as well as the interests of the Government and the Community require that he shall not be amenable to account for the opinions he may form, or the Judgments he may pronounce.'[197] It was not for his opinions that Willis merited dismissal, but for the manner in which he had published them. Instead of communicating his doubts to the government alone and proceeding with business as usual until the jurisdiction of the court was challenged, he had acted in a manner calculated to shake public confidence in the administration of justice.[198]

Willis's dismissal shook the tiny capital. Even before that, John Rolph and the Baldwins had entered the Court of King's Bench, proclaimed that Willis's opinion 'rendered painfully certain ... the apprehensions entertained respecting the due administration of public justice,' and stripped off their gowns in theatrical affirmation of their belief before stalking from the chamber.[199] On the fifth of July a public meeting at York, chaired by Dr Baldwin, adopted a petition embodying the most comprehensive public declaration yet made of Upper Canadians' grievances against the form and style of their government. The list included the Legislative Council's constant rejection of measures passed by the Assembly; the chief justice's frequent absence from the Court of King's Bench because he was either out of the province or attending the Executive or the Legislative Council; 'the undue influence which the mingled duties of Legislative and Executive advice have on the judicial function'; the existence of the so-called prerogative revenues, of which the government could dispose without parliamentary sanction; the law officers' de facto monopoly of criminal prosecutions at assize; the imperfections of the jury system; and the judges' tenure of office during pleasure, which 'subjected [them] to the ignominy of an arbitrary removal.' It vindicated Willis's position on the constitution of the Court of King's Bench in language that echoed the three lawyers' statement in court twelve days earlier. It requested various remedies, including the judges' exclusion from the Executive and Legislative Councils and the introduction of judicial tenure 'during good behaviour,' as in England.[200]

One prayer of particular significance for the future was for the Crown's advisers henceforth to hold office only as long as they possessed the confidence of the House of Assembly. This was not the first time the merits of colonial self-government had been canvassed in Upper Canada. Originally formulated in Ireland in the 1780s, the idea seems to have been contemplated as an answer to colonial misgovernment by Judge Thorpe and his circle about 1806. A few years later it had been advocated (or so it is claimed) by francophone opposition leaders in Lower Canada. Thereafter the idea disappears from the sight of historians, though it probably did not do so from the minds of contemporaries, until its re-emergence in Upper Canada in 1828. It seems to have resurfaced in March in a debate on the prerogative revenues in the House of Assembly; but the debate took place at the very end of the session and no report of it survives.[201] It was the petition of July 1828 that formally placed responsible government on the public agenda; and it is no coincidence that the precipitating event was the dismissal of Judge Willis.

For more than a century after the achievement of responsible government in the late 1840s, English-Canadian historians tended to visualize the story of their country chiefly in terms of its progress from subordinate colonial status to democratic, parliamentary self-government. It is therefore the more remarkable that they have so generally underrated the political crisis that established responsible government irremovably in the Upper Canadian political vocabulary. Even in the classic nineteenth-century account of J.C. Dent the crisis ranks only as one of a series of acts of political repression, neither more nor less important than the wrecking of Mackenzie's printing-shop, the Niagara Falls outrage, and the punishment of Francis Collins.[202]

In fact, the Willis affair was a crowning scandal, in which was concentrated the essence of the discontents that preceded it. Underlying the Niagara Falls outrage, the tar-and-feather scandal, the types riot, the Gardiner case, the punishment of Bartemus Ferguson, the banishment of Robert Gourlay, the manifold misadventures of Robert Randal, the harassment of Lord Selkirk into an early grave – underlying all these causes célèbres of the time, many of which are little remembered today, and no doubt many others so totally forgotten that we no longer know their names, was the belief that the administration of justice was habitually prostituted to the interests of the powerful. From his place on the bench a judge had finally denounced these failures of justice, only to be summarily dismissed. True, his removal did not result immediately from his criticizing the attorney general's administration of criminal justice. Still, it can hardly be doubted that after that episode the provincial government was only waiting for an excuse to get rid of him. In any event, the questions of the constitution of the Court of King's Bench and the irregular granting of official leave, technical though they were, also bore on the question of the rule of law. The connection is a subtle one, because the questions *were* technical and the government had some good arguments, but it is none the less real.

Much of the argument over the court's constitution dwelt on abstruse topics such as the difference between courts established by statute and those established by prerogative, the validity of analogies between the Upper Canadian and the various English tribunals, the precise meaning of the word 'preside' as derived from its Latin root, and so on. The major points at issue, though, were less academic.

The government relied on the intentions of the enacting legislature, the invariable practice of thirty-four years, the wording of the judges' commissions, and the 'argument from inconvenience.' Right from the start, the court had operated with less than the full bench. In 1794, when the Judicature Act had been passed, the province had possessed only the chief and one puisne justice; and Chief Justice Osgoode had left almost at once, leaving the court to be put in operation by William Dummer Powell alone. It could reasonably be inferred that Osgoode, as the bill's framer, had not intended to establish an authority that was invalid unless conjointly exercised by all three judges of the King's Bench. That from its earliest years, the court had repeatedly sat with fewer than three judges without challenge to its jurisdiction merely confirmed that its doing so was consistent with the intentions of the enacting legislature. The tenor of the judges' commissions, each of which empowered its beneficiary individually 'to hold the Court of King's Bench at such times and in such places as the said Court may, and ought by law to be holden' was a further guide to interpretation of the act. The *argumentum ab inconvenienti* was based on the dictum of the great Elizabethan and Jacobean jurist, Sir Edward Coke, that where an instrument was open to alternative interpretations, one of which entailed great inconvenience, the other was ipso facto to be preferred. Willis's interpretation of the Judicature Act would have the highly inconvenient effect of invalidating every decision ever reached by the court in the absence of a full bench, and in particular would cast doubt on many existing land titles.[203]

The arguments of Willis and his supporters were all founded on the evils of the existing system. Whenever the court sat with fewer than three judges, a single judge could reject an appeal (even if two judges were present an appeal could succeed only if favoured by both). A litigant applying for a new trial on the ground of judicial error at the assizes might find his application doomed by the very official whose judgment he was questioning. This was an evident absurdity; and if legislative intention was to be cited to help interpret the Judicature Act, the only sensible inference was that the legislature had intended to avoid such absurdity by composing the court of three judges and not fewer – it was no defence of the present system that that intention had been flouted for thiry-four years. The argument from inconvenience was dismissed as resting on the dubious premise that the inconvenience of perpetuating an unjust system was less than that of casting doubt on the judgments rendered under it in the past.[204]

To the historian, the ostensible content of these counter-arguments is less interesting than their underlying tendency; for what superficially seems a quarrel over mere technical points of law was really a confrontation between arbitrary, irresponsible power and the rule of law. This emerges clearly from the tenor of Willis's challenge to the argument from usage and the argument from inconvenience; in both cases he cited the provincial government's position on the Alien Question to refute its stand. In reply to the argument from usage, he asked:

If usage could not sanction the illegality of a very large proportion of the inhabitants of the Province enjoying civil rights, and even holding lands, granted by patent ... contrary to statutory provisions; could a shorter or less established usage sanction the illegality of any of the Judges of the Court of King's Bench attempting to hold that Court, in direct opposition to the plain and ordinary sense, to the common and natural meaning, of an Act of the local Legislature, which alone constituted the Court; – that Court by which the civil rights, the properties, and even the lives, of the inhabitants only can be judged?[205]

As for inconvenience, in his message of 15 November 1825 to the legislature Sir Peregrine Maitland had observed that the alleged aliens were 'exposed to the *inconveniences* of finding those rights denied which they have hitherto enjoyed, but which whenever they may be questioned must be decided upon ... according to Law, and without regard to *inconveniencies* [sic] which might be much regretted.' Yet many more land titles had been endangered by *Thomas* v *Acklam* than by Willis's construction of the Judicature Act.[206]

John Rolph and the Baldwins stressed that Willis's challenge to existing practice involved more than technicalities when they confronted Judge Sherwood in the Court of King's Bench on the twenty-third of June. In a statement that epitomizes the ideology of the rule of law, they proclaimed:

There are no Laws demanding a more religious observance than those which limit and define the power of individuals forming the government over their fellow creatures. And serious as must be the consequences of the temporary stoppage of the administration of justice in a whole country, we cannot help looking on it as one eventually far less dangerous to the interests of society than the sacrifice of any the least part of an important principle – and surely none can be more important than the obligation on all public functionaries to observe to the letter, the bounds of those powers, with which we are invested.[207]

This statement, which Willis repeated almost verbatim three months later in England in rebuttal to his accusers in the colony,[208] resounds like the McRuer Report's assertion of the need to safeguard civil liberties from administrative abuse in an era of 'big' government. The difference between 1828 and 1968 lay in the nature of the political institutions by which the province was governed. The malpractices alleged by Willis were essentially technical ones. In a system of genuinely open and accountable government they could not have assumed the significance they acquired under the authoritarian institutions of the colonial period. In 1828 they seemed to epitomize an irresponsible oligarchy's habitual contempt for the letter of the law.

In fact, the real matter in question in the Willis affair was nothing less than the system by which the province had been governed since its foundation in 1791. As one reads Willis's statement in court of the sixteenth of June, one is gradually possessed by a sense of déjà vu. Whether Willis is correct on the particular points at issue is almost irrelevant. What is striking is that we are face to face with yet further examples of the arbitrary and illegal practices that characterized the government of the province from the start. Sometimes, as in the Appropriations Crisis of 1806, the government flouted the law altogether; at others, as in the case of William Firth's emoluments, it merely interpreted the rules to suit itself. Sometimes, as in the Alien Question, it insisted on a strict construction of the law; at other times, as in the debate over the court's constitution, on a construction tempered by the standard of convenience. Sometimes, as in the case of the law officers' role in criminal prosecutions, it relied on a strict analogy between English and Upper Canadian law, offices, and institutions; at other times, as with the court's constitution, it argued that the different circumstances of the colony dictated different conclusions. But always the impression is of a government unchecked by any adequate system of constitutional accountability, a government ruling ostensibly by law but actually according to the convenience of itself and its friends.

Lieutenant-Governor Simcoe had promised the tiny polyglot population of the infant province English political institutions and the rule of law. Those promises had been broken by his successors. Upper Canada possessed not an 'image and transcript' of the British constitution but a travesty of it. The colony was ruled not by law but by Mammon. English laws and a professional administration of justice had not made the ordinary inhabitant more secure against dispossession than when the merchant dispossessors had sat as judges in the old courts of common pleas. The law officers of the Crown, His Majesty's attorney general and solicitor general for Upper Canada, had brought the profession and the law itself into contempt by misconduct in both their public and their private capacity. The Court of King's Bench, the temple of English justice erected in 1794, was defiled by a corrupt judiciary and informal process. It is because the Willis affair brought all these things so sharply into focus that it led directly to the inauguration of the movement for responsible government in Upper Canada.

The Willis affair was the end of the beginning. With its aftermath, the Collins case, it preoccupied the House of Assembly during the session of

1829. In an address to the king, the Assembly cited the judge's dismissal as proof that Upper Canada needed an independent judiciary and reiterated two other demands which since 1826 had become standard parts of the reform program: the chief justice should be excluded from the Executive Council, and future appointments to the Court of King's Bench should be made from the English bar, so that the bench might be freed from 'the entanglements of family connexions, the influence of local jealousies, and the contamination of Provincial Politics.' In reciting the deficiencies of the administration of justice in the province, the address dwelt on the outcome of Judge Sherwood's action against Robert Randal's tenants at the Chaudière. Christopher Hagerman, appointed to the bench in place of Willis, had refused at the assizes to admit vital evidence for the defence. Then, sitting alone in the Court of King's Bench because of Chief Justice Campbell's absence and Sherwood's disqualification as an interested party, he had heard and dismissed the appeal against his own errors.[209]

Within a few years, Whitehall had acceded to the first two demands. In September 1830 an infuriated Chief Justice Robinson learned, not through official channels but from the columns of the *Colonial Advocate*, that the imperial government intended the chief justice of Upper Canada to be henceforth excluded from the Executive Council. The Colonial Office seems to have thought it had already attained this end simply by not appointing Robinson to the council upon his elevation to the chief justiceship, but it had forgotten that the chief justice was an executive councillor ex officio. The irate Robinson protested in vain against being singled out by an edict that barred him, alone of all the colonial chief justices, from the executive council of his colony.[210] The independence of the judiciary was conceded as part of a 'package' that saw the colony's prerogative revenues placed at the disposal of the House of Assembly in return for the enactment of a permanent salary appropriation for the leading officers of the colony, including the judges of the Court of King's Bench. Independent tenure 'during good behaviour' was introduced by provincial enactment in 1834.[211]

Responsible government also found its way onto the legislative agenda, both in 1829 and 1830, in the form of motions of no confidence in the Crown's advisers. Both motions were carried by sweeping majorities, and that was the end of it: the imperial government was unwilling to sanction in the colonies the practice that subjected its own fate to the confidence of the House of Commons.[212] Except for Robinson's eventual removal, Lieutenant-Governor Colborne retained the same executive councillors who had made themselves obnoxious to the Assembly under Lieutenant-

Governor Maitland. The official oligarchy, or Family Compact, continued to dominate the provincial administration, much to the disappointment of the reform leaders, who had believed that the colony was on the verge of a new political order.

The reform leadership was further disheartened by the British government's complete repudiation of Willis when he returned home to defend himself against his colonial accusers. To Marshall Bidwell the judge was a hero who 'combined prudence and true patriotism with spirit'; his dismissal was 'one of the most flagrant acts of tyranny and oppression by which a free country was ever insulted.'[213] As Speaker of the Assembly, Bidwell had signed the lower House's address to the king, which prayed for Willis's reinstatement. Even before his dismissal, however, Willis had annoyed the Colonial Office by his public quarrel with Attorney General Robinson, and the imperial authorities declared against him on every count.[214]

The reform leaders' disappointment at Willis's repudiation by Whitehall is the more understandable in that they had probably staged the confrontation over the administration of justice as a means of advancing the case for responsible government. Both of the petitions to the Assembly that brought the subject to the forefront of the political debate early in 1828 were submitted by clients of John Rolph. Robert Randal's petition on the Chaudière case followed logically enough on his failure to gain redress in England the previous year, and it may also have been designed to influence the jury in Judge Sherwood's impending action against Randal's tenants; but the report of the select committee (chaired by Rolph) to which it was referred was well calculated to publicize inequities in the administration of justice as a whole. So too was the committee's bill, duly passed by the Assembly, investing Willis with equitable jurisdiction for the purpose of inquiring into the scandal. William Forsyth's second petition, complaining about the law officers' monopoly of criminal prosecutions at assize, even more surely emanated from the attorney's concern to dramatize the general issue than from the client's anxiety to obtain redress for a specific grievance.

If in the House in winter the guiding hand was Rolph's, in the courts in spring it was probably Dr Baldwin's. Francis Collins was close to the Baldwins, and it was to Dr Baldwin that George Rolph wrote when he wanted to get Collins down to Hamilton to report the Gore quarter sessions in April.[215] Collins could not make the trip because he was roasting the attorney general at the Home District assizes. It is hard to believe that Collins's challenge on that occasion to the law officers' monopoly of criminal prosecutions was not scripted by the lawyer-politicians he admired, and he had clearly arranged for Robert Baldwin to conduct the proceedings against H.J. Boulton, James Small, and the types rioters should occasion arise. It is also a strange coincidence that, more than two months before Judge Willis declared his opinion on the constitution of the Court of King's Bench, Dr Baldwin had complained to the government about the impending absence of the chief justice, which he feared would jeopardize the pending appeals in *Rolph v Simon* and another case. In his evidence to the select committee of 1829 on the Willis affair (which he himself chaired), Dr Baldwin stressed that the judge had learned of this protest only after he had made up his mind on the matter; yet Willis prefaced his declaration in court with the remark that he had been prompted to look into it. It is hard to believe that the prompter was neither Baldwin nor anyone close to him.[216]

Whether or not the leading reformers had chosen to fight for responsible government on the terrain of the administration of justice, they interpreted Willis's treatment by the imperial authorities as a vindication of the prevailing system of oppression. To John Rolph it seemed 'strange that in the year 1829 of the Christian era, such policy should be observed toward a dependant Colony.' William Lyon Mackenzie predicted that 'the conduct of the government of England toward her colonies will probably before long sever them from her dominion.'[217] Eight years later, both men would take leading parts in a rebellion against imperial rule, and only the rebellion crisis would stir the imperial government to begin the process of political reform that culminated after another decade of uncertainty in the concession of colonial self-government.

It must here be affirmed that the insurrections of December 1837 were a direct consequence of twelve years of verbal, constitutional, and physical violence against the reformers on the part of the provincial administration and its supporters; they flowed from a pattern of behaviour the inauguration of which has been a major topic of this chapter. Let us consider the nature of each of these three kinds of violence in turn.

By 'verbal violence' we mean a constant campaign of vilification which by inference portrayed the leading reformers as beyond the pale of society – as outlaws unworthy of the protection the law offers honest individuals in pursuit of their lawful occasions. This unremitting campaign took its tone from the very top: it reflected the views of Sir Peregrine Maitland, John Beverley Robinson, and Archdeacon Strachan. Its main voices in the 1820s were the *Kingston Chronicle*, the *Upper Canada Gazette and United*

Empire Loyalist, and George Gurnett's *Gore Gazette*. The *Chronicle* was notoriously in receipt of a government subsidy; the *Gazette and Loyalist* was the official government newspaper, edited and published by the king's printer, Robert Stanton, an old pupil of Strachan and school-friend of Robinson. When Sir John Colborne decided in 1829, in order to distance the government from such polemics, that Stanton should confine himself to official announcements, Gurnett was invited to fill the vacuum at York, where he moved to establish the *Courier of Upper Canada*.[218] It was one of the reformers' complaints against the administration of justice in 1828 that, at a time when Attorney General Robinson was prosecuting Francis Collins, William Lyon Mackenzie, and another reform editor (Hugh Thomson of the *Upper Canada Herald*) for libels against the government, he was ignoring equally libellous utterances by pro-government newspapers against the House of Assembly.[219] This alleged partiality entered the Willis affair when Robinson refused to act on Willis's complaint about a libel upon him in Gurnett's *Gore Gazette* elicited by his judgment in *Rolph* v *Simons* (in which Gurnett, of course, had been implicated).[220]

In the 1830s the chief target of such vilification was Mackenzie, who came to personify the opposition to the Family Compact. The defamation was especially intense during his term as mayor of Toronto (as York was renamed upon incorporation) in 1834, when it focused on his alleged oppressions as the city's chief magistrate and his publication of a letter from Joseph Hume predicting (as Mackenzie himself had done apropos of the Willis affair) that Britain's continued misgovernment of her colonies would soon result in their loss. In December 1834 the jailer of the Home District accused Mackenzie of having sentenced two prostitutes to two weeks' imprisonment without benefit of fire or light in late November, a charge he backed up by a forged interpolation in the warrant of commitment. George Gurnett, now a member of the Toronto city council, supported the jailer with a perjured affidavit.[221]

One effect of this incessant stream of verbal violence against leading reformers was to incite and legitimize the other types of violence. Constitutional violence is any non-violent abuse of an individual's civil rights from a political motive. The jailer's forgery and Gurnett's perjured affidavit are examples of such abuse, but Mackenzie also met it in the law courts. In April 1836 he accused the grand jury of the Home District assizes of an abortive attempt (in which Gurnett was also involved) to indict him for perjury in connection with a civil suit arising out of his feud with the district jailer. In October 1837, in a libel case at Niagara, he claimed to have barely thwarted an attempt to pack the trial jury by the district clerk of the peace, one of the types rioters of 1826 to whom Maitland had soon afterwards awarded lucrative offices. Referring to his famous victory over the types rioters, Mackenzie said that these events had destroyed the belief he had then formed that a jury of his peers could be a bulwark against oppression.[222]

The most famous example of constitutional violence against Mackenzie (one which, like the types riot, recoiled on its leading perpetrators) was his repeated expulsion from the legislature between 1832 and 1834. The general election of 1830, influenced perhaps by the more conciliatory style of Lieutenant-Governor Colborne, had resulted in the return of a conservative majority. When Mackenzie ridiculed the conservatives in his newspaper as sycophants they expelled him from the House, only to see him triumphantly re-elected with but one negative vote. When he republished the words that had prompted his expulsion they expelled him again, this time for the entire parliament – an action amounting to the partial disfranchisement of the constituency that had elected him as one of its representatives. Three times more the county of York re-elected Mackenzie, only to see him denied his place as their representative by a vote of the House. It was the persistent support for this action by Attorney General Boulton and Solicitor General Hagerman that caused their dismissal in 1833 by Lord Goderich, now colonial secretary once more.[223] Goderich had rocked the Upper Canadian establishment six years earlier by disallowing the naturalization bill of 1827 in apparent deference to the petition presented by Robert Randal. This new blow provoked George Gurnett to a celebrated editorial outburst in which he called Goderich an ignoramus and hinted that his policies were driving 'loyal' colonists to favour independence.[224]

The 1830s saw the renewal on a larger scale of the physical violence first exemplified in the types riot and the tar-and-feather outrage of 1826. While touring the province in March 1832 in connection with his expulsion from the Assembly and impending mission to Britain, Mackenzie was savagely beaten at Hamilton by ruffians led by a district magistrate. A few days later his public meeting at York was disrupted by a mob organized by George Gurnett among others.[225]

The chief well of political violence in the province was formed by the Orangemen, who had been locally strong since shortly after the war and whose numbers were greatly augmented by the surge of British immigration that began about 1827. They were particularly strong in the Brockville area, where Attorney General Jameson, himself recently arrived from

Britain to replace H.J. Boulton, stood for the Assembly in Leeds County in 1834 in partnership with the provincial Grand Master of the Orange Order. The election was marked by such violence that the two men's return was voided by the House.[226] In the summer of 1837, Orangemen disrupted Mackenzie's political meetings in the Home District before he had committed himself either publicly or privately to rebellion, and in 1839 and 1840 they attacked meetings held by Dr Baldwin and other reformers in support of the political reforms recommended by the Earl of Durham in his famous report. One Tory politician who owed his success to Orange support was Judge Sherwood's son, Henry Sherwood of Brockville, who was mayor of Toronto from 1842 to 1844 and one of the city's MPPs from 1844 to 1851. It was fitting that this convicted types rioter of 1826 should benefit from the violence for which that episode had set the pattern; and doubly so that he should lead, as Attorney General for Upper Canada, the Tory government of 1847-8, which made a last-ditch effort to stave off responsible government.

In 1823, in advocating a bill banning Orange processions, Dr Baldwin had pronounced it the government's duty to inform the newcomers that in Upper Canada, unlike Ireland, everyone was loyal and there was no need for ostentatious and intimidating displays of devotion to the Crown.[227] Instead, the government had tarred its critics as sedition-mongers and either committed or condoned abuses of their civil rights. Whether leading officials intended their verbal violence against reform leaders to produce the more outrageous of these abuses is irrelevant; Henry II may not have meant his tirade against Thomas Becket to lead to murder.

The climax of this pattern of behaviour, and the event that more than any other provoked the rebellion of 1837, was the general election of 1836. Soon after replacing Sir John Colborne, Lieutenant-Governor Sir Francis Bond Head appointed John Rolph and Robert Baldwin and a third reform sympathizer to the Executive Council pursuant to the colonial secretary's instructions to conciliate the opposition. Three weeks later Head dismissed the entire council after the newcomers had persuaded their colleagues to join their protest against his failure to consult them routinely on affairs of state. The resultant crisis ended with Head dissolving the legislature and embarking on an election campaign in which he personally denounced the opposition as disloyal and seditious. The general election itself was marred by both Orange violence and government chicanery, which may not have contributed as much to the conservative landslide as Head's propaganda but certainly served even more completely to convince the reformers that they had been routed by unconstitutional means.[228]

This conviction was reinforced the following summer. With the province in the grip of an unprecedented depression, which was wreaking havoc among its farmers, the legislature passed an act to prevent the dissolution that was constitutionally requisite upon the king's then impending death. The Colonial Office's failure to discountenance these abuses, and the extreme policy of the legislature so irregularly constituted and prolonged, made the ensuing rebellion virtually an act of self-defence. Neither the outbreak in the Home District nor that in the London District amounted to much, but the province suffered a year of intermittent border raids from the United States; had Mackenzie seized his chance to occupy Toronto the insurrection might have flared into a costly civil war. It is by the peril they brought upon the province that we must judge a dozen years of 'petty' abuses against the civil rights of the Upper Canadian reformers, and judge too the succession of attorneys general who committed or condoned those abuses in violation of their duty to uphold the rule of law.

4

Responsibility and Independence

In a small, fast-growing colony, changes can occur with startling speed. Even before the rebellions the oligarchy's hold on power was threatened by an influx of educated, ambitious British immigrants who were as hostile to the 'Yankee' farmers' pro-American sympathies as they were to the Family Compact's efforts to monopolize public office. The imperial government's decision, after the rebellions, to reunite Upper and Lower Canada under a single government merged the upper province in a broader polity which the oligarchy could not hope to dominate, although its leaders remained important in politics as long as Whitehall continued to resist the movement for responsible government.

The resistance did not last long. Originally, the Colonial Office had envisaged a 'quasi-cabinet' form of government with an executive council composed of the heads of the executive departments, all of them belonging to the legislature. Their continuance in office was not to depend on the confidence of a majority of the lower House, however, and the governor general was still to call the shots in provincial affairs. Still, not even a predominantly British population would forgo self-government indefinitely. In 1844 the Baldwinites and their Lower Canadian allies lost an election fought on the issue, after a campaign in which Upper Canada resounded with the sort of rhetoric heard in 1836. In December 1847, however, the reformers won a sweeping victory, and three months later Robert Baldwin and Louis-Hippolyte LaFontaine formed the first administration of a Canada that was independent in its internal affairs. By that time the imperial authorities had given up the struggle. Canada awaited a government willing to seize the proffered prize.

Reunion and responsible government had extraordinary consequences for the law officers of the Crown. Since each section of the new province retained its own legal system and judicial establishment, united Canada presented the oddity of a single government with two attorneys general and two solicitors general. This was singular enough, but it was exceeded in importance by the transformation wrought by responsible government in the nature of both offices, and in the attorneyships in particular.

Responsible government had both a political and an administrative aspect. Real executive authority was transferred from the sovereign's representative to the Executive Council, whose members were to hold office only as long as they retained the confidence of the people as represented in the lower house of the provincial legislature. This was the political aspect. The administrative aspect lay in the fact that, as mentioned, the Executive Council, or cabinet, as we can now begin to call it, was to consist of the heads of the different departments of government. These, so that they might be more readily accountable to the people's representatives, were expected to be members of the legislature. Thus Canada was suddenly handed over to government by politicians.

The administration of justice was peculiarly an emanation of royal grace. Unlike the more mundane functions of government, justice had never been administered by a bureaucratic department. Each court had its own administrative establishment (which, except for the superior courts of King's Bench and Chancery, consisted of no more than a clerk or two). Those ancient court officials, the sheriffs, were appointed by and directly answerable to the lieutenant-governor. On questions of policy the lieutenant-governor – representing the sovereign, the fountain of justice – had taken the advice of the judges and the Crown lawyers as he pleased. With the introduction of responsible government, the political responsibility of a minister of justice suddenly fell on the attorney general for each section. With it, as an inevitable concomitant of that responsibility, went membership in the cabinet.

This was an unprecedented development, since the attorney general in England was not considered a minister of the Crown and had never been a member of the cabinet. It was overshadowed, though, by another, even more extraordinary. The advent of responsible government fostered the growth of political parties and the emergence of a clear hierarchy of party leadership. Often the party leaders were lawyers, and it became the practice for the leader of the government party in each section of the province to take the office of attorney general for that section. In Upper Canada the tradition continued even after Confederation in 1867. Between 1841 and 1899 there were only about six years in which the leading government politician in Upper Canada and Ontario was not the attorney general, and those six years included the period from 1854-6 when Sir Allan MacNab, though officially premier of Canada, was in fact no more than a figurehead for the attorney general for Canada West, John A. Macdonald. Though these developments were unexampled in the history of England and its empire, they were logical consequences of the province's political history and social structure.

THE RISE TO PRE-EMINENCE

It will be obvious from the last chapter that John Beverley Robinson was a far more important political figure than any of his predecessors. This was partly a reflection of personal character and partly a consequence of changes in provincial politics.

Robinson clearly possessed a much stronger personality than any of his predecessors – that sadly unknown quantity, John Macdonell, excepted. John White's plaintive ineffectuality, William Firth's conceited incompetence, and D'Arcy Boulton's inert (though occasionally choleric) mediocrity have been sufficiently exposed. Less is known of Thomas Scott, but what information we have hints at no exception. Scott alone of the Upper Canadian attorneys general was appointed to the Executive Council, but his elevation in 1805 was probably less a measure of his political force and acumen than of his usefulness in the plans of his autocratic fellow-Scot, Lieutenant-Governor Peter Hunter.[1] There is no evidence that Scott made any effort to dissuade Hunter from misappropriating provincial funds, and he made no apparent contribution to settling the scandal that erupted after Hunter's death.

Soon after Scott became chief justice in 1806, Lieutenant-Governor Gore described him to the Colonial Office as 'an honourable, good man, but [so] extremely timid both on the Bench and in his political capacity [as a member of the Executive Council] that he never decides.' With Judge Powell absent in England and Firth not yet arrived in Upper Canada, Gore had had to consult Henry Allcock, now chief justice of Lower Canada, on the merits of a certain provincial enactment. Even in 1807 Gore was anxious to see Scott retired on a pension and replaced by Powell, the one truly strong and shrewd official in the colony. Scott was willing enough to go, but the financial burden of the war with France prevented the appropriation of a pension at Westminster and kept him in office until 1816, when money was provided from provincial sources.[2]

Robinson's official conduct was far more assertive than his predecessors.' This may have been partly because he was a native instead of a time-serving import, but it was probably above all a matter of sheer nous. There can be no better illustration of this than the precocious maturity shown by the twenty-two-year-old acting attorney general in handling the treason trials of 1814.

The military commander and acting governor in the province, Sir Gordon Drummond, was anxious to hang a few traitors quickly *pour encourager les autres*. At common law a criminal trial was normally held in the district where the crime had been committed, but a provincial enactment of 1814 permitted trials for high treason and related crimes to be held anywhere in the province.[3] Drummond uttered a special commission of assize to all three of the King's Bench judges to try persons accused of such crimes. He pushed Robinson for an early trial at York, fearing that to try the accused in the border districts where they had allegedly committed their crimes would be to risk their rescue by armed partisans or their acquittal by disaffected jurors.

Slowly and methodically, Robinson set about preparing the prosecutions according to the normal process, until Drummond's impatience waxed to the point where he proposed to cancel the special commission because the object for which it had issued had been lost by the delay. The young law officer also insisted on trying the accused in the districts of Niagara and London as appropriate, since the verdicts and sentences would carry more weight in the mind of the people if rendered according to the hallowed processes of common law. He did not fear recalcitrance on the part of jurors in those regions, where the ravages of the war had made the traitors' cause unpopular. The Home District, by contrast, could be expected to supply 'the worst Jurors of any in the Province.' If the trials were to be proceeded with out of district, he wished everyone to know that it was being done against his advice and not because he wanted to enhance the prospects of the prosecution.[4]

In the event, the trials all took place at Ancaster, in the Niagara District; but they were a great success from every point of view. Fifteen men were convicted by juries of their peers according to what was evidently the nearest approach to due process attainable in a war zone. Seven of the condemned traitors were reprieved, and justice was thus persuasively tempered with mercy. Drummond praised Robinson unstintingly to the secretary of state, Lord Bathurst – one reason the young solicitor general was treated so considerately at the Colonial Office during his stay in England from 1815 to 1817.[5] The effect of the trials on the solicitor's standing in Upper Canada was cited by Gore in urging his promotion to attorney general in place of D'Arcy Boulton. The operation of the provincial statute of 1814 declaring Crown land grantees who had fled to the United States during the war to be aliens[6] was 'likely to involve many questions of extreme delicacy, in which it [was] important ... that the Attorney General should possess the entire confidence of the Public.' The statute had been drafted by Robinson, 'who had the rare felicity, in conducting the Prosecutions for High Treason, under the Special Commission ... to recommend himself to all Parties, by his legal acquirements, and a zeal and firmness tempered with candour and liberality.'[7] When the young man returned to take up the attorneyship, his marriage to the niece of the under-secretary of state for war can only have enhanced his influence, which was illustrated in 1821 by his selection to represent the provincial government in London.

As attorney general, Robinson proved ready from the start to offer not only legal but political opinions on the measures referred to him. His recommendation in 1818 to postpone the proclamation ordered by Lord Bathurst on American immigration is early evidence of this trait. By the last years of his attorneyship he was routinely commenting on the policy of matters referred to him for a legal opinion. Of a bill passed in 1827 to provide for the alternate holding of local courts in each county of a district, he observed that it was a good measure and generally popular, yet it proposed 'a great alteration which perhaps should receive more deliberate consideration than circumstances have admitted ... As there is no pressing call for it, I could advise that it be reserved, which will give time for an attentive consideration of the consequences of such a change & afford an opportunity for ascertaining whether it is equally to be desired in all Districts.' A bill of 1828, which made it easier for absentee landlords to pay the tax on lands lying distant from their abode, was declared legally flawless but objectionable on policy grounds – though here Robinson admitted the undesirability of opposing the legislature in a tax matter. When, on the ground that it might involve important legal considerations, Lieutenant-Governor Maitland referred for his opinion a petition of the Roman Catholic bishop for the formation of a corporation to hold real estate on behalf of the church, Robinson disparaged it as a step that must contribute to the advance of the Roman Catholic religion in the province. His discussion of the measure was almost entirely confined to its political implications, and only in the last paragraph did he notice in passing a trivial legal objection.[8]

In addition to Robinson's self-assurance and dazzling personal attainments, three political developments helped to enhance the importance of the attorneyship in the 1820s and 1830s. The establishment of small, generally conservative urban constituencies such as York and Kingston in 1820, Niagara in 1824, and Hamilton and Cornwall in 1830 made it easier for the law officers to win election to the Assembly. The increasing politicization of public life made their duties as MPPs more important. Finally, the growing resentment of judicial interference in politics led to the exclusion of the chief justice first from the Executive and then from the Legislative Council.

Both of the English law officers were expected to be members of Parliament, and in Upper Canada it was considered desirable to have one of the Crown lawyers in the Assembly to guide the House in the execution of its legislative function; yet Robinson was the first provincial law officer to cut an important figure in politics. Among the attorneys general, John White sat only in the first parliament, from 1792 to 1796, while John Macdonell was elected to the Assembly in 1812 but died after his first session. There is no evidence that either Scott or Firth ever stood for election. Among the junior law officers, Robert Gray was an MPP from 1796 to 1804, but his presence in the House did not prevent Peter Russell from lamenting 'the want of the Attorney General's abilities in the House of Assembly, the Members of which are in general ignorant of Parliamentary Forms and Business, & some of them wild young Men who frequently require some Person of Respectability and Experience to keep them in order.'[9] D'Arcy Boulton's membership in the Assembly may be one reason he was chosen to replace Gray in 1805, but he lost his bid for re-election three years later.[10]

Political and social factors combined to keep the law officers out of the legislature. Gray and Macdonell both belonged to leading families in the intensely loyal United Empire Loyalist and military settlements in the east of the province, but most of the colony's legal talent was concentrated in counties where an official, and especially one from Britain, was not so easily elected: at York, the seat of government and headquarters of the Court of King's Bench, and at the commercial centres of Kingston and Niagara. Simcoe boasted of his success in securing White's election in the Kingston area in 1792, despite the prejudices of an electorate that favoured 'Men of a lower Order, who kept but one Table, that is who dined in Common with their Servants.'[11] Four years later, with Simcoe on leave, White, made unpopular by his advocacy of the lieutenant-governor's favourite measure abolishing slavery in the province, was unable to repeat the feat. After the failure of his bid to have White returned at a by-election in 1799, Peter Russell sadly reported to Whitehall 'that the low Ignorance of the Electors ... defeated my wish by preferring an illiterate young Man of their own level & neighbourhood.'[12]

The early law officers actually shunned politics out of distaste for the chores of parliamentary office, which were virtually unpaid. Even in 1793 White was complaining about 'how truly troublesome' his constituency was, and no doubt he found his fellow MPPs equally tedious. When invited to stand in the Niagara area at the general election of 1800, he observed: 'The [Legislative] Council complain that they are no better than clerks to the house of Assembly from the inefficiency of that body ... but who will volunteer the troublesome and disagreeable task if it is to be also unprofitable[?]'[13] When D'Arcy Boulton, now attorney general, stood for election in the Home District in 1816, he told one of his rivals, Peter Robinson (as the latter reported to his brother, the solicitor general), 'that he was much pleased to find that I was proposing myself as he would not be elected for 200 guineas being overwhelmed already with other business.'[14]

John Beverley Robinson, upon taking his seat in 1820, complained of his parliamentary chores as vociferously as any of his predecessors.[15] They did not get easier, but a loyalist's sense of duty kept him at the treadmill until his elevation to the bench nine years later. He at least enjoyed the advantage of representing the new constituency of York, with its strong pro-government interest and dearth of American farmers with inconveniently egalitarian ideas. The lack of such a seat kept H.J. Boulton out of the Assembly until 1830, when he was returned for the merchant fief of Niagara. None but a local man could hope to represent Kingston, the only town other than York and Niagara enfranchised before 1828. Christopher Hagerman's reduction from the bench to the solicitorship in 1829 may have been made in the expectation that he would win that seat, which he had held from 1820 to 1824.

The increasing intensity of provincial politics after Gore's departure in 1817 made the presence of an authoritative spokesman in the Assembly more desirable to the government than ever. As the only senior officials with any tradition of being elected to the legislature, the law officers, starting with Robinson, naturally assumed this task. The session of 1830-1 was the first in which both Crown officers sat as MPPs, but from then on they normally did so. Even R.S. Jameson, whose imposition on the colony after the dismissal of Boulton and Hagerman in 1833 made him an exception to the rule, stood for the Assembly as soon as he could, though his election was voided because of the Orange violence that achieved it. The appointment of Hagerman and Draper as attorney general and solicitor general respectively in 1837 was another landmark, being the first time since 1805 that a law officer had been chosen from the ranks of the Assembly – except, of course, for Hagerman's reappointment as solicitor general after his dismissal in 1833.

Thereafter the law officers were invariably so chosen – with one exception, which itself indicated their increasing political importance. Early in 1840 Governor General Poulett Thomson (later Lord Sydenham) was trying to rally support for Whitehall's plan to reunite Upper and Lower Canada. He elevated Draper to the attorneyship in place of Hagerman and courted the reformers by appointing Robert Baldwin as solicitor general. The 1836 election and the ensuing rebellion had emptied the Assembly of leading reformers, and Baldwin, though not an MPP, was his ageing father's political representative and heir apparent. These were the first overtly political appointments to the law officerships in the province's history.

Although the Crown officers' rise to political eminence seems natural in retrospect, it was neither smooth nor inevitable. Jameson never managed to get elected to the House. Neither he nor Boulton were the stuff of which political leaders are made. Hagerman, who did have political flair, twice lost his job for leading, or threatening to lead, the Assembly against the government. Apart from these quirks or deficiencies in the law officers themselves, there were contemporary objections to their or any other official's belonging to the Assembly. Had these prevailed, the attorney general's rise to political leadership would have been brought to a sudden stop.

The dandyish Boulton was a very different man from his predecessor. Meeting him in 1825, in the wake of Maitland's letter opposing his elevation to the bench, Robert Wilmot Horton was surprised to find him 'so *very competent* a person.'[16] Intellectually competent he no doubt was, but perhaps also intellectually arrogant in a way that was politically damaging. On his return from Newfoundland in 1840, after his dismissal as chief justice, he was to figure as an advocate of responsible government. By 1850 he would be indistinguishable on certain issues from the clearest of Clear Grit radicals. Contemporary observers ascribed his position in 1840 to political calculation and in 1850 to disappointed ambition, but one suspects that in both years it also reflected a certain perverse frivolity. One has the impression that even in the years when he symbolized everything Upper Canadians found hateful in the Family Compact, he paid only lip-service to principles that true believers such as Robinson held as articles of faith. Robinson was the Virginian United Empire Loyalist gentleman's son, Boulton the English fortune-hunting gentleman's son. Together with his enormous ambition and notorious avarice, this levity prevented Boulton from being an effective political leader.

In his very first session in the legislature, Boulton twice exposed his lightness of faith in ways that scandalized the disciples of Archdeacon Strachan. The house that was elected in 1830, though hostile to Baldwinite responsible government and still more so to the egalitarian creed of Mackenzie, was far from devoted to the Anglican exclusivism of the York oligarchy. Boulton dismayed the faithful by bringing in a bill to liberalize the marriage law which caused one more orthodox official to brand him as 'almost a "whole hog" liberal.' The Assembly embraced it, and the bill had to be quashed by the Legislative Council under the leadership of Chief Justice Robinson.

Still more disconcerting was Boulton's casual attitude towards the clergy reserves, the portion of land set aside under the Constitutional Act for the support of 'a Protestant Clergy.' Robinson, as attorney general, had held that the act intended the reserves for the exclusive benefit of the Church of England, and when the question was brought before the Assembly in 1831 Solicitor General Hagerman boldly defended the vested rights of the church. 'The Atty. Genl. on the contrary, from the sudden manner in which the question had been brought up, had not had time to give the matter much consideration, but on a hasty perusal of the statute, his present conviction was that *All* should share in the Reserves, & with this conviction on his mind he had commenced a series of Resolutions to be submitted to the House ... Oh! ye Powers,' exclaimed the King's Printer, Robert Stanton, reporting this heresy to his friend John Macaulay of Kingston. 'The King's Attorney General in this Province – the first legal Adviser of His Majesty's Representative, standing up in his place in the Assembly, & saying that he had never given "much consideration" to one of the most important subjects embraced in the Constitution of his Country and venturing an opinion, to be solemnly recorded in a Resolution, on a hasty perusal of this subject, that His Majesty in making provision for the Religious Instruction of his people in the Province, intended any other Church, than that of which he was head, & bound by sacred obligation to protect & support – fudge! – its downright nonsense! – mere popularity hunting.'[17]

This divergence between the attorney general and the solicitor general had left the House leaderless. 'All is at sixes and sevens – there is no ostensible head – every one acts for himself – there is no concert, & confusion prevails,' lamented Stanton. Leadership was expected, but leadership had not been provided. Stanton was probably unaware, since the fact had not become known in Upper Canada, that the imperial law officers had contradicted Robinson by holding that the Church of Scotland was entitled to a share in the reserves.[18] Had the attorney general shown the most ardent attachment to the Anglican cause, he might still have been unable to exert the sort of leadership Stanton wanted.

Boulton and Hagerman were soon to find out the hard way how far the law officers could lead the Assembly in directions unacceptable to the Colonial Office. Unlike Robinson, who had offered no resistance in the legislature to the naturalization bill of 1828, they persisted in pressing for William Lyon Mackenzie's expulsion from the Assembly in defiance of the secretary of state's instructions. In ordering their dismissal, Viscount Goderich admitted that as MPPs the two officials were 'bound to act upon their own view of what is most for the benefit of their constituents and of the Colony at large, but if upon questions of great political importance they unfortunately differ in opinion from His Majesty's Government, it is obvious that they cannot continue to hold confidential situations in His Majesty's Service, without either betraying their duty as Members of the Legislature or bringing the sincerity of the Government into question by their opposition to the policy, which His Majesty has been advised to pursue.'[19]

Goderich's choice of words points out an irony in the law officers' dismissal. There was a widespread prejudice in Upper Canada against the election of government officials to the Assembly, a prejudice that perhaps reflected the influence of the American constitutional doctrine of the separation of powers. The period from the 1820s to the early 1850s saw a spate of bills designed to disqualify sheriffs and other officials from membership in the legislature, and Robinson faced opposition on this score in all three of his election campaigns.[20] The scandal over his naturalization bill in 1825 provided exponents of this principle with the perfect text. 'So long as he is the servant of the Executive, and his attention is directed to the shaping of bills to meet their views, he ought not to have a voice in the representation of the people – the only constitutional check on the power of the Executive.' So wrote Francis Collins; the *Niagara Herald* drew a similar lesson from the Burlington Bay scandal.[21]

Collins and people like him feared the pollution of the people's representation by executive influence. It is doubtful if, in the heady days of popular outcry against Robinson's naturalization bill and other actual or projected inequities in the 1820s, any critic of the provincial government ever dreamed of seeing the king's attorney and solicitor general dismissed for leading an Assembly (in this respect) *plus royaliste que le Roi* in a course too illiberal for the government's liking. This is what happened in 1833, and it might have happened in 1840 if there had been no judicial vacancy to accommodate Hagerman and if Draper, like his senior colleague, had been intransigently opposed to Union.

Had the radicals ever come to power, this prejudice against mingling the different powers of government in a single person might have decisively reversed the Crown officers' movement towards political leadership. As it was, it merely helped to increase the attorney general's political importance by destroying that of the judges. We have seen how John White had played second fiddle to Chief Justices Osgoode and Elmsley and faced a challenge to his place in the official hierarchy even from Judge Powell. Powell later achieved a pre-eminence that enabled him, even before his promotion to chief justice, to raise first Macdonell and then Robinson to the attorneyship as his protégés. Under Sir Peregrine Maitland, Robinson as attorney general had replaced Powell as the pre-eminent adviser of the Crown, but this merely expressed Maitland's personal preference. What really established the political ascendancy of the attorneyship over the judiciary was the chief justice's withdrawal from politics after the House of Assembly criticized the multiplicity of his official functions.

In the short term, Chief Justice Robinson's exclusion from the Executive Council in 1831 was merely a formal change. The lieutenant-governor could still take advice wherever he wished. As long as he possessed the lieutenant-governor's favour, Robinson could continue to wield as much influence as he had as attorney general, when he had more than once refused nomination to the council from dread of adding a share of its routine administrative duties to his official burden.[22] When cabinet government was introduced in 1841, however, the chief justice was no longer a member of the committee that was henceforth, under the sovereign's representative, to direct the executive, and Robinson's vehement opposition to Union ruled out his restoration. Whenever in the ensuing years the attorney general's membership in the cabinet was criticized as inconsistent with the functions of his office, Robert Baldwin could defend it by citing the lack of a judicial presence in the cabinet, like that of the lord chancellor in England, to advise on legal questions.[23]

The failure of the rebellion of 1837 and the rise of the socially conservative Baldwin to unchallenged leadership of the Upper Canadian reformers destroyed any chance that American principles would prevail and the executive officers be excluded from the legislature. It also determined that the attorneys general would become cabinet members under the new order. Canada had no landed aristocracy like England, independently wealthy and schooled in statecraft. As in the United States, lawyers filled the gap. 'There was a sort of notion prevalent ... that there were too many lawyers in the House and Cabinet,' remarked Baldwin in 1850. 'All he could say was that it was the people who sent them there ... It was the same in the States, which some gentlemen spoke so highly of as models, all the leading public men were lawyers, and it was incident to the state of society; other professions did not provide so many men fitted to take part in public life, and there was no body of individuals in the country so independent in circumstances as to be able to devote their whole time to it, as in England.'[24] It was this that ensured that the attorneys general would normally be not only cabinet members but heads of government. 'In most cases the leading man, of whatever party may be in the ascendant, will belong to the profession of the Law ... Such person will naturally prefer the Office that keeps him, in form at least, connected with his Profession.'[25]

THE BURDENS OF OFFICE

'In form at least': the qualification was apt. By 1850 the attorney general had ceased to attend the assizes to conduct criminal prosecutions or even the Crown's civil litigation. The reform of 1841 had made him a minister of state, much of whose time was spent on the general political business of the government and most of the rest on administering his department.

The politics of the 1840s need only be sketched here.[26] They revolved around responsible government and the position of the French. Although the Earl of Durham had recommended the introduction of responsible government as practised in England, the imperial authorities tried in 1841 to implement a hybrid system in which elements of popular sovereignty were combined with the old authoritarian system. While the cabinet's tenure of office was to depend on its command of a majority in the

Legislative Assembly, real (not merely fictitious) executive authority still lay with the sovereign's representative, who was accountable for its use to the queen and Parliament of the empire. This half-and-half system was doomed to failure, but not before the reformers had lost, in 1844, a general election fought on the same principle as that of 1836 in Upper Canada: the governor general's right to make public appointments without the advice and consent of his Executive Council. Not until 1846 did Whitehall concede responsible government in principle to the North American colonies, and in Canada its implementation was delayed until 1848, when the administration of Henry Sherwood and William Badgley gave way to that of Robert Baldwin and Louis-Hippolyte LaFontaine after losing a vote of confidence. The symbolic triumph of responsible government was celebrated the following year, when the governor general, Lord Elgin, signed the Lower Canadian Rebellion Losses Act, which was designed to compensate the owners of property damaged during the rebellion. Many of its prospective beneficiaries had been rebels (though persons actually convicted of complicity were excluded), and last-ditch Tories in Montreal marked the event by invading the parliament building and burning it to the ground.

The triumph of responsible government was also the triumph of French Canadian politicians in their efforts to be accepted as equal partners in Canadian politics. A principal object of Union, as recommended by Durham, had been to destroy the French culture in Canada by assimilating it to the British. The French minority in the Assembly resisted by forming a bloc capable of controlling the legislature in coalition with either of the anglophone parties. Robert Baldwin, whose father had preached respect for French Canadian interests in the 1820s, proved the perfect partner in this endeavour. In 1841 he promoted LaFontaine's election to the Assembly for a constituency outside Toronto after the French leader's bid for election in Lower Canada had been thwarted by Orange violence. A year later, the two men formed the first reform administration. After their resignation late in 1843 over the crisis that precipitated the next year's general election, their alliance stood firm for four years against a succession of efforts by Governor General Sir Charles Metcalfe and conservative politicians to seduce LaFontaine's followers away from it. In 1848 the two men formed the first administration fully responsible to the Assembly in the history of Upper and Lower Canada.

The weapon used in vain against LaFontaine's party was patronage. The Lower Canadian as well as the Upper Canadian opposition had resented their decades of exclusion from public office. Just as the Upper

Canadian establishment had endeavoured to bolster its hegemony by proclaiming the cult of the loyalists who had stood by the United Empire in 1783 and turned back the republican invader thirty years later, so in the 1840s Baldwin hymned the glory of those who, spurning the temptations of official patronage and the terror of the post-rebellion period, had stood by the Reform party in its fight for responsible government. 'I have always been in the strictest sense of the word *a party man* and feel persuaded I shall continue as such,' he told an applicant for office in 1843. 'It is to the confidence of my party that I owe the position which I occupy and I think it is my duty to make use of the influence which that position gives me to strengthen and support that party ... Whatever influence I possess is not *mine* to be used for my own benefit or the gratification of my own feelings but a trust to be accounted for to my Country and my party.'[27]

The same theme was sounded in two form letters in Baldwin's official letter-book. The form entitled 'Unfavourable Reply to Application' stated:

... while it would be to me personally a pleasure to be able to comply with your request I cannot permit such feelings to interfere with what I conceive to be my duty to the public or to the political party to which I belong. It was the confidence of that party that placed me in the position which pointed me out to the Representative of my Sovereign as a fit person to be called to take part in the administration of the Government: And convinced as I am of the Soundness of their principles and the political integrity of their views it would in my opinion not be consistent with my duty to make use of whatever influence I possess in the Counsels of the Province to forward the promotion of those who have, I doubt not conscientiously, been avowedly hostile to both my party and its principles. Neither do I think it would be just to those who stood firm to us in the period of our political adversity to give precedence to others who, from indecision to say the least of it, have been vacillating between us and our opponents and have only become apparently settled in their views as the scales appeared to turn in our favour.[28]

Form number 16, a reply to unsolicited advice from political supporters, struck a similar note.

The press of official and Executive business renders it impossible for me to write in reply to all the communications which my friends do me the favour to address to me; but they must not on that account suppose their letters to be either disregarded or undesired. On the contrary, I feel the responsibility of my position too sensibly not to be glad of information & Counsel from any quarter. And when it comes from my political friends [& more particularly when from those who stood firm by us in the hour of our political prostration when our opponents fancied they had their feet upon our necks & could keep them there for ever] it is to me be assured ever doubly welcome.[29]

In fact, in the interests of coalition-building Baldwin was to direct patronage to many individuals whose good fortune would provoke old-time reformers to howls of anger; yet the parenthesis to be specially included in letters to those dour and devoted campaigners was sincere enough.

The long struggle in Upper Canada over the Family Compact's monopoly of public office, and the authoritarian institutions that sustained it, was only one of several such contests in the British North American colonies that imbued Canadian politics with an enduring sensitivity to patronage questions. The applications for office that swamped Baldwin as attorney general, necessitating the invention of a sheaf of form letters, was a major ingredient in the complex politics that increasingly hampered the chief law officer from attending the circuit to conduct criminal prosecutions. Not only politics but an increasing press of departmental business pinned him to his desk.

Some of this business was traditional, some of it new. The attorney general traditionally handled smuggling and other revenue cases for the government. When individuals defaulted on bonds to the government, given either by officials for the due performance of their duties or by private persons for the due performance of contracts, it was his duty to proceed against them in the name of the Crown. He also performed such duties for the post office, which remained an imperial operation until 1851, and for the Board of Ordnance, the army department responsible for administering military installations in the province. The attorney general also continued to be responsible for drafting bonds and other agreements for the government, and for issuing his fiat for letters patent. Many such agreements were routine, but others, such as Board of Works contracts, which included difficult technological language, were not. Among the fiats required of Henry Sherwood in 1847 were several for instruments proclaiming fairs, appointing coroners, establishing places as ports of entry and clearance (from which trade could be conducted with the United States), and announcing rewards for the arrest and conviction of malefactors. A growing category of such letters patent consisted of what the world today understands by the word 'patent': those awarded to inventors. The patented inventions of 1847 included a new sort of milk-churn, a machine for producing hot air for the heating of buildings, a Coiled Spring Tooth Revolving Horse Rake, and an ambiguously designated Smut Machine.[30]

As the country grew, so did the traditional sorts of business; but new sorts also crowded in on the attorney general. The foundation of the Court of Chancery in 1837 obliged him to keep an eye on litigation in that court, to see if any was in progress that affected the rights of the Crown or the public and might require his appearance. It also exposed him to applications by parties who wished to institute lawsuits in the name of the attorney general. In these relator actions, his consent was necessary because the matter at issue was one of public interest rather than one of specific injury to the plaintiff. Such litigation involved the Crown in no expense or responsibility, but each application had to be scrutinized to see if the matter merited the proceeding applied for.[31]

One sort of business the attorney general tried hard to avoid was that of advising municipal authorities. Between 1830 and 1840, the number of districts in Upper Canada grew from nine to eighteen and urban municipalities began to be formed – the city of Toronto and assorted towns and police villages. The next decade saw a much greater expansion of local government. An act of 1841 set up elected district councils; urban authorities sprang up everywhere; school-boards were established. The last step in the process was Baldwin's Municipal Corporations Act of 1849, which set up a complete system of local government, rural and urban, throughout Upper Canada. The territory swarmed with municipal officials, all wanting advice, and with a horde of local judges.[32]

Attorney General Draper brought the subject before Lieutenant-Governor Sir George Arthur in 1840. A clerk of the peace had asked him three questions concerning local taxation and two about tavern licence fees and the fine for selling liquor without a licence. When the new city of Toronto had requested Attorney General Jameson's advice on certain questions in 1834, Jameson had treated it as a matter of private practice and charged a fee for each consultation.[33] In 1840 Draper took a different tack. He gave his opinion only on the last two of the questions put to him, because the fees and fines in question went to the government. He withheld an opinion on the tax questions on the ground that they affected strictly local interests. 'According to my understanding of the English practice upon such questions,' he reported to Arthur, 'the District should procure professional advice in the ordinary manner, as in England questions relative to Parish or County rates would be submitted, upon which, I apprehend, the Attorney General there would never be called upon to advise in his official capacity.'

In referring the question to the Executive Council, Arthur doubted whether the English practice was applicable. 'The whole structure of Society in this Province, and more particularly, the constitution of all its Inferior Tribunals of Justice, seem to require, that the legal advice which Magistrates, and other servants of the Crown at Home, are obliged to procure at their own expense, should, in most instances, be afforded to them gratuitously in this country.' In agreeing with the lieutenant-governor that it was desirable that the attorney general advise municipal authorities in such cases, the council stressed the importance of fostering a uniform application of the law by local government officers.[34]

So decided the Executive Council of Upper Canada in 1840, but in United Canada the relationship between the law officers and the Executive Council was rather different. In March and April 1842 the cabinet upheld the refusal of Solicitor General Day of Lower Canada to advise two district magistrates and a district warden. It was declared inexpedient to require the law officers to advise municipal councils about contemplated actions.[35]

Baldwin happily applied the principle in Upper Canada. Replying to a query from a school trustee, he gave the desired opinion but explained that the attorney general's duty required him to give legal advice only to the government and the Legislative Assembly; his correspondent was wrong in supposing that it was incumbent on the trustees to apply to the attorney general whenever they needed advice about their duties.[36] Baldwin's response to similar applications took shape as a form letter entitled 'Special Reply to Application for Official Opinion where Party not entitled to it.' In a tone hovering between the brisk and the querulous, the letter stated: 'It would seem from the number of similar applications to me from Magistrates, Commissioners and others throughout the Country that an opinion is entertained that such Officers have the right to call for the opinion of the Law Officers of the Crown as a matter of course and that it is the duty of the latter to afford them such advice when wanted in the discharge of the duties of their respective offices. Such an opinion however I take leave to say is utterly without foundation. The Attorney and Solicitor General are public servants to advise and assist the Executive Government of the Country, but are not Counsel for every individual holding an official Situation in the Country.'[37]

Local officials of the provincial government also proliferated as the country grew, and the Crown officers tried to repel their queries too. Day again led the way, maintaining that the law officers were obliged to give opinions only to heads of department. Local officers, such as collectors of customs, had to furnish bonds and sureties for the due performance of their duties, and Day felt that in answering the queries of such officers the government was assuming a responsibility that properly rested on the individual and his sureties.

In this case too the cabinet granted the law officers some relief. They recommended that in all cases affecting the public interest generally, or where it was desirable to promote uniformity of action throughout a department, the Crown officers should continue to give their guidance. In cases of less general import, falling within 'the ordinary discretion confided in subordinate public officers,' the latter should be left to judge for themselves or to take private counsel. In no case was such an officer to write to the Crown officers directly; he should get in touch with the head of his department, who would decide whether to refer the query.[38]

Nevertheless, the increasing press of departmental and political business made it more and more difficult for the Crown officers, and the attorney general in particular, to attend the assize circuits as of old. What William Firth had declared in 1811 to be 'the chief end of the Institution of his high Office' was increasingly delegated to queen's counsel. Indeed, the attorney general found himself delegating not merely this routine function but even part of his new duties as minister of justice for Upper Canada. Two of Baldwin's form letters were to be sent to superior and inferior court judges respectively, asking for their views on proposed legislation related to the administration of justice; but such legislation was often left to be drafted and guided through the legislature by others. The act of 1845 setting fixed dates for the assizes, drafted pursuant to a decision of cabinet, was introduced and pushed through by Henry Sherwood.[39] The great reform of 1849, which remodelled Chancery and set up a second superior court of common law (the Court of Common Pleas), was the brain-child of William Hume Blake. The matching bill of 1850 that reformed the county and division courts was the responsibility of John Sandfield Macdonald.[40]

These men were all solicitor general, but important ministerial operations often took place outside the attorney general's office altogether. When, in 1860, John A. Macdonald wanted a bill drafted to improve the administration of justice, he went to J.H. Cameron, solicitor general (west) from 1846-8 but since then a private member. In 1864 a bill on the law of dower was drafted for Macdonald by W.H. Draper, by now chief justice of Upper Canada.[41] The act to amend the law of property and trusts that passed into law under Macdonald's aegis in 1865 had been drafted and first introduced into the legislature the year before by the postmaster general in the preceding administration – the distinguished equity lawyer Oliver Mowat, who was soon to become a vice-chancellor and later, for nearly a quarter of a century, attorney general and premier of Ontario.[42]

Another kind of delegation was imposed on the attorney general of Upper Canada not by the pressure of work but by the political arrangements of the new province. In the 1840s the capital of United Canada was first Kingston and then Montreal. After the riots of 1849, the capital alternated between Toronto and Quebec until it was fixed at Ottawa in 1865. The attorney general, as a member of the cabinet, had to reside at the seat of government. Since Toronto remained the judicial headquarters of Upper Canada, whenever the capital was elsewhere he had to appoint agents at Toronto to handle departmental business. In 1842-3, and again in 1848, Robert Baldwin used his own firm of Baldwin and Son, where the business was dealt with by Adam Wilson (a future mayor of Toronto, solicitor general for Upper Canada, and chief justice of the courts of Common Pleas and King's Bench of Ontario) and Larratt W. Smith. These took it over in their own right, as Wilson and Smith, when Baldwin and Son was wound up in September 1848. When the capital was switched from Toronto to Quebec in 1851, Attorney General William Buell Richards assigned the agency to his brother Stephen, who retained it until 1855. Four years later, John A. Macdonald assigned it to the retiring chief clerk of the Crown Law Department, Robert A. Harrison (later chief justice of Ontario).[43]

ECONOMY AND EFFICIENCY

The common thread in this pattern of administration was that of small-scale government. Queen's counsel conducted Crown litigation on a fee-for-service basis; the Toronto agency operated on fees and a £100-a-year retainer (the latter paid by the attorney general out of his own pocket until 1852);[44] getting bills drafted by a judge like Draper was no doubt cheaper still. The same approach would be taken when county attorneys were introduced in 1857. On the eve of Confederation, the 'Attorney and Solicitor General's Office, Canada West,' consisted of seven people: the two law officers themselves, a chief clerk (performing functions that Robert Harrison, on quitting the post in 1859, had described as those of 'Attorney General de facto'),[45] an assistant clerk, a stenographic clerk, a temporary clerk (paid per diem), and a messenger.[46]

As far as its central administration was concerned, Upper Canada was getting cheap justice.

Yet many people did not think so. The excessive cost of criminal justice was a regular theme of complaint in the Legislative Assembly throughout the 1840s and was twice raised with the Executive Council by the governor general. In consequence, the subject of the law officers' duties received more attention than ever before in the history of Upper Canada. What was in the first instance a matter of provincial housekeeping eventually expanded to include (though scarcely systematically) an important constitutional question: the nature of the Crown officers' responsibility and whether it was compatible with membership in the cabinet. When the debate was over, little had changed. As in 1811 in the Executive Council, and in the 1820s in the House of Assembly, the topic was raised, discussed, and dropped. The system established in 1841 was still in effect at the time of Confederation.

The nature of the debate in the 1840s forms a striking contrast with that of 1828. The earlier controversy revolved around large issues of fairness in the administration of criminal justice, the later one around whether the law officers were doing what they were paid to do and how they could be made to do it. It was 1828 that was the exception. In 1811, the question of the attorney general's duties had arisen because William Firth was perceived to be making too much money. In 1823, the wish to institute semi-annual assizes without too great an increase in the cost of the administration of justice had focused attention again on the attorney general's emoluments. Even in the later 1820s, the challenge to the Crown lawyers' monopoly of criminal prosecutions on civil rights grounds had gone hand in hand with concern about the cost of the justice system.

This preoccupation led in 1830 to an important report on taxable costs – the fees for services and the fixed costs of legal proceedings that lawyers were entitled to charge their clients or to claim, under a court award of costs, from the opposing party.[47] A select committee of the Assembly heard many witnesses, including Judges Sherwood and Macaulay, both of the Crown officers, and private attorneys of the stature of John Rolph, Marshall Bidwell, and W.H. Draper. The lawyers agreed, irrespective of their politics, that they were not paid too much for what they did, but that what they had to do at their clients' expense might be lessened by simplifying procedure in both the Court of King's Bench and the district courts. Costs might also be reduced by expanding the district courts' jurisdiction, thereby transferring litigation to them from the King's Bench. Several witnesses recommended abolishing those upper-class sinecures the clerkships of assize and transferring their duties to the deputy clerk of the Crown in each district. Their circuit money was a burden on the public revenue, and their fees, chargeable to the individual litigant and generally considered excessive, could be replaced by a small per-diem salary.

Amid the various witnesses, eminent and brilliant, the testimony of one stands out. Robert Baldwin Sullivan, a young man of poetic and drinking bent, was a nephew of Dr Baldwin and a cousin of Robert. Originally a reformer like them, he took a conservative turn when, after serving as mayor of Toronto in 1835, he entered the Executive Council formed by Sir Francis Head upon the resignation of John Rolph, Robert Baldwin, and the rest of the council in April 1836. Through many political vicissitudes he served in the executive councils of both Upper and United Canada until 1843. Then, reconverted to reform, he resigned his office along with Baldwin, LaFontaine, and their followers over Sir Charles Metcalfe's insistence on making public appointments without their advice and consent. During the general election campaign of 1844 he was the reformers' chief propagandist in Upper Canada, publishing a series of brilliant articles in favour of responsible government as the Baldwins conceived it. In 1848 he re-entered the cabinet along with Baldwin and LaFontaine before becoming a judge, first in the Court of King's Bench and then in the new Court of Common Pleas.

In his evidence to the select committee on the administration of justice in 1830, Sullivan took a broader approach than any other witness. He began by challenging the idea 'that any body of men should be made by law an encumbrance on the community at large, or that the law should enforce a remuneration for the services of any person superior to that, which he would obtain if his exertions were applied in a line of life in which the community would voluntarily contribute to his support.' On this principle he rejected the notion 'that there are vested rights in any office or employment: all that the Law ought to contemplate is to allow a fair compensation for labour, and every person holding an office or employment, ought to consider, that so soon as his emoluments are found to exceed his services, it is the duty of the Lawgiver to interfere and reduce them to a proper level.'

This rather wordy formula was an explicit challenge to the traditional conception of public office as a species of property, a monopoly of services for which the office-holder was entitled to claim a fee. Officers such as the clerk of the Crown and the district sheriffs and clerks of the peace should not be allowed to derive inordinate incomes from the fees yielded by their office (fees which were growing, of course, along with the population) while the bulk of the work was done by deputies whom they paid a small salary. Instead, the fees should be paid into a fee fund for the use of the government, which would pay a fair salary to the officer and his deputies.[48] Sullivan's reference to the interference of the 'Lawgiver' is interesting because it suggests that on some occasion defenders of the proprietary conception of office may have denied the power of the legislature to curtail privileges derived from royal letters patent issued by prerogative.

The Crown officers were to be early victims of Sullivan's doctrine. His evidence had dismissed them with the passing comment that their fees were far too high, especially compared with what other lawyers received for their services. Yet the committee scarcely needed telling this – as Sullivan himself remarked, the Crown lawyers' accounts were always before the House and had become a matter of public discussion. For the past decade or so, the attorney general had been making about £2,000 a year from public sources, quite apart from the yield of his private practice.[49] This level of compensation, which far exceeded what most other leading officials received, had long been a matter of regret to conservatives as well as reformers, and the regret can only have deepened when H.J. Boulton succeeded Robinson in the favoured place. As early as 1821 a bill had been introduced into the Assembly to pay the attorney general a salary instead of fees. This was actually done to the sinecure office of auditor general of land patents in 1826, the year the job passed from Henry John Boulton's brother-in-law to his brother D'Arcy Boulton Jr. Three years later the suggestion was revived as to the law officerships by an Assembly select committee.[50] In 1833, after four years of Henry John himself as attorney, the legislature acted, establishing a salary of £1,200 a year for the attorney general and £600 for the solicitor general in lieu of their annual retainers and all fees and expenses received for services performed in their public capacity. This remained their salary until Union, except for the year 1835, when the new reform majority in the Assembly exercised its muscles by cutting them back to £750 and £375 respectively.[51]

Oddly enough, it was this reform of 1833 that underlay the controversy of the following decade. After Union, the law officers of both sections – the attorneys general in particular – were immersed in the general political business of the province and the expanded chores of their respective departments. Consequently, they became less and less able to attend the assizes to conduct criminal prosecutions. Yet they still received the salary voted them by the legislature for that duty, among others, while queen's counsel had to be paid for taking their place on circuit.

The question arose in the Assembly in the autumn of 1843. On second reading of a government bill disqualifying certain provincial officials from membership in the legislature, an MPP from Lower Canada, Robert Christie, moved to extend the ban to queen's counsel and the solicitors general. Baldwin, as attorney general, opposed the exclusion of queen's counsel, since they were not government employees but a senior rank of the legal profession. True, it was normal to employ them in preference to other counsel to conduct Crown litigation in lieu of the law officers, but there was nothing to stop the government from hiring any barrister it chose for the purpose. As to the solicitors general, Baldwin readily conceded that they should be excluded not from the Assembly but from the cabinet. The solicitor general (west) would thus be able to live at Toronto instead of at the capital (then Kingston) and save the government money by taking charge of Crown business before the courts there, while his liberation from cabinet concerns would allow him to attend more assize circuits.[52]

Nothing was done at once because of the constitutional crisis that broke out in November 1843. For the next nine months Sir Charles Metcalfe governed with a skeleton Executive Council of three while trying to form a coalition that could hope to meet the LaFontaine-Baldwin alliance at the hustings. Even in February 1844, however, he kept the subject alive by referring it to the council. In September it was ordered that the solicitors general should no longer belong to the council but should reside in their respective sections, where they could attend to Crown business. The attorneys general were to attend the assizes whenever they could.[53]

The council made one other recommendation to help meet this goal. In Upper Canada one cause of increase in the cost of the administration of justice had been the reforms of 1837. The Court of King's Bench had been enlarged from three judges to five, and semi-annual assizes had been reintroduced for the first time since the experiment of 1823.[54] From then on, too many assizes were held at one time for the Crown officers to attend them all. It was after this that the first three queen's counsel – Sir Allan MacNab (newly knighted after leading loyal men of Gore to the defence of Toronto in 1837), Henry Sherwood, and John Cartwright – were appointed. In September 1844 the council wondered whether the number of circuits might be reduced, and other changes made, with a view to allowing the Crown officers to get to more of them.

When the legislature met after the election, Solicitor General Sherwood brought in a bill to implement this suggestion. It abolished the second assize in eight districts, thereby reducing the number of circuits, and put an end to the assize judge's power of naming the day his court would sit, setting instead fixed dates that would minimize the number of over-lapping sittings and make it possible for the Crown officers to attend almost all of them. One of the chief reasons behind the call for semi-annual assizes in the 1820s had been the wish to reduce the amount of time that persons accused of serious crimes would have to spend in jail awaiting trial if they could not arrange bail. To prevent the recurrence of this evil, prisoners awaiting trial in districts with annual assizes might apply to be tried in any neighbouring district with an earlier assizes.[55]

The new scheme foundered amid the complexities of Canadian politics. The 1844 election had given the governor general's supporters a lopsided victory in the western section that only slightly outweighed their defeat in the east, where Metcalfe had won virtually no support among the French. Draper now led a government with a slender majority, resting on an unstable coalition of high Tories and moderate conservatives, mainly from Upper Canada. The task of political management left him less time than he might have wished for attending the assize circuits. The government formed by Sherwood on Draper's resignation in 1847 was even weaker. Sherwood, whom Draper had dismissed from the post of solicitor general the previous year for his Tory intransigence, was offered the attorneyship only after his successor, J.H. Cameron, had turned it down. In retaining Cameron as solicitor, Sherwood felt obliged to bring him into the cabinet.[56]

Even before this, in September 1846, Governor General Earl Cathcart had responded to discontent at the law officers' continued dereliction of duty by directing a committee of cabinet consisting of every member except the Crown officers to consider the duties and emoluments of those officers before and since Union, how and by what authority their duties had changed since Union, and how the discharge of their duties should be regulated 'so that each officer may know what is expected from him and for the due performance of which he is personally responsible.' The only change the committee reported was the addition of the political duties entailed in membership in the Executive Council and in the Legislative Assembly (both of which, they stated, had been required of the law officers only since 1841). These had withdrawn them from the conduct of Crown litigation to a much greater extent than had been expected.[57]

For the future, the committee insisted that it was 'a point of the last importance that the duty of conducting the Crown business in the Courts of Law, should be discharged to the utmost extent, by the four highest Law Officers of the Crown, in person ... Their presence in Council with Colleagues who have abundant other opportunities of consulting with them and ascertaining their views, can seldom be as important to the public interest, as their habitual presence in the Courts.' The attorneys' duties as legal advisers and draftsmen to the government could not be allowed to exclude them from the courtroom. Most of the points of law on which they had to advise their fellow department heads involved questions of no great difficulty, while the business of drawing up proclamations, patents, etc. was a mere matter of routine that could be done by clerks, as in other departments. 'An adequate establishment for the routine work of the Law Officers' Department would be much more economical than the employment of Queen's Counsel in the Courts of Law: besides that it would relieve the high Law Officers of the Crown from a description of employment not suitable to their rank and position, nor apparently compatible with their full discharge of the higher class of their duties.' The committee recommended that, except when overlapping circuits made it inevitable, the attorneys general should not be allowed to assign queen's counsel to assizes without the governor general's special permission.[58]

In keeping with the knuckle-rapping tone of this report was the committee's decision on a question concerning the attorneys' emoluments. After the Upper Canadian law officers had been placed on salary in 1833, the attorney general had continued to take fees from private individuals for the issue of letters patent that were of pecuniary advantage, such as those appointing them to offices of profit. The attorney general (east) had followed this example in 1841, when the Lower Canadian law officers too were placed on salary because their residence at Kingston would prevent their continuing to draw income from Crown litigation or private practice. LaFontaine and Baldwin, on taking office, had questioned the propriety of this practice, but the council report of 1844 had sanctioned it. Now this cabinet committee of 1846, from which the law officers were absent, denounced the practice as inconsistent with the Upper Canadian statute of 1833.[59] In effect, the law officers were declared to have misconstrued for years the legislation defining their own emoluments!

The next two years brought a respite to the embattled Crown officers, but in 1849 the controversy was renewed. The province was still feeling the effects of the tremendous pan-Atlantic slump of 1846-8. The general election of December 1847 had returned a more radical Upper Canadian representation than any since 1834, and the new assembly was especially favourable to slashing government expenditure and trimming lawyers' pocket-books. Still, it was Robert Christie of Gaspé, an independent-minded Tory who had been expelled as many times from the nationalist-dominated Assembly of Lower Canada as Mackenzie had from the Upper Canadian, who led the way with a series of resolutions calling for the reduction of official salaries, the payment of all official fees into a central fund, and the assumption of the governor general's huge salary of nearly £8,000 by the imperial authorities.

In 1846 the attorney general's membership in the cabinet had been condemned as inconsistent with his constitutional duty to advise that body impartially on legal questions. Lewis Moffatt of Montreal proposed to abolish the solicitorships altogether and exclude the attorneys from the cabinet while retaining them in the Assembly. This would be an important step towards assimilating the Canadian constitution to that of England, where 'the Crown Lawyers formed no part of the Executive.'[60] One of Christie's resolutions in 1849 transcended the fiscal preoccupation in amplifying the constitutional objection. It declared:

That the Attornies and Solicitors General, as the principal Law Officers of the Crown in this Province, are in matters of law, and legal questions of public interest, the responsible advisers of the Executive Government thereof, and as such are referred to frequently by it, as well in cases where private rights are concerned, as in those of a public nature. That, in the opinion of this House, they therefore ought not to take the lead, conduct, nor participate in the political business of the Government, nor ex officio to occupy seats in the Executive Council, nor to deliberate therein as Members thereof; but to be exempt therefrom, and restricted to the official duties appertaining to their station in Her Majesty's Courts of Law, which are now, by reason of the attention of those officials to the political business of the Government, performed by substitutes, and at great additional expense to the country, and that they should be professionally consulted only in legal matters by the Executive, when for its information and guidance it may be necessary to refer to them for their opinion and report thereon, and which [opinion] should be as free of all suspicion of political bias, as are and ought to be the decisions of the Judges in Her Majesty's Law Courts.[61]

Christie's resolution touched on a seminal point of constitutional doctrine pertaining to the office of attorney general: it is his duty to advise the executive dispassionately on questions of law, and by doing so to restrain it from breaches of legality or constitutional principle to the injury of individuals. In addition, the attorney general was invested with quasi-judicial powers that were as incompatible with membership of the supreme executive committee as those of the chief justice. They included an absolute discretion in authorizing relator actions, in disposing of the applications of persons wishing to sue the Crown, and in staying criminal prosecutions by entering a *nolle prosequi*. When such discretion had to be exercised on politically contentious subjects, any decision that seemed to favour the government was bound to be suspect, no matter how impartially achieved.[62] From this point of view, Christie's declaration echoed the criticism of the Upper Canadian law officers who in 1828 had acted for supporters of the government in suits arising from civil rights outrages.

Christie's sweeping proposals failed, but a new assault in 1850 persuaded the government to set up a select committee on public income and expenditure to investigate the operations of the provincial adminis-tration as a whole.[63] The witnesses on the subject of the Crown officers concentrated on two main questions: how many officers were necessary, and whether they, or any of them, should belong to the cabinet. Both questions bore on the committee's fiscal preoccupation, since the law officers' cabinet membership was a cause of absence from the assize circuit. The constitutional issue was noticed, though, both in the witnesses' testimony and in the legislature.

Baldwin waxed plaintive on the burdens of office. 'No one who has not filled this office ... can have any just conception how thoroughly every moment of time is occupied,' he said. Despite the tiny establishment set up by order in council four years previously to handle the routine tasks judged to be beneath an attorney general's dignity, he predicted it would soon be necessary to make a new arrangement for the conduct of routine legal business – 'that part of the business of the Crown, which more properly belongs to the profession of a Solicitor, than to that of a Counsel.' He alluded to the system in England, where each government department had its own solicitor and only exceptional or difficult matters were referred to the law officers of the Crown. For Upper Canada he proposed a single solicitor at Toronto, the section's judicial headquarters, and another at each county seat.[64]

This cut no ice with H.J. Boulton in his 'Clear Grit' mood. He personally had no objection to a cabinet full of lawyers, he declared, 'but as for the Attorney General, he should have to go on the circuits; it was due to the lives and rights of the subject, that the first law officers of the crown should be in attendance ... It was monstrous to see the ... Attorney

General paid large sums for assize business when their duties were performed by young and inexperienced men, and lives and property jeopardized.'[65]

In 1850, as four years previously, Baldwin had defended the attorney general's cabinet membership by citing the lack of a Canadian equivalent to the lord chancellor. In 1846 the Orange leader, Ogle Gowan, had suggested meeting Baldwin's argument by making the vice-chancellor a member of cabinet and Speaker of the Legislative Council (thereby also emulating the lord chancellor's position as Speaker of the House of Lords).[66] The proposal was futile, since it would have offended reformers by bringing a judge back into both councils, and Lower Canadians by creating a cabinet office that only an Upper Canadian could fill; while few Tories were likely to support the political elevation of the then vice-chancellor, R.S. Jameson (Gowan's old running mate in Leeds and Grenville in 1834), above Chief Justice Robinson.

From time to time during the 1840s, though, W.H. Draper had made a similar proposal that was free from these objections. As imparted to the select committee in 1850, it entailed the creation of a single cabinet law officer who would be responsible for advising the government on all questions of a 'general or political' character, for the drafting of government legislation, for advising the cabinet on the merits of private bills passed by the legislature, and for the routine administrative work now performed by the attorneys general. This officer would not be expected to represent the Crown in court, except in state trials of special importance. The non-cabinet law officers would have general responsibility for Crown litigation, both criminal and civil, and would advise the government on matters of law when required to do so. They would be paid fees and a small retainer. Since they would reside not at the capital but at the legal headquarters of their respective sections, they would be able to engage in private practice.[67]

J.H. Cameron also thought one cabinet law officer enough, but the moderate reformers who dominated the government tended to argue the need for two. Baldwin, as we have seen, noted the predominance of lawyers in the party leadership of both sections, which made the status quo inevitable as long as stable government depended upon 'what may be called the separate confidence of each section of the Province.'[68] Three others, R.B. Sullivan, Lewis Drummond (solicitor general for Lower Canada) and S.B. Harrison (Lord Sydenham's premier, as provincial secretary, in 1841), declared that the existence of two systems of civil law in the province made it necessary.[69]

Everyone agreed that there should be two non-cabinet law officers, but there was some question whether they should continue to sit in the Assembly. Baldwin thought they should, since the attorneys' political duties made it impossible for them to pay adequate attention 'to what may be called the Law Legislation of Parliament.' Draper and James E. Small (solicitor general for Upper Canada, 1842-3) agreed. Even Cameron and Harrison, who dissented, thought they should hold office on a political tenure, Cameron because the law officerships were a stepping-stone to the bench and 'each political party should in its turn, as it obtains power, have the right to appoint [the law officers] with a view to promotion to the Bench.'[70] By contrast Louis-Joseph Papineau, leader of the Lower Canadian rebellion in 1837, had objected to the law officers' being cabinet members precisely because they were so often promoted to the bench, taking their political prejudices with them.[71]

It was left to R.B. Sullivan, who twenty years earlier had so eloquently challenged the old conception of the Crown officerships as vested monopoly rights in the provision of services, to provide a historical perspective on the issue. In 1844 the attorney general's salary had been cut from £1,200 to £1,100, and by 1850 it was down to £1,000. Under the old system his income had been far greater, although the population was then much smaller and the public business less important, leaving him time to enrich himself further by private practice. 'No one who has not had much experience in the practical working of the Executive Government, can have a correct notion of the multiplicity of cases in which legal advice is necessary,' Sullivan told the committee. 'Besides the framing of many, and the accurate consideration of all measures introduced into Parliament upon the responsibility of the Executive, questions are daily arising in the Executive Council, in the Department of Public Works, Crown Lands, Customs, Excise, Education, and regarding the Magistracy, and complaints against Magistrates and other public functionaries, as well as relating to Provincial relations with the Imperial Authorities, and even sometimes with foreign countries.' If the attorney general received, instead of a salary, even a moderate fee for every consultation, his income would be large. Instead, he was 'the worst paid lawyer, in proportion to the extent of his professional services, of any in the Province, or probably in North America.'[72] How things had changed in twenty years!

During the 1850s the attorney general continued to languish under an ever-increasing load of administrative responsibility, part of it unnecessary. A report by cabinet minister Thomas D'Arcy McGee in 1863 deplored the tendency of ministers to refer to the law officers questions of a purely administrative nature. 'That either of the chief law officers may happen to be Premier – and therefore to be consulted on grounds of public policy – cannot of itself relieve the head of any department from his own proper official responsibility,' the report declared. 'It is neither desirable for the sake of the department, nor for the political head of the government, if he should happen to be also an Attorney General, that the former should shelter themselves under the written opinions of the latter.'[73]

The burdens of the attorney general for Upper Canada were further increased by statutory innovations. In 1853, when the clergy reserves question was finally settled by using the reserves to create a fund for municipal loans in aid of railway construction, it became his duty to report on the legality of every municipal by-law passed under the act.[74] Two years previously Upper Canada's first criminal appeal statute, in providing for appeal on a point of law to either of the superior courts of common law against conviction at assizes or quarter sessions, had required the attorney general or his representative to appear in the court of reference to argue the matter. John A. Macdonald found he was often not told of such cases, and in 1856 he had to secure an order in council requiring the Crown counsel involved to draw up a brief for him in time for the appeal.[75]

On top of all his other duties (or perhaps below them) came the attorney general's responsibility to oversee the growing volume of legislation imposed by population growth and the rise of big business, which demanded many innovations in provincial law and institutions. This duty was often slighted because of overwork; James Small had anticipated in 1850 that the attorney's exclusion from the cabinet 'would tend to prevent errors from creeping into our Statute Book to the extent that has heretofore prevailed.'[76] In this branch of duty, the attorney general's failure was made good to some extent by an officer inherited from Lower Canada, the law clerk to the Legislative Assembly. In the person of Gustavus Wicksteed, one of the province's distinguished civil servants, this officer drafted public and private bills upon request, put amendments into proper language, made sure that the text that came to third reading was internally coherent, and oversaw the printing of the final document.[77] This was mostly work which the Crown officers had done in the old days, and it was not work that Robert Christie of Gaspé – who in 1818 had been the first law clerk of Lower Canada – thought the clerk should be doing. Every year the legislature was asked to vote special sums to Wicksteed for drafting public bills. If the law officers could not do the work themselves, Christie maintained in 1853, they should pay for it themselves.[78] This was hard on the poor attorneys, who only a year earlier had seen their salaries cut to £900 and who had enough to do in advising the government on the merits of bills once they were passed and in trying to avert new legislation that was inconsistent with existing law.[79]

Despite the carping of Christie and other critics, there were no sound objections to the costs arising from the attorneys' cabinet membership, least of all those accruing to criminal prosecutions at assize. Prior to 1833 the attorney general of Upper Canada alone had received about £2,000 a year from public sources; in 1849, despite a much increased load of criminal and civil business, both Upper Canadian law officers were receiving £1,765 in total, including contingencies, and disbursements to queen's counsel were only £1,085.[80] If there was one sound ground for complaining about the cost of criminal prosecutions, it had nothing to do with the Crown officers: 1849 and 1850 saw two more vain attempts to abolish the clerkships of assize. In 1851 an act was at last passed to transfer the assize clerks' duties to the deputy clerks of the Crown – that veteran conservative politician, Attorney General Baldwin, resisting to the last. The terms of the debate had not changed in twenty-five years: one MPP supported the bill because 'the sons of the judges and the relations of the ministry received these clerkships as mere sinecures'; another complained that the clerks went on circuit merely to have a good time. The new act exempted the clerkship of assize at Toronto as long as the present incumbent continued to hold it. The late Chief Justice Campbell's son had filled that job since 1825.[81]

THE PLAGUE OF PATRONAGE

If there was no rational basis for complaints about the cost of criminal prosecutions in Upper Canada, what did underlie the reiterated attacks on the law officers of the Crown? It may partly have been displaced malice flowing from the final triumph of Baldwinite reform: there was a wish to strike back at the victor and a special satisfaction to be gained from assailing the neurotically conscientious Baldwin for dereliction of duty. But there was more to it than this. One could hope by such accusations to activate prejudices that were deeply ingrained in the political culture of Upper Canada – the prejudices attached to the concepts of monopoly, sinecure, and patronage.

When Robert Randal addressed the voters of Lincoln from the hustings in 1820, he had urged them to spurn 'that influence that strengthens the strong arm of aristocracy, by favouritism and patronage ... that makes a monopoly of all places of profit or honour.'[82] He was referring to the authoritarian political system that allowed a small group of powerful men to control official appointments to the benefit of themselves, their families, and their political affiliates throughout the province. Many of the offices subject to this collective monopoly were themselves monopolies, since they invested the possessor with the sole right of performing certain services, for each of which he was entitled to a fee. Sometimes much of the work of the office was done by deputies, or the fee was far higher than the service justified. In such cases the office was a sinecure.

Such a system was bound to be resented by the ordinary Upper Canadian. It forced him to contribute to the enrichment of the favoured few, not only indirectly by paying taxes that went into salaries, but directly by the payment of fees, all too often for services that did him no good. When Randal's Chaudière estate was sold by the sheriff at the suit of H.J. Boulton, the proceeds went to pay not only Randal's debt to Boulton but also the sheriff's fees; part of the debt to Boulton, moreover, represented fees payable to the clerks of the successive courts of assize at which Randal had tried in vain to reclaim the Bridgewater estate from Clark and Street. Losing litigants still face having to pay court costs today, of course, but these are a trivial proportion of the total costs of litigation and go into a central fund. In those days they could be a burden to the ordinary farmer or other impecunious inhabitant, and they went straight into the private piggy banks of the officials entitled to claim them: Randal's went to a sheriff connected by marriage to his despoiler, Boulton, and to clerks of assize who were kin or protégés of the judges who denied him justice.

The distribution of offices was regarded with jealousy both within and without the privileged circle. The Executive Council tried to deprive William Firth of the sinecure portion of his income as attorney general – the fees claimable for his fiat; the over-ample emoluments of the clerkships of assize were snatched from John Small by judges with hungry mouths to feed; H.J. Boulton regretted the enjoyment of those emoluments by youths with no family to support or dignity to maintain; George Rolph was stripped first of his clothes and then of his office as clerk of the peace. In each instance there was a feeling that rewards were going to the unworthy, but Rolph's case is especially interesting. One use of the official clique's monopoly of appointments was, as Randal declared, to 'strengthen the strong arm of aristocracy by favouritism and patronage.' To ambitious men beyond the privileged circle, their best chance of getting inside it was to earn the favour and patronage of those who presided at its centre. The participation of Allan MacNab and George Gurnett in the attack on Rolph was an ill-judged manifestation of that motive. In all probability, the misjudgment stemmed from a sense of injustice at seeing such a covetable office as Rolph's in the hands of someone so backward (as they saw it) in strengthening the strong arm of aristocracy.

The use of patronage to reinforce the status quo made it the main focus of the political struggle – so much so that the two major crises in the movement for responsible government occurred in 1836 and 1843, when reformers in the Executive Council insisted that they should influence or control appointments to office. So sensitive was the electorate as a whole to the issue that on both occasions government propagandists were able to smear the reformers as being no better than themselves – as being just as greedy for jobs. There was more than a grain of truth in the charge. While some of the Upper Canadian reformers, such as William Lyon Mackenzie, were quixotic idealists who might have aspired to public employment but instead spurned the whole system, many of them worked for responsible government in the hope that a more open system would give them a better chance at the trough. Such a motive, imperfectly concealed, was not likely to win the support of the rank and file, who had no hope of a government job under any system. It was this mistrust of the reform politicians that Baldwin's enemies tried to activate in 1849-50 by complaining of his dereliction of duty.

The hostility of people like Randal and Mackenzie to monopoly of services went beyond government to embrace the professions. Responsible government may have been achieved, but the monopolies maintained by the Law Society of Upper Canada and the Medical Board of Upper Canada were still intact. The early 1850s saw many petitions presented to the legislature and several bills introduced there to allow anyone to practice law or medicine who could sell his services as a practitioner. In 1853 John Rolph, now a Clear Grit representative in the Hincks-Morin cabinet and the founder of a private medical school, would exploit this feeling to secure the abolition of the faculties of law and medicine at the University of Toronto.[83] Although the attorneyships had ceased to have any taint of monopoly or sinecure about them in 1846 at the latest, when the incumbents had at last stopped taking fees for fiats, in such a climate of opinion the attorneys' failure to perform the most public part of their job made it possible to denounce them as getting £1,000 a year for nothing – or, worse, for plotting ways to stay in office.

Of course, in the complex bilingual, multicultural society called Canada the tasks of political management that helped to keep the attorneys away from the circuits were essential to stable government; but this was of no consideration to those who were not getting what they wanted from the government – those who were beginning to see Robert Baldwin not as the leader of the reform movement but as a conservative who was more strongly committed to maintaining professional monopoly, clerkships of assize and a cumbrous and expensive system of justice than to abolishing the clergy reserves. The attorneys' absence from the assizes was also attacked by those who felt they had a better right than Baldwin to be leading a conservative government. In 1851 the two sides would combine to force his resignation by voting to condemn his remodelling of the Court of Chancery.

To these enemies, radical and conservative alike, the attorneys' failure to attend the circuits was doubly offensive because it freed them to perform their political manipulations and created patronage for that purpose. The attorney general's ability to nominate Crown counsel as he wished, circuit by circuit, just as the judges nominated clerks of assize, was deeply resented. The nominees were often MPPs, a fact that stimulated the old prejudice against the pollution of the popular branch of government by executive influence and led to Robert Christie's attempt in 1843 to disqualify queen's counsel for election to the Assembly. Baldwin resisted the proposal, as we saw, by arguing that queen's counsel were not government employees but a senior rank of the legal profession, and though it was usual to select Crown counsel from their number the government was not obliged to do so by law. When, later in the decade, he acted on this view by appointing barristers who were not queen's counsel to conduct Crown business, the opposition shifted its ground and tried to bar the appointment of MPPs as Crown counsel. Oddly enough, the clamour of resentment was now swelled by indignant Tory QCs, who maintained that the government *was* obliged to employ them in preference to their juniors and that Baldwin's failure to do so amounted to an unconstitutional discrimination against them on political grounds.[84]

Indeed, the fuss over Baldwin's neglect of the circuits and the appointment of substitutes was mostly cynical and factitious, with the loudest complaints coming from insatiable seekers of patronage. One was H.J. Boulton, of whom no more need be said. Another was Sir Allan MacNab, whose political credit, already tarnished, was ruined in 1846 when he tried to make a political deal with Baldwin. Henry Sherwood, whose brief taste of high office in the 1840s was all too little to satisfy him, was a third. John Prince, who made nearly twice as much in Crown counsel fees during the decade as any other Upper Canadian barrister, was a temperamental malcontent whom Baldwin stripped of his silk gown in 1850 after Prince publicly advocated Canadian independence from the empire. Henry Smith of Frontenac would still be dissatisfied after serving as solicitor general from 1854 to 1858 and Speaker of the Assembly from then until 1861; not even the knighthood he received in 1860 would prevent him from deserting the party of his lifelong friend John A. Macdonald the following year.[85] Unlike these political has-beens and never-wases, Macdonald himself was quite ready to admit that the attorney general could no longer attend the circuits; he complained only that incompetent reformers were appointed as substitutes instead of efficient Tories.[86]

MINISTERIAL RESPONSIBILITY

Indirectly, this cynical opposition to Baldwin led to an extension of the debate over the nature of the attorney general's constitutional responsibility. Despite the evident utility of an equity jurisdiction in cases such as Robert Randal's, the more radical reformers had never been in favour of setting up a separate Court of Chancery, with its elaborate and expensive procedure. Their aversion was enhanced by William Hume Blake's reform of 1849, which simplified the procedure but constituted a costly bench of three judges instead of the single vice-chancellor who had presided since the court's founding in 1837. When Blake resigned as solicitor general to assume the chancellorship of the remodelled court, patronage-conscious enemies accused him of reforming the court to create a job for himself, though the post had first been offered to W.H. Draper.[87]

Two years later a new onslaught against the court caused Baldwin to resign, the first minister in Canadian history to do so individually on grounds of confidence. In June 1851 William Lyon Mackenzie moved for a committee to look into abolishing the court and transferring its jurisdiction to the common-law courts. The motion was narrowly defeated, but the Upper Canadian members split 25 to 9 in its favour. The Tories joined the radicals in supporting Mackenzie. Even Solicitor General John Sandfield Macdonald, who voted with the government, expressed sympathy for the opposition.[88]

However opportunistic the motives of many who took part in it, this decisive condemnation of an Upper Canadian measure by the section's representatives was something that Baldwin felt obliged to treat as a vote of no confidence in himself, if not in the government as a whole. He had not framed the enactment, but he was head of the department from which it issued and had decided to push it through in the face of opposition that had made Blake ready to desist. 'The more I thought of it,' he explained to his son-in-law, 'the more convinced I became that, even supposing that there did not exist an abstract necessity for my resigning, it was not only justifiable but that ... I could best serve my country by doing so. I felt that if unable to protect measures such as the Judiciary Acts of 1849 from becoming the sport of demagog clamour before they had been 2 years in operation I could have no hope of being able to sustain any of the Institutions of the Country or procure for any measures for their improvement, no matter how deliberately framed, anything approaching to a fair trial.' Recognizing that the support given to Mackenzie by the likes of H.J. Boulton, Henry Sherwood, and Allan MacNab represented a ganging-up of old enemies against him personally, he dissuaded his cabinet colleagues from resigning with him.[89]

Baldwin's resignation embarrassed Francis Hincks, his heir presumptive as leader of the Upper Canadian reformers and premier of the province. An election was pending, and Hincks had no wish to remodel the cabinet in the meantime. In particular, he wanted to replace Baldwin as attorney general not with Sandfield Macdonald, who as solicitor general had a traditional (though fast obsolescent) reversionary claim to the promotion, but with W.B. Richards, who was less of a political threat and who shared his own sympathy for big business. This was best left until after the election. He therefore prevailed on Baldwin to retain his portfolio until then while resigning the premiership and his place in the cabinet.[90]

This arrangement focused attention once more on the attorney general's cabinet membership. H.J. Boulton introduced resolutions declaring that the attorneyship had 'been regarded in every successive change of Ministry in this Province as one of the highest in the administration of public affairs, to which a seat in the Provincial Government has undeviatingly been attached.' Baldwin's new status was inconsistent with the practice in Britain, where a resigning minister who was administering his office as caretaker pending the appointment of a successor necessarily continued to bear 'all the political responsibilities of the Cabinet ... of which he cannot relieve himself so long as he continues, however temporarily, to discharge the duties of his high official station.' Baldwin's position was therefore inconsistent with the principles of ministerial responsibility he had advocated throughout his career. In the ensuing debate Boulton noted that unlike his English counterpart, who was not a minister, the attorney general in Canada performed many duties which in England belonged to the secretary of state for the Home Department. John Prince thought that the attorney should not be in the cabinet at all; he stirred the pot by asserting Sandfield Macdonald's right to succeed to the attorneyship as in England. Few people cared to trample on the beaten Baldwin, and Boulton did not press his resolutions to a vote.[91]

Two other controversies during these years also highlighted the question of the constitutional propriety of the attorney general's presence in the cabinet. Canada was moving out of the age of clergy reserves and clerkships of assize into that of capitalist economic expansion, and it is no coincidence that both controversies were implicated with the most contentious subject of the new era: railways.

Like the Constitutional Act of 1791, the Canadian constitution of 1840 authorized the governor general at his discretion (and in certain cases required him) to withhold the royal assent from bills passed by the legislature and refer them to the imperial government for its decision.[92] In 1849, on the advice of his two attorneys general, Lord Elgin reserved several bills, one being a charter of incorporation for the Ontario, Simcoe and Huron Railroad. Robert Baldwin was deeply alienated from the expansionistic, speculating spirit that seemed to be taking the country over, and he was unhappy that the company's charter permitted a lottery form of subscription by which the equity would be shared among a number of subscribers chosen at random.[93]

When the next session began, H.J. Boulton, who had pushed the bill through the Assembly, moved for the production of all the correspondence on the reserved bills between the imperial and the provincial government. When Baldwin objected on the ground that the documents in question included the official opinions rendered by the law officers of the Crown, which were confidential, Boulton rejected his argument as inconsistent with the principles of responsible government. The provincial administration should not be able secretly to induce the imperial government to withhold the royal assent to colonial bills, and then escape responsibility by withholding the necessary information from the legislature; on the contrary, it should be under a constitutional requirement to inform the legislature before or during discussion of a measure if it intended to recommend reservation. In the present case, Boulton wished the Assembly to see 'not an opinion given by the law officers of the Crown, which he had no objection to consider as confidential; but ... the grounds on which the head of the government gave their [sic] advice to Ministers to reserve several of the bills of last session, and for which advice they [*sic*] have not made themselves responsible to the country.' Baldwin replied that, while the Crown officers' legal opinions were confidential, he was willing to state the government's reasons for recommending the reservation of any of the bills in question.[94]

The confusion surrounding the attorney general's dual political personality was illustrated again in 1852 in connection with the planned building of the Grand Trunk Railway from the New Brunswick border to the Detroit River. The railway was supposed to be part of an intercolonial line terminating in the east at Halifax. A Canadian enactment of 1851 had authorized the construction of the Grand Trunk in any of three ways, which it listed in order of preference: by means of an imperially guaranteed loan; failing that, by financial co-operation between the government and the province's municipalities; or, if neither of these methods proved feasible, by the co-ordinated action of private companies formed to build lines along different sections of the proposed route. Two such companies, the Montreal and Kingston Railway and the Kingston and Toronto Railway, had been incorporated in 1851 with a proviso suspending the operation of their charters until put in force by special proclamation.[95]

In 1852 the negotiations for an imperial loan guarantee collapsed and the intercolonial scheme with them, but Hincks decided to push ahead with the Grand Trunk. He had made up his mind to have the line built by a large British concern; but rather than have the 1851 act amended for that purpose, he had the Montreal-Kingston and Kingston-Toronto charters proclaimed in the expectation that the British firm would be able to take them over by subscribing for a majority of the shares. The Montreal-Kingston promoters thwarted his scheme, however, by subscribing the entire capital themselves, and he was forced to declare war on them by promoting the incorporation of a rival company to build a line from Montreal to Toronto. The Montreal-Kingston group protested against this proposal as an infringement upon their rights. The whole affair was investigated by the Legislative Assembly's standing committee on railways (whose chairman, Allan MacNab, had greeted the new era with the motto 'All my politics are railroads'). The committee concluded that the Montreal promoters' stock subscriptions had not been made in good faith, and that the new scheme was not an infringement upon their rights, but the battle continued until it was eventually settled by compromise.[96]

There was obviously something dubious about the government's first proclaiming the private companies' charters and then promoting a rival corporation. It was this suspicion that brought the attorney general's constitutional status once more before the Assembly. The government's critics moved for the production of all papers bearing on the decision to abandon the provincial-municipal funding option and put the companies into business, including any opinions the law officers had rendered on the legality of the government's actions. A debate ensued on the nature of the law officers' responsibility to the legislature and how it could be reconciled with their claim to confidentiality in rendering opinions to the Crown.

Opponents of the motion relied on British practice. The law officers, they maintained, were the confidential servants of the Crown, and the legislature had a right to the disclosure of their opinions only in certain special (but in the report unspecified) cases; in all others, disclosure was an act of grace on the part of the executive. In no case, however, were the law officers responsible for their opinions to the legislature, though the government was responsible for any actions taken on the basis of those opinions. In the present case, as it happened, there was no official opinion for which the law officers could be called to answer, since they had given their views orally in cabinet.[97]

Supporters of the motion rejected the British analogy because the Canadian law officers, unlike the English, were cabinet ministers. They were not independent of the executive and could not shelter behind it. As cabinet ministers they must be responsible for all their public acts; and in order that their responsibility might be enforced, it was necessary that their opinions be disclosed to the legislature upon request, unless the government could make a case that disclosure was not in the public interest. The present case, in which the law officers had been able to give an informal oral opinion on a highly controversial matter affecting private rights, constituted exactly the sort of circumstances that made their membership in the cabinet undesirable.

Of course, this sort of debate was unlikely to settle the question of the Crown officers' cabinet membership, or that of the confidentiality of their opinions, except in the most ad hoc fashion. On the second matter, the government imposed its views by defeating the motion for disclosure. The position first taken by Baldwin in 1850, and defended in 1852 by both William Badgley and Lewis Drummond (past and present attorneys general for Lower Canada) would be asserted as a general principle by John A. Macdonald in 1860.[98] The question of cabinet membership came up repeatedly during the next sixty years, both in the self-governing dominions and in Britain itself, but for Ontario it was settled by the British North America Act of 1867, which constituted the Dominion of Canada, with Ontario as one of its provinces. The act specified that the attorney general for Ontario was to belong to the Executive Council of the province.[99] In the new federal government the precedent was established by John A. Macdonald's assumption of office as attorney general and minister of justice.

Although these qualms about the attorney general's cabinet status were inconclusive, they may have had a saving side effect in influencing the Court of Chancery to take a broad view of the private citizen's standing in matters of public interest that might otherwise have been pursued only by means of a relator action. The occasion was another railway scandal. The mayor of Toronto had engaged in a highly profitable speculation in City of Toronto debentures issued to help the construction of the Ontario, Simcoe and Huron railway. His partner in this secret speculation had been none other than Premier Hincks. By-laws and a statute had been passed without which the profit could not have been made. As far as the mayor was concerned, it was a classic case of breach of trust by an officer of a corporation; yet when it was exposed in 1853 the city council refused to sue him on behalf of the municipality.

The outraged ratepayers' normal recourse would have been to apply to the attorney general for permission to institute a relator action. But the attorney general was W.B. Richards, the friend of big business and favourite cabinet colleague of the premier. Instead, five ratepayers sued the mayor for restitution of his share of the profit to the city. The mayor challenged their standing on the ground that the only proper form of action was a relator action, but the court allowed the case to proceed on the basis of a slender English precedent. The corporation later took the case over in order to prevent the case failing on appeal on the issue of the plaintiffs' standing; but *Paterson* v *Bowes* (later *Toronto* v *Bowes*) has subsequently been cited as a leading case on that issue. Victory on the substantive issue also went to the plaintiffs, who were represented by a brilliant young counsel called Oliver Mowat. When Richards, now a judge, heard the case in the Court of Appeal, he rendered a strong judgment against the mayor.[100]

A FOOL NO MORE

Between 1833 and 1846 the office of attorney general for Upper Canada had been transformed. From a lucrative vested interest, yielding a potentially limitless income to the possessor in fees for services, it had been converted into the sort of salaried employment enjoyed by ministers of the Crown today. In the process it had acquired a host of new duties, which caused it to diverge widely from its English prototype.

The attorney general had become the member of cabinet responsible to the legislature for the administration of justice – in a phrase, minister of justice. He had done so by adding to his traditional duties others which in England either pertained to the lord chancellor and the home secretary or (as also was true of legislative drafting) were subject to no effective ministerial supervision. Pre-eminent among such duties, as we shall see in the next chapter, were criminal prosecutions. In England in the 1850s the need for a single responsible minister of justice was to be proposed, in connection with the establishment of a system for the public supervision of criminal prosecutions, by jurists of the eminence of the former Lord Chancellor Brougham and Sir Alexander Cockburn, attorney general and later lord chief justice of England; but nothing much was done. The law officers continued to perform their traditional functions out of private chambers with the aid of their private clerks for another forty years, and they continued private practice until it was banned in 1894.[101] The attorney general for Upper Canada, by contrast, was already in the 1850s operating out of public offices with a publicly paid staff (although a small one). He had no time for private practice, although it was not forbidden, and had given up even prosecutions at assize, which had never formed part of his English counterpart's duties. Indeed, while the attorney general of England normally did appear for the Crown in important cases of crime against the state, the attorney general for Upper Canada would not appear even in the treason trials that followed the Fenian raids of 1866.[102]

The attorney general's rise to cabinet rank aroused controversy after it had happened, but it proved irreversible. Could it have been prevented?

Resisting a similar change in the status of the office in his colony, a South Australian judge of the 1860s noted that colonial executive councils commonly included the law officers of the Crown. His explanation was that such councils were merely advisory and the Crown officers therefore had no power to compel the adoption of their advice. The grant of responsible government automatically turned them into cabinet members for lack of a decision at that point to exclude them.[103]

This cannot fully explain the case of the Canadian law officers. It is true that their exclusion must have depended on a decision at Whitehall: specifically, a decision to devolve the executive responsibility for the administration of justice onto someone other than the attorney general. There was evidently no such impulse, either in 1840 or at other times; in

1851 the colonial secretary, Earl Grey, condemned Robert Baldwin's retention of the attorneyship after quitting the cabinet as 'very objectionable.' Yet Canada differs from the Australian model in that, except for Thomas Scott in 1805-6 and James Stuart in 1827-31, the law officers of Upper and Lower Canada did not belong to the Executive Council.[104] Their rise to cabinet rank in 1841 was not the result of mere institutional inertia – of prior membership in a body which then had executive responsibility thrust upon it; it flowed from a deliberate decision to include them in the cabinet – a decision that registered not only the predilections of the lawyers who led the contending factions but the exigencies of political management, which brought in the solicitors as well as the attorneys.

The same pragmatic considerations sustained the status quo against the criticism that surrounded both offices during Union. The solicitorship was not an essential office; in Upper Canada it was vacant from June 1841 to July 1842, from December 1843 to October 1844, and from August 1858 to February 1860. After 1867 the new province of Ontario would have only a single law officer, the attorney general.[105] But while not indispensable, the office was very useful. The solicitor could assume duties for which the attorney had no time; when the legislature was not in session he could take the busiest assize circuits, which cost the most in Crown counsel fees. To abolish the solicitorships in order to save £500 or £600 apiece a year would be a false economy, R.B. Sullivan told the select committee of 1850. Yet, useful as they were in these respects, the solicitors' survival seems to have been due to their political value. The goal of excluding them from cabinet was never achieved; D'Arcy McGee's report of 1863 reiterated the old recommendation to do so in order to free them to conduct the Crown litigation.[106]

During the 1840s the modern ministerial attorney general, just hatched from the chrysalis of the ancient proprietary officer, was drying and flexing his wings amid a carnivorous political fauna. The essence of the new office was twofold. First, the attorney general had acquired the constitutional responsibility of a minister of the Crown for the administration of justice in Upper Canada. Second, he was now responsible for the constitutionality of public administration in general – responsible not to the queen and Parliament in London but to the people of Upper Canada (and of the province as a whole) as represented in the legislature.

The resignation of Baldwin in 1851 brilliantly illuminated the importance of both innovations. The Upper Canadian members had manifested a lack of confidence in him as minister of justice for Upper Canada. But he resigned not because of the actual vote on the Court of Chancery, but because of its broader implication that he 'could have no hope of being able to sustain any of the Institutions of the Country' or procure a fair trial for measures designed to improve them.[107] This was a significant formula. The first part of it was potentially just as applicable to his traditional duty as attorney general as to his new role as minister of justice; for, as attorney general, he was responsible for sustaining not merely the institutions but the constitution of the country. A second implication was that the attorney general must resign if his inability to perform this vital function proceeded from any source at all – not only from the legislature, but equally from his colleagues in the Executive Council or cabinet. Mr Attorney was King Lear's fool no longer.

In fact, rather confusingly, he had become King Lear – or at least a member of the supreme executive committee that had succeeded King Lear. This raised doubts as to whether the attorney general could be relied on to advise impartially, or admonish effectually, a body of which he himself was a part, and often the head. The advent of responsible government had created conditions in which he could play an independent watchdog role in ensuring the constitutional administration of public affairs. How could his cabinet membership be reconciled with that role?

5

The Public Peace

The attorney general's neglect and eventual abandonment of the assize circuit had institutional as well as political consequences. It revived interest in the old question of appointing local Crown attorneys, and this time the debate resulted in legislation. The County Attorneys Act of 1857 instituted a system of liaison between the central and local authorities for the administration of justice, and above all for the conduct of criminal prosecutions, that lasted with little change for nearly a century. It was one of a number of important changes in the administration of criminal justice in the course of the nineteenth century. This chapter concentrates on three that are particularly relevant to themes that have already been sounded.

Like the County Attorneys Act, both the Felon's Counsel Act of 1836 and the formation of a provincial police force bore on the attorney general's duty to uphold law and order. In dealing with these topics in chronological order, we place them in anti-chronological order in terms of the process of law enforcement. The Felon's Counsel Act reformed trial procedure in criminal prosecutions at assize. The County Attorneys Act, in so far as it affected assize prosecutions, bore on pre-trial proceedings. The creation of a provincial police force, which was first debated in the mid-1850s but not fully achieved in Ontario until 1909, has to do with an earlier stage still. The chronological pattern is no accident; it reflects a gradual broadening of the attorney general's practical responsibility for law and order in the course of the century as the administration of law enforcement became more regular and centralized.

CAPITAL PUNISHMENT AND THE FELON'S COUNSEL ACT

The Felon's Counsel Act of 1836 was a major step towards establishing a more equitable balance between the Crown and the defendant in criminal trials.[1] It was only the latest in a series of steps that had gradually mitigated the rigour of criminal procedure as it existed in England in the late seventeenth century. At that time a person accused of a crime faced severe constraints in defending himself. He had no right to see the indictment by which he was accused, and he could learn its tenor only when he heard it read in court. He could not count on being able to call even friendly witnesses, let alone compel the attendance of unwilling ones, and his witnesses were not allowed to testify under oath. He had no advance knowledge of the witnesses the Crown intended to call. The rules of evidence were much less strict than they later became and gave undue weight to hearsay and the testimony of the defendant's alleged accomplices. The accused was denied the help of legal counsel in defending himself. After the Glorious Revolution of 1688, a more liberal current of opinion in procedural matters eventually led to the alleviation of most of these handicaps. Individuals charged with treason or misdemeanour became entitled to full defence by counsel. In the early 1830s, however, defence counsel in felony trials were still barred from addressing the court on the defendant's behalf, although by this time they were allowed to examine and cross-examine witnesses and to advise the accused on what to say in his own defence.[2] This was the system of criminal procedure that existed in Upper Canada by virtue of the imperial and provincial statutes establishing the criminal law of England in the province.[3]

In the 1820s this last remaining anomaly became a matter of concern to the Upper Canadian reformers. There are several possible reasons for this, but two stand out. First of all, in the United States the right to 'the assistance of counsel' was federally guaranteed by the Bill of Rights. Although the extent of that assistance was not specified, accused felons in both federal and state courts were generally entitled to full defence. The denial of such a privilege to accused felons in Upper Canada therefore appeared a glaring example of colonial tyranny.[4] Second, the gradual liberalization of criminal procedure after the Glorious Revolution was accompanied by a trend towards increased harshness in the substance of the criminal law. The number of capital statutes had grown tremendously by 1792, and it was the criminal law of England as it stood then that became the law of Upper Canada by the reception statute of 1800.[5] By the

1820s, the inability of an accused felon on trial for his life to enjoy the advantage of full defence by counsel was a goad to humanitarian consciences in England and Upper Canada alike.

By this time, in fact, the severity of the law was itself a matter of embarrassment. Partly it had developed as a concomitant of the liberalization of criminal procedure, since it could be argued that the harder it was to secure a conviction the more terrible the penalties of conviction ought to be. Partly it was due to the absence of effective punishments other than death, since in the eighteenth century there were no facilities for long-term imprisonment and transportation was considered no deterrent to the young and rootless malefactor. Partly it facilitated a paternalistic style of social control, since the sentence was often remitted as an ostentatious act of charity. Yet the tempering of justice with mercy was in practice all too random, and the randomness of the legal process was magnified when juries, fearing to trust to the judicial dispensation of mercy, refused to convict in capital cases where the defendant's guilt was clear. By the 1820s there was a widespread feeling in England in favour of a more rational, less arbitrary system of penalties, whereby crimes would be punished by graded sentences of imprisonment to which a jury would have no reluctance to commit a prisoner. These would be served in institutions of a penitentiary or reformatory nature in which hard labour would contribute to the redemption of the criminal.[6]

The same feeling was evident in Upper Canada. The comparative rarity of serious crime may have made the question press less heavily on the public conscience, but in thoughtful minds the anomaly was accentuated by the utter irrelevance of many of the punitive statutes to the state of provincial society. In 1823, William Warren Baldwin brought in a bill to declare that the provincial statute of 1792, which had received the English law as the rule of decision in matters relating to civil and property rights, had not been intended to import *every* English statute but merely that part of the law which was 'reasonable, fair and applicable.' He was especially concerned at the growing recourse to the criminal penalties attached to breaches of the game, excise, and stamp laws and at the tendency to use English criminal statutes such as the infamous Black Act of 1723, which had been passed in order to repress by capital punishment the popular resistance in forest regions to landowners' encroachments on the traditional economic rights of the common people. That act had provided for the punishment of individuals who committed certain crimes while armed and disguised, but it had been wrenched by judicial interpretation to apply to anyone who, while *either* armed *or* disguised, did almost anything which could be construed as a breach of the peace, if he or his action were obnoxious enough to the authorities.[7] In Upper Canada the act had recently been used to prosecute one man who had stolen a steer to feed his starving family, and another who had shot at a charivari party that beset his house one night. Baldwin feared that if the reception statutes of 1792 and 1800 were to be so broadly construed as to admit this and other irrelevant English statutes, it would afford scope for the discriminatory application of the law for repressive purposes.[8]

Baldwin's effort to stifle this 'serious and growing evil' was thwarted by Robinson and Hagerman, who misrepresented his bill as being calculated to exclude English statute law entirely and retain only the common law; this, they declared, would be tantamount to depriving the province of all law. Robinson suggested that it would be more sensible to consider the merits of all the questionable statutes one by one. Still, two years later he brought in a copy of the English act of 1823, which dispensed with the pronouncement of the death sentence except in cases where it was likely to be carried out. This was after his visit to England in 1825, where the need to find a proper substitute for the death penalty in cases of felony, when banishment meant only a one-way ticket to the United States and the colony lacked the funds to build and maintain a penitentiary, was one of the topics he raised at the Colonial Office on the instructions of Lieutenant-Governor Maitland. Within a few years the need for a provincial penitentiary had become widely recognized, and one was opened at Kingston in 1835.[9]

Given this climate of opinion, it was no coincidence that the first attempt, late in 1823, to enact a felon's counsel bill in Upper Canada arose from a debate in the Assembly on capital punishment. The mover was the American-born farmer from the Gore District, John Willson of Saltfleet, who was to be chosen as Speaker by the anti-government majority elected in 1824. In introducing resolutions calling for reform of the criminal law, he appealed both to the greater humaneness of the American criminal code and to the recent improvements in England, where Sir Robert Peel, in the first phase of a far-reaching reform that was to take several years, had just secured the repeal of a number of capital statutes and the enactment of the death-sentence statute mentioned above.[10] In his speech Willson advanced most of the arguments used to sustain the abolitionist cause in Britain. The death penalty was no deterrent to crime; it made society callous; it was contrary to Christian teaching; to prescribe it for offences of widely different magnitude brought the law into contempt by encouraging jurors to shirk their duty; appropriate penalties uniformly imposed would do more to suppress crime than excessive ones haphazardly applied.

John Beverley Robinson responded with the array of stand-pat arguments he trotted out whenever reform of the criminal law was proposed. To act before the text of the English statutes was available would be premature; he believed capital punishment was a deterrent; if Willson brought in a bill dealing with particular statutes he would be willing to discuss these one by one, but he would never assent to an attempt to reform the criminal law wholesale.[11] This resistance by the attorney general prompted Dr Baldwin to urge Willson to drop his resolutions and introduce a bill giving defendants in felony trials the right of full defence by counsel, and for the next dozen years the felon's counsel bill became an annual cause célèbre, like the bill to repeal the Sedition Act. Each year it was passed either unanimously or by lopsided majorities with only the Crown officers and one or two others dissenting. The election of a conservative Assembly in 1830 made no difference. And yet, as in the case of the sedition act repeal bill, as often as the bill was passed by the Assembly it was turned down by the Legislative Council.[12]

The tenor of the debate did not vary much from year to year. Opponents of the bill argued that it would import a confrontational aspect into felony trials like that which allegedly characterized them in the United States. According to Robinson, the Crown counsel's role in criminal prosecutions in Upper Canada was a neutral one: 'He confined himself to a statement of the evidence, and always laid before [the court] every thing that he knew favourable to the prisoner.' Full defence by counsel would only force him to use greater ingenuity in addressing the jury, and the prisoner might be worse off than he was now. 'Counsel would no doubt make strong appeals to the feelings of the Jury, and as the due administration of Criminal Justice might be interfered with by such appeals, it would become the paramount duty of a Crown prosecutor ... to address the Jury in a different manner, from that which he now found ... necessary.' If Robinson thought there was any chance of an innocent man being convicted under the present system he would support the bill, but experience showed that this was not the case; if ever a prisoner was convicted on doubtful evidence, he could depend on the clemency of the executive.[13]

Proponents of the bill rejected all of these arguments. Unjust convictions were not infrequent, maintained Christopher Hagerman in 1823, especially when the defendant was confronted with false and malicious testimony. The notion that Crown counsel played a neutral part in criminal trials was nonsense, declared John Rolph two years later. 'He never knew the crown officers to slacken their duty, or to interest themselves in the slightest degree for the prisoner.' How could they? The Crown officer came from York knowing nothing of the case; he was briefed on it by the magistrates responsible for committing the prisoner for trial; but did he ever visit the prisoner in his cell to get the other side of the story?

The reformers also heaped scorn on the other main justification for the present system – the notion that the judge served as counsel for the prisoner in protecting him from any abuse of due process. They maintained that this sort of ring-holding function, even when the judge practised it conscientiously, gave the prisoner no protection against the adversary eloquence of the Crown counsel; he could receive that only from a professional advocate. The reformers dwelt on the hardship even an educated man must feel in having to address the court in defence of his life and liberty. To a poor, uneducated man, unused to public speaking and perhaps conscious of being surrounded by hostile strangers, it was doubly cruel.[14]

The Upper Canadian debate survives only in fragmentary newspaper reports, but all these arguments were voiced in England too, and we can use English sources to amplify our understanding of the issues. The evidence heard by the Criminal Law Commissioners, and the report they based on it, stressed the defendant's difficulty in rebutting false evidence when it was sprung upon him in court. The notion that the judge was the defendant's counsel was 'too extravagant to require comment,' since the judge had no prior knowledge of the case and was too preoccupied during the trial with making notes on the evidence to examine it critically from the defendant's point of view. The supposed neutrality of the prosecuting counsel's address was of no benefit to the prisoner; a dispassionate yet coherent statement of the facts that had led to the prisoner's arraignment could be more telling than impassioned rhetoric, and it was much harder to counteract it by cross-examining the prosecution witnesses than by presenting a similar statement from the prisoner's perspective. Sometimes the defendant's counsel furnished a written statement for him to make in his defence; but if prepared before the trial it might not deal adequately with the testimony given in court, and if prepared during the trial it might suffer from undue haste. If the prisoner was illiterate, the statement would have to be read by the clerk of the court, and this was often incompetently done.[15]

English authorities were sometimes cited in Upper Canada. The reformers liked to quote Blackstone's disparagement of the rule as denying a man on trial for his life the aid that was allowed him in prosecutions for petty trespass. When the editor of a new edition of Blackstone, Sir John Taylor Coleridge, presumed to question the author's opinion, Robert Stanton, the king's printer and an old friend of Robinson's, hastened to publish the note in his newspaper. Since Coleridge relied heavily on the notion of the Crown counsel's impartiality and the judge's sympathy for the prisoner, his argument was not likely to convert reformers, and his alternative proposal to abolish the prosecutor's opening address seems to have received little air in either country.[16]

From time to time the controversy in Upper Canada was fuelled by a sensational trial. One such was that of Michael Vincent in 1828 for the murder of his wife. The evidence was circumstantial, and its uncertainty was increased by the coroner's failure to have the corpse professionally examined. The accused man, asserting that his wife had died of a fit, protested his innocence to the last. Two medical witnesses testified that the condition of the corpse was consistent with a violent death, but Vincent's counsel, John Rolph, insisted with all the authority of a London-trained surgeon that it was equally consistent with the prisoner's story.

Despite these uncertainties the presiding judge, Christopher Hagerman, delivered a charge to the jury that openly stated his belief that Vincent was guilty. In the process he displayed his difficulty with medical evidence by instructing the jury that a 'chronic' disease was one that affected the spine. Francis Collins remarked, 'We never felt the loss of that admirable measure proposed by Mr. Bidwell, and strenuously opposed by the Attorney General, the Felon's Counsel Bill, so forcibly as upon this occasion, when we saw the learning, the science, and the eloquence of Mr. Rolph stifled at a time when we thought the ends of justice demanded that they should be freely exercised. We do not see how any body of legislators, professing Christianity, could be so callous to every feeling of humanity as to deny the full benefit of defence by counsel in the last struggle for his life, no matter how atrocious the crimes with which he may be charged.' The final scene was in keeping with this travesty of justice. The knot slipped, and Vincent's life came to an end in fifteen minutes of tortured convulsion – much as his wife's may have.[17]

Usually, plenty of voices were to be heard on both sides of a case like Vincent's. Even in 1836, when the felon's counsel bill finally became law, one of its supporters cited a recent murder trial at Niagara only to be contradicted by another, the foreman of the jury on that occasion, who maintained that the defendant had been justly convicted. Still, it was widely held that innocent persons were convicted under the present system, and in Vincent's case at least the issue was less the defendant's guilt than his defencelessness in the face of a biased charge by the judge, who was supposed to be his protector against such abuses of process. By 1836 the hollowness of this and other arguments against the bill was so obvious that even Archibald McLean of Cornwall, formerly a diehard opponent, had stopped believing them. The measure had not yet been adopted in England, but the House of Commons had approved it and it was possible to predict its imminent enactment (which occurred later in the year). A similar enactment of the Lower Canadian legislature had been reserved for the consideration of the imperial government, but it was known that it was to receive the royal assent.[18] When reform was advocated by such an authority as the English attorney general, Sir Frederick Pollock, there could be no credible reply to Marshall Bidwell's denunciation of the existing law as a relic of the barbarous era when an accused person was presumed guilty until he could prove his innocence.

Of course, the Felon's Counsel Act did not completely remove a poor man's disabilities in court. Counsel normally expected to be paid. In England before 1836 the judge might at his discretion assign counsel to a penurious prisoner without fee, although only with the practitioner's consent. The Prisoner's Counsel Act as originally presented to the House of Commons bound the judge to assign counsel, subject to consent, but this provision was removed in committee and things stayed as before.[19] How things worked in Upper Canada, where the legal profession was less crowded and there was no great throng of counsel at the assizes hoping for business, remains to be seen. No doubt a prisoner on trial for his life always managed to obtain professional defence whether he could pay for it or not, since the barrister's oath was considered to impose an obligation like that of the Hippocratic oath.[20] Even in England, though, most defendants in the 1860s continued to face the court without counsel. In Ontario a generation later a defendant appearing at the assizes or before the county judge would 'often' be assigned counsel by the court, but the full benefits of the Felon's Counsel Act were not available to the poor until 1966, when the Legal Aid Act set up a publicly funded plan to assist needy litigants.[21] Three years earlier the u.s. Supreme Court had declared that the Bill of Rights obliged state governments to provide counsel in non-capital cases if the defendant could not obtain it himself.[22]

THE CROWN'S RIGHT OF REPLY

In Upper Canada one aspect of the debate over the Felon's Counsel Act was particularly relevant to the office of attorney general. It concerned trial procedure. In England, one of the leading points of discussion was the precise order of proceeding to be introduced by the new measure. The obvious answer was that it should be the order that prevailed in trials for misdemeanour and in civil actions at common law. The prosecuting counsel stated his case and then adduced evidence in its support. If the defendant intended to produce evidence, his counsel would follow a similar course, after which the prosecuting counsel was entitled to make a closing speech commenting on the case as a whole. To this the defence could not reply. If, as happened in Robert Randal's trial for perjury in 1825, the defendant produced no evidence of his own, the case went to the jury after his counsel's statement without any reply by the prosecution.

The bill's most enthusiastic proponents felt that this was unfair to the accused, since he could not call witnesses in his defence without exposing himself to the detrimental effect that a closing statement for the prosecution might have on the jury – a statement that might contain misrepresentations of the evidence which the judge might overlook and the defendant be unable to correct. Sir Frederick Pollock averred that unless the defence was allowed to reply to the prosecution's closing remarks, he would consider the existing system, unjust as it was, preferable to the reform; the glaring injustice of the present procedure might at least benefit the defendant by gaining him the jurors' sympathy. Despite the support of Lord Chancellor Brougham, however, the clause giving the defendant the final word to the jury was eliminated by the House of Lords.[23]

In Upper Canada, the question of the final word had special importance because criminal prosecutions at assize were normally conducted by the law officers of the Crown, who enjoyed a traditional but ill-defined right to the last word in cases in which they appeared, regardless of the normal procedure. The extent of the right was the subject of sporadic controversy in eighteenth- and nineteenth-century England because it was hard to justify on grounds of equity. In the eighteenth century there was a tendency to limit it to state prosecutions, but in 1837, after the Prisoner's Counsel Act was passed, the judges resolved in conclave that 'in cases of public prosecutions for felony, instituted by the Crown, the Law Officers of the Crown, and those who represent them, are, in strictness, entitled to the reply, although no evidence is produced on the part of the prisoner.'

The 1840s saw a tendency also to admit the right in civil actions in which the Crown was directly concerned. After mid-century, trial judges tended to restrict the right to the law officers in person and to deprecate it as unconscionable even in that case. The limitation was officially embraced by the judges in 1884; and though the right was claimed by the law officers as late as 1922, it has since fallen into disuse.[24]

Although the evidence is scanty, it seems that the Upper Canadian law officers exerted the right to the last word more generally than was admitted in England even by the formula of 1837. Even that rule extended the right only to 'public prosecutions for felony, instituted by the Crown.' In Upper Canada, though, it seems to have been invoked habitually, even in the privately instituted prosecutions that the Crown officers conducted (as in England they did not) in exercising their monopoly of prosecutions at assize. At any rate, the practice was cited more than once to show why the benefit of full defence by counsel was even more urgently needed in Upper Canada than in England.[25]

To be sure, the precise extent to which the right was relied upon is uncertain. In 1823, John Beverley Robinson denied that he ever claimed it when the defendant produced no evidence.[26] He limited himself to a personal denial, however, and this, together with the fact that the reason was still being urged in 1836, suggests that other Crown officers were less scrupulous. One clue to the extent to which the right was claimed is given by Randal's perjury trial. This was a case of misdemeanour, and Randal enjoyed full defence by counsel; yet the prosecution was instituted not by the Crown but by private persons. J.B. Macaulay was conducting the prosecution expressly as the solicitor general's deputy, Boulton having stepped aside because of his personal imbroglio with Randal. Macaulay's claim to address the jury after Rolph had done so was turned down because he was not a law officer. The case does not prove that the Crown officers regularly invoked the right of reply in private prosecutions for felony, in which the defendant's counsel was not allowed to address the court; however, it does suggest that they claimed it in private prosecutions for misdemeanour, and even this was a broader assertion of the right than was admitted by the English formula of 1837.[27]

In this question, as in others having to do with the administration of criminal justice, the inability of the law officers after 1837 to attend every assize created uncertainty. The matter came to a head in 1863 as a result of a burglary trial at the Huron and Bruce assizes. The prisoner called no witnesses, and his counsel accordingly addressed the jury. The Crown counsel claimed the right of reply as the representative of the attorney general. The defence protested but was overruled by the chief justice of Upper Canada, Archibald McLean. On an application for a new trial, the judges of the Court of Common Pleas were divided on the question. Chief Justice Draper admitted that Crown counsel enjoyed the right of reply in cases where the Crown was directly concerned, such as state prosecutions or a prosecution for assault upon a customs or other public officer. In ordinary prosecutions like the present he had always ruled against the claim unless the attorney general was prosecuting in person. Draper was supported by Justice Joseph Curran Morrison but opposed by Justice W.B. Richards, who relied on the English formula of 1837.[28]

As noted above, however, the 1837 rule applied only to 'public prosecutions for felony *instituted by the Crown.*' This hardly appears to justify Richards's reasoning, and the cases cited also contradict it. In 1829 in England, in a prosecution for malicious libel on the prime minister, the Duke of Wellington, the defence contested the right of reply on the ground that the prosecution had been initiated by Wellington in his private capacity, but the attorney general replied that he himself was appearing in his official capacity and made good his claim to reply. That same day, though, in a prosecution for a libel on the lord chancellor, he stated that he was appearing in a private capacity and did not claim the right. In a case decided in 1845 on which Richards also relied, on the ground that it had been decided by a former English attorney general, who ought to know what he was talking about, Chief Baron Pollock allowed the Crown counsel the last word on his claiming to represent the attorney general; but that case concerned a postmistress stealing money from letters delivered to her office. In other cases the controversy over the right to reply either turned on different points or went against the Crown.[29]

This controversy of 1863 is evidence of a deviation from English practice, and it casts retrospective light on Upper Canadian practice before 1836. Even Draper, who was less ready than Richards to give the last word to the Crown, went beyond the 1837 formula in his willingness to allow the right of reply to the attorney general in person in ordinary prosecutions. This suggests that the law officers had regularly claimed the right in ordinary prosecutions before 1836. It is noteworthy, too, that the divergence from English practice was entrenched in legislation three years later.

In England the Common Law Procedure Act of 1854 had altered procedure in civil actions at common law in a way that prompted efforts to remedy the defects in the Prisoner's Counsel Act by introducing a similar reform in criminal procedure.[30] The Criminal Evidence and Practice Act of 1865 provided that, if a prisoner defended by counsel did not intend to produce any evidence, the prosecuting counsel was to address the jury a second time before the defending counsel delivered his address. If the defence did call witnesses, though, the prisoner or his counsel was to be allowed not merely an introductory address but a closing address in summary of the defence case. This applied whether or not the prisoner was assisted by counsel.[31]

The civil procedure reform of 1854 had quickly been copied in Upper Canada.[32] So in its turn was the act of 1865; but with two significant exceptions in favour of the Crown. First, the licence to the prosecution to address the jury a second time in closing its case was not limited to occasions when the prisoner was defended by counsel. Second, the right of reply was allowed in every case 'to the Attorney and Solicitor General, and to any Queen's Counsel having written authority from either of them for that purpose.'[33] The English act, by contrast, merely stated that 'the Right of Reply ... save as hereby altered, shall be as at present.' The effect of the English legislation, then, was to prolong the uncertainty evident in the case law and to foster the trend towards a more restrictive interpretation of the right to reply until, in 1884, the judges limited it to cases in which the attorney general or solicitor general appeared in person. The Canadian statute, by contrast, defined the scope of the right precisely and in a way that established the right both of the Crown officers in person and of their deputies, even in ordinary (as opposed to state) prosecutions. The federal Criminal Procedure Act of 1869 repealed the requirement for written authority.[34]

The change did not pass unchallenged. In 1880 Thomas Robertson of Hamilton, a Conservative backbencher, introduced a bill in the House of Commons to restrict the right to the law officers of the Crown, as in England. Robertson had been born in Ancaster in 1827, the very year in which his father and grandfather, Alexander Robertson and Titus G. Simons, were sued by George Rolph in the tar-and-feather case. In 1857 he had become the first county attorney for Wentworth.[35] At the time he brought in his bill, criminal defendants had not yet been granted the right to testify on oath at their trial. Robertson argued that it was unfair to a defendant so handicapped, if he had no witnesses to call in his defence, to have his (or his counsel's) statement to the jury subsequently undermined by the Crown prosecutor. If the Crown were always represented by experienced counsel, who appreciated their position 'as standing between the prisoner and the people,' the right of reply might safely be left with them. In fact, though, Crown prosecutors were often young men who seemed to think that their reputation was compromised if they failed to secure a conviction.[36]

Despite his credentials as a former county attorney, Robertson did not get a sympathetic hearing. Malcolm Crooks Cameron, a future Ontario High Court judge, denied that Crown prosecutors ever departed from the canons of impartiality that ought to govern them; if they did they should not be Crown prosecutors. He dwelt on the difficulty of securing a conviction. 'As a general thing,' he told the House,

the prisoner is tried by his peers, and he has the advantage of every technicality of the law that is open to him. He has the advantage of being zealously defended by the ablest men of the Bar. He has the right of challenge [to jurors], and he almost always has the sympathy of the people ... After the usually able and impassioned appeals that are made to juries by prisoner's counsel on behalf of their client, it is only fair that the Crown should have a chance of calmly, deliberately, fairly and honestly stating the facts and of analyzing the testimony submitted to the jury.

Every other speaker supported Cameron, and Robertson's effort to adjust the balance in criminal trials was defeated. In 1892 the Criminal Code extended the right of reply to all Crown counsel (not merely to queen's counsel as previously) representing the attorney general in a criminal prosecution.[37]

From time to time the right of reply continued to be resisted. In 1893 the chief justice of Manitoba, Thomas Wardlaw Taylor, interpreted the Criminal Code as conferring a right to address the jury at the close of the evidence, not after the closing speech for the defence. The report of the case rightly noted that Taylor's decision was questionable and went on to review some of the precedents and authorities. In 1905, after extensive discussion, the Ontario Court of Appeal decided that the right belonged to every Crown prosecutor on the ground that every Crown prosecution was under the direction of the attorney general.[38] A notable instance of its baneful use occurred during the trial of the Finnish communist Aaro Vaara in 1929 for seditious libel. Vaara, the editor of a Finnish-language newspaper, had published an article that dared to suggest that the king's health was of little concern to the exploited workers of the empire. He was convicted, despite a masterly defence by a future attorney general of Ontario, Arthur Roebuck, and later deported. The Crown's right to the last word to the jury remained in the Criminal Code until the revision of 1968-9.[39]

CRIMINAL PROSECUTIONS AND THE COUNTY ATTORNEYS ACT

Even before the Felon's Counsel Act was passed in 1836, the putative felon was not devoid of procedural advantages; they were not ones on which he could rely, however. The chief of them was the minute accuracy of detail demanded by the common law in an indictment. Even the most trivial error or omission in the description of parties or circumstances could lead to the acquittal of the most palpably guilty defendant. So could the omission of time-hallowed Latin formulae that had long since lost their raison d'être. In England in 1800 a prisoner convicted of forgery escaped punishment when, just as the judge was about to utter the death sentence, it was noticed that the forged note was not signed 'Bartholomew Browne,' as stated in the indictment, but 'Bartw. Browne.'[40] Since pre-trial proceedings commonly took place under the aegis of the unpaid lay magistrates who were responsible for local petty justice, such inaccuracies were common. In Upper Canada, where the magistrates were often ill-educated and indifferently literate (or where, as William Dummer Powell had nicely put it, 'the Selection for the administration [of justice] in detail was necessarily made from a population which affords none better'), the problem was that much worse.[41]

The problem was not limited to the drafting of indictments. The magistrates were also responsible for examining the complainant and any witnesses, preparing written depositions of their evidence, and binding them by means of monetary recognizances to appear in court on the appointed day to perform their part in the trial. This was often slackly done; and, according to Powell, negligence was even more common in the case of major offences than minor ones because prosecutions at assize, unlike those at quarter sessions, were conducted at the Crown's expense and not at that of the complainant or the district. Even if the indictment was in good order, the Crown counsel might have to go into court improperly briefed, and once in court he might find that the complainant (the prosecutor, as he was called) or a vital witness was absent. These defects could be dealt with by instituting a public officer, properly qualified, to take charge of pre-trial procedure.[42]

A third reason for such an office was the prevention of malicious prosecutions. Unfettered initiative in instituting criminal prosecutions allowed personal vindictiveness to be gratified by frivolous or unconscionable proceedings. The desirability of sifting out such cases was one of arguments that John Beverley Robinson and his supporters urged in 1828 against allowing prosecutors at the assizes to proceed by counsel of their choice. They were able to cite a speech of Sir Robert Peel's in the House of Commons two years earlier that had recommended the appointment of public prosecutors on this ground.[43]

Certain charges, such as assault and perjury, especially lent themselves to the gratification of malice. The persecution of Singleton Gardiner included a malicious prosecution for assault and that of Robert Randal a malicious prosecution for perjury. Perjury charges often issued from litigation in other courts, as when William Lyon Mackenzie was presented to the grand jury of the Home District assizes in 1836 after the jailer had unsuccessfully sued the city of Toronto for money he claimed Mackenzie had promised him when mayor.[44] Chancery litigation was an especially fruitful source of perjury prosecutions because proceedings in equity entailed the alternate submission of sworn statements by the contestants.[45] In the 1840s, James E. Small was one Crown counsel who made it a rule never to draw an indictment for perjury on an unsubstantiated personal complaint; he insisted that the charge should first be investigated by a magistrate or authenticated by a grand-jury presentment. To Chief Justice Robinson only a magistrate's hearing would do, since the grand jury heard complaints in secret and often without the accused party's knowledge.[46] Such rules of thumb helped to impose discipline on the vengeful prosecutor, but they were no substitute for a careful sifting of the evidence by a public prosecutor resident in the locality.

The early statements of the need to make pre-trial proceedings more regular and efficient differed as to whether the task should be assigned to the clerk of the peace or to a special officer. Powell's memorial at the beginning of the century proposed a special officer, a 'young Gentleman of the Bar,' in each district, with the rank of king's counsel and a £100-a-year retainer, who would assist and advise the magistrates in their judicial functions and take charge of the documents in cases pending at the assizes. He would act as the attorney general's assistant in protecting the interests of minors, orphans, and other traditional Crown wards in the locality, and provide the government, through the attorney general, with information as to 'what was passing ... as to general manners, and the observance, or non observance, of positive Laws.' He would 'point [the magistrates'] attention to the objects of police which want regulation and hold a hand to the execution of the laws in those respects.' ('Police' meant the general regulation of matters of public safety, health, welfare, and morals, for which the magistrates were responsible as the local government and petty judiciary.) The House of Assembly also embraced the idea of a special officer in passing the district attorneys bill in 1823. In

1811, though, Powell suggested merely that the responsibility for certain preliminary proceedings should be distinctly assigned to the district clerk of the peace: namely, taking charge of the papers in trials pending at the assizes, making sure that the prosecutor and witnesses in each case were properly bound over to appear, and preparing a brief of each case for the information of the Crown counsel when he arrived on circuit.[47]

As we saw in chapter 3, there is an important ambiguity about the early proposals to put preliminary procedure in assize prosecutions in charge of a special officer. It is unclear whether his duties were to be confined to pre-trial proceedings or were to include conducting the prosecution. Neither of Powell's proposals specified the conduct of prosecutions, but his first suggestion of a 'king's counsel,' entitled to wear silk, certainly implies it. No details survive of the bill of 1823, but its title also implies the conduct of prosecutions – if, as seems reasonable, 'district attorney' meant the same as in the United States. All three proposals have come down to us in a historical context that implies the conduct of prosecutions – the discontent at the amount of money paid to the law officers of the Crown for travelling the assize circuits.

There was a third option. Even if his duties in assize prosecutions were restricted to the preliminary phase, the local Crown attorney might still act as public prosecutor at the quarter sessions, where there was no equivalent to the Crown counsel and prosecutors proceeded by their private counsel or with none, as in England. When the question of appointing local Crown attorneys arose again at mid-century, the main area of doubt would be whether they should prosecute in both courts or at quarter sessions alone.

In the 1840s a variety of circumstances made the question of appointing local Crown prosecutors at once more pressing and less controversial. Even after their fees were commuted in 1833, the law officers had retained an interest in travelling the assize circuit because of the private business it generated. After Union this ceased to be a practical consideration, for the attorney general in particular. At the same time the attorney general had to find Crown counsel for an increasing number of assizes, which meant going through his personal list of eligible practitioners to find someone willing to attend at this, that, and the other assize town. Since Crown counsel received no travel allowance, the assignments often depended on who had private business at the place in question. The problem was magnified when the legislature was in session and MPPs could not take assize work.[48]

The resulting ad hoc system weakened the administration of justice by its lack of continuity. Robert Baldwin devised reporting forms for Crown counsel and a routine for handling assize papers,[49] but the chaotic situation described by James Patton (a future solicitor general) in 1855 differed little from that depicted half a century previously by Powell. The Crown counsel would appear at the assizes knowing little or nothing of the business he had to conduct. In cases held over from the last assizes, his precursor might have left no notes to guide him. New cases had to be hastily mastered from preliminary documents that often left it unclear what charges the evidence would sustain. Witnesses and vital papers might be missing, leading to delay in the preparation of indictments for the grand jury. Often the case had to be held over until the next half-yearly assizes.

At the quarter sessions, according to Patton, things were in some ways worse for lack of any public prosecutor at all. The clerk of the peace prepared indictments to the best of his ability, but he often lacked the thorough knowledge of criminal law and procedure necessary to deciding what charges the evidence would sustain and what other evidence must be gathered to support the charges that seemed apt. His lack of skill often appeared in defectively framed indictments that allowed wrongdoers to escape on a technicality. In the absence of a prosecuting counsel, the task of examining witnesses for the Crown fell to the chairman of the court, who was forced thereby to combine the offices of judge and Crown prosecutor. If the defendant was represented by counsel, the chairman might find himself having to decide in his judicial capacity challenges to his own proceedings as prosecutor.

True, the prosecutor might employ counsel privately; but why should private citizens have to pay for the efficient prosecution of crime, which was a matter of public interest, even if they could afford it? As it was, individuals were often deterred from reporting crimes by the knowledge that they themselves would be bound over to prosecute the offence and would either have to pay for counsel or leave the case to the talents of the court. The keenest in coming forward were often the least desirable – the malicious prosecutors who should not be allowed to proceed. In those prosecutions especially, but even in legitimate ones, privately retained counsel often flouted the supposed duty of a prosecuting counsel to present the facts dispassionately and impartially.[50]

It is hard to believe that the administration of justice was quite as inefficient at mid-century as it had been fifty years previously, but in 1866 John A. Macdonald could still speak of 'illiterate magistrates' in the rural parts.[51] In any case, even if the magistrates and clerks of the peace were generally of a higher calibre than their forerunners, they bore a greater responsibility. The court of quarter sessions now had a much broader jurisdiction, with power to sentence convicts to up to seven years in the penitentiary. Individual magistrates enjoyed extensive powers of summary conviction, subject to appeal. When, in the 1840s, the call for the institution of public prosecutors began to be heard again, the act of 1841 that had started this extension of jurisdiction was cited as a reason for appointing local Crown attorneys to conduct prosecutions at the quarter sessions as well as the assizes.[52]

It is probably no coincidence that the revival of interest in the idea occurred in 1846, the year after the Criminal Law Commissioners in England published their report on criminal procedure. In the context of rapid urban growth and a rising crime rate, the inefficiency of the English police system had become a matter of increasing concern. The idea of appointing public prosecutors had been recommended to Parliament as early as 1798. In the 1820s it had been advocated by Jeremy Bentham, whose theoretical writings on government were by mid-century the strongest influence on proponents of administrative reform. Lord Chief Justice Denman told the commissioners: 'Our procedure for the purpose of preliminary inquiry is open to great objection. The injured party may be helpless, ignorant, interested, corrupt. He is altogether irresponsible; yet his dealing with the criminal may effectually defeat justice. On general principles, it would evidently be desirable to appoint a public prosecutor.'[53] The report went out of its way to make a case for the innovation but concluded that the subject needed more consideration.

This did not happen for another decade; but in 1854 the House of Commons appointed a select committee to look into the matter. Their report exposed a state of affairs much like that in Upper Canada but in many ways worse. Although by the 1850s the cost of a prosecution was partly reclaimable from public funds, the initial outlay still fell on the prosecutor himself and might not be reimbursed unless he was able to carry the action to a conviction. The effort of undertaking the process of detection, capture, and prosecution often deterred victims from pursuing offenders, and it was said that the expense was sometimes a deterrent to poor people even when they wanted to prosecute. As in Upper Canada, the trouble was least likely to deter the vindictive prosecutor; but the select committee also heard about the extortionate prosecutor who instituted proceedings in order to be bribed to drop them (offences such as keeping a bawdy-house or gaming-house were especially subject to this abuse). Even a prosecutor who instituted proceedings with honest intent might succumb to a bribe, if he was poor and feared that his attorney or his witnesses were corruptible.

Apart from the value of having genuine prosecutions efficiently conducted, these loopholes and abuses argued for the provision of a 'superintending mind' – a public officer who would institute inquiries into crimes where necessary, pursue suspects, ensure that the evidence was enough to secure conviction, take steps to stay proceedings if it was not, and take care that no prosecution, once instituted, should founder owing to the corruption of the prosecutor or his attorney. He would also institute proceedings in cases where no private citizen was interested in or capable of doing so; for instance, in the murder of a stranger or in the abuse of children by their parents or of servants by their masters.[54]

It is doubtful that things were as bad in Upper Canada in the 1840s and 1850s as they were in England. For one thing, at the assizes at least, prosecutors did not have the right to choose their own counsel (unless the case was one in which the Crown counsel thought it improper to proceed; but such a case was unlikely to be accepted by the grand jury). For another, the legal profession was not as overcrowded as in England, where a host of hungry attorneys and barristers clustered at the assizes, ready to take on any prosecution without inquiring too closely into the motives of the prosecutor.[55] Still, James Patton's editorial of 1855 shows that the defects in the administration of criminal justice in the province went beyond the fiscal and political concerns that loomed largest in the reported remarks of the politicians – remarks that tended to focus on the law officers' failure to attend the assizes and their alleged choice of substitutes according to political criteria instead of professional competence.

The idea of creating local public prosecutors may have been first revived by Sandfield Macdonald. In 1846 he proposed establishing district attorneys on the American model to prosecute at the quarter sessions, where many offenders were getting away for want of a prosecutor.[56] The select committee on public income and expenditure in 1850 heard three more proposals. William Hamilton Merritt, entrepreneur of the Welland Canal and now (though a cabinet minister himself) a vigorous campaigner for economy in government, suggested 'that an Attorney should be appointed in each County, to be called the County Attorney, who should have the conduct of all the ordinary criminal prosecutions, both at the Assizes and at the Sessions.' A resident prosecuting counsel at each assize town would speed up the pre-trial process and greatly reduce the delay the present system imposed on prosecutors, witnesses and grand jurors. James E. Small proposed that such an official, whom he called 'a resident Counsel for the Crown ... in each County,' should be paid out of local funds, not the central treasury. S.B. Harrison, the former provincial secretary, in a throwback to Powell's proposal of 1811, suggested merely that 'In many cases, where they are competent to the performance of the duty, I think the Clerks of the Peace in the several Counties might be advantageously employed to perform the Crown business at the Assizes as well as at the Quarter Sessions.'[57]

A year later the cynical Tory attack on the ad hoc system reached its height. Amid the hungry bray of Allan MacNab, John Prince, and the like, however, more realistic contributions were made by John A. Macdonald and by Joseph Curran Morrison, who was shortly to become solicitor general under Hincks. Macdonald, as we saw in chapter 4, was ready to admit that the attorney general could no longer attend the assizes, and merely called for a more discriminating selection of substitutes.[58] Morrison went further in proposing that the ad hoc system be abolished in favour of resident local prosecutors. Two months later H.J. Boulton brought in a bill for the appointment of 'county barristers.' The bill was supported in principle by ex-Solicitor General Cameron but opposed by both Crown officers (Baldwin and Sandfield Macdonald), and Boulton withdrew it. There was another abortive attempt at legislation in the session of 1854-5, before John A. Macdonald brought in the bill that became law.[59]

The increasing support for the concept both in Upper Canada and England suggested that its time had come; yet Macdonald's measure did not escape controversy. Criticism was focused both on its scope and on the proposed method of appointment. The county attorney was to be the public prosecutor as a matter of course at the quarter sessions, but he was to prosecute at the assizes only when the attorney general made no special appointment. While the appointment of resident prosecutors to the assizes as well as to the quarter sessions would have abolished all the patronage provided by the ad hoc appointment of Crown counsel, this half-measure preserved all that patronage and created a large number of new offices for him to fill. In typical style, the Toronto *Globe* branded the measure 'The Wholesale Patronage Bill.'

When we read the title of this Bill, we supposed these County Attorneys were to take the place of Crown Counsel at the Assizes. We were prepared to admit that a permanent local officer, if competent to take charge of the criminal business before the higher Courts, would be preferable to the half-fledged legal deputies whom the Attorney General now sends into the counties to bungle the criminal business for a few days, and who are, perhaps, never seen again in the neighbourhood. The expectation that the proposed system would put an end to the *sopping* of members of Parliament who happen to be lawyers with a 'circuit' induced us to suspend our opinion until we saw the bill. But we find the 'County Attorney' is not to supersede the Crown officer.[60]

Macdonald defended the bill as a scheme 'to introduce a complete local system for the efficient administration of criminal justice.' He played on his critics' disagreements. One school believed that the office of county attorney should be merged with that of clerk of the peace. Macdonald adopted this position in preference to a radical's argument that to restrict the clerkship to lawyers was undesirable since they 'had too much of a monopoly of affairs already.' He promised that the new officer would normally act at the assizes as well as the sessions, but refused to say so in the act lest he limit his discretion to appoint special prosecutors in cases where local jealousies or other circumstances required it. As to the mode of appointment, his critics were divided between those (such as William Lyon Mackenzie) who favoured the American elective principle and those who would leave the matter to the county council. Macdonald argued that 'the government were responsible for the administration of justice, and how could they be responsible if the officers who administered justice were appointed by other and irresponsible parties?' Solicitor General Henry Smith quoted the maxim that 'wherever the Queen prosecuted, she ought to appoint the officer who prosecuted.'[61]

The officer created by the County Attorneys Act was to be a barrister of at least three years' standing, resident in the county, and was to be appointed by the governor during pleasure. He was to be a part-time official, paid by fees for the services he performed and entitled to conduct private practice as long as it did not interfere with his official duties. The proviso meant that, unlike queen's counsel, he was barred from acting as defending counsel in any criminal trial, a ban that applied also to his partners in practice. Clerks of the peace who were barristers were to be eligible for the office, and henceforth all new clerks of the peace were to be barristers of the requisite standing and county attorney ex officio.

The new officer's duties were numerous and important. The county attorney was to receive from the magistrates and the coroner all the papers connected with criminal charges and, upon examining them, to institute further investigations and gather additional evidence as appeared requisite. He was to compel the attendance of witnesses and the production of papers by subpoena if necessary, so that prosecutions might not be unduly delayed. He was to institute and conduct prosecutions at quarter sessions on the part of the Crown in the same manner as the law officers at the assizes and with the same privileges, save that of entering a nolle prosequi to stay proceedings. He was to watch over prosecutions brought by private prosecutors at quarter sessions 'wherein it is questionable if the conduct complained of be punishable by law, or where the particular act or omission presents more of the features of a private injury than a public offence; and without unnecessarily interfering with private individuals, who wish in such cases to prosecute, to assume wholly the conduct of the case where justice towards the accused seems to demand his interposition.' At the assizes, he was to deliver the papers to the Crown officer or his appointed substitute, assist him with the criminal business as required, and take charge of it himself when no outside counsel was appointed. He was also to institute and conduct proceedings before the magistrates for a variety of offences of a police nature punishable on summary conviction. He was to advise the magistrates on criminal matters upon receipt of a written request stating a particular case. Finally, he was to perform certain non-legal functions connected with the courts; in particular, he was to supersede the county treasurer as the receiver of fees paid in the local civil courts.[62]

The County Attorneys Act can be seen as the last act of the era of reform in the administration of justice that began with the Judicature Acts of 1849 and took in the Common Law Procedure Act of 1856 and the criminal appeals statutes of 1851 and 1857.[63] The office of county attorney was a distinctive Upper Canadian creation, and like other distinctive Canadian institutions it was a blend of American and British ideas. The idea of a local public attorney drew on both American and Scottish examples; a general British influence is evident in the rejection of the elective principle and a distinctively English one in the preservation of the private citizen's right to conduct a criminal prosecution by counsel of his own choosing (although, as we saw in chapter 3, in Upper Canada this right had always been limited to the quarter sessions). Perhaps English influence is also evident in the timing of the measure: the idea had been in the air since William Dummer Powell floated it early in the century, but it was not effected until English opinion seemed to be moving decisively in the same direction.

'Upper Canada is greatly dependent upon England in matters of law reform,' generalized a professional journal in 1858. 'It is the policy of our Legislature to await the working of a reform in England before hazarding an experiment here.'[64] This is not quite what happened in the case of the County Attorneys Act. As with the Felon's Counsel Act of 1836, the legislature jumped the gun; but this time Parliament remained glued to the starting-blocks by a combination of vested interest in the status quo and constitutional scruple at interfering with a traditional private right. As a result, divergence between Upper Canadian and English practice in criminal prosecutions became wider still. In England prosecutions remained substantially in private hands. In Upper Canada the new law did not authorize the county attorney to assume the conduct of all criminal proceedings at the quarter sessions as a matter of course in the way that the attorney general or his deputy had always taken them over at the assizes, but the fact that he was to be paid out of public funds for conducting them created a strong incentive for the prosecutor to waive the privilege of proceeding by private counsel.

This divergence of practice reinforced the difference in attitude towards the rights of the private prosecutor in England and in Canada. In Ontario it could be said by 1895 that 'no county judge will try a person accused unless the prosecution is conducted by a crown officer; neither will a judge of assize.'[65] In England, no public supervision of the prosecutorial process was instituted until 1879, and then it was strictly limited. The power was vested in a single officer, the director of public prosecutions, who was to have no more than six assistants and was to intervene only in cases of exceptional importance or difficulty, or where special circumstances or a failure to proceed seemed to imperil the due prosecution of an offender. If the director instituted a prosecution and then abandoned it, any party interested in the prosecution was entitled to appeal to a judge for permission to assume it himself or for an order to the director to resume it. The legislation provided that nothing in the act was to interfere with the right of any person to institute, undertake, or carry on any criminal proceeding.[66] In the twentieth century, the private prosecutor in England experienced a significant diminution of his powers, starting with a statute of 1908 that entitled the director of public prosecutions to take over any prosecution at his discretion and abolished the right of appeal against his abandonment of proceedings. Nevertheless, English judges long continued to cite the right of an individual to carry on a prosecution as an important constitutional safeguard of individual liberty, whereas their Canadian counterparts tended to condemn the practice for its propensity to produce uncertainty and unfairness.[67]

Although the County Attorneys Act undoubtedly contributed in the long term to a deterioration in the position of the private prosecutor, an effort has been made to interpret it in a libertarian light. Critics of the increasing centralization of the administration of criminal justice in Ontario in the 1960s argued that the county attorney was conceived as a semi-autonomous officer, who compensated for the attorney general's cabinet membership by distancing him from the prosecutorial process and thereby lessened the danger of political interference.[68]

We noticed in chapter 4 the anxiety lest the attorney general's cabinet membership prevent his impartial discharge of his office. While this anxiety was applicable to his quasi-judicial functions with respect to relator actions and criminal prosecutions, however, it always tended to be voiced in reference to another aspect of his duty: that of giving the cabinet impartial legal advice. The incompatibility of cabinet rank with the attorney general's prosecutorial functions was mentioned only in deploring the fact that his political duties were keeping him away from the assizes. The controversy in the 1820s over the law officers' allegedly biased performance of their prosecutorial duties was not renewed at mid-century.[69]

Certainly, nothing is reported to have been said on the subject during the discussions of the 1850s on the setting-up of local Crown prosecutors. In the legislature, the debate always revolved around three familiar preoccupations of the era: economy, efficiency, and the elimination of patronage. The comments of the *Upper Canada Law Journal* were confined to efficiency. The *Globe* saw the measure as far from devolutionary: 'It seems to be admitted that under our system the administration of justice should be controlled by the Executive, that it should be centralized in the hands of the general government, in order that there may be uniformity of interpretation and equal enforcement; that there may be prompt and efficient responsibility on the part of the local administrators of the law, and a complete independence of popular feeling.'[70] Indeed, the impulse behind the County Attorneys Act seems to have been no different from that which underlay the later centralizing push of the 1960s, which a judge saw as expressing a current belief 'that decentralization leads to a lack of uniformity of service and application of standards, and that centralization promotes those objectives.'[71]

Admittedly, the act did not specifically state the relationship that was to obtain between the attorney general and the new officer, but none of its language strongly implies autonomy. He was to be appointed by the governor, not by the attorney general; but the governor would act on the advice of his ministry, of which the attorney general was the member with general responsibility for the administration of justice – and, more often than not, premier into the bargain. His tenure of office was to be during pleasure, not during good behaviour (arguably a prerequisite of autonomy, since he would then have been dismissible only by impeachment). John A. Macdonald was quoted in some reports of the debate on second reading as saying that the county attorney was to hold office during good behaviour;[72] if this was the original design, the final arrangement was a major departure from it, though hardly one indicating an intention to create an autonomous local officer. The purpose of the new officer was 'to aid in the Local Administration of Justice': language that in no way derogated from the attorney general's traditional authority in the sphere of criminal prosecutions. That authority had never been exerted at the quarter sessions, but arguably only because there was no point (or no fee). Finally, the responsibility of the new officer in criminal prosecutions did not extend to the assizes, where the old ad hoc system remained in force.

It is hard to say for certain why the old system at the assizes was continued. One obvious answer is the usefulness of the patronage, but that may not be the whole story. In 1895 a provincial commission was told that in 'the small county towns the County Attorney had too little experience in the criminal law to be entrusted with the prosecution of grave offences.'[73] This was probably no less true a generation earlier in places like Perth, for instance, where the address presented to Mr Justice Adam Wilson by the bar of the town at the opening of the autumn assizes in 1863 bore but five signatures.[74] Given the residence requirement and the part-time nature of the job, it was necessary to award the county attorneyship to a local man; the officer had still to be chosen, in William Dummer Powell's words, from a population that afforded none better.

This necessity was the more confining when the appointee had to combine professional skill with a certain financial competence and integrity. The bill of 1857 had made the county attorney responsible for the financial supervision of the local civil courts, apparently because the clerks of these courts were prone to extend credit liberally to their patrons and it was thought desirable to replace the supervision of the county treasurer, who was appointed by the county council, with that of an officer responsible to the central government.[75] One or two members had questioned the wisdom of looking for legal competence and accounting skills in the same man, and before long their doubts were justified. In 1863 and 1864, the cabinet had to provide for the defalcations of four county attorneys – a task that meant succouring the unfortunate county judge, whose salary the county attorney was supposed to pay from the fees received by the local courts. When the county attorney of Lanark and Renfrew fell short in 1863, he was replaced by one of Perth's other four barristers. A year later the judge was still looking for his salary and the new officer's dismissal was recommended (though apparently without result – perhaps the local professional population afforded none better).[76]

In part the problem was structural. The remuneration of the office meagre at first, since the county attorney was assigned a fee only for prosecutions and received on top of this only a 4 per cent commission on the court monies he handled. This disappointed the new officers, some of whom may have accepted the post in the belief that the government would pay any reasonable account rendered for the other statutory duties, whereas in fact it intended to pay nothing. In 1861 the cabinet set up a more comprehensive tariff,[77] but this solved only part of the problem – it did nothing about the shortcomings of the clerks of the local courts, who were inclined not only to an indiscriminate extension of credit but also to 'small pillage' on their own account. The correspondent who brought this problem to John A. Macdonald's attention in 1861 suggested that the county attorney should make a quarterly audit of each clerk's books.[78] Whether the suggestion was acted upon is uncertain, but a statute of 1864 put the county attorney firmly in control of the clerks, and the government firmly in control of the attorneys, by setting up a stamp system. All court fees were to be paid by affixing stamps of a certain value to the relevant legal documents. The county attorneys were to be the local agents for the sale of these 'law stamps,' which they themselves were to buy from the government at a 5 per cent discount. This reform effactually denied both the clerks and the county attorneys any scope for either 'small pillage' or the injudicious extension of credit at the public expense.[79]

Even allowing for institutional deficiencies, though, a large part of the system's early shortcomings lay with the government and the political culture it reflected. The *Upper Canada Law Journal* had stressed the importance of appointing the best man, not the strongest partisan, to be county attorney; but the greatest concession the government favoured was to appoint the best partisan.[80] In 1864 the chief justice of Upper Canada, W.H. Draper, drew Macdonald's attention to defects in the administration of criminal justice of which, he delicately hinted, the attorney general was doubtless unaware since the Crown officers no longer attended the circuits. Because of increasing pressure on the attorney general to appoint both Crown counsel and county attorneys according to political considerations rather than professional merit, assize prosecutions were 'but too frequently conducted in a very unsatisfactory and inefficient manner – and occasionally the Counsel entrusted with them exhibit a painful deficiency of adequate legal knowledge, the want of which they sometimes endeavour to conceal by an over-zeal in pressing Juries to convict, as they would press for a verdict in a civil case.' Draper found himself obliged to assist the prosecuting counsel in the examination of witnesses rather than 'see the administration of public justice rendered contemptible and the risk incurred of encouraging crime by the facility with which conviction was evaded.'

Draper suggested that the attorney general should set up six rules to be cited in refusing inappropriate requests for patronage. The number of queen's counsel should be limited, since the distinction lost value as it became more common, 'and still more if professional ability, reputation and standing, as well as individual character, are not all indispensable qualifications for its attainment.' No one but a queen's counsel should be retained to prosecute at the assizes, and a local resident never. Crown counsel should always be appointed for an entire circuit and forbidden to send substitutes, since only thus could the best men be acquired. The Toronto assizes should be taken by the solicitor general if possible ('I do not presume to suggest that the Attorney General should attend, tho' I should like to see the Crown more frequently represented by its officers in our Courts'). County attorneys should never be allowed to prosecute at the assizes.[81]

A month later a motion in the Assembly obliged Macdonald to speak to the subject. The mover focused on Crown counsel appointments, asserting that for years past they had degraded the profession and allowed criminals to escape, while the county attorneys were unjustly deprived of the assize business in favour of 'mere sucklings at the Bar.' Macdonald admitted submitting to pressure in these appointments and agreed (as in 1857) that county attorneys should have the work wherever they were fit for it. After deprecating the unprofessional conduct of barristers who begged business from the Crown, he read out Draper's recommendations, stating his personal disagreement that the number of queen's counsel should be fixed and county attorneys never allowed assize business.[82]

'John A. modestly acknowledged having allowed himself to make improper appointments ... but promised better behaviour in future,' reported the *Perth Courier*.[83] It sounded as if Macdonald had eaten humble pie, but he may well have arranged for the motion in order to air the subject and publicize Draper's letter. Two years later he became prime minister and minister of justice in the new dominion government, leaving the administration of criminal prosecutions to his personal and official namesake, the attorney general for Ontario. 'With respect to the County Attorneyship of Lambton, and Crown business on Circuit I am powerless,' he told an importunate correspondent in October 1867, 'inasmuch as this patronage belongs to my friend John Sandfield McDonald.'[84]

Before John A. quit the provincial stage, though, the office of county attorney had been given the opportunity of proving its value in a crisis. A secret society dedicated to the independence of Ireland had been formed in the United States. Early in 1866, its underground activities in Ireland led to the suspension of habeas corpus in the island. In the northern cities of a war-weary United States, its ranks swelled by rootless veterans of the civil strife, the Fenian Brotherhood conceived and elaborated the curious strategy of liberating Ireland by invading Canada. As armed brigades drilled unchecked just south of the border, the Canadian government called out 10,000 militia volunteers to guard the frontier. In April there was similar alarm in New Brunswick, punctuated by a couple of trivial border incidents.[85]

On 1 June 1866 the threatened invasion came. The village of Fort Erie, opposite Buffalo, was seized by a thousand Irishmen. The ensuing three-day fiasco was dramatic only by comparison with the events in New Brunswick, but it lasted long enough, and caused the death of enough young Canadians, to rouse public feeling in Upper Canada to fever pitch. On 8 June the provincial legislature hastened through all its stages an act suspending habeas corpus.[86]

This emergency measure was as mild as an instrument suspending civil rights could reasonably be. It permitted the detention of persons captured by the armed forces or the militia, or arrested on a warrant of two magistrates, and charged with certain acts against the state. The suspension of civil rights in any particular case was to continue only if authorized by the cabinet within fourteen days, and the law that empowered magistrates to issue a warrant of arrest in an indictable offence only on receiving sworn information of wrongdoing remained in force.[87]

Unfortunately, the continuance of this last safeguard was not stated expressly but was left implicit in the statute. All over the province magistrates assumed the power to arrest persons on mere suspicion, sometimes with violence towards the victims and their property.[88] Macdonald had to send a public circular to the county attorneys instructing them to discourage the practice. 'No arrests should be made on mere suspicion, nor without information on oath stating specific facts to establish a *prima facie* case of treason or of some of the criminal acts specified in the act.' It was undesirable to arrest even known Fenians, for the collapse of the invasion would probably destroy the Brotherhood. Macdonald directed the county attorneys to intervene on behalf of any party wrongfully arrested and to report the circumstances to him, the attorney general, at once. The government had no intention of invoking the suspension of habeas corpus against any prisoner except those involved in the raids.[89]

'I am glad you liked my Circular to the County Attorneys,' Macdonald told an Irish Catholic newspaperman four weeks later. 'I found it to be absolutely necessary to issue it for the purpose of reassuring the Roman Catholics, who were a good deal bullied by indiscreet and bigoted men in several parts of Canada, especially among the magistracy.'[90] Indeed, the government's handling of the Fenian affair was a model of discretion. No one was hanged. Partly to mollify the Americans, nearly every convict was released long before his sentence was up, despite the most certain proof of his treasonous acts.[91]

Two documents in addition to Macdonald's circular epitomized the government's concern for legality. In July 1866 Robert A. Harrison, the attorney general's Toronto agent, drew Macdonald's attention to the possible illegality of the detention of certain prisoners who had not been captured in battle or arrested on a warrant, but taken up as suspected stragglers from the raiding parties. There was no moral doubt of their connection with the raiders, and it would be possible to establish a prima facie case against the great majority of them, but Harrison felt uneasy about holding them unless an information was laid against each and a warrant for his arrest issued and authorized by cabinet under the Habeas Corpus Suspension Act.[92]

The second document was an easy-going but uncompromising rebuke by John A. Macdonald to a friend. 'I have yours of the 26th and am rather surprised at your advice to allow parties to be arrested on mere suspicion of Fenianism. Now this is a country of law and order, and we cannot go beyond the law. The Habeas Corpus Suspension Act gave no authority to the Government or the Magistrates of the Country to proceed without information on oath. All that it did was to prevent any application for bail or Habeas Corpus after final commitment ... The consequence of allowing illiterate magistrates to arrest every man they chose to suspect (and that would be, in rural districts, every Roman Catholic) would be to drive all that class out of the Country, to ruin many a respectable family by forcing them to sacrifice their property, and to swell the ranks of the Fenian organization in the United States by every man who has been obliged to leave.'[93]

This canny and unaffected private homily shows the attorney general vindicating the rights of a victimized minority in exemplary fashion. It is interesting for other reasons as well. Macdonald's opinion of the provincial magistracy makes it clear why he established the county attorneyships. The fact that his correspondent was a county judge suggests how tenuous the rule of law might still be in Upper Canada without an authoritative example.

After 1867 complaints about the conduct of Crown prosecutions faded away. This may be partly because the ascendancy gained by the provincial Liberals under Oliver Mowat reduced the pressure on the government to make unsuitable appointments. Even requests from the federal Liberal leadership to award patronage on their behalf, and the temporary loss of the provincial power to create QCs in 1879, did not outweigh this basic political fact.[94] Mowat's personal integrity also helped. When the *Canada Law Journal* at last published a criticism of the conduct of Crown prosecutions in 1891, the writer made a point of acknowledging Mowat's conscientious administration of justice in general and his care in the appointment of Crown counsel in particular. It was the system that was at fault.

The article advanced two basic criticisms. First, it was inherently undesirable that Crown counsel should be appointed on a political basis, since it exposed them to considerations other than the conscientious discharge of their duty. Second, the ad hoc system still suffered from some of the defects that had led to the establishment of county attorneys in 1857. There was a lack of continuity from one assize to the next. Cases might be insufficiently prepared because they involved questions of law that the county attorney had not previously encountered. Appointments of Crown counsel were made too late for counsel to master the cases they had to argue – one cause of cases being pressed unfairly, rather than in the judicious manner ideal in a prosecuting counsel. Since in criminal matters no latitude was allowed to the Crown while the defence was often allowed great scope, to assign prosecutions to counsel mainly conversant with civil business was bound to handicap the Crown unduly.

The writer saw permanent appointments as the answer to these defects. 'The more permanent we can make our judges and all other Crown officials, the better it will be for all parties concerned in the law and its due enforcement. A man who knows that his position is secure will be more likely to perform his duty in a freer and more independent manner than he whose tenure depends, to some extent at least, on considerations other than the faithful discharge of his official functions.'⁹⁵ A professional Crown counsel would have more time to master the niceties of criminal law and procedure and work up his cases. In order to maximize administrative continuity, the writer suggested appointing one counsel for each assize circuit, to be available for consultation as well as for the actual conduct of prosecutions.

The proposal envisaged that the circuit counsel would be paid in fees, yet it pointed to a further step in the professionalization of the criminal justice system. As such it was a harbinger of the late twentieth-century arrangement whereby every Crown attorney in the province is a full-time salaried employee of the Ministry of the Attorney General.

A PROVINCIAL POLICE

One motive behind all the reforms discussed here was the wish to bring greater certainty and uniformity of effect to the administration of criminal justice. John Willson had condemned the application of the death penalty to crimes of widely differing gravity as deterring juries from an impartial and consistent performance of their duty. The Felon's Counsel Act was supposed to achieve not only more certain acquittal of the innocent but also (by exposing the spuriousness of a false defence) more certain condemnation of the guilty. County attorneys were intended to bring greater efficiency to criminal prosecutions and control the vindictive prosecutor. The extension of the Crown's right of reply and the proposal to appoint permanent circuit counsel were also intended to promote efficiency in the prosecution of crime.

The wish for more certain and uniform law enforcement underlay efforts to reform the police. The process did not result in a provincial police force until 1909, although the creation of such a body was suggested as early as 1855. The delay might have been less had the province not managed to achieve most of the desired reforms within the framework of local institutions, but it occurred partly because public opinion and municipal vested interests resisted centralization as they did not in respect of criminal prosecutions.

In eighteenth-century England the local nature of the police power was one of its essential elements. It was exercised by the local magistrates, who commanded for the purpose a constabulary. The constable was an officer of the quarter sessions or other local court embodying the police power. It was his duty under the magistrates to maintain public order, suppress dangers to public morality such as illegal drinking, gambling, and prostitution, and enforce local regulations for the prevention of fire and public nuisances – a wide category that might include blocking the highway and polluting the water or the atmosphere. He also served the magistrates by keeping order in court, guarding prisoners, and serving warrants, summonses, and other process. It was an inefficient system, especially in the cities, but the struggle against royal absolutism in the seventeenth century had left the ruling class distrustful of any sort of state police power.[97]

This local system was imported into Upper Canada. The magistrates in quarter sessions assembled would appoint a number of men to be constables for the year. The duty was part-time, unpaid, and irksome, and often had to be enforced by coercion. As the population grew and urban communities began to flourish, the system was increasingly deficient and had to be replaced by a more intensive form of organization. After the incorporation of Toronto in 1834, for instance, a small force of full-time salaried constables was appointed each year by the city council.[97]

This system was extended piecemeal to other urban places during the 1840s, but soon it proved inadequate in its turn. Municipal councils did not want to spend the money needed to establish a large enough force. Annual appointment by council led to selection according to political affiliation and popular influence rather than competence and integrity. Worse still, in a politically polarized society like that of Upper Canada in the 1830s and 1840s, where a threatened élite was trying desperately to hold on to the remnants of political dominance, there was a strong temptation to prostitute the police force to party purposes. We saw in chapter 3 how in 1839 and 1840 the provincial establishment encouraged or connived at Orange violence against reformers demonstrating in favour of the Durham Report. In Toronto after the rebellion of 1837 the constabulary became virtually the legal auxiliary of militant Orangeism, and Toronto policemen were implicated in the most notorious of these outrages, which occurred just north of the city in October 1839. Even when they did not take part, they could be counted on not to prevent the excesses of their brethren.[98]

Whether active or passive, the constables were simply following their masters' lead. Toronto aldermen and the district sheriff (a cousin of the types rioter Samuel Jarvis) were prominent in the affair of October 1839. Two years later, after an election that was essentially a referendum on Union, the mayor and aldermen were condemned by a provincial commission of inquiry for failing to restrain Orange violence both during and after the polling. That election resulted in the narrow defeat of the Orangemen's darling, the types rioter Henry Sherwood, who next year became mayor of Toronto. His brother Samuel, who egged on the rioters, later became Toronto's chief of police.[99] North of the city, in Simcoe County, W.B. Robinson, the chief justice's brother, benefited from violence which his successful opponent denounced to Robert Baldwin as 'really astonishing in a country having any pretension to Civil Liberty ... The desperate Struggles the Party are prepared to make to retain their much abused power can only be known by Experience.'[100]

In 1849 it was the same. In Toronto the mayor was George Gurnett of tar-and-feather fame. With the Baldwinite reformers in power and the rebellion losses bill before the legislature, the Tories were loaded for bear. Just as Gurnett had hinted at the merits of independence in 1833 after hearing of the dismissal of Boulton and Hagerman as law officers of the Crown, many were now threatening rebellion if the bill passed and advocating annexation to the United States.[101] When William Lyon Mackenzie returned to Toronto early in March after twelve years' exile, a mob burned Baldwin, Solicitor General Blake, and Governor General Elgin in effigy while the police authorities stood by. 'About 10 the mob of 1500 drunken infuriated yelling demons sat down before J. McIntosh's home, where I was, burnt my effigy, beat it with clubs, swore they would burn the premises if I was not brot. out to them, fired guns & pistols, and threw vollies of stones at every part of the building,' reported Mackenzie to his son. 'The police did nothing – and their captain, an orangeman, said – "If you want McKenzie, go in and take him out." *Gurnett*, the mayor, went to bed at 1/2 past 8 o'clock to be out of the way of pres[erv]ing peace, tho' he is clerk of the peace!' Another old reformer remarked to Baldwin: 'It is wonderfull to think of, a most singular thing in deed, that the Mayor of the city ... a most efficient magistrate at other times, should not interfere to keep the peace, and so many good and Loyal Justices of our Lady the Queen in that great City to be looken on when tar barrels are Burning in the streets of Toronto.'[102]

The fact was that while for a quarter of a century the Upper Canadian élite had exploited the existence of popular violence and turned it to their purposes, they had not invented it. The tar-and-feather culprits could not have camouflaged their attack on George Rolph as a charivari had charivaris not existed. Neither George Gurnett, nor the Sherwoods, nor the Jarvises, Robinsons, and Boultons had invented the Orange Order, and they could not control it. Gurnett had found this out the hard way in

1844. After the Baldwin government had secured an act banning political processions, he had tried to enforce the new law on 12 July only to end with footprints up his coat.[103]

After 1849 the Tories came to terms with responsible government and no longer had much use for political violence. From 1854 on, when they joined the Baldwinites and their Lower Canadian Bleu allies in a new 'Liberal Conservative' coalition, they had an extra incentive to scotch it, since it was likely to be directed against Upper Canada's growing Roman Catholic community and would alienate the Bleus. As for other expressions of popular rowdiness, the Tories began to see those as an unredeemed threat to law, order, and property – the disorder that was endemic near large-scale construction projects such as railways and canals, where large gangs of workmen and their families were housed in camps or the temporary hovels they themselves built from filched materials; the disgraceful episode in Toronto in June 1855, when rival fire companies, supposedly fighting a blaze, began fighting each other instead; the blatantly insubordinate riot that erupted in the same city four years later when the corporation tried to encroach on plebeian turf by extending a street across the College Avenue, a popular grassy promenade.[104]

This sort of disorder required a large and efficient police force of a kind that did not exist in the province. At first the government tried to provide it on an ad hoc basis. A statute of 1845 authorized the government to form a body of not more than 100 men, to be called 'the Mounted Police Force,' to serve in districts where public works were in progress, and forbade the possession of firearms without a licence in any area where the act had been proclaimed in force. Originally passed for two years, it became a permanent feature of the statute book and in 1851 was extended to the policing of large private construction sites after labour unrest disrupted the building of the Great Western Railway. An act of 1892 applied the statute to northern Ontario's new mining frontier.[105]

Large-scale disorder among the permanent residents of a locality evoked further legislation. In 1850 and 1851 the south shore of the St Lawrence was disturbed by widespread resistance to efforts to impose a modern public school system, which the inhabitants feared would be used to undermine their traditional values. This so-called *guerre des éteignoirs* was merely an exceptional flare-up of a disaffection that was endemic among the common people of Upper and Lower Canada alike. At first it was dealt with by military detachments, but later a temporary mounted police force was raised, as in Montreal in 1849.[106] These emergency measures were costly, and an efficient permanent peace-keeping establishment seemed essential, but meanwhile the British and Canadian governments resorted to a temporary expedient. The imperial authorities proposed to settle British military and naval pensioners on military reserves in Canada, to be available for five years as an emergency police force mobilizable by the province at the request of local authorities. In 1851 the legislature authorized the government to mobilize these veterans in aid of the civil power.[107]

Emergency peace-keeping was only one problem, of course; the other was the provision of an efficient permanent police. In some rural neighbourhoods Orange or criminal bands had pursued their purposes with little check throughout the 1840s, and a charivari could go on for a week or more and involve up to sixty rioters at a time.[108] In the cities, the root of the problem lay deeper than municipal parsimony and constabulary indiscipline; it lay in the fact that the constables came from the same social class and community as the rioters and shared their prejudices. In Toronto, for instance, the fire brigade, like the constabulary, was of a strong Orange hue. In the brawl of the fire companies the police had intervened ineffectually; worse still, their few arrests came to nothing because the arresting officers fudged their testimony in court to ensure the defendants' acquittal. Similar complicity was evident a month later, when a crowd led by a fire company was allowed to wreck a circus in order to settle a grudge arising from a brawl in a brothel. This sort of thing suggested that the police force must not only be removed from municipal control but must also be isolated from the community that was to be policed.[109]

Two models of such a reform had been implemented in Britain in the 1820s by Sir Robert Peel. One was London's metropolitan police, an efficient uniformed local force of career constables controlled by an appointed board of commissioners. The other was the Irish constabulary, a force controlled by the central government through a hierarchy of officers.[110] In 1855 the mayor of Toronto backed the London system,[111] but from a provincial viewpoint this solution was open to objection: it might do very well for any municipality that adopted it but it would not address the problem of disorder in the rural areas; nor would it meet rioting on the scale Montreal had experienced in 1849, which required a much stronger force than any municipality could be expected to maintain. The traditional recourse in such emergencies had been to the army, but by mid-century the British government was reluctant to sanction the use of troops to quell civil disturbances.[112] The answer seemed to be the Irish model of a centralized constabulary whose members could legally act anywhere in the province and be quickly concentrated, using the new railways, wherever an emergency arose.

When in 1854 the new Liberal-Conservative ministry set up a commission to look into reorganizing the militia and providing an efficient and economical means of public defence, it added a mandate to report on 'an improved system of Police for the better preservation of the public peace.'[113] Under the leadership of the premier, Sir Allan MacNab, the commissioners dismissed the existing municipal police with brisk contempt, condemning the system of annual appointment by council, the failure to isolate the constabulary from the community, and the lack of rules, discipline, or any means of rewarding the deserving or punishing the disobedient officer.

The answer was a provincial force, which 'should be armed, clothed, equipped and lodged in Barracks; the men should be required to go to any part of the Province, and prevented as much as possible from acquiring local feelings or sympathies; they should be trained to such movements as would enable them to act effectively together in Streets or Fields, and accustomed to the use of arms, which should always be kept at their Barracks ready for use at any emergency, but not carried when on ordinary duty.' The force was to be concentrated in the nine major urban centres of Upper and Lower Canada, and its men were to perform all the duties currently executed by the municipal constabularies it was to supersede. The municipalities were to pay two-thirds of the expense of the detachments stationed within their bounds and to supply barracks and stations, but constables were to be appointed, and forces allotted to the different centres, by the provincial commissioners of police. In addition to this force, the volunteer militia, like the u.s. National Guard, were henceforth to be mobilizable in aid of the civil power upon the written requisition of any two magistrates or the head of any municipality.[114]

The commission's proposals were controversial. Even the interim police bill of 1851 had been resisted by MPPs who, in the words of W.H. Merritt, 'did not want to see Canada made a second Ireland by the introduction of an organized police force and a standing army; for the latter would follow as a matter of course.' The distinguished tribune Henry John Boulton had decried the proposed force as potentially subversive of the liberties of the people.[115] Now, four years later, Merritt thought he saw his prediction realized: 'He had always considered it an essential principle to leave to the inhabitants themselves the responsibility of preserving peace and order

... If they adopted the proposed Police system, and placed them all under a central authority, a pretty state the country would be in.'[116]

The militia bill of 1855 became law despite strong resistance.[117] The next year's police bill was swamped by the protests of municipal councils before it reached second reading.[118] The bill was well designed to provide efficient permanent municipal policing on the one hand and to deal economically with riot control and other police emergencies, both urban and rural, on the other; but the combination of extended government patronage, flouted local *amour propre*, and a potential menace to civil liberties was fatal. The Toronto city council denounced the scheme by 19 votes to 3, with only those pillars of the establishment, Alderman John Hillyard Cameron and Mayor John Beverley Robinson Jr, speaking in its favour. One member denounced it as typical of the military and despotic spirit of its author, MacNab: 'Instead of creating a single police force, it established almost a standing army.' Another condemned it as 'opposed to the enlightened genius of the present age.'[119]

Many of these aldermanic strictures had been anticipated by the *Globe*. George Brown's organ deprecated the centralizing tendencies of the scheme, which gave the government too much power over the liberties and privileges of the people. Municipal control was preferable because municipal councils were more amenable to popular control than the government was; the patronage entailed in appointing 500 officers was better diffused among such bodies than concentrated in the government. Particularly interesting is the *Globe*'s distinction between the two major functions of the police, the maintenance of order and the suppression of immorality. 'A favourite argument on behalf of the centralizing system is, it works well in England, but those who use it forget the difference between Canada and the mother country. In the densely populated British Islands, abounding in large cities, whose hundreds of thousands embrace a large proportion of the very poor and the vicious, the police force is not merely an instrument for checking the immorality of society, it is an important engine in the preservation of peace and order ... It is, in its organization, rather military than civil.' Canada had no need of such a force.[120]

The characterization of the English police as military was in those days more accurately applicable to the Irish constabulary, and once thwarted in its effort to bring in the Irish system it was to the English model that the government turned. The Municipal Act of 1858 removed the police force from the control of the city council and vested it in a board consisting of the mayor, the police magistrate, and the recorder (the salaried judge who had superseded the mayor and aldermen at the city quarter sessions). The board had the right to stipulate a minimum strength for the force, and the council retained only the authority to fix a reasonable rate of pay for its members.[121]

In Toronto, the new board retained less than half of the old constables and recruited many of the new officers, along with the new chief of police, from Britain. The strict regime the new chief imposed on his men led to frequent clashes between the board and the council, as did the board's attempt to ban Orangemen from the force. This controversy was settled by a compromise by which only men active in the order were excluded; but municipal parsimony thwarted some of the new chief's more military schemes, such as a barracks for the unmarried constables. At last, in 1866, it struck at the chief himself when the commissioners failed in an attempt to obtain a judicial injunction binding the council to pay him what the commissioners thought was a proper salary. Next year the power to set pay was shifted from the council to the board. Discontent within the force reached a climax in 1872, when the men publicly voted no confidence in their chief and reproved the commissioners for constantly taking his side. The board had to fire the whole force to bring the malcontents to heel.[122]

The early troubles of the new police system kept the idea of a provincial force alive. Some time in the mid-1860s, John A. Macdonald was addressed by a friend on the advantages of an Irish-type constabulary, especially in view of the civil war south of the border and the social disruption that might ensue on the demobilization of the contending armies. On top of this, the manner in which the office of constable was discharged in Upper Canada was 'a standing farce, a heavy hindrance in the administration of the criminal law.'[123] In 1869 Sandfield Macdonald introduced a bill into the Ontario legislature that differed only in detail from that of 1856. He did so at the very end of the session, so that the members and the public could consider it during the recess and let the government know their views. The *Globe*, responding with alacrity to the invitation, dismissed the bill in a few dispassionate sentences as redundant. This may have been the general feeling, since the legislature saw no more of it.[124]

In the wake of the troubles of 1872, the Toronto police magistrate sent J.G. Scott (chief clerk of the Provincial Law Office and soon to become Ontario's first deputy attorney general) a copy of the 1869 bill with a note urging its enactment. The city council should have nothing to do with the police, he declared (not that, by this time, the council had much to do with it).[125] But the concept of a provincial police force was about to assume a different guise – that of a government-controlled and government-funded force for frontier areas where there was no municipal organization or where municipalities were unable to meet the need. One act of 1874 authorized the government to appoint constables 'for any provisional, judicial, temporary-judicial or territorial district, or for any portion of the province not attached to a county for ordinary municipal and judicial purposes'; another authorized it to appoint constables for the border area along the Niagara River, where the encroachments of American lawlessness were too much for the local authorities.[126]

In the rest of rural Ontario, things remained much as before. In 1882 a government circular asked county officials whether they thought the county constabulary was sufficient, or whether a significant number of criminals were avoiding detection and conviction. Opinions varied, though most respondents agreed that the police would benefit from the presence of a salaried detective in the county. The generally cautious Mowat decided to do nothing. Not until 1896 was it even made incumbent on county councils to appoint and pay a chief constable.[127]

The police in Upper Canada and Ontario in the nineteenth century remained decentralized in comparison with the administration of criminal justice. There was no tradition of centralization to build on as in the case of criminal prosecutions, where the law officers of the Crown had conducted proceedings at the assizes from the very start, nor was there even a fictional English precedent like the notional responsibility of the attorney general in England for the prosecution of crime. On the contrary, the English example pointed to localism. Public opinion in mid-nineteenth-century Ontario did not share that English fear of state power which had retarded the advent of efficient policing in London, but it was not about to admit that the province needed Irish remedies. The expense of a provincial police force, the slight it entailed to municipal self-esteem, and resentment at the prospect of municipalities having to pay for a force they did not control also encouraged resistance.

In the end the police force was removed from municipal control; municipalities continued to have to pay only for the force needed in the locality. Emergency police continued to depend on special legislation like that governing construction and mining sites and the Niagara frontier. Labour unrest not covered by this legislation was often dealt with by calling out the militia. It took the gold rush on the province's northern mining frontier to bring the Ontario Provincial Police into being in 1909, initially as little more than a single administrative system for the assortment of ad hoc units the government by then had under its control.[128]

6

In Right of Ontario

In 1867 the British North America Act combined the provinces of Nova Scotia, New Brunswick, and Canada into a federal polity, the Dominion of Canada.[1] The maritime provinces entered the confederation in their old form, but the province of Canada was split into two new ones, Ontario and Quebec, which corresponded in territory to Upper and Lower Canada. Since these territories had remained judicially distinct throughout the period of political union from 1841 to 1867, the office of attorney general for Upper Canada was not much affected by this rupture. What did affect it was another sort of split: the assignment to the dominion government of many of the executive and legislative powers previously exercised by the provinces.

This distribution of powers affected two major functions of the office – the administration of justice and the provision of legal advice to the provincial executive and legislature. Much of the former function was assigned to the dominion; but the dividing line was far from clear, and matters constantly arose that could not confidently be assigned to one jurisdiction or the other. As we shall see in the next chapter, from 1867 on the attorney general for Ontario could not exercise his remaining responsibility for the administration of criminal justice without close attention to the terms of the act.

This was, however, only a special instance of the general problem that was to preoccupy him in his role as law adviser to the provincial executive and legislature. With unobtrusive but arresting art, the draftsmen of the act had contrived the distribution of powers in terms that created an almost infinite potential for dispute between the dominion and the provinces. Easily surpassing the apocryphal committee that set out to design a horse and achieved a camel, the Fathers of Confederation, aided by the Colonial Office, created nothing less than the legislative equivalent of an optical illusion: look at the act one way and it seemed to say one thing; look at it another way and it seemed to say the opposite. This ambiguity set the stage for a long struggle between two great men of late nineteenth-century Canada. John A. Macdonald, prime minister of the dominion from 1867 to 1873 and from 1878 to 1891, vigorously asserted Ottawa's authority in his efforts to mould Canada into a thriving nation – or, some would say, into the empire of a thriving Montreal business community.[2] Oliver Mowat was also committed to a thriving Canada, but as Ontario's attorney general and premier from 1872 to 1896 he started from the premise that what was good for Canada was what was good for Ontario.

An account of their struggle belongs in this book for two reasons. First, it had always been the attorney general's duty to advise the executive and legislature of the province on its relations with external jurisdictions, but the ambiguity of the BNA Act raised that function to an unprecedented importance – so much so as to make the addition of dominion-provincial relations to his advisory responsibilities the main late nineteenth-century innovation in the attorney general's office. The point is worth stressing, since Mowat's simultaneous tenure of the premiership and the attorney-ship has obscured the fact that his preoccupation with the subject, and in particular with provincial rights, pertained especially to his administrative portfolio. It was as law adviser and chief legislative draftsman to the provincial executive and legislature that Mowat plotted and executed his triumphant campaign. It was as the Crown's chief legal counsel 'in right of Ontario,' as it is formally expressed, that he twice appeared in person before the Judicial Committee of the Privy Council on behalf of the province. Both of the cases in which he did so bear the name of the attorney general for Ontario; two others – the Ontario Assignments Act reference and the prohibition reference – are formally entitled *Attorney General for Ontario* v *Attorney General for Canada*.

Second, Mowat's campaign for provincial rights has never yet received full and fair appreciation. After the First World War Canada's anglophone nationalist intelligentsia railed against the country's continuing subordination to Westminster in international affairs and to the Judicial Committee of the Privy Council in constitutional interpretation. The Statute of

Westminster ended the former grievance in 1931, but the latter was intensified by the dominion government's impotence in tackling the economic crisis of the 1930s – an impotence perceived to stem partly from the committee's progressive curtailment of Ottawa's authority over a period of four decades. From about 1930 to 1960 a chorus of constitutional lawyers, political scientists, and historians excoriated Mowat, the committee, and their chief Canadian acolyte, Chief Justice Sir Lyman Duff of the Supreme Court of Canada, for unravelling the glorious tapestry of nationhood woven by the Fathers of Confederation. While this view has never gone unchallenged, and has ceased to inform the analysis of experts, modern historical writing continues to reflect its influence sufficiently to warrant revisionary discussion.[3]

The BNA Act contained three main sources of dissension between the partisans of dominion and provincial power. One was the power it gave the dominion government to disallow acts of the provincial legislatures, just as the imperial government had disallowed those of colonial legislatures. Another was the incomplete definition of the relationship between the lieutenant-governor as the personification of the provincial executive, the governor general of Canada as the personification of the dominion executive, and the British Crown as the ultimate source of executive authority in the empire. The third was the language of the clauses that distributed legislative power between the dominion and the provinces. It is on the last two questions, which were resolved in the law courts and which chiefly engaged Mowat as a legal strategist and tactician, that this narrative is focused. The discussion is technical in parts, but law is a technical subject and neglect of the technicalities condemns a historian to superficiality even if by chance he escapes egregious error. More to the point, it is historical; for abstract analysis of the individual 'cases' by constitutional experts, neglecting the historical context and the dynamics that link them in causal succession, is largely to blame for the errors that still mar historical writing on the subject. Only a historical account of the legal battle over provincial rights can explain the outcome and reveal the magnitude of Mowat's achievement as attorney general for Ontario.

THE BATTLE FOR SOVEREIGNTY

The earliest strains between Ontario and Ottawa occurred over disallowance, but the first of the primary legal issues to flare up was that of executive power. The fight began, several months before Mowat became premier, with a dispute over the right to appoint queen's counsel. The Ontario government made several appointments in March 1872, not knowing that the dominion had just obtained the English law officers' opinion that a lieutenant-governor had no power of appointment unless it was specially conferred on him by provincial enactment. They found out only in October, when the dominion government informed the provincial patentees that their standing was dubious and offered to regularize it by conferring a dominion patent.

Affirming its belief that the lieutenant-governor could make such appointments as an expression of the royal prerogative, the Ontario government proposed that Ottawa and Ontario jointly refer the question to the Judicial Committee of the Privy Council. The dominion side-stepped this challenge, using the excuse that Ontario's expressed intention to confer statutory power on its lieutenant-governor as the imperial law officers prescribed made the reference inappropriate. Ottawa proposed that dominion patents be recognized in the provincial courts and provincial patents in those of the dominion by mutual agreement. (There were no dominion courts as yet, but the erection of a supreme court for the dominion was contemplated.)[4]

Mowat became attorney general and premier just after Ontario challenged Ottawa to take the matter to the Privy Council. He had quit politics eight years previously for a seat on the Chancery bench, and his return in 1872 followed dominion legislation barring members of Parliament from sitting in a provincial legislature. The two leaders of the Ontario government, Edward Blake and Alexander Mackenzie, both decided to stay at Ottawa. They joined George Brown, dean of Upper Canadian liberalism and proprietor of the *Globe*, in persuading Mowat to quit the bench and take over the provincial leadership from Blake.[5]

Early in 1873 Mowat had two provincial acts passed to remove doubts as to the lieutenant-governor's authority to appoint queen's counsel. One concerned the power of appointment, the other the power to award patents of precedence in the courts of Ontario to members of the provincial bar. Significantly, both acts were declaratory in form: that is, they did not *confer* the power on the lieutenant-governor but *confirmed* that he possessed it already.[6] There the matter rested for six years, chiefly because Macdonald's Conservative ministry at Ottawa gave way in 1873 to a Liberal administration led by Alexander Mackenzie.

The power of appointing queen's counsel might seem a trivial occasion for a constitutional row, especially since no one denied that provincial governments could assume it by legislation. Indeed, the status of queen's counsel was starting to become a fairly trivial matter by the 1870s, in Ontario at any rate. True, much Crown assize business was awarded to QCs, and occasionally, when no superior court judge was available, one would even be commissioned to preside at an assize.[7] Generally speaking, though, the patent was merely honorific, conferring a certain precedence over mere barristers (and over QCs of later creation) in addressing the court. The political instability of the pre-Confederation decade led to this honour being conferred with the same abandon as Crown counselships and county attorneyships. When Sandfield Macdonald added his quota in 1863 to the pool John A. had created over the preceding decade, the *Upper Canada Law Journal* observed that it was a wonder he did not appoint every man at the bar while he was about it and so practically destroy the honour he had done so much to degrade.[8] One senses a political bias in this pronouncement by a journal that had been founded by a friend of John A.'s and boasted among its editors his former chief clerk and Toronto agent, Robert A. Harrison, and Harrison's successor as chief clerk, Hewitt Bernard. Certainly the standard was to sink much lower in the next three decades as John A. scattered patents in batches among practitioners more at home in the police and division (petty debt) courts than in the higher reaches of litigation.[9]

Still, a police-court lawyer might be a valuable political ally, and the power to make him a queen's counsel was worth having. In addition, the dispute over the power to create queen's counsel involved a constitutional issue of the greatest importance.[10] Under responsible government the governor general and the lieutenant-governors, like the monarch in England, had the power to do very little except with the advice and consent of their ministers, who held office through the support of a majority of the elective legislature. In debating whether a power belonged to the governor general or the lieutenant-governors, the real issue was whether it belonged to the executive of the dominion or the provinces.

With respect to the appointment of queen's counsel, the argument was complicated by the BNA Act's express grant to the provinces of legislative authority in relation to the administration of justice and the establishment and appointment of provincial offices and officers. Since queen's counsel were arguably (in theory at least) royal officers for the administration of justice, Macdonald was willing to admit that a provincial legislature could pass an act authorizing the lieutenant-governor to appoint them. But Macdonald could not admit that the lieutenant-governors possessed that power independent of legislative sanction, since such power could spring only from the royal prerogative – the reservoir of original rights and powers that the Crown, as the fountain of executive authority, still retained, unimpaired by legislative regulation. The royal prerogative was an attribute of sovereignty, and Ottawa insisted that, although the lieutenant-governors were expressly assigned particular prerogative functions by the BNA Act, the great residue of sovereign power lay with the governor general – the personification of the dominion executive – as the sole representative of the Crown in Canada. Ontario contended that the dominion enjoyed only those prerogative powers assigned to it by the BNA Act, while the residue rested with the provinces.

Each side relied on the language of the act. The centralists referred to the clauses dealing with the distribution of legislative powers, which assigned authority in specified matters to the provincial legislatures and left the rest to Ottawa; this was evidence of a centralist bias in the act which was inconsistent with the notion that the provinces were sovereign. They also cited the clauses constituting the dominion and provincial governments. The dominion executive power was said to be vested in the queen and carried on by the governor general in her name and on her behalf; the dominion legislature consisted of the queen and the two houses of Parliament. The provincial executives, by contrast, were to be headed by 'an Officer, styled the Lieutenant Governor, appointed by the Governor General in Council' (that is, by the dominion government) and holding office during the governor general's pleasure. The provincial legislatures were to consist of the lieutenant-governor and two houses (one in Ontario, which had dispensed with an appointive upper chamber).

There was, then, no mention of the queen in connection with the provincial constitution, an omission emphasized in the clauses relating to the distribution of legislative powers. Section 91 described the lawful authority of 'the Queen, by and with the advice and consent of the Senate and House of Commons,' while section 92 defined that merely of 'the Legislature.' On the basis of this pervasive trend of language, centralists argued that the lieutenant-governors were divorced from the sovereign power and partook of the attributes of sovereignty only to the degree specified in the act. This limited them to such trivial functions as appointing members of the provincial upper house and summoning the provincial legislature 'in the queen's name.'

Provincialists tended to rely less on the wording of individual clauses and more on the tenor of the whole. The centralist error was to think of the act as creating and completely defining an entirely new political entity: a sovereign Dominion of Canada, divided for the purposes of local government into four subordinate provinces with powers that were specified in full in the act. That was not quite what the act did. It did create the Dominion of Canada, and it did completely define the dominion power, but the clauses defining the shape of the provinces and their relation to the federal power were *not* complete. This was because the provinces had existed prior to Confederation, and their constitution was also defined by earlier imperial legislation, such as the Constitutional Act of 1791 and the Act of Union of 1840, that the BNA Act had left unrepealed.

It was therefore immaterial that the act vested the appointment of lieutenant-governors in the governor general and contained no general expression of their relation to the queen. That relation was implicit in the wording of sections 64 and 65, which stated that the executive authority in the provinces of Nova Scotia and New Brunswick was to continue as constituted at Confederation and that the lieutenant-governors of Ontario and Quebec were to exercise all the powers, authorities, or functions vested in the governor of the province of Canada at Confederation as far as they were applicable to a provincial government. The governor of Canada, and the lieutenant-governors of Nova Scotia and New Brunswick, had incontestably been the queen's representatives and as such had wielded prerogative powers which included the appointment of queen's counsel. Was the status inherent in the office to be abolished by the mere omission of unnecessary verbiage from the BNA Act, or by the fact that the lieutenant-governors were now to be appointed not by the queen's government in England but by her dominion government in Canada?

Granted this premise, the provincialists had an easy time of it. They could argue that the legislative process of the provinces was exactly analogous to that of the dominion; therefore the queen's participation was implicit, although not expressly mentioned in the BNA Act. Moreover, the lieutenant-governors represented the queen in ways that were not expressly provided for in the act; for example, they presided over the administration of justice and disposed of the Crown lands in her name, often acting by means of instruments under the great seal of the province – a traditional emblem of sovereignty that was mentioned in the act. It could even be contended that administrative government was in itself an act of prerogative right. Over the centuries, to be sure, the executive authority in many matters had been regulated by legislation, and in those cases the source of authority was no longer the royal prerogative but the regulating statute (a joint act of monarch and legislature). In regard to everything else, however, the administrative authority was still rooted in prerogative right, and the BNA Act assigned some such matters to the legislative power of the provinces. Did the act intend lieutenant-governors to have no executive authority in those matters until the provincial legislature had conferred it upon them? Had the entire administration of justice since 1867, except as regulated by provincial legislation, been ultra vires? Had all appointments of provincial officers, unless sanctioned by legislation, been null and void? If the centralist case was correct, how could they not be, resting as they did on the words of the BNA Act that sustained the prerogative appointment of queen's counsel?

These questions of statutory exegesis may seem academic, but they touched on the realities of political power. Provincial legislation was subject to disallowance by the dominion government. If the provinces were sovereign entities which had created the dominion by mutual compact, a basis existed for resisting the dominion's use of the disallowance power in ways that were inconsistent with their sovereignty. Furthermore, the larger the reservoir of authority vested in the provincial executive, the less need there was for the executive to acquire powers by legislation that might be vetoed by the dominion.

In a way that was intangible yet real, the question of sovereignty impinged on the other major focus of the dominion-provincial contest, the distribution of legislative power. Underlying the dispute was a disagreement over the intentions of the Fathers of Confederation – the provincial leaders upon whose resolutions, passed in conclave at Quebec in 1864 and confirmed with minor changes in London two years later, the BNA Act was based. Macdonald had favoured reducing the provincial powers to a minimum ('municipal' and 'local' were the words often used, implying by the analogy with city, county, and lesser corporations an absence of royal participation and hence of sovereignty). At conferences overshadowed by the civil war in the United States, he had been able to command broad assent for the proposition that the flaws that sectional tension had exposed in the U.S. constitution should be avoided in that of the new confederation. This assent was reflected in the distribution of legislative powers in the BNA Act, which reversed the United States' arrangement by assigning specific powers to the provincial legislatures and the residue to the federal authority. Since 1867 Macdonald had done his best to impose a centralist interpretation of the Act and in doing so had enjoyed the consistent support of Whitehall, which belittled the status of the lieutenant-governors symbolically in a dozen ways as well as by explicit utterance (they were merely 'a part of the Colonial Administrative staff,' said the colonial secretary in 1875 in a phrase much quoted by centralists).[11]

But words can have different meanings. Mowat had been at Quebec, and in his view the BNA Act did not mean half of what Macdonald said it did. As the mover of the resolution conferring the disallowance power on the dominion government, Mowat wielded special authority when he told provincial premiers at another Quebec conference in 1887 that it had been understood in 1864 that the power was to be used with the same reticence the imperial government observed towards the legislation of colonies enjoying responsible government.[12] Even if Mowat was wrong in this (which is unlikely), it is quite possible that in 1864 he and Macdonald may have agreed on words while disagreeing on the vision those words all too imperfectly described. And whether or not a majority of the Fathers of Confederation shared Macdonald's vision rather than Mowat's, in 1887 the premiers of all but the two smallest provinces, neither of which had been a party to the original agreement, shared Mowat's – or at least rejected Macdonald's.[13]

The point is that the controversy over the BNA Act was not essentially a struggle to establish contrary absolutes, though as a subject of litigation and political controversy it often assumed that form. At bottom the question was not whether lieutenant-governors were sovereign, but how large the provinces' share of the total executive and legislative power was as against the dominion's. The judges' understanding of the sovereignty issue might well influence their interpretation of the clauses that distributed the legislative power between the provinces and the dominion.

The first opportunity to develop the provincial case in detail arose not upon the appointment of QCs but upon another subject equally trivial and even more arcane: the right of escheat. Oddly enough, the battle was joined not with Macdonald's Conservative government but the new Liberal ministry of Alexander Mackenzie. Escheat is the ancient common-law principle by which the property of persons dying intestate and without heirs is taken over by the Crown. In 1874 the Ontario legislature passed an act to regulate the mode in which such property, and any forfeited to the Crown by virtue of the proprietor's conviction for treason or felony, was to be administered by the provincial government.[14] The act was duly reviewed by the dominion minister of justice, Télesphore Fournier, under section 90 of the BNA Act, the disallowance clause. Fournier declared the Escheats and Forfeitures Act to be ultra vires the province and proposed its repeal. Mowat refused, and the act was disallowed.[15]

Although the smiting hand was Fournier's, the prompting mind was that of his deputy minister, who had written a report which Fournier had merely countersigned. Fournier's deputy was none other than John A. Macdonald's brother-in-law, Hewitt Bernard, whom Macdonald had appointed as chief clerk of the Crown Law Department in place of R.A. Harrison in 1859 and retained in Ottawa in 1867 on becoming dominion minister of justice.[16] Mowat exploited the link in his reply: he had considered the report of the *deputy* minister of justice, he wrote, and trusted that, after considering the provincial reply, the Minister 'would not hesitate to withdraw the concurrence which, in the absence of any statement of the provincial view, he was led to express in the forcibly stated but exparte opinion and recommendation of his deputy.'[17]

Bernard had argued that lieutenant-governors possessed no prerogative rights except those expressly vested in them by the BNA Act. The right of escheat was not so vested; neither was it among the subjects assigned to the provincial legislatures. Forfeitures for crime were matters of criminal law and procedure, subjects expressly assigned to the dominion. Mowat replied that the lieutenant-governors had retained all the incidents of sovereign executive power that were not transferred to the dominion by the BNA Act. The act confirmed the provincial ownership of public property in general, and all lands belonging to the provinces at Confederation in particular; this included the right of escheat, an incident of territorial sovereignty like that which gave the Crown the ownership of lands exposed by the retreating sea. As to forfeitures for treason or felony, these came to the province as an incident of the administration of justice. Mowat ended with a general review of the case that provincial governments were receptacles of prerogative rights.[18]

Fournier rejected Mowat's invitation to distance himself from his deputy, but he was soon appointed to the new Supreme Court. His successor was Edward Blake, the brilliant young equity lawyer whom Mowat had replaced as premier of Ontario. Blake, a son of the former solicitor general and chancellor William Hume Blake,[19] agreed with Bernard that forfeitures for treason or felony belonged to the dominion, but he concurred in Mowat's position on prerogative rights in general and on escheat for want of heirs in particular; indeed, it may have been he rather than his attorney general Adam Crooks who worked out Ontario's position on the appointment of queen's counsel in 1872. He felt it improper to abandon Fournier's position, but he readily accepted Mowat's suggestion in 1876 that Ontario and Ottawa jointly submit a case for adjudication by the Supreme Court.[20]

Mowat's proposal attests to his confidence in his case, for Fournier was one of the six judges and there was no appeal in special references of the sort proposed.[21] The reference was never made, however, for now the Quebec Court of Queen's Bench (Appeal Side) rendered a judgment on the subject of escheat in favour of provincial rights. Although the judgment was based on narrower grounds than those of provincial sovereignty, Blake declared that the Supreme Court ought more properly to take cognizance of the matter through an appeal from the Quebec judgment. He abandoned the special reference and recommended that, pending its reversal, Ottawa should assume that the right of escheat for want of heirs lay with the province.[22]

The other matter, that of forfeiture for crime, was not essential to Mowat's case for provincial sovereignty. Either it came within the words of the BNA Act that assigned the administration of justice to the provinces, or it came within those that assigned criminal law and procedure to Ottawa. In neither case could it affect the question of what the act *implied* concerning the location of prerogative rights and powers, and as a distribution-of-powers question it was not worth fighting over. In 1877 Mowat reintroduced his disallowed act without the provision relating to such forfeitures, and it became law without interference from the dominion.[23]

It was soon afterwards, in 1879, that three judges of the Supreme Court of Canada declared war on provincial rights. The occasion was a revival of the controversy over the power of lieutenant-governors to create queen's counsel. Nova Scotia had copied Ontario in passing laws empowering its lieutenant-governor to appoint QCs and regulate precedence at the provincial bar. A QC appointed by the dominion prior to these acts challenged the award under one of them of patents giving precedence to certain QCs appointed under the other. The Supreme Court of Nova Scotia upheld his challenge on the ground that the statute regulating precedence was not retroactive. On appeal to the dominion tribunal, a majority of the court seized the chance to denounce the provincial pretensions to sovereignty.[24]

This characterization of a judicial decision may seem inappropriate, but several circumstances tend to confirm it. First, the lower court could have been upheld without going into the constitutional position at all. The two other judges who heard the appeal, Samuel Henry Strong and Télesphore Fournier, did precisely this and protested against their colleagues' course, declaring that the court ought never to pronounce on the constitutional power of a legislature to pass a statute unless such adjudication was essential to the decision of a case. Of the three judges who did, only one – William A. Henry of Nova Scotia – professed it as the sole ground for his decision. The other two, one of whom readily admitted the superfluousness of the discussion, were the most vehement up-holders of dominion supremacy: John Wellington Gwynne and Henri-Elzéar Taschereau.[25]

The majority judgment in *Lenoir* v *Ritchie* need not be reviewed in detail. In essence, the decision was as follows. The power of appointing queen's counsel formed part of the royal prerogative. Even a legislature in which the queen was represented could trench on the prerogative only by legislation that did so 'by express words or necessary implication'; the provincial legislatures, in which the queen was not represented, could not do so by any means. They might still have been able to pass laws on the subject if the BNA Act had expressly empowered them to do so, or if the power were a necessary implication of the provincial authority to legislate in relation to the administration of justice (this latter ground was the basis of the imperial law officers' opinion of 1872). But the BNA Act had not expressly conferred such power, and a queen's counselship was not a necessary office in the administration of justice; rather, it was an honour or dignity like a knighthood or baronetcy. The power of awarding such patents was not implied in the BNA Act.

The majority judgment was a serious setback to the provincial-rights position. By invalidating legislation passed by the provinces at the suggestion of John A. Macdonald himself, based on the imperial law officers' opinion, it transferred the power of appointing QCs from the provinces, where Alexander Mackenzie had been content to leave it, to the dominion. Macdonald proceeded to rub this in by awarding patents to fifteen men honoured by Ontario four years previously.[26]

Worse than this, three of the six judges of the Supreme Court of Canada had revealed themselves as totally committed to the centralist position on provincial sovereignty, and Mowat knew that Fournier too was un-reliable. Not only could the court be counted on to deny the lieutenant-governors any prerogative powers beyond the meagre scraps expressly assigned them by the BNA Act, but it had confined the authority of the provincial legislature to confer such powers more narrowly than the imperial law officers' opinion of 1872. Who could tell how tightly the court might construe the 'implied' jurisdiction of the legislature in future decisions on matters of greater substance?

Worst of all, it had all been unnecessary and injudicious. The respondent's challenge to the constitutionality of the legislation had taken the appellant by surprise; the case in its favour had been poorly argued; no provincial government had been represented in court; the issue was arguably superfluous to the judgment.[27] Yet three of the judges had seized the chance to trample the provincialist position with cleated boots. The shock to Mowat is demonstrable: a week before the *Lenoir* judgment he had proposed to Macdonald's minister of justice, Alexander Campbell, that they refer to the Supreme Court the question of jurisdiction over the grand jury; after *Lenoir* he delayed the reference repeatedly and at last refused to go on with it as long as such references could not be appealed to the Privy Council.[28]

Lenoir was unappealable too, since the appellant had no case even if the prerogative issue was omitted. Yet the current situation was intolerable. Mowat counterattacked on the escheat front. His original legislation had been prompted by the death of a wealthy Torontonian in 1871. Though he had long been a provincial issuer of marriage licences, Andrew Mercer had never got around to marrying the mother of his children, and he had left no will. The twice-disappointed concubine and her son had fought off a host of pretended heirs in the courts only to lose the estate in 1878 to the attorney general for Ontario, the officer appointed by the Escheats Act of 1877 to act for the provincial government in such matters. In 1880 the Chancery decision in favour of the province was unanimously confirmed by the provincial Court of Appeal, after pleadings that seem to have been a replay of the controversy between Mowat and Bernard in 1875.[29] The case moved on to the Supreme Court of Canada. Here Mowat might expect to lose, but in a case like this he could appeal to the Privy Council.

Mercer v The Attorney General for Ontario was fought with big guns. Ottawa was represented by Zebulon Lash, deputy minister of justice and later a law partner of Edward Blake. The family retained William McDougall, former Clear Grit cabinet colleague of Mowat before Confederation but now a Conservative and soon to become leader of the Ontario opposition. Edward Blake, now leader of the Liberal opposition at Ottawa, led for Ontario. He was supported by his former law partner James Bethune, a leading Liberal member of the Ontario legislature. Especially striking was the intervention of Quebec, represented by the constitutional expert T.-J.-J. Loranger, former *Bleu* cabinet minister and judge and now a professor of law at Laval University.[30]

The trial was remarkable for the scope of the argument. Lash used the words of the BNA Act to establish the case that sovereignty resided solely in the governor general and that the provincial claim of implicit sovereignty was groundless. McDougall amplified this argument with all the authority of a statesman who had represented Upper Canada at the founding conferences of the confederation. Confederation had not been the work of the British North American peoples themselves but an act of absolute imperial power; it had not been a coming together of bodies politic, sovereign or otherwise, but their annihilation and reconstitution on the anvil of imperial might.

No one can doubt the power of the Imperial Parliament to have deprived Canada (so far as an Act of Parliament could do it) of representative government altogether ... They could assign such powers of legislation for the future as they thought fit without respect to the 'rights' of the past. There were no rights in the question which a court of law can recognize. The people of the four provinces, united together in the new form, were endowed with even greater rights and larger powers than before, but the legislative control and direction of affairs was placed under two distinct legislative bodies ... The full and complete exercise of that power was vested in the Parliament of the Dominion, but certain geographical distinctions were retained, and the provinces were allowed, under the machinery provided in the act, to legislate upon certain specified local subjects as a matter of convenience.[31]

How then could Ontario claim to have brought into the new union a corpus of existing rights and powers? 'What rights could Ontario have had? There was no such political entity or corporation; there was no such province in a legal sense. It was a geographical expression.'

Anticipating the argument Loranger was there to make, McDougall admitted that French Canadians might have brought into Confederation some rights derived from imperial recognition of their special status, but these had nothing to do with the province of Quebec as constituted by the BNA Act. 'Those rights were not secured to Quebec according to her present limitary lines. They were conceded to the French population who were scattered at that time over the whole northern part of this continent ... They extended to the *people*, and not to any geographical or territorial circumscription or boundary.'[32]

For Ontario, Blake stated the provincialist approach to the BNA Act in plain words.

Here when it is intended to grapple with the conjunction of four provinces and the establishment of separate legislative powers, and when it has been attempted to deal with all these subject-matters in a few printed pages, it would be a fatal error to stick to the letter of the act. It is the duty of this court to look around in order to get at the proper construction to put on the different paragraphs of the act ... One section cannot be taken by itself, but all must be read together in order that, by a broad, liberal and quasi-political interpretation, the true meaning may be gathered.[33]

Dismissing as a legal fiction McDougall's contention that the dominion had been created from a political chaos, he proceeded to interpret each clause of the act in the light of the historical reality that three corporate entities, comprising four distinct communities, had come together by their own will – or at least by that of their lawful representatives. Bethune followed with the case that provincial sovereignty was implied in the act, and Loranger argued that the BNA Act represented not an act of absolute imperial might but a treaty binding the empire and four provinces, combined in compact, to form a joint authority vested with specific powers for specific purposes. Any other interpretation was contrary not only to history but to reason: 'Why should the province of Quebec, for example, have abandoned its rights, the most sacred, guaranteed by treaties and preserved by secular contests, and sacrificed its language, its institutions and its laws, to enter into an insane union, which, contracted under these conditions, would have been the cause of its national and political annihilation? And why should the other provinces, any more than Quebec, have consented to lose their national existence and consummate this political suicide?'[34]

The court split 4 to 2 in favour of the appeal, with Fournier joining the *Lenoir* majority and Chief Justice Sir William Ritchie siding with Strong. It was to be expected, but Ontario could appeal to Whitehall. In July 1883 Mowat appeared in person before the supreme judicial tribunal of the empire on the first of two occasions when he crossed the Atlantic to plead in his capacity as Her Majesty's attorney general for Ontario (not the lieutenant-governor's, surely, although appointed by him). Joining him in support of a leading English equity specialist, Horace Davey, was the future deputy attorney general of Ontario, John R. Cartwright. The dominion was represented by Lash in support of the English solicitor general – the latter acting on private retainer, of course, not in his official capacity.

It is always good to win, but to Mowat the provincial victory may have been tinged with disappointment. The Privy Council judgment avoided the grand constitutional issue and decided the case on the narrower one that had formed the basis for the Quebec judgment of 1876. Section 109 of the BNA Act gave each province 'all lands, mines, minerals and royalties' belonging to it at Confederation, and the Judicial Committee decided that escheat was a royalty incidental to the provincial tenure of Crown lands.[35] The case for provincial sovereignty remained in the balance a decade longer.

When the row over provincial sovereignty resumed at the end of 1885, it was at the initiative of Ottawa. In the meantime Macdonald had lost three more major battles with Mowat before the Judicial Committee of the Privy Council. One was a long-standing dispute over the Ontario-Manitoba boundary. On returning to power in 1878, Macdonald had refused to ratify the line drawn by a board of arbitrators set up during the Mackenzie administration. The arbitrators, before whom Mowat had represented the province in person, had accepted the provincial case in almost every respect; so did the privy councillors when it came before them in 1884.[36]

The other two provincial victories, which were gained in 1884 and 1885 respectively, concerned Macdonald's use of the disallowance power. One, which had to do with liquor licensing, is described below in connection with the distribution of legislative powers. The other stemmed from a dispute between two Ottawa Valley lumbering firms. Boyd, Caldwell and Son had begun floating sawlogs down a stream that had been improved by a downstream proprietor, Peter McLaren, to facilitate the passage of his own cut. McLaren applied to the Court of Chancery for a restraining injunction. A provincial statute of 1849 had established the right of lumbermen to use all streams 'during the Spring, Summer and Autumn freshets' for the transport of lumber, but McLaren relied on a judicial decision of 1863 which had held that the right applied to streams capable in their natural state of transporting lumber, not to those that could do so only after being improved for the purpose. While *McLaren v Caldwell* was proceeding through the courts, Mowat carried through a provincial act to establish the rights of upstream proprietors. McLaren successfully appealed to Ottawa to disallow the act as an unacceptable infringement upon the rights of private property.

Four years in a row, Mowat's disallowed bill was re-enacted by the legislature. The first three times Macdonald disallowed it again. Before he could do so a fifth time, the Privy Council intervened. The courts of Chancery and Appeal had both confirmed Caldwell's right, only to be reversed by the Supreme Court of Canada; but the Judicial Committee sustained Caldwell on the basis of the 1849 act, concluding that the judgment of 1863 on which McLaren had relied was mistaken. Thus the provincial statute that Macdonald had disallowed four times as an atrocious interference with private rights was authoritatively declared to have been merely an affirmation of the law of the land.[37]

The Conservatives sustained so much damage from Macdonald's use of the disallowance power from 1880 to 1884 that he never employed it again in his contest with Mowat. For Mowat, the three Privy Council decisions of 1884-5 were a resounding vindication.[38] More important, the Judicial Committee's judgment in the licensing case had produced a first and hopeful sign of its attitude towards the question of provincial sovereignty. The Crooks Act had been challenged on the ground that it created boards of licence commissioners with the power to pass by-laws. It was argued that the provincial legislature was not sovereign but a mere municipal wielder of powers delegated by Westminster and therefore, on the maxim that 'a delegate may not delegate,' incompetent to devolve any of its lawmaking powers. According to the Judicial Committee, this contention was

founded on an entire misconception of the true character and position of the provincial legislatures. They are in no sense delegates of or acting under any mandate from the Imperial Parliament. When the British North America Act enacted that there should be a legislature for Ontario, and that its legislative assembly should have exclusive authority to make laws for the Province and for provincial purposes in relation to the matters enumerated in sect. 92, it conferred powers not in any sense to be exercised by delegation from or as agents of the Imperial Parliament, but authority as plenary and as ample within the limits prescribed by sect. 92 as the Imperial Parliament in the plenitude of its power possessed and could bestow. Within these limits of subjects and area the local legislature is supreme, and has the same authority as the Imperial Parliament, or the Parliament of the Dominion, would have had under like circumstances to confide to a municipal institution or body of its own creation authority to make by-laws or resolutions as to subjects specified in the enactment.[39]

Coming only a few months after the Mercer judgment, this declaration hinted strongly at how the committee might have decided the sovereignty issue on that occasion had it chosen to do so.

Macdonald therefore had ground to recover late in 1885 when he moved to reopen the question of provincial sovereignty. The reason for the dominion initiative was plausible enough. Canadian queen's counsel were beginning to appear before the Judicial Committee, who could not be expected to know their rightful precedence; it was desirable to prepare an accurate list for their guidance and that of the Supreme Court of Canada, who might also be unaware of the minutiae of each provincial bar. In asking the provincial governments for a list of QCs belonging to the bar of their province, however, Ottawa requested that it be informed only of pre-Confederation patentees and those subsequently appointed by the governor general. Post-Confederation creations by the provinces were pointedly ignored.

Ottawa's initiative soon stood revealed as a blunder. Mowat replied with a reasoned statement of Ontario's position on provincial sovereignty in general and the right to appoint QCs in particular. It was obviously intended for the eyes of the Judicial Committee: it was after all important for their lordships to know that what purported to be a full list of queen's counsel at the bar of Ontario might be defective. In addition to repeating the general case, therefore, Mowat stressed that the question had never been fully considered by competent authority. The imperial law officers' opinion of 1872 against the provincial power to create QCs by prerogative had been rendered on the basis of a 'very imperfect case' submitted by Ottawa after Nova Scotia had expressed doubt in the matter; the law officers had known only that one province questioned the lieutenant-governor's prerogative, not that others confidently maintained it, and they had not been fully apprised of the provincial case; the statutes passed in accordance with the law officers' opinion had been condemned by a judgment grounded on an equally defective case, one that unfortunately was unappealable.[40] What Ottawa had done, in fact, was give Mowat the chance to draw *Lenoir v Ritchie* to the Privy Council's attention and let their lordships know that the underlying issue of provincial sovereignty was very much alive. He again invited Ottawa to refer this question to the Privy Council, but – as in 1872 – in vain.

In 1887 Mowat moved forward on the political front. A conference of provincial premiers met at Quebec under his chairmanship in what was billed as a re-enactment of the Confederation conference of 1864. Only the tiny peripheral provinces of Prince Edward Island and British Columbia, neither of them a party to the original agreement, spurned the invitation. In a conclave that was in itself an endorsement of the compact theory of Confederation, the other five premiers unanimously adopted a series of resolutions on provincial grievances against Ottawa, including several proclaiming the provincialist position on sovereignty and disallowance.

Macdonald ignored the conference, but he could not counter-attack. He had fatally overreached himself in his passages of arms with Mowat during the first half of the decade, and the execution of the Métis leader Louis Riel in 1885 had further alarmed a Quebec already anxious for the safety of French Canada within Confederation. Manitoba resented the economic dominion of the Canadian Pacific Railway much more than Mowat's success in the recent boundary dispute, in which the real loser was the dominion, since Ottawa in establishing the province in 1870 had retained ownership of the natural resources within its territory. The maritime provinces had their special grievances and fell in with Mowat. Rome and her allies were on the march; the Carthaginian could parry but not strike back.[41]

Mowat chose to deliver the coup de grâce on his enemy's strongest ground. In 1888 he carried through the legislature 'An Act respecting the Executive Administration of the Laws of this Province.'[42] The act cited the provisions of the BNA Act that confirmed the lieutenant-governors of Ontario and Quebec in the powers exercised by their predecessors back to 1791 and invested the provinces with legislative authority over the administration of justice. It declared that the lieutenant-governor of Ontario had executive authority over every matter within the legislative authority of the province, and that that authority extended to the commutation or remission of sentences imposed for offences against provincial laws and laws pertaining to matters within the provincial jurisdiction.

It was declaratory legislation in the style of the queen's counsel statutes of 1873, but the choice of subject was especially noteworthy. The Quebec conference of 1864 had agreed that the pardoning power should reside in the lieutenant-governors. As Mowat well knew, this agreement had not been reflected in the BNA Act because the Colonial Office insisted that the power must belong to the governor general as the sovereign's immediate representative.[43] In asserting that section 65 of the BNA Act invested lieutenant-governors with that power none the less in respect of matters within the competence of the provincial legislature, he was subjecting his view of the act to the sternest test yet.

After launching this legislative ironclad on its long voyage through judicial waters, Mowat went again to London. In the summer of 1888 he and Edward Blake presented Ontario's case in *St Catharine's Milling and Lumber Co.* v *The Queen, on the information of the Attorney General for Ontario*, a dispute arising from the decision of the Manitoba boundary dispute four years previously. That decision had confirmed Ontario's political authority in the disputed territory, but Ottawa claimed to own the land and its valuable timber. Part of the provincial case was a restatement of the compact theory of Confederation and the contention that the BNA Act should be construed 'in a large, liberal and comprehensive spirit, considering the magnitude of the subjects with which it purports to deal in very few words.' In awarding Ontario the land as well as the territory the committee followed *Mercer*, again reserving judgment on the sovereignty question; but the argument may well have impressed Lord Watson, now sitting for the first time in a major Canadian constitutional case, for it was he who was to write the decisive judgment four years later.[44]

   Mowat's Executive Administration Act passed the test of the provincial Court of Appeal, where it benefited from the advocacy of Edward Blake.[45] It was awaiting the decision of the Supreme Court of Canada in the summer of 1892 when the Judicial Committee gave judgment in the case of *The Liquidators of the Maritime Bank of Canada* v *The Receiver-General of New Brunswick*. The subject of the case is unimportant; the judgment was critical. The object of the BNA Act, it authoritatively declared, had been 'neither to weld the provinces into one, nor to subordinate provincial governments to a central authority, but to create a federal government in which they should all be represented, entrusted with the exclusive administration of affairs in which they had a common interest, each province retaining its independence and autonomy.'[46] Within their reduced sphere of competence, the provincial governments were fully as sovereign as those of Nova Scotia, New Brunswick, and Canada before Confederation. After this judgment the Supreme Court had no choice but to confirm the Executive Administration Act.[47] Later in 1892 Mowat launched a reference that led to judicial confirmation by the Privy Council of the queen's counsel statutes of 1873, thereby reversing *Lenoir*.[48] All this was merely mopping-up, though; after *Maritime Bank* it could no longer be doubted that the provinces were sovereign and responsible governments.

THE DISTRIBUTION OF LEGISLATIVE POWERS

The question of provincial sovereignty was capable of absolute decision: either the provinces were sovereign within their allotted sphere of jurisdiction or they were not. The distribution of legislative powers was a more complex problem, since new matters of legislation could arise ad infinitum. As a theoretically inexhaustible subject it did not lend itself to any kind of grand strategy, but within the limits of possibility Mowat's victory was to be as immense as his victory on provincial sovereignty.

   Mowat showed a kind of genius in devising legislation that exercised the provincial powers to their limit, particularly the power to legislate concerning property and civil rights in the province – a subject that was Mowat's special area of expertise as an equity lawyer and judge. His notable achievements in this vein were an act that established standard terms for fire-insurance policies in the face of the dominion power to legislate in relation to the regulation of trade and commerce, and two others that made up for defects in the law relating to bankruptcy and insolvency, a subject specifically assigned to the dominion.[49] None of the acts touched on politically sensitive issues, though, and none caused much friction between Ontario and Ottawa.

The liquor trade was different. The prohibition movement was approaching its full strength in the 1870s and 1880s. Prohibitionists were moral crusaders with little regard for constitutional niceties, and they badgered both levels of government impartially. In addition to the inherent political importance of the liquor trade, a further consideration in Ontario was the political patronage created by the Crooks Act of 1876,[50] which set up a licensing system administered by a horde of local commissioners and inspectors appointed by the government.

In Ontario, by virtue of a statute of 1864 called the Dunkin Act,[51] prohibition was operative in any municipality where a majority of the electors opted for it in a referendum. In 1878 the Mackenzie government introduced a similar system across Canada by a law known as the Scott Act.[52] In 1882 the Privy Council confirmed the validity of the Scott Act in the case of *Russell* v *The Queen*.[53] This decision subsequently became the centralists' lodestar by virtue of its solution to the problem of the distribution of legislative powers as laid down by sections 91 and 92 of the BNA Act. The negation of *Russell* was to be Mowat's outstanding achievement in this field of constitutional struggle, matching his negation of *Lenoir* in the field of provincial sovereignty.

Section 92 conferred on the provinces the exclusive authority to make laws pertaining to the province 'in relation to matters coming within' sixteen 'classes of subjects,' which it enumerated. Fifteen of them were specific classes of wider or narrower extent, such as municipal institutions, property and civil rights, and the solemnization of marriage. The sixteenth class of subjects was stated to be 'Generally all matters of a merely local or private nature.'

Section 91 was more complicated. It began by empowering the dominion 'to make laws for the peace, order and good government of Canada, in relation to all matters not coming within the classes of subjects' reserved to the provinces in section 92. It then amplified this general definition of the dominion sphere by enumerating twenty-nine classes of subjects which, 'notwithstanding anything in this act,' it declared to lie within that sphere: classes such as fisheries, postal service, marriage and divorce, and the regulation of trade and commerce. This enumeration was introduced by a clause stating that it was made 'for greater certainty, but not so as to restrict the generality of the foregoing terms of this section' (those terms being the general grant of power to legislate in relation to all matters not assigned exclusively to the provinces by 92). After the enumeration, section 91 closed by enacting that 'any matter coming within any of the classes of subjects enumerated in this section shall not be deemed to come within the class of matters of a local or private nature comprised in the enumeration of the classes of subjects by this act assigned exclusively to the legislature of the provinces.'

Essentially, this scheme of distribution established two mutually exclusive spheres of power: a provincial sphere of specific powers enumerated in section 92, and a dominion sphere consisting of everything that was not within the provincial sphere. It was simple enough, but with the simplicity of incompleteness, and the incompleteness caused difficulties. The general extent of the dominion power could be determined only by defining the extent of the provincial powers, and some of these were of broad and uncertain extent. The extent of the specified dominion powers was also problematic; the enumeration of certain classes of subjects as comprising matters belonging to the dominion legislative authority left the courts to decide whether any given matter actually did fall within one of the enumerated classes. Such decisions could be controversial. In considering the validity of Mowat's fire-insurance legislation, for instance, the Privy Council had to decide whether the matter in question came within the dominion power to regulate trade and commerce. This in turn depended on how broadly that power was to be construed. The Judicial Committee's analysis of this question in *The Citizens' Insurance Co. v Parsons* (1881) gave rise to fifteen years of uncertainty.[54]

Citizens' Insurance also laid down a system of analysis for assigning the subject-matter of an impugned statute to the proper part of sections 91 and 92. First, one should ask if it fell within one of the classes of subjects enumerated in 92. If it did not, it was clearly ultra vires the provincial legislatures and within those of Parliament. If it did, but fell also within one of the classes enumerated in section 91, it was still intra vires Parliament, since it was removed from the force of section 92 by the declaration that all matters coming within those classes lay within the exclusive legislative authority of the dominion. Only otherwise was it a proper subject of provincial legislation.[55]

In applying this system to the Scott Act, the Privy Council reached a conclusion favourable to the dominion. The validity of the act had been challenged as contravening three articles of section 92. The provinces were entitled to regulate liquor licences for revenue purposes, a power with which prohibition must interfere. The act was also challenged as an interference with property rights unwarranted by any enumerated power in section 91, and as an infringement upon the provincial jurisdiction in relation to matters of a merely local or private nature.

The judgment vindicated the act against all three charges. Its purpose was prohibition; this clearly did not come within the class in section 92 that allowed the provinces to raise a revenue from licences, since prohibition was the direct negation of that power. Neither was it clearly enough within the meaning of 'property and civil rights' to encroach upon the provincial powers under that vast and general head. Last, it did not come within 'matters local and private' on the grounds alleged by the appellant, who had not denied that the dominion could enact a general prohibitory law but merely asserted that the 'local option' aspect of the act made it local rather than general legislation. Since the act did not fall within any of the provincial powers specified in section 92, it was a valid exercise of the dominion's power to legislate for the peace, order, and good government of Canada – this despite the fact that it might incidentally affect matters within the bounds of section 92, such as the provincial taxing power and the individual's right of ownership.[56] The court reserved judgment as to whether the act was also a valid exercise of the dominion jurisdiction over the regulation of trade and commerce, as the Supreme Court of Canada had declared in *The City of Fredericton* v *The Queen*.[57]

Russell encouraged Macdonald to challenge the Crooks Act, Ontario's liquor-licensing law. In 1883 Parliament passed the McCarthy Act,[58] which established a system of regulation along the lines of the Crooks Act for the professed purpose of promoting temperance throughout Canada. But Macdonald had moved too soon. The Crooks Act had been upheld by the Ontario Court of Appeal a year previously, and in December 1883 that judgment was upheld by the Privy Council.

In *Hodge* v *The Queen*, the Crooks Act was ineptly attacked on the ground that *Russell* had placed the regulation of the liquor trade in general within the dominion power to regulate trade and commerce. In its judgment the Judicial Committee pointed out the error: *Russell* had upheld the Scott Act under Ottawa's general authority to make laws for the peace, order and good government of Canada. But *Russell* and *Citizens' Insurance* both illustrated the principle 'that subjects which in one aspect and for one purpose fall within sect. 92, may in another aspect and for another purpose fall within sect. 91' (and vice versa).[59] The Crooks Act, in setting up local boards of licensing commissioners, came within the articles of section 92 empowering the provinces to make laws in relation to municipal institutions and matters of a merely local nature.

Hodge did not of itself render the McCarthy Act ultra vires, but it made its legality doubtful and did Macdonald some political harm. Even the leader of the Ontario Conservatives, W.R. Meredith (later chief justice of Ontario), disowned the act, and Mowat exploited his enemies' confusion by slapping a heavy tax on licences issuing under it. Macdonald felt compelled to defend the integrity of the act by disallowing Mowat's tax as a scheme to punish licensees for complying with a valid law. In doing so he ignored the advice of his minister of justice that, as long as it was not so heavy as to be prohibitive, the tax was a valid exercise of the provincial power to raise revenue from liquor licences.

Eventually Macdonald was forced to refer the McCarthy Act to the Supreme Court, which disallowed it. This blow was quickly reinforced by the Judicial Committee's concurrence. At that time neither court gave its reasons in special references, but it is clear that Russell had given a misleading impression of the extent to which the courts would permit Ottawa to legislate for the peace, order, and good government of Canada in terms that were within the competence of the provinces to enact for themselves. The refusal to permit regulation of the retail liquor trade under the dominion 'trade and commerce' power was consistent with the decision in the Citizens' Insurance case, which had assigned to the provinces jurisdiction over the manner in which a trade was to be conducted within a province.[60]

Russell, Hodge, and the McCarthy Act reference settled the jurisdictional issue for the moment, but they left a conundrum. It had been quite reasonable to assume that if the courts would let the dominion legislate on prohibition, they would also let it do so on licensing. The only difference between the two cases was that Hodge had confirmed the provinces' jurisdiction in licensing, while Russell had left the question of their jurisdiction in prohibition unresolved. In deciding that Ottawa could promote temperance by the imposition of uniform prohibition laws, but not by setting up a uniform licensing system in localities that had not adopted prohibition, the Judicial Committee had ruled inconsistently.

That inconsistency gave Mowat an opening by which to put Russell to the test and achieve its modification – once it had stopped being politically useful. In the short run it was very useful. Nothing short of prohibition was going to satisfy the prohibitionists, and Mowat judged theirs to be a minority position, though strengthened by their tendency to be single-issue zealots. *Russell* helped him steer a middle course, gradually tightening the Crooks Act while staving off demands for prohibition on the ground that it was Ottawa's business. As prohibitionism grew in strength, though, so did the demand that Mowat put the jurisdiction issue to the test. Just before the provincial general election of 1890, he took the decisive step by amending the Crooks Act to include a local option similar in principle to the Scott Act.[61]

The new law was tactically ingenious. It showed good faith with the prohibitionists without conceding anything substantial. It allowed Mowat to bring *Russell* up for review without jeopardizing any serious legislative issue, much as he had launched the Executive Administration Act, another practical redundancy, in order to reopen *Lenoir*. It allowed him also to challenge *Fredericton*, the Supreme Court judgment that had confirmed the Scott Act under the unacceptably broad definition of the trade and commerce power on which the Privy Council, in *Russell*, had suspended judgment. Finally, it set up a ground of attack on the Scott Act that had not been used in *Russell*. A preamble to the enacting clause noted that identical legislation had once prevailed in Ontario as part of the province's municipal and licensing laws but had been omitted from the post-Confederation consolidations because of the similar provisions in the Dunkin Act; this, however, had been repealed by the Scott Act, and it was expedient that municipalities should enjoy again their old powers. This language established a basis for arguing that the provinces could enact prohibitory laws by virtue of their jurisdiction in matters relating to municipal institutions – ground that had not been taken in *Russell*, a case originating in New Brunswick, where the municipal law had contained no prohibitory power.

Mowat was all patience and all cunning. During the 1890 session he had procured an act authorizing the government to refer doubtful constitutional questions to the provincial Court of Appeal, a tribunal that had showed itself much more favourable than the Supreme Court to the provincialist position. When, predictably, his local option amendment was challenged as ultra vires, he referred the matter to the court 'in order to avoid a multiplicity of appeals' on the question. Later in 1891 the court gave him the judgment he wanted, one that discounted *Russell* on the ground that it had not been decided in the light of a full statement of the provincialist case.[62] This was the same ground on which Mowat had discounted *Lenoir* v *Ritchie* five years previously in his dispatch on the power to appoint QCs.

Eventually, of course, the Ontario act was challenged in the Supreme Court. But that challenge was not to form the basis of the crucial decision, for events overtook it. During the early 1890s Mowat continued to repel the prohibitionist agitation by arguing that the province's power did not certainly extend beyond retail prohibition. In 1893, however, the Conservatives tried to outbid him for the prohibitionist vote by introducing a total measure into the legislature. Mowat outwitted them with a motion of confidence in the government's intention to secure an authoritative judgment on the extent of the provincial jurisdiction. The motion also provided for a province-wide plebiscite on total prohibition. The plebiscite rendered a substantial majority in favour of prohibition, and Mowat accordingly submitted seven questions on the subject to the Supreme Court of Canada. This he was now willing to do, since a dominion act of 1891 had made such references appealable to the Privy Council.[63]

Mowat's seven questions were intended to elucidate the whole range of provincial options with respect to prohibition. One of them specifically concerned the validity of the Ontario local option law, but the others asked whether the provincial power applied only to the retail trade or extended to wholesale and manufacture and to the banning of imports into the province. Manitoba and Quebec intervened on the provincialist side, while the Dominion Distillers' and Brewers' Association aligned itself with Ottawa. An appeal against a conviction under the Ontario act was before the court at the same time, and there was an overlap of counsel, since J.J. Maclaren, who represented Ontario and Manitoba in the reference, was also retained to defend the Ontario act in the appeal. In the reference Ontario was also represented by Deputy Attorney General John R. Cartwright.[64]

In both hearings, the arguments and judgments turned on three aspects of the general distribution of legislative powers in sections 91 and 92 of the BNA Act: the extent of the general dominion power under section 91 to legislate for the peace, order, and good government of Canada; the breadth of the specific dominion power to legislate in relation to the regulation of trade and commerce; and the principles to be followed in assigning matters to the dominion or provincial legislature. The force of three previous cases was also in question. The provincialists wanted to reverse the Supreme Court decision in *Fredericton* v *The Queen* and to undermine the Privy Council decision in *Russell*. The centralists wanted to discredit the Privy Council's reasoning in *Citizens' Insurance Co.* v *Parsons*, which in confirming Mowat's fire-insurance legislation had defined the trade and commerce power more narrowly than they would have liked.

The provincial contention that retail prohibition came within the power to legislate in relation to municipal institutions was based on *Hodge,* which had upheld provincial regulation of the retail trade under that head. The difference between regulation and prohibition, argued Ontario, was only one of degree; therefore, the analysis that applied to the one must encompass the other. This argument impugned *Russell* by completing the analogy between it and the McCarthy Act reference: both cases concerned legislation by the dominion that was intra vires the provinces under the same subsection of section 92 (or subsections, since here as in *Hodge* the local matters provision was cited in addition to the municipal institutions power); consequently, the Judicial Committee's vindication of the Scott Act under the dominion general power was false.

Since section 92 might be held invalid if retail prohibition were within the specific dominion powers enumerated in section 91, the provincialists also denied that it fell within the trade and commerce power – the only part of section 91 that was relevant. Here they could rely on the McCarthy Act reference, which had complemented *Hodge* by holding that Ottawa could not regulate the sale of liquor. If prohibition was merely an extreme form of regulation, as Ontario maintained, how could Ottawa prohibit under the trade and commerce power what it could not regulate under it? This argument posed a challenge to *Fredericton.*

Cartwright contended further that even if the trade and commerce power were a valid location for prohibition, it should still give way to section 92. This was an attack on the *Citizens' Insurance* approach to the distribution of powers, which accorded the enumerated powers of section 91 primacy over those of section 92. It had been advanced for Ontario as early as the McCarthy Act reference of 1885 and is traceable to an important memorandum (of which more later) written by Mowat four years before that. The argument is best expressed in Mowat's own words:

The general object of the British North America Act as stated in its 91st section was to give the Federal Parliament authority 'to make laws for the peace order & good government of Canada in relation to,' not all matters absolutely, but to 'all matters not coming within the classes of subjects by this Act assigned exclusively to the Legislatures of the Provinces,' and it was declared to be only for greater certainty that an enumeration of particulars is afterwards made, not (as the section cautiously provided) 'so as to restrict the generality of the foregoing terms of this section.' The subsequent enumeration is in form by way of declaration, not enactment ... The enumeration may contain some particulars which unless so specified would not have been held to be included in the general words; but, having reference to the general object which is so stated, & to the form of the section, each article in the enumeration is, where possible & as far as possible, to be so construed as not to include the rights assigned exclusively to the Legislatures of the Provinces.[65]

Chief Justice Strong summarized the argument in affirming its applicability to retail prohibition: 'As the subjects enumerated in section 92 are exceptions out of those mentioned in section 91, it follows that if a ... power is included in ... the former section, the power itself and all appropriate means of carrying it out are to be treated as uncontrolled by anything in section 91.'[66]

Fredericton, relying as it did on a broad interpretation of the trade and commerce power, was a major strategic target, but *Russell* was the greater tactical challenge because it was a Privy Council decision and hence irreversible, no matter how erroneous its premises. The Judicial Committee had already confirmed Ottawa's power to pass a law identical in principle to the Ontario local option act: to get around this the provincialists relied on the 'Aspect Doctrine' – the declaration in *Hodge* 'that subjects which in one aspect and for one purpose fall within sect. 92, may in another aspect and for another purpose fall within sect. 91' – and especially on its application in the Ontario Assignments Act reference of 1894. In that decision the Judicial Committee had confirmed Mowat's act of 1885 permitting a debtor to make a voluntary assignment of his assets in order to share them fairly among his creditors regardless of the priority that current or pending litigation might establish among them. The committee had admitted that Ottawa might legislate in identical terms under its power to pass laws in relation to bankruptcy and insolvency, but it had justified the Ontario act on the ground that such a scheme, being voluntary, was ancillary rather than essential to bankruptcy and insolvency legislation, the essence of which was compulsion.

The Assignment Act decision was helpful to the defence of the Ontario local option act because it established that Ottawa and the provinces might have a *concurrent* power to legislate in respect of some matters falling within sections 91 and 92. Yet it left one difficulty: it laid down that in the case of a conflict of legislation, the provincial law must give way to the dominion's. How could this help Ontario's local option law when the Scott Act had already set up a local option scheme applicable to every municipally organized acre of the province?[67]

The centralists assailed these weak points in the provincialist case. They denied that the Ontario act was valid under section 92, for the municipal institutions power could not implicitly authorize the provinces to legislate in relation to matters the BNA Act did not assign to them expressly. Even if that power did include a quantity of implicit authority, it could hardly extend to prohibition, which had been only a recent addition to the municipal law of Upper and Lower Canada at the time of Confederation and had not existed at all in the maritime provinces. But even if prohibition was admitted to lie within section 92, the Scott Act's comprehensive local option scheme occupied the whole field of legislation and must override the Ontario act.

The centralists' major concern, however, was to place retail prohibition within the dominion trade and commerce power and so vindicate *Fredericton*'s broad interpretation of that power. The most comprehensive and powerful effort to do so was the judgment of the octogenarian Supreme Court justice, John Wellington Gwynne, who had been proclaiming an extreme centralist dogma since the days of *Lenoir* and *Mercer*. More than forty years earlier, he and Mowat had confronted each other in *Toronto v Bowes*, the 'Ten Thousand Pound Job' case of 1853. The rematch was no coincidence: then as now, Gwynne was aligned with forces working to contain Toronto, and Upper Canada in general, within the sway of Montreal finance, while Mowat represented Toronto-led resistance to those forces.[68] An Irishman of the same cultural stamp as W.W. Baldwin and William Hume Blake, Gwynne now received a strong assist from Robert Sedgwick, a Scottish-born Nova Scotian recently appointed to the Supreme Court after five years as deputy minister of justice at Ottawa.[69]

The BNA Act, declared Gwynne, must always be interpreted in the light of its framers' intentions as revealed by contemporary report. He quoted the words of John A. Macdonald, George-Etienne Cartier, George Brown, and the Earl of Carnarvon, colonial secretary in 1866-7, to show the centralist intent of Tory and Grit, of Upper Canadian and Lower, of colonial leaders and imperial. Part of that intent had been to avoid the fatal flaws of the u.s. constitution, one of which was the federal government's lack of authority over intrastate commerce. 'If the framers of our constitution had contemplated conferring upon the Dominion Parliament only such a limited jurisdiction as that possessed by the Congress of the United States they would have had no difficulty, and doubtless would not have failed, in so expressing themselves,' affirmed Gwynne. 'On the contrary, the language they have used is of a most unlimited character.'[70] On this basis he denounced *Citizens' Insurance* for its undue constriction of the dominion trade and commerce jurisdiction and the Assignments Act reference for unduly extending the provincial power with regard to property and civil rights.

The Judicial Committee had based its narrow construction of the trade and commerce power in *Citizens' Insurance* on the fact that certain subjects that might have been comprehended by the term 'trade and commerce' had been separately specified in the enumeration of dominion powers: banking, weights and measures, bills of exchange and promissory notes, bankruptcy and insolvency, and interest. The committee deduced from this that the framers of the BNA Act had placed a narrow construction on 'the regulation of trade and commerce,' which did not comprehend those matters and might therefore not comprehend others. Such a narrow construction might, it rather fancifully surmised, reflect the sense attached to the term 'regulations of trade' in the Act of Union of 1707 between England and Scotland.[71]

Gwynne and Sedgwick responded that these matters had been mentioned in order to extract them from the scope of the provincial power respecting property and civil rights; their specification did not, therefore, imply that they were not also comprehended within the term 'trade and commerce.' It was inconceivable that the British North American statesmen who framed the act could have had the Act of Union in mind while doing so: their guide must have been the u.s. constitution, the only federal constitution they knew and the awful example from which they were so anxious to learn, said Gwynne; their terminology, added Sedgwick, must have been that of contemporary British North American legislation, not borrowed from antique British statutes.[72]

To discredit the Assignment Act decision, Gwynne cited Carnarvon's statement to the British Parliament in 1867 that concurrent jurisdiction was shared by Ottawa and the provinces in respect of only three subjects, each specified in the act: agriculture, immigration, and public works. The notion that it could exist in respect of other matters was by inference delusive. It could at any rate never be stretched to establish such jurisdiction in relation to prohibition. This was not an extreme degree of regulation (as the provincialists claimed) but its negation, since the power to regulate a trade presupposed that the trade was lawful. Provinces could no more prohibit the retail sale of liquor under their regulatory power than the dominion (following *Hodge* and the McCarthy Act reference) could regulate it under its prohibitory power.[73]

Only after unfolding this lengthy case for a broad interpretation of the trade and commerce power did Gwynne notice the effort to justify

Ontario's local option law under the municipal power. He dismissed it in a page, thereby vindicating *Russell*; but it was *Fredericton* he was most concerned to uphold, with its broad construction of the trade and commerce power. 'That judgment has never been reversed, nor, in my opinion, shaken,' he said. 'If ever it should be reversed it will in my opinion be a matter of deep regret, as defeating the plain intent of the framers of our constitution and imperilling the success of the scheme of confederation.'[74]

The members of the Judicial Committee spiked poor Gwynne with his own pike. They agreed with him that regulation was inconsistent with prohibition but concluded that the Scott Act could not therefore be valid under the power to regulate trade and commerce – so much for *Fredericton*. But their main purpose was to isolate *Russell*. That decision had relieved them 'from the difficult duty of considering whether the [Scott Act] relates to the peace, order and good government of Canada, in such sense as to bring its provisions within the competency of the Canadian Parliament' – ominous language, since their predecessors of 1882 had so concluded without difficulty. They further disparaged the decision by noting that neither Ottawa nor the provinces had been represented in the argument, which had arisen between a private prosecutor and a person convicted at his instance; still, it 'must be accepted as an authority to the extent to which it goes.' Where brought into effect by referendum, the provisions of the Scott Act 'must receive effect as valid enactments relating to the peace, order, and good government of Canada.'[75]

After this grudging concession to their own irreversibility, their lordships paused briefly to garotte *Fredericton* and commend the narrow construction of the dominion trade and commerce power in *Citizens' Insurance*. Then they banished *Russell*, like Ishmael with his mother into the wilderness, by declaring both the sale and manufacture of liquor subject to provincial prohibition under the local matters provision of section 92 – or possibly under the property and civil rights provision; it was not necessary in the present case to decide which was more appropriate (each had been considered and ruled out in *Russell* fourteen years before). The committee denied that the Scott Act excluded the Ontario local option by occupying the whole field of legislation: it excluded it only from those municipally organized acres where it had been brought into effect by referendum; everywhere else the two laws stood side by side. Oliver Mowat's two legislative ironclads, the Executive Administration Act and the Ontario local option, ruled the waves together.

Mid-twentieth-century critics denounced the prohibition reference both for rejecting *Russell's* broad view of the dominion general power to legislate for the peace, order, and good government of Canada and for affirming, in preference to *Fredericton*, the restrictive view of the dominion trade and commerce power enunciated in *Citizens' Insurance*. The criticisms in relation to the dominion general power rest on a highly schematic analysis, which portrays the judgment as absolutely bad in contrast to the absolute good of *Russell* and makes much of the apparent inconsistency of its reasoning.[76] Considered as the result of a historical process, however, the judgment appears rather as an attempt to treat the problem of the dominion general power more thoroughly than in *Russell*, and its seeming inconsistencies flow from the fact that it dealt with a subject of legislation – retail prohibition – that *Russell* had confused by its incomplete handling of the problem. 'Your Lordships do not overrule, you explain,' said Sir Horace Davey in the McCarthy Act hearings, discussing whether the committee should or could contradict its decision in *Russell*. Now at last their lordships 'explained' – but they did not overrule.[77]

Russell had confirmed the Scott Act on the basis that the act 'did not fall within any of the classes of subjects assigned exclusively to the Provincial Legislatures' and must therefore be valid under the dominion general power even if *Fredericton* erred in placing it within the trade and commerce power. The general power was precluded by its very terms from matters belonging to section 92, and the appellant had argued that the provinces could pass for themselves under section 92 a local option act like the Scott Act as a matter of a merely local nature. The Privy Council did not deny this, but asserted that the declared object of the Scott Act, that of establishing uniform laws throughout Canada for the promotion of temperance, shifted it from section 92 into the scope of the general power.[78]

In procuring the McCarthy Act (the dominion licensing law) in 1883, John A. Macdonald had acted quite in accord with this reasoning. If it was desirable to establish uniform laws throughout Canada for the promotion of temperance by prohibition, why was it less desirable to set up a uniform system of regulation for the promotion of temperance in localities that had not adopted prohibition? In discountenancing the McCarthy Act (without stating reasons), the Supreme Court and the Judicial Committee denied the logic of *Russell*. The only difference between the two cases was that *Hodge* had already decided that the provinces could regulate retail sale, while *Russell* had left undecided the question of whether they could prohibit it. This difference could not save the Judicial Committee from inconsistency. *Russell* said that, even if the provinces could prohibit, the Scott Act was still a valid exercise of the dominion general power because its generality of purpose and application lifted it out of section 92. By analogy, the provincial licensing power was no bar to the McCarthy Act.

By his local option law and prohibition reference, Mowat compelled the committee to confront this inconsistency. *Russell* was a complete contradiction of the approach to the dominion general power laid down in his memorandum of 1881. We have noticed the memorandum's insistence on a narrow interpretation of the dominion powers enumerated in section 91. The next paragraph extended that insistence to the general power, arguing that the enumerated classes of subjects in sections 91 and 92 were intended to embrace all possible subjects of legislative action and that the general power was merely a residual authority to cope with the unforeseen. 'An unnecessary reference to the general words in order to give or support a wider interpretation of the enumerated powers of the Federal authority than these might otherwise bear, is contrary to the intention and (it is submitted) to the proper construction of the Act.'[79] *Russell's* casual confirmation of an act of Parliament which each province could have enacted for itself represented the antithesis of Mowat's approach, and one from which the Judicial Committee, and even to some extent the Supreme Court, backed away once the McCarthy Act reference gave Mowat the opportunity to contest it.

Obliged by the prohibition reference finally to resolve the contradiction, the Judicial Committee did so by refining *Russell's* reasoning in a way that substantially adopted the approach laid out in Mowat's memorandum. Since the dominion general power was precluded by definition from matters confided to the provinces by section 92, the committee concluded that it must 'be strictly confined to such matters as are unquestionably of Canadian interest and importance.' It could not justify dominion legislation on matters normally within the provincial competence unless the matter in question had attained 'such dimensions as to affect the body politic of the Dominion.' The committee did not prescribe any test of that condition but implied the need for one by remarking that to allow Ottawa to legislate on such matters merely 'upon the assumption that these matters also concern the peace, order, and good government of the Dominion' – as Macdonald had attempted with the McCarthy Act – would 'practically destroy the autonomy of the provinces.'[80] The Scott Act was not necessarily ultra vires, but it should not have been confirmed without some test of its necessity.

As well as defining the scope of the dominion general power, the committee determined the relationship between the enumerated dominion powers of section 91 and those assigned to the provinces by section 92. The former were introduced by a declaration that the exclusive legislative authority of the dominion extended to them 'notwithstanding anything in the act.' This language might seem to imply that such matters were ultra vires the provinces. In concluding that they were not, the Judicial Committee did not discuss this introductory language but relied on the final clause of the section, which stated that no matter belonging to the enumerated classes was to be 'deemed to come within the class of matters of subject of a local or private nature comprised in the enumeration of the classes of subjects by this Act assigned exclusively to the legislatures of the provinces.'

This final clause was ambiguous in several ways. It could be construed as defining the relationship of the section 91 enumerations to all of the classes enumerated in section 92, or merely to the class specifically designated as 'matters of a merely local or private nature.' The committee had already opted for the latter definition in *Citizens' Insurance*, and now it had to confess an error. But even if the clause were held to apply to the whole of section 92, it could still be read in two ways. It might be construed as reinforcing the introductory language in excluding the provincial legislative power from matters belonging to any of the section 91 enumerations; alternatively, it might be seen merely as protecting Ottawa's right to legislate on such matters even when they seemed also to fall within section 92. It was this latter meaning, which did not limit the provincial power, that the committee put on it in the Prohibition judgment. The clause 'was not meant to derogate from the legislative authority given to provincial legislatures ... save to the extent of enabling the Parliament of Canada to deal with matters local and private in those cases where such legislation is necessarily incidental to the exercise of the powers conferred upon it by the enumerative heads of clause 91.'[81]

The Judicial Committee's treatment of this final clause of section 91 has been dismissed as 'legerdemain'; together with the committee's alleged neglect of the introductory language, it has been implicitly but unambiguously ascribed to a design to pervert the BNA Act. One recent writer denounces the committee's analysis of the clause as entirely newfangled and unjustified; another admits puzzlement at the reading.[82]

In fact, although their lordships did not cite the introductory language at this point, they did not ignore it; they merely assumed tacitly that it supported rather than contradicted their construction. In doing so they were following the view propounded in Mowat's memorandum of 1881, advanced by Deputy Attorney General Cartwright in the prohibition reference and upheld in the Supreme Court by Chief Justice Strong. The key contention was that the declaration introducing the enumerations was itself governed by the proviso that it was made 'for greater certainty, but not so as to restrict the generality of the foregoing terms of this section.' Those terms were the general grant of authority to Parliament (as Mowat put it) ' "to make laws for the peace order & good government of Canada in relation to" not all matters absolutely, but to "all matters not coming within the classes of subjects by this Act assigned exclusively to the Legislatures of the provinces." ' In abusing the Judicial Committee for supposedly extending the scope of the provincial legislative powers at the expense of the dominion enumerated powers that supposedly annihilated them, mid-twentieth-century critics consistently ignored this crucial proviso, and their error lingers on.[83]

GUARDIAN OF PROVINCIAL RIGHTS

We have reviewed Mowat's struggle for provincial rights chiefly in terms of a succession of cases and the reasoning they evoked. Mowat's success was partly a victory of forensic reasoning, but it was also very much a triumph of forensic strategy and tactics. His main strategic weakness was his inability to control the flow of litigation into the Supreme Court or the Privy Council. He did all he could as attorney general for Ontario, however, to ensure that constitutional questions came before the Judicial Committee as often as possible and in the shape best suited to provincial interests.

The critical influence on his strategy was *Lenoir* v *Ritchie*. To Mowat this case represented all that was uncontrollable in the process of constitutional construction. It was private litigation originating in another province, and the provincialist case was so ill-founded in substance that it was unappealable when the constitutional issue was decided adversely. In order to prevent constitutional issues from reaching the courts in such a form in future, Mowat used two instruments: the special reference and the loaded statute.

The special reference brought a doubtful constitutional question to the Privy Council or the Supreme Court so that it could be fully argued by the governments concerned rather than left to the haphazard exertions of private litigants and their counsel. It was also a way of avoiding the uncertainty that sprang from private litigation such as *Lenoir* and *Mercer*, which often entailed a variety of questions in addition to the constitutional one. Given a good case and a sound bench, it was a handy tool of constitutional construction, but institutional flaws limited its value. Reference to the Supreme Court could be made only by the dominion government, and to the Privy Council only by the imperial government; in effect, neither tribunal could be consulted without Ottawa's approval. Moreover, references to the Supreme Court were unappealable, and after *Lenoir* that court was unacceptable to Mowat as a tribunal of final judgment. Finally, neither the Privy Council nor the Supreme Court gave reasons for their decisions in special references.[84]

In 1887 Mowat promoted a provincial act allowing the attorney general for Ontario or his dominion counterpart to launch an action in the High Court of Ontario (the provincial superior courts of common law and equity as combined by his Judicature Act of 1881) for a declaration as to the validity of any Ontario enactment. The judges were to give reasons for their decisions, which were to be appealable to the Privy Council. Since such an action required the consent of both parties, however, it too depended on Ottawa's compliance. In 1890, therefore, Mowat brought in his act allowing the provincial government to refer constitutional matters to the Court of Appeal for a reasoned decision appealable to London. This enabled him to make an appealable reference without Ottawa's consent should he wish to forestall an unappealable reference by Ottawa to the Supreme Court.[85]

It is significant that Mowat introduced the unilateral reference at the same time as his local option measure. This was his second resort to the loaded statute – that is, a statute designed to bring a specific constitutional question before the courts in the most desirable form. The dominion minister of justice, Sir John Thompson, had chosen to test the first, the Executive Administration Act of 1888, in the High Court of Ontario in order to get a reasoned decision;[86] but the loaded statute was a risky ploy as long as Ottawa could opt to test it instead by an unappealable reference to the Supreme Court. Mowat made sure he could forestall such a reference before he launched his ironclad against *Russell*.

In 1891 Thompson, stimulated no doubt by Mowat's legislation, amended the Supreme Court Act to require reasoned judgments in reference cases and to permit appeal to London.[87] But reference to the court still depended on Ottawa's consent. This did not matter as far as Ontario legislation was concerned, since that could be referred to the provincial Court of Appeal; but in 1891 a case like *Lenoir* arose. The constitutionality of a Manitoba law based on his Assignment Act of 1885 was unexpectedly challenged in a case originating between private parties on other issues. Anxious to have the constitutional question decided on a full discussion of its merits rather than left to the hazards of private litigation, Mowat at once proposed to Thompson that they refer it to the Supreme Court. Thompson refused, saying that it was proper to leave it to be decided on the basis of the pending litigation.[88]

It was the same ground on which Mowat and Edward Blake had abandoned their proposed reference on escheats in 1876; but that had been before *Lenoir*. Mowat's reaction was vitriolic: 'I observe that you attach little importance to a good argument by counsel as a means of securing a sound judgment by the Court; and I remember that you intimated a like view some years ago in our correspondence about Provincial Q.C.'s. If this view has been the consequence of your judicial experience in Nova Scotia the fact must have arisen from local causes. The contrary is, I am sure, the view of the Ontario Bench and Bar, and in fact of every other Bench and Bar of which I have knowledge.' In England a second argument was often called for by the court in a difficult case if the first argument was insufficiently full; everywhere large fees were paid to first-class counsel in order to secure thorough preparation and full argument; Thompson's refusal to make the reference was a deplorable emulation of the laissez-faire approach to constitutional construction prevalent in the United States.

Thompson replied that the government could hardly be expected to take the lead in litigating on all doubtful constitutional questions, but he would be glad to consider a reference if the case was decided on some other point than the constitutionality of the statute. This was no comfort to Mowat, whose aim was to avoid the constitutional question being wrongly decided because of inadequate presentation, as in *Lenoir*. Luckily, his reference statute of 1890 enabled him to force the issue by referring his own Assignments Act to the Ontario Court of Appeal, and the question was finally decided to his satisfaction by the Privy Council in 1894.[89]

The lengths to which Mowat was willing to go, after *Lenoir*, in order to influence private litigation are revealed by *Citizens' Insurance Co. v Parsons*. This was one of three lawsuits involving Mowat's fire-insurance law, two of them launched by Parsons and the third by another plaintiff, which the Supreme Court of Canada decided simultaneously in 1880. The decision was rendered a couple of months after *Fredericton* had placed its broad construction on the dominion power to regulate trade and commerce. The decision was 3 to 2 in Mowat's favour, but Gwynne, dissenting, denounced it as inconsistent with *Fredericton*.[90]

Mowat was anxious to have his law upheld by the Privy Council, but to his alarm the insurance companies tried to buy off their adversaries in order to present an ex parte (unopposed) appeal. They were aided by the fact that Parsons, at least, had been reduced to insolvency by the delays resulting from the litigation. Mowat therefore asked the province's London solicitors whether Ontario could intervene in the case. They reported that the province could not intervene as of right but might petition for leave to do so. This they recommended, since the petition, even if refused, would allow the province to present its case and lodge it in the judges' mind.

Whether or not Mowat took this advice, he finally followed a different but highly efficacious course. Instead of intervening formally, the province funded Parsons's response to the appeal and Mowat collaborated with Parsons's solicitors and counsel in the preparation of their case. Although Mowat had visited Europe the previous year he went there again. In May 1881 he conferred with Parsons's solicitors in London. A prolific correspondence ensued while Mowat toured Scotland; it included a detailed memorandum by him on the respondent's brief. He authorized the retainer of Sir John Holker, lately attorney general, at the province's expense to lead for Parsons. When the Judicial Committee heard the case in July, Mowat was present.[91]

On the lowest estimate of its importance, Mowat's memorandum reveals *Citizens' Insurance* in a new light, for the Judicial Committee followed it directly in rendering that narrow construction of the dominion trade and commerce power which neutralized *Fredericton* and allowed Mowat ultimately to destroy it. What has appeared to be just another of those early private lawsuits, unaffected by government intervention, through which the BNA Act received its first, haphazard interpretation stands revealed as Mowat's first big win. Yet Mowat's commentary may have been less important in this respect than in its influence across fifteen years on the judgment that overthrew *Fredericton*; for it was this very memorandum, twice quoted above, that first adumbrated for the Judicial Committee the doctrines recognized by the prohibition reference in defining the limits of the general and enumerated dominion legislative powers under section 91.

In the latter respect, to be sure, the influence of the memorandum was scarcely instantaneous, since *Russell* contradicted it only six months later; yet even on *Russell* it probably had its effect. *Russell*, like *Lenoir*, was private litigation originating in another province, the sort of case Mowat could not influence. The appellant's bungled argument resulted in that broad interpretation of the dominion general power which it took Mowat fourteen years to rectify. But for *Citizens' Insurance*, the Judicial Committee might have followed *Fredericton* in confirming the Scott Act under the trade and commerce power.

Once the constitutional battle was joined in earnest before the committee, Mowat did not rely on the ad hoc measures that had sufficed to win *Citizens' Insurance*. Sir Horace Davey, first retained in *Mercer* in 1883, accepted a general retainer from the province, which thereby obtained the right to first refusal of his services; in November 1884 a second general retainer went to R.B. Haldane, initially Davey's chosen junior. These arrangements ensured that Mowat's influence on the judicial construction of the BNA Act lasted long after he passed from the scene and went beyond the case law created during his attorneyship. Davey was appointed to the Judicial Committee in 1893. Haldane became a personal friend of Lord Watson, the judge who wrote the *Maritime Bank* and prohibition judgments. In 1912 he joined the Judicial Committee himself as lord chancellor and subsequently wrote some of the judgments that most irked mid-twentieth-century centralists.[92]

This is far from saying that Mowat's victory was somehow gained against the substantive merits of the case. That view has often been stated in reference to *Maritime Bank* and the prohibition reference in particular, along with allegations that both somehow reflect a bias on Lord Watson's part – perhaps introduced by his friendship with Haldane. *Maritime Bank* has been presented as a sudden reversal of twenty-five years' constitutional practice and the prohibition judgment as the virtual repeal of the BNA Act, each undertaken without due (or any) attention on Watson's part to the centralist case. Watson's declaration that the final clause of section 91 applied not only to the last subsection of section 92 but to all sixteen is singled out as a particular perversity – one exacerbated by his failure to justify it.[93] Our historical review of the provincial rights struggle allows us to refute these contentions, both a priori and in detail.

The centralist interpretation of Confederation, in both the late nineteenth and the mid-twentieth century, was founded on the resolutions of the Confederation conferences and on the surviving discussion and explanation of them by British North American politicians of the time. Some of these politicians were of strongly centralist bent, but arguably their version of what Confederation was about has received too much play – Macdonald's in particular. As for the apparently centralist utterances of some later opponents of Macdonald, these have been too readily treated as Holy Writ rather than the expressions of a historical moment, expressions that cannot be understood without reference to their context. At any rate, if the provincialist or compact view of Confederation was as groundless as centralist commentators have made out, it is unlikely that we would find politicians of the intelligence and probity of Edward Blake and Oliver Mowat making it the basis of opposition to Macdonald's centralism almost from the start (Blake did so as early as 1869).[94]

In addition to the contemporary record, two main arguments were urged against the compact view. One was the legalistic contention that Confederation (as William McDougall declared in the escheats case) was achieved not by agreement between the lawful representatives of the participant provinces but by an act of absolute imperial power. This argument relied heavily on the words of the act in order to deny that the provinces ought to be seen as continuing entities (on the tense, for instance, of section 5, which states that 'Canada *shall be* divided into four provinces, named Ontario, Quebec, Nova Scotia, and New Brunswick').[95] The second argument was the reverse of legalism; it was an argument from political realism. It relied on the observation that there was strong opposition to Confederation in the two participant maritime provinces and that the consent even of their governments, let alone their legislatures, was obtained only after a good deal of political chicanery and arm-twisting by Whitehall. From this point of view Confederation was indeed and not only in theory an act of absolute power, and the idea that it represented a compact of the participant provinces was a risible fiction.[96]

But none of these arguments, even if true, can sustain the proposition that the Privy Council ought to have enforced a centralist construction of the BNA Act thirty years later on a country largely antagonistic to it. The legalistic argument fails because it ignores an essential fact: the internal independence of the provinces before Confederation, and that of the dominion after it, was founded not on the letter of the law but on the decision of the imperial government (a decision politically expedient, uncertain in its implications, unevenly applied in practice, yet morally binding) to stop interfering in the provinces' affairs. For the Judicial Committee to have imposed Macdonald's centralism on Canada on such a legalistic basis would have been highly inequitable and a contradiction of the constitutional fiction called responsible government.

So too would have been its imposition on the ground of the other two arguments. Even if the lawful representatives of the participant provinces had been united in centralist intent in the mid-1860s, to have imposed that centralism on their unwilling successors thirty years later would have been to exalt ignorance above experience. And to have enforced a centralism imposed by imperial bullying would have been to compound the abuse of responsible government entailed in that bullying. Once these things are considered, *Maritime Bank*'s confirmation of the compact theory appears not as an indefensible whim but a reasonable decision as to which of two interpretations of the BNA Act was the fairer. It was an exercise in constitutional equity, and the willingness of the Ontario government to refer the issue to the Judicial Committee in 1872 and 1886, and to the Supreme Court in 1876,[97] may reflect the fact that Blake and Mowat (like their English counsel, Davey and Haldane) were specialists in equity.

Certainly *Maritime Bank* was not a sudden reversal of twenty-five years' orthodoxy. It was the termination of twenty-five years' effort by Macdonald and his Colonial Office supporters to impose a particular notion of the constitution – one, perhaps, that best suited the interests of the Montreal business community and its British financiers. It was not a reversal of any settled constitutional doctrine, unless the flawed Supreme Court decision in *Lenoir* can be taken to have settled anything. And although it was sudden in the sense that any judicial decision is sudden, it was not precipitate. By 1892 the committee had been exposed to the controversy repeatedly: in *Mercer* and *Hodge* (1883), the McCarthy Act reference (1885), and *St Catharine's Milling Co.* (1889 – a case, like *Mercer*, in which Mowat represented Ontario before the committee in person), and perhaps also in the dispatch on the appointment of queen's counsel that Mowat had prepared for the committee in 1886. Their lordships had had ample opportunity to make up their minds.

No more was the prohibition judgment whimsical or perverse. We have cleared it of the charge that in defining the relation between the provincial legislative powers in section 92 and the dominion powers enumerated in section 91 it ignored the declaratory clause introducing the latter. Neither did it ignore, as alleged, Mr Justice Gwynne's centralist Supreme Court judgment. It adopted his contention that prohibition was the negation of regulation – though, as we saw, it did not draw the desired conclusion – and it also followed his interpretation of the final clause of section 91. Watson's allegedly perverse application of that clause to all sixteen subsections of section 92 constitutes one of the main charges against the Prohibition judgment; yet it merely emulated Gwynne. The other major charge is that the judgment emasculated the dominion general power by sundering it from the enumerated powers, ignoring the fact that the clause introducing those powers stated that they were enumerated merely in order to illustrate the extent of the general power; but Mowat's memorandum of 1881, to which the judgment gave effect, was in part based on precisely that understanding of the enumeration.[98] Things like this expose the futility of basing criticism of the Judicial Committee's approach to the BNA Act on the wording of the act. It bears repeating that, as regards both sovereignty and the distribution of legislative powers, the act was an optical illusion that could be clarified only by reference to considerations of equity.

The resolution of these uncertainties was an enterprise in which the Judicial Committee was not the only (and, except in an institutional sense, not even the most important) participant. The credit belongs also to the Canadian statesmen, judges, and counsel – men just as conversant with the meaning of Confederation and the needs of the polity as John A. Macdonald and the centralist justices of the Supreme Court – who developed the provincialist case. Above all, perhaps, it belongs to the quarter-century campaign of Oliver Mowat as Her Majesty's attorney general for Ontario – a masterpiece of forensic craft which, by harping on the case for provincial sovereignty, created a favourable context for the resolution of the distribution-of-powers problem.

Oddly enough, the decisive judgment of 1896 came a few days after Mowat had resigned the attorneyship to become minister of justice in the new Liberal government at Ottawa – the first since 1878. One of his first acts in his new job was to cancel the list of 173 names submitted to the governor general by the outgoing ministry for creation as queen's counsel.[99]

7

Minister of Justice

Provincial rights was the most dramatic of the attorney general's concerns during the last third of the century, but it was not the only important one. The others lay principally within the administration of justice. In the drive for greater economy and certainty, the antiquated system of distinct common-law and equity jurisdictions was abolished and the role of the jury diminished in both the civil and the criminal sphere. Although a campaign to abolish the grand jury came to nothing, the ancient role of the criminal trial jury as a shield against oppressive prosecution underwent major revision, virtually without controversy.

THE BNA ACT AND LAW REFORM

The attorney general for Ontario had to concern himself with the BNA Act in other capacities than his role as guardian of provincial rights. The act assigned to the provinces 'the administration of justice in the province, including the constitution, maintenance and organization of provincial courts, both of civil and criminal jurisdiction, and including procedure in civil matters in those courts.' However, 'the criminal law, except the constitution of courts of criminal jurisdiction, but including the procedure in criminal matters' was assigned to the dominion. So was the appointment of judges of the superior, district, and county courts in each province, and the fixing of their salaries, allowances, and pensions. The resulting division of responsibility gave rise to great uncertainty.

John Sandfield Macdonald ran into this almost at once. In 1868 and 1869 he undertook a number of important reforms in the administration of justice that were focused on the duties and status of the county court judges. In 1853 these judges had been given a limited jurisdiction in equity in order to allay contemporary discontent with the Court of Chancery, until then the only tribunal of equitable jurisdiction. Four years later their tenure of office had been altered from tenure during pleasure to tenure during good behaviour. At the same time a court of impeachment had been set up to enforce good behaviour by investigating charges of corruption against them.[1] By the late 1860s it was clear that the chief problem of the county court judges was not corruption so much as incompetence and negligence. Macdonald decided to abolish their equity jurisdiction as being beyond their capacity and to restore them to tenure during pleasure.[2]

At the same time Macdonald increased their responsibility in their sphere of greatest competence, petty criminal jurisdiction. He reduced the annual sittings of the Court of General Sessions of the Peace, over which the county court judge or his deputy generally presided, from four to two (incidentally abolishing the reason for calling them quarter sessions). To make up for this he brought in a new system of criminal procedure, the so-called speedy trial, whereby an accused person, rather than waiting (probably in jail) until the next sessions or assizes, might elect immediate summary trial (that is, without grand and petit jury) in what soon became known as the County Judge's Criminal Court.[3]

This reform marked a major shift away from jury trial in criminal matters. Justices of the peace had always exercised summary jurisdiction in trivial offences. The scope of this jurisdiction had been extended in the 1840s and 1850s, and in 1850 Robert Baldwin, in one of his liberal reforms, had made it subject to appeal to a jury at quarter sessions.[4] Now summary jurisdiction was extended to all offences triable at sessions. Since jury trial for such offences was available only four times a year, at the semi-annual sessions and assizes, and since an accused person might face a longish spell in custody before obtaining it, most defendants henceforth availed themselves of the speedy process in the County Judge's Criminal Court.[5]

Macdonald's reforms required no fewer than four separate acts of legislation – three at Toronto and one at Ottawa.[6] Because the new 'speedy trial' was a matter of criminal procedure, Macdonald carried that part of the package as a dominion measure. He was able to do so in person, since he was a member of Parliament and of the Legislative Assembly. At the initiative of Quebec members, the measure was extended to their province.

Despite splitting the reform in this fashion, however, Macdonald still stumbled among the pitfalls of the BNA Act. The provincial act adjusting the county judges' tenure specified that they were to hold office during pleasure and be subject to removal by the lieutenant-governor 'for inability, incapacity, or misbehaviour, established to the satisfaction of the Lieutenant Governor in Council.' John A. Macdonald, as dominion minister of justice, objected to this provision as vesting the power of removal in two officials; the BNA Act vested the appointment of county court judges in the governor general, and if they were to hold office during pleasure whose pleasure could it be but that of the appointing officer? The power of the lieutenant-governor to dismiss for cause must create a distinct and co-ordinate authority. Under threat of disallowance by Ottawa, Sandfield Macdonald had to amend the act to restore tenure during good behaviour. By this means removability by the lieutenant-governor 'for cause' was ensured without creating a co-ordinate power of dismissal in the governor general.[7]

This sort of hitch made for extreme caution even in petty matters of administration. Sandfield Macdonald burnt his fingers again in 1869, when the provincial budget tried to give the Ontario superior court judges an extra $1,000 a year in contravention of the section of the BNA Act that made Ottawa responsible for paying them.[8] When Oliver Mowat wished to appoint Stephen Richards QC to preside at the Perth assizes in the autumn of 1875, he took care to clear Richards's demand for twenty dollars a day with his friend Edward Blake, now minister of justice at Ottawa. When he wanted to pass a law on the transportation of convicts to the penitentiary, he made sure in advance that Blake did not consider this a dominion concern.[9] This sort of correspondence between the two men was typical, but it earned Blake a rebuke from his deputy minister, Hewitt Bernard. John A. Macdonald's brother-in-law deprecated 'the tendency, often unavoidable, to communicate direct on any official subject with the Provincial Minister' when centralist constitutional propriety required such communication to pass through the lieutenant-governor, an officer of the dominion government.[10]

Where small matters had to be dealt with so tactfully, larger ones had to be handled with the greatest care. The consolidation of the public general statutes of Ontario, launched by Mowat in 1874, took nearly three years because of the obstacle presented by the many pre-Confederation laws on matters that were not intra vires the province. The process of consolidation entailed going through the statute book, sorting out all the legislation that was still in effect, and condensing everything on a given subject into a single concise and lucid text. When the whole body of public statute law was thus reduced, the entire text was adopted by the legislature as a single corpus of 224 chapters embodying the statute law of the province. If any chapter had contained matter that in Ottawa's opinion encroached substantially on the dominion jurisdiction, the consolidation might have been disallowed by the governor general.

This did not happen, partly because the consolidating commission took great care and partly because the work was completed while the Mackenzie ministry was in office. The minister of justice accepted the provincial declaration that the revision included only matters within the provincial jurisdiction. Where a matter was politically controversial and Ontario and Ottawa were at loggerheads, reform might be blocked completely. This was the case with reform of the grand jury, as we shall see.[11]

This first Ontario consolidation, which became law as the Revised Statutes of Ontario 1877, was one of Mowat's important achievements as provincial minister of justice. It was no small task to reconcile all the contradictions and inconsistencies that clogged the unrevised statute book after years of private-enterprise legislative drafting by back-benchers, and legislative camel-building by select committees and committees of the whole, all unchecked by attorneys general too preoccupied by politics to perform their official duty of preventing such gaffes. Luckily, there was less than two decades of havoc to remedy because an earlier consolidation had been undertaken in the late 1850s. Mowat had taken part in that exercise, which was influenced by earlier efforts in England, New Brunswick, Nova Scotia, New York, and Massachusetts.[12] He gave the new commission a similar mandate, authorizing the commissioners to simplify the language of the statutes as much as possible and to suggest – but not incorporate on their own initiative – the amendments they thought requisite. The donkey-work was done by three young lawyers under the constant supervision of Mowat himself and the three judges of the Court of Appeal – Chief Justice Draper and puisne justices George W. Burton and Christopher S. Patterson. In the course of the work Draper was replaced by Puisne Justice Thomas Moss, and the number of commissioners was increased by adding Vice-Chancellor Samuel Hume Blake (Edward's brother) and James R. Gowan, judge of the county court of Simcoe.[13]

The consolidation venture casts a revealing sidelight on Mowat's later course in the constitutional struggle with Ottawa. As the commissioners, Mowat among them, noted at the time, to decide what to include in the consolidation and what to omit as ultra vires the legislature meant resolving many problems of jurisdiction that had not yet come before the courts. The commissioners' principle was to include every statute that was not clearly ultra vires; yet Mowat at first excluded the Dunkin Act, the pre-Confederation local option act, as an unwarranted interference with Ottawa's power to regulate trade and commerce. He eventually included it on the unanimous advice of his colleagues.[14] Their advice was vindicated twenty years later by the prohibition reference of 1896, which concluded, among other things, that the repeal of the Dunkin Act by the Scott Act had been beyond the powers of Parliament.[15]

Another glimmer of the same sort is supplied by the municipal law consolidation of 1873. This exercise, which served as a trial run for the general revision of 1874-7, was executed by Adam Crooks, attorney general under Blake and now provincial secretary, and John G. Scott, chief clerk of the provincial law office and soon to become the province's first deputy attorney general. In a reading of the BNA Act quite at odds with the future attempt to justify the Ontario local option as forming part of the municipal law of Upper Canada at Confederation, this consolidation included a schedule of legislation that had been omitted as being ultra vires the province.[16]

The inclusion of the Dunkin Act in the revised statutes exemplifies the potentiality for friction had the statutes come under review by a centralist Conservative government at Ottawa. Mowat's doubts as to its inclusion, and the omissions from the consolidated Municipal Act, show that he had not at this time worked out all the ramifications of the distribution of powers, although his position on provincial sovereignty was fully formed. Of course, in the mid-1870s it suited Mowat very well to consider prohibition as ultra vires the province. One wonders whether it was the lawyer or the politician who at first decided to leave out the Dunkin Act.

REFORM OF THE CIVIL JUDICATURE

One area of law reform that was mercifully uncomplicated by constitutional conundrums was civil procedure and the shape of the law courts. Here Mowat carried out a two-stage reform, the most prominent feature of which was the abolition of the age-old division of civil jurisdiction between common law and equity, two self-contained systems based on fundamentally different principles.

The autonomy of the two systems flowed from their historical origins. Jurisdiction in equity had grown up in order to make up for flaws in the common law, so that where by the letter and forms of the law a sufferer might not be entitled to a remedy he could obtain one in equity.[17] By the mid-nineteenth century the institutional reasons for their separate existence were long past and the division of the civil law into two jurisdictions, each with its special powers and procedure, neither of which could take cognizance of all wrongs or offer a complete range of remedies, was a ludicrous anomaly; yet the conservatism of the legal profession in general was such that, in Upper Canada as in England, palliation was preferred to cure. William Hume Blake's reform of Chancery in 1849 and John A. Macdonald's Common Law Procedure Act of 1856 each provided such palliation, but it remained possible for a just cause to come to grief through being launched in the wrong court, and the course of litigation in each jurisdiction was still hampered by the absence of procedures available in the other. As economic growth and the consequent rise of limited-liability corporations engendered an increasingly complex commercial law, this barrier to the efficient settlement of disputes became intolerable.[18]

Ontario did not lead the way in this any more than in most matters of legal reform. The state of New York had accomplished a complete fusion of common law and equity in 1848, the year before Blake's and Baldwin's Judicature Acts.[19] In the early 1850s there had been much discontent with the defects of the divided jurisdiction in England; the Common Law Procedure Acts of 1852 and 1854 – the model for Macdonald's act of 1856 – were an attempt to remedy them. By the late 1860s these remedies, which were less thorough in the equity sphere than Blake's in Upper Canada, were clearly inadequate. In 1867 a royal commission was set up to look into more radical measures.

The commission reported in March 1869, and two years later it was clear that its recommendations would be passed into law. In Ontario this prospect led Edward Blake to move for changes in the system his father had done so much to install at mid-century. Sandfield Macdonald, who had been lukewarm to that system on its introduction, proposed that the province should set up a commission of its own to look into the matter.[20] Late in 1871, just before leaving office, he named puisne justices Adam Wilson and J.W. Gwynne, Vice-Chancellor S.H. Strong, Judge Gowan of Simcoe County, and Christopher S. Patterson. On assuming the premiership, Blake added Thomas Moss (soon, like Patterson, to be elevated to the bench) in order to strengthen the equity representation.[21]

The commissioners' labours were short and fruitless. The new ministry was anxious for swift action, while most of the commissioners favoured careful investigation; their other duties made it unlikely that they would report within two or three years. Attorney General Crooks considered this sort of deliberation redundant in view of all the thought that had been devoted to the question in other countries. The basic issue was one of policy, not inquiry, and the government was ready to recommend measures to the legislature on its own responsibility. On Crooks's recommendation the commission was cancelled within a year of its appointment.[22]

This move probably reflected real differences of opinion and interest between common lawyers and equity specialists. The government wanted not just swift but thorough reform: the complete fusion of law and equity into a single jurisdiction administered by a single superior court commanding the full range of substantive and procedural remedies. This prospect was unwelcome to many common lawyers because it meant the obsolescence of the particular, artificial form of question that common-law courts dealt with and the redundancy of the artful forms of pleading that had been developed for dealing with it.

At common law the issue always was whether B, the defendant, had done A, the plaintiff, the particular wrong alleged in the action. This made possible a variety of technical defences: that the wrong person was suing, or the wrong person was being sued, or even that the offence that had been committed was not that which was alleged. This sort of technicality, half a century earlier, had hampered Robert Randal in his quest for justice against Thomas Clark and caused Singleton Gardiner to lose his action for wrongful imprisonment against Mahlon Burwell. Equity asked a different question: has wrong been done, and by whom to whom? To answer this question it had developed a more flexible procedure which allowed third parties to be joined to the action as plaintiff or defendant. It also allowed a defendant to urge a counterclaim in answer to the plaintiff, whereas at common law he would have to start separate proceedings on his own account.[23]

Common-law practitioners comprised perhaps three-quarters of the provincial bar. They did not relish the prospective redundancy of their special skills and the need to master a new procedure. These sentiments may have struck a sympathetic chord in the common lawyers on the commission, partly because the latter, as judges, would have to learn the new procedure and partly because they had risen through mastery of the arcane craft that fusion would destroy. At any rate, most of the commissioners were less eager than the government to go ahead with thorough fusion, and their reluctance may have contributed to the decision to dissolve the commission.[24]

If equity men thought that Mowat's succession as attorney general and premier meant instant and total fusion, they were in for a surprise. Like all successful politicians, Mowat knew how to count. The Ontario Administration of Justice Act of 1873 was far from the whole-hog measure passed that year at Westminster;[25] it did not fuse the courts but merely allowed lawsuits to be transferred from one court to another when appropriate. The procedure of the different jurisdictions also remained distinct, although the common law-courts received an enhanced equity jurisdiction and were allowed to alter the parties to a suit, as in Chancery.

Mowat's half-measure made him a target for whole-hog men. He had resisted the pressure for total fusion by citing the flaws that practice had exposed in the English reform. This provoked an anonymous writer in the *Canada Law Journal* to lament the presumption that nothing more could be done by way of law reform 'than merely hunt up and copy some English statute, changing the word "England" into "Ontario," wherever it occurs; and that if every English statute fails ... that failure while it lasts must estop every one in Canada from attempting, even in the proper way which ensures success, anything similar ... I confess it often troubles me and other of Mr. Mowat's personal friends to reconcile his very satisfactory record as a judge, his judicial courage and determination in pushing aside as far as he could, and so frequently as he did, the many inane technicalities which continually strove to interpose themselves between him and justice, with his far less satisfactory role of a legislative legal reformer.'[26]

But Mowat knew that in this case the views of the Upper Canadian bar were more accurately reflected in the *Canada Law Journal*'s editorial columns than in its anonymous correspondence. The journal had been founded in 1855 as the *Upper Canada Law Journal* by Judge Gowan (one of the ousted law commissioners), and it still reflected his enlightened common lawyer's viewpoint. In 1871 it had questioned the advisability of pushing ahead precipitately in advance of England, and in 1873 it had applauded Mowat's moderation in eschewing fusion; had thorough fusion been imposed at a stroke and equity procedure made universal, as in England, all the business of the united court would have fallen to the Toronto equity specialists and two-thirds of the judges would have had to administer an unfamiliar procedure without preparation.[27] By advancing at a safe distance behind England, Mowat was able to cite the imperial example in answer to doubters. When in 1881 he passed his own Judicature Act (having first cautiously introduced it a year previously in order to test the reaction), what opposition there was lacked all credibility. Objectors were understood to be reactionaries who opposed a beneficial simplification of organization and procedure out of mercenary motives or an archaic sentimentalism.[28]

The Ontario Judicature Act of 1881 introduced the thorough fusion for which reformers had been pressing.[29] The courts of Queen's Bench, Common Pleas, Chancery, and Appeal were united into one Supreme Court of Judicature for the province, to consist of two branches: the High Court of Justice and the Court of Appeal. The High Court was to consist of three divisions: Queen's Bench, Common Pleas, and Chancery. It incorporated not only the jurisdiction of the old superior courts but also that of the assizes, which, although normally presided over by a superior court judge, had until then been a distinct institution. A schedule to the statute endowed the new court with a uniform code of procedure. In the process of establishing a comprehensive system of judicature, the act made many other innovations, including the restoration of equity jurisdiction to the county court judges. Two that are particularly relevant to the history of the attorney general's office were the creation of two new administrative posts – the official guardian and the inspector of legal offices. The official guardian was to act in legal matters on behalf of infants who had no other competent representative. Formerly, a solicitor had been appointed by the Court of Chancery, as required, to perform this function for a fee; now the office was made a salaried government employment, and either the government or the High Court was empowered to turn it into a full-time position by barring the incumbent from private practice during tenure. The inspector of legal offices was appointed to ensure the orderly administration of sheriff's, county attorney's, and court offices throughout the province by regularly inspecting their books and reporting annually to the government on the efficiency of their administration. A particular concern of the inspector was to ensure that uniformity of administrative practice prevailed in the various court offices.[30] Nowadays both offices are to be found in the organization chart of the Ministry of the Attorney General: the official guardian in the civil law division and the inspector of legal offices in the courts administration division.

THE DECLINE OF TRIAL BY JURY

A remarkable feature of both Sandfield Macdonald's and Mowat's reforms was their reduction of the layman's role in the administration of justice. In effecting this, the two ministers followed the lead of the County

Attorneys Act of 1857, which in due course virtually wiped out private prosecutions. The target of Macdonald and Mowat was the layman as juror.

Juries were an affront to the rationalizing spirit of the age, with its emphasis on establishing law as a science administered by trained professionals whose skilled operations would achieve predictable results. As long as juries formed part of the judicial process, law could be no more a science than bridge or poker, games in which even the fullest mastery of principle still left the player subject to the uncertainty of the deal or the luck of the draw. Nevertheless, lawyers were no more unanimous in wanting to rationalize this part of the process than in wanting to rationalize the court system. Those who were skilled in the art of swaying juries had no wish to see their art made obsolete. Moreover, the right of trial by jury had always been much more strongly insisted on by Upper Canadian public opinion than the right of private prosecution, and it offered a more tenacious resistance to the onslaught of the reformers.

In criminal matters trial by jury was even older than the province, having come to the old province of Quebec along with the rest of the English criminal law. In civil matters it was introduced by statute in 1792, along with the English civil law, by an Assembly anxious to curb the power of the merchant judges of the old courts of common pleas in advance of their abolition by the Judicature Act of 1794.[31] Another statute of 1794, drafted, like the Judicature Act, by Chief Justice Osgoode, established a system of jury selection that lasted with little change until 1850.[32]

Because trial by jury was so highly prized, faults in the system introduced by Osgoode gave rise to discontent. Joseph Willcocks and Benajah Mallory, two MPPs who were soon to join the United States in making war on Canada, brought in two bills on the subject in 1811 and 1812.[33] The bill of 1812 'to restrain sheriffs from packing juries in this province' addressed the grievance that the district sheriff, an officer of the government, had absolute discretion in composing the roll of jurors for the assizes or quarter sessions from the eligible householders. The bills of 1811 and 1812 on so-called special juries may have attacked the right of the Crown to demand such a jury, which was chosen from the wealthier freeholders of the district, in trials for misdemeanour.

Another focus of concern was the jury's freedom to render a verdict according to conscience. Their right to do so with impunity had been established in England by *Bushell's Case* (1670). Edward Bushell was the foreman of a jury that had acquitted two Quakers (one being William

Penn, the future founder of Pennsylvania) accused of preaching in public. They had broken the law, and the Crown had many witnesses; when the jury refused to convict, its members were heavily fined for their contumacy by the judge. Imprisoned for not paying his fine, Bushell sued out a writ of habeas corpus. The resulting judgment of Chief Justice Sir John Vaughan established the impropriety of punishing jurors for any verdict that could not be proved to have been induced by bribery or menaces. Vaughan reasoned that it was the jury's duty, not the judge's, to decide whether, on the facts, a defendant was guilty beyond a reasonable doubt of the charges against him, and without proof of subornation one could never be legally certain that the jurors had deliberately decided against the facts. In particular, however much their verdict might appear to contradict the evidence given in court, one could never know what knowledge they had brought as inhabitants of the locality to their evaluation of the evidence.[34]

Bushell's Case ensured that no one could be convicted in the face of the jury's wish to acquit him; but it went further. Practically speaking, it established the jury's right to decide, as representatives of the community, whether the law the defendant was accused of breaking was a just law and whether, if just, it was justly applied in the given instance. In *Bushell's Case* the jurors may have felt that the statute against sectarian preaching was itself unjust; in the case of Robert Randal's trial for perjury in 1825, they probably had no objection to the law against perjury but may have felt that the properties he had sworn he owned were his in justice if not in law. In the one case they were acting as censor of the law itself and in the other as censor of its application.

But while *Bushell's Case* conceded the censorial role in practice, Vaughan's judgment did not authorize it explicitly – although in the first efflorescence of Whig constitutionalism it was interpreted as doing so even by such an 'establishment' figure as Sir John Hawles, solicitor general from 1695 to 1702; Hawles's tract *The Englishman's Right* (1680) was one of the most radical and most influential statements of the time on the jury's rights and duties.[35] Throughout the next century the jury's functions continued to arouse controversy. Was it to 'judge of the law' or merely to 'judge of the fact'? Was it to decide only whether a defendant had committed the acts alleged against him, or also whether those acts amounted to a crime? Was its decision as to fact to be based solely on the evidence given in court, or was it to be influenced by the local knowledge of persons and circumstances that was traditionally one of its raisons d'être?[36]

This debate was reproduced in Upper Canada. While there is no evidence that Chief Justice Powell's threats to the jury in *Randal* v *Phelps* caused a fuss, D'Arcy Boulton's conduct at the Gore District assizes in 1823 did reach the newspapers. In *Milne* v *Tisdale*, an action for ejectment, he rejected the jury's verdict for the defendant and ordered them to reconsider it. Like Randal's suit, this was a civil action and the verdict was subject to revision by the Court of King's Bench; but we have seen that people like Randal viewed the seizure of a man's property by judicial process as a blow to his civil rights, and the superior court's reversal of jury verdicts that favoured the small proprietor was itself a source of grievance.[37]

In this case the role of the jury was debated in general terms. The judge admonished the jurors that they were 'not judges of the law, but of the fact.' They had only to attend to the evidence 'as it comes from the witnesses in open court,' taking the judge's statement of the law as part of that evidence. John Rolph, for the defendant, averred that the jurors were judge of both law and fact and questioned the judge's right to insist that they reconsider – though he might *request* reconsideration as a mark of respect to the court. The jurors retired again but returned with the same verdict, whereupon Boulton reproved them as before and demanded to know their grounds. The foreman explained that they relied on the testimony of one of the defendant's witnesses, whom they knew to be honest. When Boulton persisted in trying to coerce the jury, Rolph protested against his 'unconstitutional' attempt 'to destroy the only barrier betwixt the law and the people, betwixt tyranny, oppression and good government, the only protection for life, liberty, and property.'

The plaintiff's counsel, Solicitor General Boulton, now stepped in to suggest that a disinterested third party draft a 'special verdict' for the jury's consideration: that is, a finding as to fact only that did not entail a declaration in favour of one suitor or the other. The 'disinterested' party he had in mind was J.B. Macaulay, lately his law clerk. Rolph insisted that if the solicitor wanted a special verdict he should draw one himself; but when the younger Boulton did so Rolph objected to its terms. Eventually the jurors were sent off to draft their own special verdict; but they returned to say that they lacked the expertise to do so and must stick to their general verdict for the defendant.[38]

The affair had an interesting sequel. The king's printer, Charles Fothergill, had just declared his candidature for the Assembly in opposition to one of the solicitor general's brothers and was running a campaign that was anti-oligarchy, anti-lawyer and, above all, anti-

Boulton. As an Englishman of Whig leanings he was well versed in the ideology of the rule of law and its texts. Within a month he had published an edition of *The Englishman's Right*, Hawles's radical version of the jury's rights and duties. In his introduction, addressed 'To the People of Canada,' Fothergill declared that the ends of justice were 'frequently obstructed or delayed, and sometimes wholly defeated, through the ignorance of Juries as to what concerns their rights, duties and privileges.' He adjured his readers to set the tract next to their Bibles and study it nearly as often.[39]

With the jury already so much in the public mind, it was natural that the renewed flare-up of political unrest in the mid-1820s should produce new demands for reform. The lead was taken by Bartholomew Beardsley, a friend of W.W. Baldwin's who was also to take a leading part in the attack on the law officers' monopoly of prosecutions at assize. Jury-packing was constant in his district of Niagara, alleged Beardsley, and he proposed to stop it by making householders serve in strict rotation. Attorney General Robinson supported the idea in principle, observing that the sheriffs would probably be glad to be relieved of the suspicion thrust upon them by the present system.

Robinson may have guessed, though, that Beardsley's proposal was not supported by all the reformers and could be counted on to fail without his opposition. John Matthews of Middlesex opposed the change because it would cause hardship to freeholders from the outlying parts of the district, when under the present system the sheriff could select the pool from individuals living close to the district seat.[40] Nevertheless, in 1827 and 1828 jury-reform bills were passed by lopsided majorities and had to be scotched by the Legislative Council.

Robinson's true views can probably be found lurking between the lines of a characteristic comment to Robert Wilmot Horton in December 1828 in a discussion of the strictures of the House of Commons select committee on the government of the Canadas: 'Our Juries are taken in a manner prescribed by a Statute of the Provincial Legislature, which has existed, without complaint, for 35 years,' he told the under-secretary. 'It is the same in principle as that which prevailed in England, under a comparatively modern Statute up to the time of Mr. Peel's act. To this moment no individual in the Province has ever asked the Legislature to alter it; but for two or three sessions past, a Member of the Bar who happened to be also in the Assembly, has proposed to change the system by a bill so incomplete, and so absurd both in its principle and its details, that the Legislature could not pass it, and would have been disgraced if it had ... I think the system may be improved, and will cheerfully attempt it, but in the mean time there is no *grievance* in the system, and any man who thinks there is, may have a Special Jury chosen by ballot from the whole District.'[41]

The events of the 1820s also discredited the grand jury, the panel of freeholders who reviewed the evidence for the prosecution in order to ascertain that it warranted bringing the defendant to trial. The assize grand jury always consisted of leading inhabitants of the district, usually magistrates, and could be relied on in politically contentious cases to support the establishment. We saw how the Middlesex grand jury quashed Singleton Gardiner's complaint of perjury against Mahlon Burwell in 1823. After the Rolphs' protracted clash with the Gore District magistrates a few years later, their supporters complained to Lieutenant-Governor Colborne in May 1829 that the assize grand jury was invariably composed chiefly of magistrates.[42]

Despite Attorney General Robinson's conviction that no grievance existed, leading reformers such as Beardsley and Dr Baldwin continued to bring in jury bills which the Legislative Council had to quash. In their endeavours the Council soon had the help of Chief Justice Robinson; his stamp is evident upon the report of a Council select committee on the Assembly bill of 1836, a report clearly destined for English eyes. Grand juries were selected precisely as in England, it noted: 'The sheriff selects twenty-four from among the persons of greatest intelligence, most considerable property and established character in his District. The greater number usually, (perhaps always,) are Justices of the Peace; Merchants and respectable Farmers are also returned ... when their estimation in society makes them eligible for the duty.' The mode of choosing petit juries likewise emulated the English. The Assembly bill threatened to politicize the selection of the jury pool by imposing the task on the elected officials of the townships – the tax assessors, tax collector, town clerk, and highway commissioners – and was also objectionable in making every adult male eligible for jury service and abolishing the right of the Crown to demand a special jury in either civil or criminal cases. It was far preferable to leave the selection of jurors to the sheriff, the king's chosen officer, who was responsible to the Court of King's Bench and free from popular influence. The report affirmed 'that if there is any one part of our social fabric which above all others it would be injudicious to subject rashly to the chance of experiments, it is the Trial by Jury – the corner stone of freedom – the best security for order – and the distinguishing boast of Englishmen and their descendants.'[43]

It was not as the cornerstone of liberty that William Lyon Mackenzie, for one, perceived the Upper Canadian jury system. It was about the time this report was penned, in the spring of 1836, that he accused the grand jury of the Home District assizes, led by George Gurnett, of plotting to frame him for perjury. In October 1837, just before his rebellion, he claimed to have detected an attempt to pack the petit jury at the Niagara assizes in a libel action against him. Allegedly, the clerk of the peace, Charles Richardson – one of the types rioters of 1826 – had excluded potential sympathizers of Mackenzie's from the list of freeholders used by the sheriff for choosing the jury pool.[44]

As with other things, reform was delayed until the advent of responsible government in the late 1840s. In 1850 Robert Baldwin brought in a comprehensive jury law, which among other things shifted the task of composing the jurors' roll to certain elected officials of each municipality within the district (the mayor or town reeve, assessors, and municipal clerk). They were to choose from among the top three-quarters of the ratepayers in their municipality, ordered by amount of assessment, those who, 'from the integrity of their characters, the soundness of their judgments and the extent of their information,' appeared 'most discreet and competent' for the office.[45]

Now a curious thing happened. The royal assent was barely dry on Baldwin's instrument of perfection when the jury itself became the object of sustained attack by the legal profession. Forgotten was its reputedly age-old role as guardian of individual liberty. Suddenly it was a medieval relic, costly and inefficient, that continued to clog the machinery of justice only through inertia of the public will. 'The argument to be drawn from prestige and habit merely is of little avail,' protested the *Upper Canada Law Journal* in 1856, 'when speed, cheapness and certainty of decision are in the opposite scale.' A year later it had 'come to the deliberate conclusion that Mr. Baldwin's jury scheme, fair in theory, in its practical application has proved a complete failure.' Another year passed and the *Journal*, quoting the English historian Hallam's denunciation of trial by jury as 'a preposterous relic of barbarism,' was ready to admit 'that trial by jury, if not defensible on reason, ought not to be supported on prestige; if not compatible with the safe, speedy, and economical administration of justice, ought not to be bolstered up and preserved solely because of its antiquity.'[46]

There were two main aspects to this assault on the jury. One concerned its use in civil trials in the superior courts of common law, where the growing complexity of commercial litigation in the modern era of corporate financial and industrial enterprise was throwing up more and more causes of the sort laymen were considered unfit to decide. The English Common Law Procedure Act of 1854 had allowed litigants to dispense with the jury by mutual consent, but this provision had been left out of the Upper Canadian act of 1856. Reformers argued that there could be no objection in principle to such a change, since the Court of Chancery had never operated with a jury (although it was able to refer disputes of fact to the common-law courts for determination by a jury). They also cited the evidence of the division court, the lowest civil court, where petty debt causes were tried. Its Upper Canadian precursor, the court of requests, had never had a jury, but the act of 1841 setting up the division court had given either party (except where the amount in question was fifty shillings or less) the right to demand a five-man jury. Experience showed that the option was generally waived, and it was declared absurd that the jury could be dispensed with in an inferior but not in the superior courts.[47]

The second line of criticism concerned the requirement for a unanimous verdict in both civil and criminal trials. On the one hand, it was urged, unanimity allowed a single dishonest juror to thwart the administration of justice; on the other, unanimity forced the fullest discussion of the facts, since a dissenting view, if not effectual in preventing a verdict, might pass unconsidered. Unanimists noted that less than one jury in a hundred was discharged for failing to agree, but an assortment of compromises continued to be canvassed, such as allowing a three-quarters or two-thirds majority verdict in cases where the jury failed to agree after a certain time (in civil cases at least).[48]

In 1858 Oliver Mowat introduced a bill to eliminate the jury from civil trials in the county and superior courts unless one of the parties demanded it. The bill earned him the plaudits of the *Upper Canada Law Journal*, though the journal preferred the less radical formula which would make jury trial the norm unless the parties agreed to waive it. The government took a different line from either, however, preferring to try to improve the jury rather than diminish its role. The Jury Act of 1858 increased the property qualification in furtherance of its stated intention 'to obtain a better class of jurors than are now obtained,' but it expressly affirmed the generality of jury trial in civil causes.[49]

Sandfield Macdonald's Law Reform Act of 1868 changed all this. As well as enacting part of the reform in criminal procedure described earlier, it abolished jury trial in civil causes in the superior and county courts unless it was requested by one of the parties or, in absence of such request, ordered by the judge. In 1873 Mowat's Administration of Justice Act made two slight modifications in this reform. In the trial of certain causes that concerned persons rather than property – libel, slander, criminal conversation (adultery), seduction, malicious arrest, malicious prosecution, and false imprisonment – trial by jury was to be the norm unless the parties agreed to waive it. In all other matters, the right of a party to demand a jury was subjected to the judge's discretion.[50]

Once this major reform was instituted, the movement to introduce majority verdicts lost its impetus. Unlike the measures to reduce or abolish the jury's role, it did not promise to diminish administrative costs. Attempts by James Patton in 1859 and 1861 to bring in the majority verdict in civil cases had been opposed by the *Upper Canada Law Journal* as possibly foreshadowing a similar reform in criminal procedure, 'an alteration which would be fraught with danger to public liberty and individual safety.' In the spirit of John A. Macdonald's jury reform of 1858, the journal now affirmed that 'that which has existed for ages should not be disturbed unless it be shown affirmatively that the practical result of the rule is injurious; and those who advocate a change deal only in generalities and abstract arguments.'[51]

Further efforts in the 1870s by James Bethune foundered on Mowat's opposition. The attorney general affirmed that he himself (an equity man) had always favoured the change, but he cited the opposition of public opinion and successful jury lawyers. There was no practical grievance that required the remedy, and venerable institutions ought not to be disturbed without clear evidence of need.[52] And so unanimity survived the century.

The movement to abolish the grand jury aroused rather more excitement, because lay participation in criminal justice was traditionally valued as a bulwark of individual liberty. In seventeenth- and eighteenth-century England the grand jury had done much to shield political opponents of the Crown from efforts to repress them by judicial means. In the United States its power of deciding whether criminal proceedings should ensue on any indictment was included, along with trial by petit jury, in the Bill of Rights of 1791. In nineteenth-century England the local élites who manned it valued it both as a means of asserting their will in the criminal matters that came before it and as a channel for communicating their political and social views to the government by a presentment to the judge.[53] In Upper Canada too, if the experience of Singleton Gardiner and George Rolph is any guide, assize grand juries were an institution of the local élite, although quarter-sessions grand juries might sometimes aid a litigant in dispute with members of the local élite.

In mid-nineteenth-century England, the spirit of Benthamite reform was as hostile to the grand jury as to the private prosecutor. Both were part and parcel of the old, haphazard, paternalistic law enforcement the reformers wished to replace with a rational, impartial, and efficient system of criminal justice – one that would serve the bourgeois proprietor as well as the country gentleman. From the Benthamite standpoint, the secrecy of deliberation that had once helped grand juries to shield the targets of executive oppression was now merely a screen behind which local élites could exert their own oppressive hegemony. The cities now had professional police magistrates, and it was absurd that cases committed for trial by those magistrates on a preliminary hearing of the evidence should be subject to review by laymen with no expertise in examining witnesses. It was worse than absurd that cases which those magistrates dismissed as groundless, after hearing evidence both for and against, could be revived by the prosecutor simply by laying a complaint before the grand jury, which decided on its merits after reviewing only the favourable evidence. Now that freedom of the press was established, the best security for the impartial administration of criminal justice was a competent corps of stipendiary magistrates and professional prosecutors, such as existed in Scotland and France, performing their duties in public. These views were given currency by the eighth report of the Criminal Law Commissioners in 1845, which reprinted an article critical of the grand jury, and by the Select Committee on Public Prosecutors ten years later, which heard and printed much testimony to the same effect.[54]

This sort of argument was soon to be heard in Canada. During the debate on Baldwin's jury reform in 1850, the English controversy was cited by William Badgley, lately attorney general for Lower Canada, in expressing his preference for a public prosecutor, who would be responsible to public opinion and the press, over the grand jury, which was entirely irresponsible owing to the secrecy of its deliberations 'and in fact protected the criminal to the injury of the innocent.' There was no grand jury in Scotland, Badgley noted; but both Baldwin and J.H. Cameron observed that its abolition in Upper Canada would be unacceptable to public opinion.[55]

Badgley's opinion may have reflected a Lower Canadian anglophone response to francophone grand juries, but it was to be echoed in Upper Canada. As an important reform of preliminary criminal procedure, the County Attorneys Act of 1857 encouraged review of the grand jury's role in that procedure. One of the abuses the act was designed to prevent was malicious prosecution, which was encouraged by the prosecutor's right to go directly to the grand jury without any preliminary investigation by a magistrate. The *Upper Canada Law Journal* observed that the county attorney could control such proceedings at the quarter sessions, but he had no counterpart at the assizes (though we have seen that Chief Justice Robinson, for one, disapproved of complaints for perjury being presented to the grand jury without preliminary review by a magistrate).[56] In any case, even at quarter sessions 'a controlling power [was] requisite as much for the institution of criminal procedure as for watching it when instituted.'[57] The journal referred to Lord Chief Justice Campbell's pending bill in England, soon to become law as the Vexatious Indictments Act. Campbell's bill was designed to prevent grand-jury indictment upon mere presentment, without any preliminary hearing by a magistrate, for certain offences commonly alleged in malicious or extortionate prosecutions.

Two years later, in 1861, a similar law was passed in Canada. It prohibited prosecution for perjury, subornation of perjury, conspiracy, false pretences, keeping a gambling-house or bawdy-house, and indecent assault, unless the complainant had been bound over to prosecute and the accused party to defend himself, or unless the prosecution was consented to in writing by a law officer of the Crown, a judge of the county or superior courts, or a recorder (the title of the professional magistrate whose quarterly court had supplanted the quarter sessions in the cities of Canada). This rule ensured that such charges would normally receive preliminary investigation and be communicated to the accused party. As a safeguard against the hasty dismissal of complaints, the act provided that when a justice of the peace refused to commit the case for trial after the preliminary hearing, the complainant could insist that the justice bind him over to prosecute and transmit his recognizance to the county attorney.[58]

Of course, the grand jury did not pass undefended in England, and these voices too were heard in Canada. In 1860 the *Upper Canada Law Journal* reprinted an article that epitomized the case for the grand jury from *The Jurist*, an English law journal. Based on the speech of a prominent judicial officer of the City of London (the common serjeant, Thomas Chambers), it attacked the Benthamites with arguments stressing the institution's traditional importance as a safeguard of individual liberty and an instrument of social control. The grand jury prevented a subject from being exposed to criminal trial for a serious offence 'by mere action of the officers of the Crown, or of any tribunal appointed by it.' It guaranteed his right to bring an oppressor to justice, even if that oppressor was a servant of the government acting in accord with its wishes. It enabled representatives of 'the upper classes' to apprise the government of evils and abuses that were prevalent in their district.

Reviewing the case for abolition, *The Jurist* noted that police magistrates, however efficient, were still servants of the Crown and ought for liberty's sake to be subject to the check of the grand jury. Improper prosecutions were better prevented by taking proper security from would-be prosecutors as provided for in the Vexatious Indictments Act. A recent effort to exempt committals by police magistrates from subsequent review by the grand jury except in the case of offences against the state was dismissed with the remark that the state was well able to harass an opponent judicially without indicting him for state offences. In conclusion, *The Jurist* quoted Chambers to the effect that the distinguishing feature of the administration of justice in England was its 'popular element' – an element modern reforms were tending to diminish by substituting professional administrators. The grounds for these changes-- impartiality, efficiency, economy – were plausible enough, but the changes might have unforeseen and detrimental consequences. 'Cheapness and speed may be attained at a cost incalculable.'[59]

After this flurry of discussion in the late 1850s, Upper Canada heard little about the grand jury for a decade, until Sandfield Macdonald's criminal justice reforms of 1869. Macdonald's new 'speedy trial' eliminated most of the grand jury's business at a stroke, yet had the paradoxical effect of reviving agitation for its complete abolition. The initial impetus was given by Justice J.W. Gwynne in an address to the assize grand jury at Kingston, in which he decried the notion that any review of magistral committals was necessary – except possibly in the case of state offences, 'if the days for the Government acting in the *role* of tyrants are not passed away.' After becoming chief justice of Ontario in 1875, Robert A. Harrison lent his authority to the movement, and a year later an abolition bill was brought into the legislature. In the debate Mowat granted that there was much to be said on both sides of the question, but he had not made up his mind and knew of no common-law jurisdiction in which the grand jury had been abolished; in any case, the constitutional uncertainty as to jurisdiction made it unwise to legislate at present in Ontario.[60]

Despite his temporizing, Mowat took the idea of reforming the grand jury, if not abolishing it, seriously enough to propose to Edward Blake in 1877 that Ontario and Ottawa refer the jurisdiction question to the Supreme Court. Blake agreed, but nothing was done. Two years later

Mowat revived the proposal after his chief ministerial lieutenant, Arthur Hardy, had carried a bill through the legislature reducing the number of grand jurors from twenty-four to fifteen. The act contained a proviso delaying its operation until it was proclaimed by the lieutenant-governor; presumably Mowat reasoned that regulating the size of the grand jury was within the provincial powers relating to the constitution of criminal courts, but prescribing the size of the quorum required to authenticate a bill of complaint came within the dominion power in relation to criminal procedure. The impossibility of reducing the complement to fifteen as long as the quorum remained twelve made it essential to resolve the jurisdiction question before the Ontario act could be implemented; but even before Ottawa consented to the reference the *Lenoir* judgment turned Mowat against unappealable constitutional references to the Supreme Court. A move to abolish the grand jury by act of Parliament in 1880 came to nothing, and the Ontario statute was never proclaimed.[61]

The last attempt of the century to abolish the grand jury was launched in 1889 by Senator James R. Gowan, the former county judge and a long-time campaigner for the cause. Gowan was also an energetic advocate of codifying the criminal law, and late in 1890 his initiative persuaded Sir John Thompson, the dominion minister of justice, to circulate a questionnaire on the grand jury to all the attorneys general and dominion-appointed judges in Canada in connection with the preparation of the Criminal Code (eventually enacted in 1892). In the meantime, the case for abolition was exhaustively canvassed in the *Canada Law Journal* (which Gowan had founded).[62]

When the 111 returns to Thompson's questionnaire were published in 1891, they revealed a wide difference of opinion on the subject. Forty-eight of the respondents favoured abolition, 41 opposed it, and 12 were uncertain. Of 47 returns from Ontario, 23 were in favour, 18 opposed, and 6 undecided. A remarkable feature of the Ontario return was that the county judges strongly favoured abolition while almost all of the superior court judges advocated retention.[63]

Gowan and his adherents may have been disappointed by the resistance to their cause, although they did their best to discount it. Gowan himself described the result of the questionnaire as a 'very considerable majority' in favour of abolition. The *Canada Law Journal* contended that the higher judiciary were not the best judges of the question – one 'on which those who, as Crown prosecutors, are practically dealing with grand juries ... may be permitted with all deference to express a dissenting opinion'; the county judges too, living not in Toronto but throughout the province, were closer to the grass roots.[64]

Gowan expressed particular disappointment at Mowat's position. The attorney general had evidently made up his mind since 1876, but his reply to the questionnaire had discussed the subject not on its merits but purely as a political matter. After challenging Ottawa's jurisdiction, Mowat observed that the consensus of informed opinion in Ontario was against abolition; a majority of the government concurred. If the grand jury were abolished, its place would have to be taken by a public official, and this the government opposed. Citing the unproclaimed provincial statute of 1879, Mowat proposed that Ottawa and Ontario legislate concurrently on the size of the grand jury and its quorum so as to achieve an economical reform without stumbling over the jurisdiction issue. Gowan commented: 'I certainly felt surprise when I saw the name of Hon. Mr. Mowat ... opposed to this change; for he has been for many years ... a great law-reformer, and the obstacles in the way of justice which "the wisdom of our ancestors" had placed in his way – all these technical absurdities, he bore down and toppled over without the slightest hesitation ... he was almost like a hippopotamus rushing through a cane-break in his desire to make direct and plain the path of ready justice.'[65]

Mowat had drawn much the same reaction fourteen years previously for his reluctance to impose total fusion of common law and equity. His position on the grand jury may have reflected a similar caution, since it was hardly a resounding endorsement of the ancestral wisdom. It was certainly influential, though, in protecting the grand jury from Thompson's pending revision of the criminal law.

The controversy over the grand jury is a handy guide to social perceptions among the leaders of the legal profession in late nineteenth-century Ontario. An institution of several hundred years' growth, it was at the start of the century an essential element in the system of judicial administration that sustained the dominance of the landed interest – the nobility and the gentry – in the shires of England: the system of local government by lay justices of the peace drawn from the gentry and meeting in quarterly conclave at the general sessions of the peace. At the county assizes the justices of the peace themselves comprised the grand jury and by their secret deliberations played a part in an elaborate rite of social authority – the impartial administration of justice. At the quarter sessions, where the justices presided on the bench, the farmers who made up the grand jury were confirmed in their social importance by being chosen to emulate in the forum of petty justice the duties performed by the leaders of local society in the arena of grand justice.[66]

The object of the rite was the solemn celebration of the rule of law, an ideal that had thrived as the basis of the landed gentry's resistance to the arbitrary power of the Crown in the seventeenth century. That power, rooted in the age-old royal prerogative, had been expressed in two main ways: in the levying of taxes without parliamentary sanction, and in the arraignment of individuals for political offences, often of an indeterminate nature, in the prerogative court of the Star Chamber, where a harsh summary justice was dispensed informally and in private.

In the fiscal realm, the rule of law meant that the Crown could not levy or spend taxes without parliamentary authorization by statute. In the administration of justice, it meant freedom from arbitrary and prolonged arrest without trial, for this struggle saw the invention of the writ of habeas corpus. It meant that innocence was presumed until guilt was proved. It meant the enforcement of fixed, knowable laws by a fixed process – 'due process' – administered by a judge who was not subject to dismissal at the royal whim. It meant the administration of due process in public, so that justice was not only done but seen to be done. And it meant not only public witness but public participation: the secret review of complaints by the grand jury to ascertain that they contained well-founded allegations of offence against a fixed and certain law; the secret review of the evidence by the petit jury to establish, beyond a reasonable doubt, whether the accused had committed the alleged offence. In this freedom from arbitrary taxation and arbitrary process lay the essence of English liberty.

In exalting the law above the Crown, the landed interests exalted it above themselves. The rule of law became a part of the ideology of the English state – the secular counterpart of Anglicanism. It was the sanction on which the gentry based their right to prosper while the poor man laboured for a crust. The rich might be few and the poor many, but all were equal in the eyes of the law. The poorest man could not be condemned without a fair trial by a jury of his equals according to a procedure so rigid that even a trivial failure of form might suffice to thwart the most strongly grounded prosecution.[67] Such an error was irreversible, since magistrates, judges, the king himself were mere ministers of the sovereign law – a law that was ultimately God's. The course of justice could be interfered with only to mitigate the severity of its consequences for the unfortunate: perhaps by a wronged party's decision not to press charges, or a judge's discretionary mercy in sentencing, or the Crown's forbearance in softening the sentence or pardoning the offence.

This ideology of the rule of law as the foundation of English liberty was imported into Upper Canada along with the English law itself. Its rhetoric permeated the political struggles of the first half of the nineteenth century. According to the official oligarchy and its adherents, the province possessed that 'image and transcript' of the English constitution which Lieutenant-Governor Simcoe had promised the first House of Assembly – the utmost in rational liberty a colony could enjoy. Opponents of the oligarchy denounced the constitution as a travesty, not a transcript, of the English and descanted passionately on its flaws: the dependence of the Legislative Council and the judiciary on the executive; the existence of the prerogative revenues, which the government could collect and spend without the sanction of the House of Assembly; the monopoly of prosecutions at assize by the law officers of the Crown; the defects of the jury system. As evidence for their indictment they pointed to repeated abuses of the rule of law: the persecution of Singleton Gardiner, the types riot, the tar-and-feather outrage, the illegal sittings of the Court of King's Bench. These abuses, as well as political grievances such as the oppressive sedition law, the attempted discrimination against the American-born, the various forms of preference accorded the Church of England, and the monopoly of office by a clique of incompetents, could all be remedied if the provincial executive, like that of England, was made responsible to the people.

Moderate reformers like the Baldwins, many of them lawyers, harped on the efficacy of responsible government as an antidote to the grievances of Upper Canada until it came to be thought of as something like a universal panacea. And to those whose idea of heaven was railways, economic growth, and rising land prices, it was a panacea. True, the new order could not reach the acme of perfection as long as Upper Canada was yoked to the economically backward, Roman Catholic, French Canadian masses in a legislative union that subjected its destiny to the will of Montreal-centred business interests and a Montreal-centred Catholic hierarchy. But for this problem another panacea was swiftly devised: confederation, which severed the unnatural union by restoring to each community its separate legislature. The new federal order took twenty-five or thirty years to perfect, but Ontario and Quebec co-operated in this enterprise and gradually secured the adherence of most of the other provinces. The Interprovincial Conference at Quebec in 1887 was a landmark on the road to perfection.

The arguments of those who wished to abolish the grand jury were thoroughly imbued with this sense of approaching perfection. In the era of responsible government, who were the oppressors against whom the grand jury was a necessary safeguard? 'The idea that the grand jury system constitutes in the present day the palladium of British liberties and serves as a shield interposed between the subject and the crown ... partakes altogether of too mediaeval a character to justify its receiving a moment's consideration in the present day,' wrote Mr Justice Gwynne, himself once an enthusiastic railway promoter. 'No perils to the due administration of criminal justice do, or can, in modern times arise from any interference, due or undue, upon the part of the crown.'

Gwynne's confidence in the perfection of modern liberty was shared by several county court judges. 'The grand jury, as is well known, was originally brought into existence for the protection of innocent citizens from interference by the crown, or by powerful subjects causing unjust prosecutions, but as these proceedings have long become practically things of the past, the grand jury as an institution is no longer necessary and has outlived its usefulness' – thus John Deacon of Renfrew. John Ardagh of Simcoe, an ex-editor of the *Upper Canada Law Journal*, concurred: 'In this country, and in this, the end of the 19th century, such a question [as the grand jury's value as a safeguard against executive oppression] hardly deserves consideration.'[68] Such opinions reflected what has become known as the Whig interpretation of history: the idea that the English genius for liberty, exemplified in the rule of law and the predestined progress of every civilized (that is, predominantly white) part of the empire towards self-government under free parliamentary institutions, was fast approaching perfection.

Few of those who defended the grand jury envisaged a possible renewal of executive tyranny. They tended to stress perils of a lesser order, in particular the incompetence of the rural lay magistracy. While Gwynne derided the grand jury's services as 'now reduced to an enquiry, more ludicrous than real, whether the evidence upon which the justices had after careful investigation ... committed the accused parties to gaol to stand their trial, was sufficient to warrant the proceedings,' several of his colleagues belied his dismissive sarcasm. 'Where there is not a trained magistracy, that is, a magistracy who by means of a legal education have become conversant with the rules of evidence, there should ... be another tribunal to which committals should be subjected before the accused is put on his trial.' So thought Hugh MacMahon of the Common Pleas Division, an experienced Crown counsel. Other judges reasoned likewise – G.W. Burton of the Court of Appeal, who had rendered strongly provincialist judgments in the escheats case and the local option reference, William Falconbridge of the Queen's Bench Division, and Chief Justice Sir Thomas Galt of Common Pleas.[69]

The weakness of the lay magistracy did not worry Gwynne, since justices of the peace had access to expert advice from the county attorney. Other respondents, however, stressed the impropriety of an officer whose business was prosecution deciding on the merits of an indictment, either in the capacity of an adviser to the committing magistrate or (as some abolitionists recommended) in that of an official successor to the grand jury. It was thought improper that an official who received fees for conducting criminal prosecutions should assume the grand jury's power to decide if a prosecution should take place.

This aspect of the debate touched on the nature of the prosecutor's duty. If one accepted that the Crown prosecutor was detached and impartial in his approach to the evidence, Gwynne's argument was indisputable; but two judges above all scorned the notion. John Rose of Common Pleas declared, 'The tendency of employing any officer to prosecute appears to be, in the course of time, to create a bias against accused persons ... In certain police circles the formula in fact is "guilty, prove yourself innocent."' Judge James Reynolds of Leeds and Grenville averred that 'public prosecutors are apt to become *persecutors*, [and] instead of following the trite maxim of the English law, "every man is innocent until he is proved guilty," rather view the accused as guilty, and taking the role of the detective, seek only for such evidence as will strengthen their view.' No other judge committed himself explicitly to this notion of a prosecution or police mentality, but Sir Thomas Galt and John H. Hagarty, chief justice of Ontario, joined Reynolds and Rose in deprecating the idea of the county attorney assuming the judicial duty of the grand jury. Oddly enough, Thomas Robertson of Wentworth, now a puisne justice of the Chancery Division, did not address this question at all, although it formed the ground on which he had tried to end the Crown's right to the last word in criminal trials in 1880. Yet he may well have thought of it, since he affirmed, with all the authority of a former county attorney, 'I have never yet heard a sound, logical reason for doing away with the grand jury.'[70]

While these allusions to magistral incompetence and the danger of the prosecution mentality contradicted the brash confidence of the perfectionists, they were not incompatible with the underlying perfectionist premise that social tranquillity and civil liberty were here to stay. Today's rural justices might not be up to par, but future generations might well be, given the continuing progress of the Upper Canadian mind. The notion that the prosecution mentality made a man unfit for the judicial task of assessing the strength of a criminal complaint merely recognized that there were limits to human perfection and that checks and balances would always be essential to the protection of individual liberty.

Only three judges took the view that perfect liberty might not be near at hand, or that the existing social tranquillity might be transitory. One was Mr Justice Burton, the English admiral's son who was to succeed J.H. Hagarty as chief justice of Ontario. 'Should a period of intense political excitement ever again unfortunately arise,' he wrote, 'and result in inflammatory harangues and writings, it might be of great importance to interpose such a body as the grand jury as a protection to persons prosecuted for such offences.' Judge Reynolds of Leeds and Grenville concurred: 'Besides that tyranny which was known as the "tyranny of kings," there are other kinds of tyranny which require to be guarded against, and from which the subject should be saved. There is the tyranny of the people, the tyranny of the mob, the tyranny of morbid sentiment. Hitherto the great protector in all these cases has been the grand jury, and who can say how soon, in the rapid tide of time with all the changes it brings, we may have to rejoice if haply the grand jury system has been preserved[?]'[71]

Burton and Reynolds were unusual in assuming that Canada's current social condition might not be permanent. The perspective of William Aird Ross of Carleton was unique among the judiciary of Ontario. Ross was a former law partner of R.W. Scott, author of the Scott Act and now leader of the Liberal opposition in the Senate. He was a septuagenarian Scotsman, and he denounced the grand jury from the standpoint of a mid-nineteenth-century Scottish radical.

To Ross the idea that the grand jury was a guardian of liberty was hogwash. It was a medieval relic, a virtual Star Chamber in its secrecy and irresponsibility. Above all it was an instrument of class domination. 'It is an English institution composed in England of high caste people, members of the so called county families, very useful for the protection of such families and for smothering scandals in high life, as well as for doing strict and impartial justice to the poor, especially where the interests of landlords and poachers come in conflict ... In England and in Ireland, where the English system has been made the means of great oppression, grand juries have municipal and other powers of great extent, of which the governing class have no scruple in availing themselves.' Things were not so bad in Ontario, where the grand jury was less important, but even there it was an instrument for the perversion of justice. 'It is before the secret inquisition that the wealthier criminal has his tremendous advantage over his poorer fellow, the outcast, who has no friends or money to buy them ... Cases are smothered in secret which could never be met in the full blaze of an open trial.'[72]

To Ross the abolition of the grand jury meant the elimination of a means of social oppression. Was it a last, etiolated snake in a garden of otherwise perfect liberty? Did the wealthy have no other means of ensuring that the rule of law, before which all men were supposedly equal, worked to give them a preference over the poor? Ross did not say.

It was not, in any case, the grand jury that was to be the victim of Thompson's draftings but the petit jury – or rather the protection it represented against oppressive criminal proceedings. For forty years, while the grand jury was attacked and the petit jury's role in civil proceedings vastly curtailed, this safeguard had survived relatively unscathed. True, Sandfield Macdonald had reduced its occasions from six a year to four – and rather cynically at that, since he had first halved the sessions in the legislature and then pleaded the plight of prisoners awaiting trial as his reason for asking Parliament to bring in speedy summary trial. However, the merest hint of introducing majority verdicts had long since been condemned even by the reform-minded *Upper Canada Law Journal* as 'fraught with danger to public liberty and individual safety,'[73] and in 1892 the safeguard still existed, for those who desired its protection, much as it had for more than two centuries.

Thompson's draft Criminal Code did not further curtail access to trial by jury, but it seriously compromised the integrity of that safeguard as it had existed since *Bushell's Case* in 1670. Chief Justice Vaughan's judgment could not have established the jury as community censor of the law and its application but for a time-honoured rule of the common law that precluded trying a defendant a second time for an offence of which a jury had acquitted him.[74] Thompson's draft code proposed to abolish this rule by enabling the prosecutor as well as the defendant to appeal on a point of law and empowering the Court of Appeal, upon hearing such appeal, to direct a new trial. It also compromised trial by jury in another way, in empowering the trial court, if of the opinion that the point at issue depended on a question of fact, to require the jury to render findings on the relevant fact or facts.[75]

Four or five MPs criticized these proposals in committee of the whole, and the Liberal constitutional expert David Mills was not alone in condemning the proposed legislation, in words that echoed the u.s. Bill of Rights, as a contravention of 'the old rule ... that once a man is put in jeopardy he cannot again be put on trial.'[76]

The proposal allowing the court to question the jury as to facts was disparaged as threatening to reduce the jury to a mere finder of facts. Thompson denied any intention to render defendants liable to retrial after acquittal and offered to strike out certain clauses. This got rid of the proposal concerning findings of fact, but a comparison of the draft code and the final act suggests that the omissions as to appeal against acquittal were merely cosmetic. The Criminal Code as enacted permitted either the Crown or the accused to ask the court, either during or after a trial, to reserve any question of law pertaining to it. If the court consented, a case was to be stated for the opinion of the Court of Appeal; if it did not, the applicant could refer the question to the Court of Appeal upon receiving written leave from the attorney general. The Court of Appeal was empowered to direct a new trial if it concluded that the ruling in question was erroneous and the error had led to a mistrial. In effect, therefore, a motion of the Crown could result in the retrial of a defendant after acquittal.[77]

The government's motives in bringing in this reform are unrecorded; indeed, if Thompson's disclaimer can be believed, its introduction may have been inadvertent. The draft code was based on contemporary English proposals that had not been enacted; one of these had included provision for appeal from acquittal, though in a tentative, almost dubious, fashion. The hasty preparation of the Canadian draft led to much of the English material being shovelled in without thoughtful evaluation. As for the form in which the code was enacted, that owed much to the government's strategy of repeatedly playing down its innovations in the hope that Parliament would pass the bill without closely scrutinizing the massive text. In introducing the legislation, Thompson had referred to appeal from acquittal in a single sentence immediately before a lengthy digression on the desirability of abolishing the grand jury. This has been interpreted as a ploy to draw opposition fire towards a proposal that was not even in the bill.[78]

The subsequent legislative history of appeal from acquittal certainly smacks of parliamentary incompetence. In 1923, during a piecemeal revision of the code, it was repealed by mistake. An attempt two years later to restore it failed in the Senate, but in 1930 it was brought back in a form that weakened the safeguard of trial by jury still further, since the Court of Appeal was empowered not merely to direct a new trial but to substitute a verdict of guilty and return the defendant to the lower court for sentencing. In introducing the bill the minister of justice, Ernest Lapointe, mentioned the clause in passing in a reference to 'certain amendments in the matter of procedure which have been suggested and recommended by the attorneys general and other persons entrusted with the administration of justice in the province[s].' It passed without a syllable of debate in either House. Although the ground of appeal was restricted to 'a question of law alone,' in practice it has permitted the reversal of jury acquittals that were based on ample knowledge of both the law and the facts.[79]

Conclusion:

Law and the Constitution

At the end of the nineteenth century the office of Attorney General for Ontario probably enjoyed greater prestige than ever before or since. Mowat's monumental incumbency was chiefly to thank for this, but he was only the latest in an eighty-year succession of illustrious office-holders whose memory easily effaced that of the early lesser lights. Even in the 1820s the attorney general, in the person of John Beverley Robinson, had been the most influential official in the province. As soon as cabinet government was introduced in 1841, the attorney's ex officio headship of the legal profession, the province's social élite, made the office all but synonymous with the political leadership of the province.

When Upper Canada regained full provincial autonomy in 1867 as Ontario, the identification of the attorneyship with the premiership was enhanced. Under Mowat the two offices became fused to such an extent that the first three deputy attorneys general, J.G. Scott, E.F.B. Johnston, and J.R. Cartwright, combined their office with the clerkship of the Executive Council, the provincial cabinet. Mowat's successor, Arthur Hardy, continued the tradition of combining the attorneyship and the premiership. When Hardy retired in October 1899, the attorney general of Upper Canada and Ontario had been the province's political leader for all but half a dozen years since 1841. Until the former schoolteacher George Ross succeeded Hardy, Francis Hincks was the only non-lawyer premier the province had known, except for George Brown, who occupied the post for four days in 1858.

Almost from the start, then, the attorney general in Upper Canada had enjoyed a political importance unknown to his English prototype. This was probably one cause of his acquiring administrative duties that would have been equally unfamiliar to the latter. When cabinet government was instituted, it was taken for granted that the attorney general would belong to that body. There was therefore no reason to assign ministerial accountability for the administration of justice to any other officer.

The attorney general's assumption of that duty was expressed symbolically as well as practically by Robert Baldwin's responsibility for the Judicature Acts of 1849. Chief Justice Osgoode, not Attorney General White, drafted the act of 1794; Lord Chancellor Selborne, not the attorney general of England, was responsible for the English Judicature Acts of 1873. And since Upper Canada had no equivalent to the British home secretary, the provincial attorney general also tended to assume responsibility for aspects of the administration of justice which in England belonged to that officer. Except for Allan MacNab's ill-fated police bill of 1856, all police legislation came out of the attorney general's office. After its foundation in 1909, the Ontario Provincial Police also found its way into the attorney general's sphere.

One important area of the administration of justice in which the attorney general assumed a much more substantial duty than his English counterpart was the prosecution of criminal offences. From the very start he was personally responsible for assize prosecutions. When, after 1837, he and the solicitor general could no longer attend every assize, the attorney general assumed the responsibility of finding substitute prosecutors and ensuring administrative continuity between the successive assizes in each district and (after 1849) county. In 1857 the County Attorneys Act set up a permanent, province-wide organization to provide administrative continuity and brought criminal prosecutions at quarter sessions within the Crown's purview, practically as well as in theory. England, by contrast, had scarcely the rudiments of public supervision of prosecutions until the office of Director of Public Prosecutions was created in 1879.

All these duties were added to the traditional functions of the attorney general. He continued to be responsible for advising both the executive and the legislature on legal and legislative matters, for conducting the Crown's civil litigation, and for exercising a quasi-judicial discretion on behalf of the Crown – in the civil sphere with respect to relator actions and suits against the Crown and in the criminal sphere with respect to instituting proceedings by information ex officio and terminating them by nolle prosequi. During the period of Union from 1841 to 1867, the press of political and administrative preoccupations led to these duties being more or less neglected. The new province of Ontario was more manageable both politically and administratively, and under King Oliver nothing was neglected.

The benign King Oliver was indeed the 'elective monarch' of Ontario – one of the most pronounced manifestations of a pattern that was to become common in Canadian politics, especially at the provincial level. Such political longevity is never fortuitous. It was Mowat's fortune to be a talented lawyer of impeccable probity, and thus acceptable to the provincial élite, at the same time as his values and achievements made him a hero to the ordinary citizen, and especially to the farmers of the province. The first of these characteristics underpinned the second, since his legal talents carried him to repeated victories on behalf of Ontario over John A. Macdonald, the representative of Montreal business interests. Although Mowat himself was a conciliator rather than a bigot, his special constituency comprised those who resented Macdonald's being foisted on them, first as attorney general of Upper Canada and then as prime minister of Canada, by Lower Canadian allies whose support was largely francophone and Roman Catholic. At a time when Toronto was struggling to escape from the economic hegemony of Montreal, Mowat's success in acquiring the greatest possible provincial jurisdiction over trade and commerce must also have helped him in business circles.

For many Ontarians, at any rate, it was for a long time a case of Good King Oliver versus Bad King John. After Macdonald's death in 1891 this juxtaposition no longer availed Mowat, and rural resentment of the underlying political and structural disadvantages of agriculture as opposed to finance and industry led to the rise of an agrarian-populist third party, the Patrons of Industry. This party, though short-lived, did well in the provincial general election of 1894, more at the expense of the Conservatives than of Mowat's Reformers.[1]

Of course, Mowat's long tenure occupied less than half the period during which the attorneyship was pre-eminent in Ontario politics, and we must look for other causes to account for the phenomenon as a whole. As noted by Robert Baldwin at mid-century, one cause was the pre-eminence of lawyers in society and politics; but there was more to it than that. From a governmental point of view, the great preoccupations of the nineteenth century were matters particularly within the sphere of the attorneyship, especially as it was developing in Canada. These were constitutional questions, the construction and adjustment of institutions of justice and local government, and the shaping of the law to meet the exigencies of social and economic change. The fiscal and social issues that predominate in the modern era of economic management and the welfare state were seen as relatively trivial. Even 'class' issues tended to turn on legal matters such as imprisonment for debt – witness Robert Randal's call for 'an equal distribution,' not of wealth but of justice. After Confederation, the provincial rights struggle may have contributed to the continued combination of attorneyship and premiership under Mowat (in contrast to Nova Scotia, a province conscious of economic decline, where after 1867 the premier was almost never attorney general).[2]

What made for the pre-eminence of the attorneyship made also for a remarkable continuity of tenure in the office, even in the earlier, politically less stable period. From 1840 to 1851 the attorneyship alternated between W.H. Draper and Robert Baldwin, except for Henry Sherwood's nine-month tenure in 1847-8. From 1854 to 1871 it alternated between the two Macdonalds. Less than a year after Sandfield Macdonald's ouster, Mowat took it over.

Unsurprising though it is in retrospect, the attorney general's rise was a matter of concern in mid-nineteenth-century Canada. His membership in the cabinet, and still more his premiership, seemed at odds with his duty to advise the executive impartially and dispassionately on the legal dimension of policy issues. They also raised a question about his effective accountability in the execution of his quasi-judicial duties in the sphere of criminal and civil law. 'In our system of responsible government,' as Mr Justice Riddell put it in 1924, in a decision affirming the attorney general's absolute discretion in advising for or against an application for leave to sue the Crown, 'the duty of the advisers of [the Lieutenant-Governor] ... is to exercise their best judgment in all matters of State ... In the exercise of that duty, they are not subject in any wise to the supervision or interference of the Courts or of any other power except the representatives of the people in the Legislative Assembly.'[3] This means that, if the attorney general fails in his duty, the public must rely for protection on a legislature that probably contains a majority of his political companions.

The ambiguity of the attorney general's constitutional position as a politician and cabinet member was expressed with probably unconscious subtlety by the governor general, the Marquis of Dufferin, at the time of the Pacific Scandal of 1873. When John A. Macdonald's government was found to have begged and received large sums for political purposes during the general election of 1872 from entrepreneurs seeking a charter to build the Canadian Pacific Railway, Dufferin told Macdonald: 'In acting as you have, I am well convinced that you have only followed a traditional practice and that probably your political opponents would have resorted with equal freedom to the same expedients, but as Minister of Justice and the official guardian and protector of the laws, your responsibilities are exceptional and your personal connection with what has passed cannot but fatally affect your position as minister.'[4] Dufferin all but said that an attorney general's duty was incompatible with the exigencies of electoral politics.

Such scandals do not occur daily, and the Pacific Scandal itself ended in a triumph for responsible government. Macdonald's exertions had won him only a slim majority, and the exposure of his methods provoked enough of his supporters to desert him to cause the government's collapse. Still, it is a fact of political life that governments have links to special interests, and matters affecting those interests are bound to crop up which require the attorney general to give impartial legal advice or to exercise impartially the quasi-judicial discretion that is constitutionally vested in his office. Should he declare himself in favour of the interest in question, the suspicion must linger that he has been influenced, perhaps even unconsciously, by his political connections. It is only common sense to admit that on such occasions a legislature with a majority of one party cannot command complete confidence as an agent of retribution. Neither can it command confidence as a tribunal of last resort should the Crown visit injustice on members of an unpopular minority or on the target of some large and determined ideological interest.

In the twentieth century no attorney general for Ontario has been premier, excepting James Whitney for a few months in 1905 and Gordon Conant for a few more in 1942-3. This is so partly because more premiers were non-lawyers and partly because the growth of the provincial government fostered a tendency for the premier not to hold an administrative portfolio. One lawyer who did, Howard Ferguson, adopted the ministry of education, believing it to be the most important and politically sensitive area of provincial jurisdiction during his premiership from 1923 to 1930.[5] Nevertheless, the growth of 'big government' in Ontario only enhanced the importance of the attorney general's duty to ensure that the administration of public affairs did not burst the bounds of constitutionality at the expense of the individual's civil rights. The McRuer Commission of 1964-71, in addition to its substantive proposals to aid the attorney general in performing this duty, recommended (though in vain) that the importance of the office be symbolically recognized by making its occupant next in precedence to the premier of the province.[6]

The attorney general's duty of ensuring the constitutional administration of public affairs has historically been the more important because the constitution of Canada, like that of Britain, was largely unwritten. The BNA Act defined the relations of the different Canadian governments with each other and with the imperial government, and it assigned specific powers to each level of government; but only recently has it acquired, in a form not casually amendable, anything equivalent to the guarantees of individual liberty and security found in the u.s. constitution as amended by the Bill of Rights.[7] The right to trial by grand and petit jury, for instance, which is entrenched in the latter (though not immune from compromise by the informal means of plea-bargaining), has in Canada, as in England, always been subject to annihilation by act of the competent legislature, notwithstanding its time-honoured status as a safeguard of individual liberty.

Mr Justice Riddell addressed this distinction in the decision quoted earlier.

In the United States, 'the Constitution' is a written document ... which authoritatively and without appeal dictates what shall and what shall not be done; in Canada, 'the Constitution' is 'the totality of the principles, more or less vaguely and generally stated, upon which we think the people should be governed' ... In the United States anything unconstitutional is illegal; in Canada to say that a measure is unconstitutional rather suggests that it is legal, but inadvisable.[8]

The distinction between what is legal and what is constitutional has cropped up constantly in this book. In the 1820s no one complained that it was illegal for the Crown to appropriate the so-called prerogative revenues, or for the Legislative Council to be largely subservient to the executive, or for the judges of the King's Bench to hold office during the royal pleasure. In each case the objection was one of constitutionality, of a deviation from what reformers took to be implied in Lieutenant-Governor Simcoe's promise of an 'image and transcript' of the English constitution. The same was true of the questions affecting the attorney general. The law officers' monopoly of prosecutions at assize, and later their membership in the cabinet, were assailed as dangerous deviations from English constitutional practice, not as breaches of law.

These were all matters affecting the relation between Crown and people within the province, but the same distinction between legality and constitutionality marked the dispute over the relation between Upper

Canadians and the empire. The British government always maintained the Blackstonian position that colonial legislatures were not sovereign bodies and, consequently, that Parliament could legislate for the colonies without restriction. But to colonial reformers like William Warren Baldwin this was nonsense: how could the people of the province be said to enjoy English liberties if they were not represented, like the English themselves, in a sovereign legislature? In 1822, when the Colonial Office hatched its scheme to reunite Upper and Lower Canada, Baldwin contested Westminster's right to do so unilaterally. Taking colonial internal sovereignty as his premise, he argued that the Constitutional Act of 1791 was essentially a treaty between the imperial government and the people of the province. It could be altered only with the consent of the people as represented in the legislature.[9]

In the 1840s Britain conceded internal sovereignty and responsible government as a matter of constitutional practice, without a syllable of legislation, by the expedient of refraining from interference in the colony's internal affairs. Because of this, a legalistic basis persisted after Confederation for arguing that the BNA Act was an expression of absolute imperial power, not of a compact or treaty between the participant polities and the empire: one had merely to deny that the constitutional fiction called responsible government had had an effect on the law. The confrontation between Macdonald-style centralism and provincial rights was a replay of the confrontation between narrow legalism and constitutionalism set up by the Union scheme of 1822.

The struggle against legalism drew on the eighteenth-century Irish Whig tradition of resistance to English imperialism. Baldwin was born into that tradition and passed it on to his son; Edward Blake, the first exponent of the compact theory of Confederation, came from the same Irish background and ended his career as an Irish nationalist MP at Westminster. From the will of Parliament, expressed in statute, which Blackstone upheld as supreme, the Irish Whigs had appealed to a fundamental law of civil and political rights, grounded in equity and reason, which Parliament could not alter. Unwritten but transcendent, it endowed colonial subjects with the same political rights as those who lived in England.[10] What we here call 'constitutionality' was in fact a counterpart in civil relations to the branch of law called 'equity' in property relations. Both were grounded in the premise that 'the law' could be unjust.

The struggle of the Upper Canadian reformers was very much a struggle for constitutional equity against narrow legalism. It was one that occurred at several levels, since acceptance of the Blackstonian viewpoint reflected and reinforced a broad reverence for English values, while rejection of it reflected and reinforced a broad scepticism towards them. In relation to internal legislative sovereignty and responsible government, the struggle was against the narrow legalism that would deny Upper Canadians liberties considered essential to the English constitution. In the Alien Question the struggle was against an inequitable application of the English law of alienage to a large class of inhabitants. The scandal over the treatment of Robert Gourlay and Francis Collins focused on the constitutional inequity of laws that were inherently oppressive to the individual. The campaign against official favouritism towards the Church of England opposed what might be called 'narrow constitutionalism,' since its goal was to fend off a part of the English constitution – the establishment of the Church of England – that was inequitable when applied to a colony where most of the inhabitants were not Anglicans.

All these grievances could be blamed on the colony's lack of practical legislative sovereignty, which precluded reforms not sanctioned by the imperial government. To the reformers, therefore, or at least to those – the Baldwinites – who became the mainstream, responsible government appeared to be the panacea for the province's ills. Its attainment in the 1840s was felt to be an epic victory of liberty over oppression, and this feeling of liberation had ironic consequences. Once responsible government had been conceded, constitutionalism was more and more reserved for Upper Canada's external relations; in the province's internal affairs, it was increasingly submerged in legalism. Despite the fuss of the 1820s over the law officers' monopoly of prosecutions at assize, no thought was given to extending to Upper Canadians the constitutional safeguard entailed in being able to prosecute at the assizes by private counsel. That other important source of grievance in the administration of justice, the jury system, had scarcely been reformed by Robert Baldwin before the jury itself was being derided as inefficient and obsolete.

From one point of view this reaction was natural. With the whole community perfectly represented in a sovereign legislature under responsible government, it was inconceivable that the law could be unjust. Surely there could now be no objection to withholding or abolishing constitutional safeguards that were a cause of inefficiency, desirable as they may have been in the past. In the new Canada the grand jury was redundant, public control of prosecutions beneficent, the prosecution's procedural advantage of the last word to the jury unexceptionable. The introduction of Crown appeal from acquittal in 1892 was simply one more manifestation of a tendency to submerge the constitutional in the legal.

One modern defence of the Crown appeal legislation of 1930 reflects today's uneasiness with Justice Riddell's distinction between the legal and the constitutional, echoing the rhetoric with which late Victorian commentators sought to lay the distinction to rest. Quoting Blackstone's characterization of the jury as a palladium of English liberties, the writer expresses the hope that Canadians will repel 'any erosion of the liberties which are preserved by a proper functioning of the jury system.' But, he avers, appeal from acquittal is not an erosion of those liberties; rather, by allowing the reversal of verdicts rendered against the evidence, it preserves them. Protesting against 'the proposition that the jury system is being undermined by a law which is in effect insurance that jury verdicts will continue to rest on a foundation of truth,' the writer denounces opposition to appeal from acquittal as 'a relic of thought from the time of trial by battle where the accused was acquitted forever by his victorious rush at his accuser.' The censorial jury is 'neither now the law nor appropriate to the modern expectation that a court of law can reasonably be expected to attempt to ascertain the truth.' It is 'a retrograde philosophical step,' which amounts to believing that an accused party is 'entitled to escape the consequences of his crime by illegal means.'[11]

Readers will note the derisive reference to trial by battle, so reminiscent of the historian Hallam's dismissal of trial by jury as 'a preposterous relic of barbarism' and of Justice Gwynne's contempt for the idea that the grand jury still had value as a shield against executive oppression.[12] The important thing for our argument is the use of this rhetoric to discredit, as an assertion of the defendant's right 'to escape from the consequence of his crime by *illegal* means,' the ancient *constitutional* compunction against Crown appeal from acquittal. A similar perspective on the distinction between constitutionality and legality can be detected in the Ministry of the Attorney General Act. While the McRuer Commission stressed the attorney general's duty to prevent unconstitutional laws being enacted in the administration of public affairs, the act does not mention the constitution but speaks only of a duty to 'see that the administration of public affairs is in accordance with the law.'[13]

Natural though it may have been to see responsible government as inaugurating an era of perfect liberty, this was not the only possible view of the event; and the hold that the ideology established on public opinion marks a major shift in Ontario's political culture.[14] Its associated perspectives on private prosecutions and trial by jury had their advocates in England – indeed, as we have seen, they originated there; yet in England there was no rush to act on them. Though in the last fifteen years the safeguard traditionally contained in the right to trial by jury has been significantly eroded there too, appeal from acquittal is still taboo and the importance of the jury's censorial role is evident in recent prosecutions connected with the coal-miners' strike of 1984-5.[15]

The decline in Ontario of the sense of a distinction between the constitutional and the legal reflects the absorption of the ideology of the rule of law in that of responsible government. The older ideology emerged out of social and political strife; it was the product and mirror of a complex balance of power between different elements of a highly stratified society – a balance of power known to history as the eighteenth-century Whig or 'mixed' constitution. Blackstone captured its essence in his famous depiction of the state as a machine: 'Every branch of our civil polity supports and is supported, regulates and is regulated, by the rest ... Like three distinct powers in mechanics, they jointly impel the machine of government in a direction different from what either, acting by themselves [sic], would have done; but at the same time in a direction partaking of each, and formed out of all.'[16]

Expecting the continuance of the strife that had engendered it, but anxious to control that strife, the Whig constitution included rules that restricted the use of the criminal law as a weapon. Of these rules, the right of the jury, representing the local community, to act as censor of the law and its application was probably the most radical. A cherished principle of mid-seventeenth-century radical commentators on the law, the doctrine of the censorial jury dramatizes the fragmented, adversarial nature of contemporary society. Emanating from the sense of unjust disfranchisement produced by a highly restrictive property-based franchise, which precluded ordinary Englishmen from the law-making process, it alone, of all the tenets of the rule of law, limited 'the divine right of Parliament' to establish laws favouring the dominant social interest. Advocates of the doctrine justified it by an appeal to a notion that contested the supremacy of Parliament – the notion of an unwritten but transcendent fundamental law, grounded in a principle variously defined as experience, reason, or equity (or some combination thereof), which Parliament could not alter.[17] This fundamental law was in some minds identified with the common law and in other minds distinguished from and elevated above it, but always it was supreme and immutable.

The doctrine of the censorial jury was, then, symmetrical in form with the Irish Whig doctrine of colonial internal sovereignty that underlay the Baldwinite demand for responsible government. Both doctrines appealed from the will of Parliament to an unwritten fundamental law which stood above statute; both upheld the will of a notional local community against the same central legislative authority, in which the community was represented inadequately or not at all. In the doctrine of colonial legislative sovereignty, the disfranchised local community was the colonial community as a whole; in the English doctrine of the censorial jury, it was the ordinary folk in each locality whose interests suffered because of lack of representation in the House of Commons.

In Upper Canada, the latter community had its counterpart in the ordinary farmers, who suffered under a system of law and political economy that favoured mercantile capital. The farmers' hopes for responsible government varied greatly from those of the Baldwins – land speculators and bank shareholders whose social values differed little, if at all, from John Beverley Robinson's; as the farmers' tribune, William Lyon Mackenzie, noted, the social order was 'quite as dependent on the laws which regulated the distribution of wealth as on political organization.'[18] In 1828, the year in which all things seemed possible, the Baldwinite political effort was disrupted by the rift in the anti-government ranks. Robert Baldwin was beaten in the county of York by Mackenzie and another radical; in Lincoln the Baldwins' friend Bartholomew Beardsley, so ardent in assailing jury-packing and the law officers' monopoly of prosecutions at assize, was defeated by the hostile propaganda of Mackenzie and Robert Randal; Dr Baldwin owed his victory in Norfolk partly to Randal's bane Thomas Clark, who shared Baldwin's aversion to the government's policy of taxing large speculative landholdings.[19]

Nevertheless, as an ideology of the disfranchised, Baldwinite responsible government had a strong appeal for agrarian populism. The farmers could vote, of course, but their representative chamber was paralyzed by the authoritarian political system that enveloped it. And because the impotence of the House of Assembly was the grand symbol of their disadvantage, their animosity was diverted from the substance of the law towards institutional grievances that were real but secondary: the oligarchic officialdom that the system sustained; the government-dominated upper chamber that thwarted the Assembly's efforts at egalitarian reform. The farmers were induced to associate their feeling of disfranchisement not with their identity as a social class but with the colonial community as a whole, and aspirations that were basically economic and social were subsumed in the quest for an institutional panacea – colonial internal sovereignty and responsible government.

Responsible government did not alter the social balance of power that placed the lawyer and the financier above the farmer, yet fortuitous institutional factors helped to prolong for forty years the farmers' fusion (or confusion) of their class interest with that of the community as a whole. The upsurge of populist aspirations during the Baldwin and Hincks administrations was contained with difficulty, but 1854 saw the advent of a new 'liberal-conservative' hegemony in the shape of an alliance between the Baldwinites, the Macdonald conservatives, and the Lower Canadian *Bleu* bloc. Clear Grit radicalism was channelled into a campaign to rescue Upper Canada from the political union that subjected it to the domination of Montreal business interests and francophone Roman Catholics. Since the Liberal-Conservative parliamentary majority rested on the provision of the Act of Union that gave Lower Canada as many seats as the increasingly more populous upper province, the grand goals of the campaign were alternately 'Representation by Population' and dissolution of the union. Confederation was embraced as the remedy for Upper Canada's grievances, but – lo and behold – it reproduced the conditions of twenty years before, with Macdonald centralism playing the imperial ogre and provincial rights the panacea. King Oliver's campaign for provincial sovereignty, fought under the standard of 'Responsible Government,' made him a hero.

At different times, a variety of social and economic influences operated to contain the threat that rural populism posed to the political and social stability of Upper Canada: the ethnic and cultural diversity of the rural population, the prosperity of the rural economy, the opening of the prairie to agricultural settlement, and – not least – the farmers' real, though limited, influence as voters under responsible government. These, in reciprocal reaction with the political circumstances that induced farmers to identify their hopes with the Upper Canadian community and their grievances with an external enemy, were highly propitious to their acceptance of responsible government. The remarkable unifying power which – despite its failure fully to satisfy rural populist aspirations – this ideology attained in Ontario was reflected in the support farmers gave to a series of conservative Torontonians: those aristocratic land speculators the Baldwins, the big businessman George Brown, the lawyer Mowat.

The conception of society associated with the new ideology differed greatly from that associated with the ideology of the rule of law. The old conception (witness Blackstone's metaphor) was that of a mechanism designed to contain the play of adversarial social forces. The new conception was organic, playing down class distinctions by fostering identification with the whole community. The binding principle of the old conception was deference – the acceptance of one's place in a hierarchy; that of the new conception was consensus – an organic concept drawn from physiology and connoting in politics the harmonious co-operation of equals.[20] The organic nature of the new conception may explain the complacency with which the sense of a distinction between legality and constitutionality was permitted to atrophy. *Vox populi, vox dei*: with the whole community perfectly represented in a sovereign legislature under responsible government, what objection could persist to the divine right of Parliament? As defined and administered under such a system, how could the law be unjust?

Nothing like this sudden shift in political culture happened in England. There the evolution of responsible government was a protracted process, and its establishment in the context of a narrow franchise did nothing to smother social conflict that had as its political focus the question of extending the franchise; nor was there anything like the colonial political predicament to induce the submergence of sectional sentiments in a common cause. Social tension remained high, and rich and poor alike had an incentive to affirm the value of the rule of law. Thomas Chambers's vindication of the grand jury (quoted in chapter 7) reflects this persistence of eighteenth-century values. Envisaging the return of social strife to a level that might goad the government into high-handed action against popular leaders or even into calling in the military, with the result that blood was 'spilt on the scene of some immense gathering,' Chambers descanted on how

the bitterness of the strife is allayed, when the rulers and the populace are in angry collision with each other, by a court so constituted as to have sympathies with both parties and fitted, therefore, to act as mediator between them. The harshness of authority is mitigated by its acting through such an organ; the lawless impulses of the disaffected subside when they have the opportunity to appeal to a proper tribunal ... Both parties change the weapons of their warfare – both appeal to the law. The demagogue stops his inflammatory harangue to advise with his lawyer; the Government recalls its troops and instructs the Attorney General. The result is, that the greatest political questions come on for discussion in the criminal courts, and come on under circumstances very favourable for their correct solution.[21]

What was preserved in England by the continuance of the social tension that had engendered it was preserved in the United States by the federal constitution. The Glorious Revolution was conducted by conservative politicians anxious to pretend that it was not a revolution at all but an impeccably legal response to unique circumstances – the revolution was itself the first and greatest of the constitutional fictions (colonial responsible government among them) that subsequently marked the development of the British polity. In a fashion consistent with the grudging nature of the revolution, the social compromise embodied in the Whig constitution reflected the pragmatic maxim 'least said, soonest mended'; it conceded as little as possible to mid-seventeenth-century radicalism and as little as possible of that in writing. The notion of a transcendent fundamental law was shunned and the divine right of monarchy superseded by the divine right of Parliament.[22] Revolutionary America, by contrast, having successfully revolted against Parliament, established its polity on a basis that combined the ideological bent of New England puritanism with the philosophic idealism of the French Enlightenment. It adopted what it liked of the Whig constitution in the systematized form of the *philosophe* Montesquieu, and the notion of a transcendent fundamental law in the form of a Rousseauvian social contract. The existence of principles of constitutional equity unrepealable by statute was rendered incontestable.

The difference between a written constitution and an unwritten one is like that between a written and an unwritten contract: the unwritten instrument is enforceable at law, but only if you can prove its existence. Canada, its rebellion against Parliament having failed, had to accept independence on the terms offered – those of an unwritten constitutional convention. The messianism that marked the new political culture was incongruously applied to a system whose hallmark was tight-lipped pragmatism. Instead of being entrenched as fundamental law, the principles of constitutional equity retained the precarious status of conventions whose infringement was (in Riddell's significant phrase, so redolent of calculation and expediency) 'inadvisable.'

In the context of a political culture that favoured their disparagement, that status offered only uncertain protection to the constitutional safeguards traditionally embraced in the ideology of the rule of law. All, of course, were subject to annihilation by the legisature, but some had at least been established by the authority of statute – habeas corpus, for instance, and judicial tenure during good behaviour; these turned out to be the strongest. Others such as the grand jury, which rested only on the common law, were more vulnerable. The most radical of all those protections, the censorial role of the criminal trial jury, turned out to be the weakest of all, for it rested on silence. As we saw in chapter 7, it was conceded in practice by *Bushell's Case* but never authoritatively admitted as constitutional doctrine; its progressive annihilation by Parliament in 1892 and 1930, far from being 'inadvisable,' proved to be scarcely controversial.[23]

Of course, no constitution is worth the paper it is (or is not) written on unless the community it organizes is determined to uphold it. Hitler came to power under a democratic constitution; Stalin bestowed one on his empire at the height of his reign of terror; the Bill of Rights coexisted with slavery for seven decades. It is in the gap between theory and practice that those who would dismiss political democracy and the rule of law as a confidence trick have historically sought their justification.

At the very moment in 1930 when the Crown appeal amendment was passed, responsible government was meeting the worst expectations of its detractors; civil liberties were then undergoing abuse remarkably like that of a century previously. The essence of the persecution lay in the exploitation of an assortment of oppressive laws in combination to harass, imprison, and deport individuals for the expression of political ideas. Some of those laws had been passed by Parliament in the panic aroused by the Winnipeg general strike of 1919; others were already on the statute books. The former included the notorious section 98 of the Criminal Code, which made mere membership in the Communist party punishable by twenty years' imprisonment, and an amendment to the Immigration Act which rendered any unnaturalized immigrant convicted of a criminal offence liable to deportation;[24] the latter included the sedition clauses of the Criminal Code, which were used against the Finn Aaro Vaara, and the vagrancy section, which was frequently invoked against communist street orators.[25]

The elements of this repression are strikingly reminiscent of the Robinson era in Upper Canada. Just as Robert Gourlay was liable to deportation under the Sedition Act of 1804 because, being British, he had not taken the oath of allegiance in the province, so British immigrants convicted of vagrancy were liable under the amended Immigration Act because they could not be naturalized. Just as the terms of the Sedition Act contravened the principle that an individual is presumed innocent until proved guilty, so did those of section 98. Just as the House of Assembly tried for years to repeal the Sedition Act, only to be thwarted by the Legislative Council, so the House of Commons tried repeatedly in the 1920s to repeal both section 98 and the Immigration Act amendment, only to be blocked by the Senate.[26] Indeed, the last of these efforts was embodied in (and struck out of) the bill of 1930 that restored appeal from acquittal. Members of Parliament and senators neglected the latter partly because they were debating the merits of section 98!

The resemblance between these two periods of repression was more than superficial. In each case the repression stemmed from the fear felt by the dominant social interests at the threat posed by a large alien element which espoused different political values and was thought to have ideological and sentimental ties to a powerful foreign country – in one case the United States, in the other the Soviet Union. In each case there was the same tendency to treat the advocates of a new order as sedition-mongers, whose ideas placed them beyond the pale of decent society and the protection the rule of law was supposed to extend to all. And in each case there was a process of escalation: the persecutors grew bolder as they became sure of their impunity.

During both of these episodes, the process of repression had the same two distinct aspects: the state and its agents often resorted with impunity to perversions of the law and abuses of procedure, but underlying the force of the repression was the illiberality of the law itself. In the 1820s it was possible to imagine that both the law's maladministration and its inherent defects would be rectified under responsible government, but in 1930 the communists knew better: the laws then used to repress them were laws that had been enacted under responsible government and a democratic franchise. This fostered cynicism about the system itself, despite its ostensibly democratic and libertarian processes. The elaborate ceremonial of democratic election and due process was seen as a trick which served to deceive an exploited working class into believing that they were governed according to canons of equity. Responsible government, universal suffrage, and the rule of law together comprised no more than an ideology by which a ruling class justified its hegemony to the ruled.[27]

Historically speaking, this perspective on the rule of law was incontestable. We have referred more than once to ways in which the administration of justice in eighteenth-century England was set up to justify the hierarchic social order of that time and place and to provide the colour of equity to the operation of highly inequitable laws. The disparity between appearance and reality is strikingly revealed by reference to the standard work on the history of the law officers of the Crown. In documenting the growth of new standards of objectivity and fairness in the discharge of these offices, the author singles out three incumbents: Sir Philip Yorke, Sir John Scott, and Sir Thomas Denman. Yet Yorke was a co-author of the

Black Act, that charter of terror, and as Lord Hardwicke he became an instrument of its extension and merciless enforcement, first in a judicial capacity as lord chief justice and then in a political capacity during his protracted service as lord chancellor. Scott prosecuted the shoemaker Thomas Hardy for high treason in 1794 for propagating republicanism and democracy; twenty-five years later, as Lord Chancellor Eldon, he applauded the infamous massacre of 'Peterloo,' when a mounted militia under the orders of the Manchester magistrates charged a peaceful mass meeting. The humanity of Sir Thomas Denman, later lord chief justice, was evinced during his prosecution of the agricultural labourers whom starvation had driven to join in the 'Captain Swing' risings of 1830. Only some of them were hanged.[28]

Thomas Chambers's account of how the grand jury worked to soothe social passions fits this cynical perspective on the rule of law admirably, confirming in the process the most sardonic observations of William Aird Ross, the old Scottish county judge. It is extraordinary to witness Chambers's conception of how social equity is satisfied by processes calculated to stall the momentum of the popular movement while its leaders are tied up in court defending themselves against an assortment of nasty charges; how that process would have helped to fill the starving bellies of Captain Swing's followers is not evident. Nowhere does Chambers recognize that both the government and the grand jury were instruments of the country's social élite. On the most famous occasion when blood was 'spilt on the scene of some immense gathering,' the Peterloo massacre of 1819, the spilling was done by the very sort of people who formed the grand jury: the magistrates and mounted yeomanry.[29]

In Upper Canada too the law served an ideological function. John Beverley Robinson had a strong sense of the importance of appearances and a proper attention to the forms of justice. In preparing the treason trials of 1814 he refused to take advantage of the act just passed to allow such trials to be held outside the district in which the alleged crime had occurred. After the trials he joined Chief Justice Scott and Mr Justice Powell in urging the wisdom of not hanging too many of the convicts, since a judicious display of lenity was better calculated to convince the public of the justice of the proceedings.[30] In 1818, after he had failed to get the grand jury of the Western District to authenticate a rather far-fetched indictment for conspiracy against the Earl of Selkirk, Robinson was reluctant to accede to a request on behalf of the North-West Company to proceed against the earl by information ex officio, which would have dispensed with the need for a grand-jury indictment. The proceeding was legal but extraordinary, and it was bound to have the appearance of oppression (the more so since the filing of ex officio informations was banned in the United States under the Bill of Rights).[31]

Of course, the fact that in a case like Selkirk's the grand jury could dig in its heels merely enhanced the ideological effectiveness of the system. Much of the time grand juries acted independently, and much of the time John Beverley Robinson performed his office dispassionately. But what worked for an earl in a non-political case at the periphery of the province, in a district where he had some influence, would not necessarily avail a critic of the establishment engaged in politically sensitive litigation at York, or Hamilton, or Niagara.

Indeed, even in Selkirk's case the system did not work very well, for the earl was perceived as a threat to the commercial interests of the Upper and Lower Canadian élites. Chief Justice Powell abruptly terminated the Western District assizes to prevent the grand jury from rejecting Robinson's indictment and preferring others against agents of the North-West Company; the legislature was railroaded into passing an act allowing offences committed in the wild parts of the province to be tried in any district; Robinson shifted the venue to York, where a more pliant grand jury could be expected. It was the reverse of his wise restraint in 1814, but that had been based on the justified assumption that he could get the verdicts he wanted from jurors in the districts where the crimes had been committed. In any case, Robinson cited an English legislative precedent to support the change in venue: the Black Act.[32]

In Ontario, then, as in England, the rule of law, and later responsible government, served the establishment as an ideological justification for its pre-eminence, and in times of crisis agents of the establishment could be false to those ideals in ways which showed that they valued other things more highly than their ostensible creed, the secular faith of the polity. Yet not all of them betrayed that creed, and even those who did were somewhat held in check by it. Even in the authoritarian polity of Upper Canada, men with a will to repression, such as John Beverley Robinson, were constrained by the fact that too great an abuse of the canons of constitutionality meant moral bankruptcy, and the likes of John Rolph and William and Robert Baldwin were ever at hand to recall them to their duty. True, George Rolph was tarred and feathered, and Robert Gourlay and Judge Willis driven from the province, and Singleton Gardiner and Francis Collins thrown into jail, and William Lyon Mackenzie harassed in a dozen different ways, and reformers all over the province beaten up by Orangemen when they tried to vote; but no one was simply shot and thrown into the lake. Repression was impeded because the repressors' ostensible purpose was to preserve the constitution from republican, democratic subversion; they needed to conform as closely as possible to the constitution even as they flouted it.

A hundred years later the same was true; and in the more open society of the twentieth century there were judges such as William Raney (a former attorney general of Ontario), and lawyers such as Arthur Roebuck (soon to be the province's attorney general), and a small army of other officers of state and articulate critics who refused to be stampeded by a climate of repressive hysteria. They would have no truck with abuses of the constitution even when the victims were people whose ideas they deplored.[33]

Since in this chapter we have taken the censorial jury as a benchmark of libertarian sensibility, it must be conceded that the introduction of appeal from acquittal into the Criminal Code made no contribution to the persecution of the communists. The censorial jury works as a safeguard only in prosecutions (like that of Penn and Mead in 1670, and of Robert Randal in 1825) that are offensive to the community from which the jury is drawn; it is useless when public opinion is bent on persecution (as in 1866, for instance, when John A. Macdonald had to uphold the rule of law in the interest of suspected Fenians), and unreliable when the rules of qualification tend to draw juries from social elements unsympathetic to the accused. During the persecution of the 1930s, vagrancy offences were tried under summary jurisdiction, and in trials for more serious offences juries did not distinguish themselves.

The point about institutional safeguards of this sort is that their efficiency lies partly in their multiplicity. None is an infallible guarantee. When the state is intent on repression, all of the safeguards together may not suffice to protect its targets. But each symbolizes the public commitment to the rule of law. Each, as it is overthrown, triggers an alarm in the public conscience, provoking more people to question the persecutors' motives, focusing more attention on the underlying causes of the conflict.

For this reason the ideology of the rule of law, and the culture of constitutionality of which historically it has formed a part, have been esteemed even by people who admit that they function as ideologies to mask, justify, and perpetuate social inequity. In concluding his study of the origin of the Black Act, the English historian and civil libertarian E.P. Thompson acknowledged that ' "the law," as a logic of equity, must always seek to transcend the inequalities of class power which, instrumentally, it is harnessed to serve. And "the law" as ideology, which pretends to reconcile the interests of all degrees of men, must always come into conflict with the ideological partisanship of class.' As the English novelist E.M. Forster, first chairman of the National Council for Civil Liberties, put it fifty years ago: 'The fact that our rulers have to *pretend* to like freedom is an advantage … If Britannia goes a-whoring, she can be the more easily found out because of her professions of monogamy in the past. That is why, with us, the *forms* of government and the *forms* of justice are so important, and need watching so zealously.'[34]

As Forster's remark implies, institutional safeguards are useless unless sustained by a libertarian political culture; indeed, it is only in such a cultural context that those safeguards can work at all or are even understood. Libertarian cultures generate extra-governmental bodies to watch over the forms of government and justice – bodies like the National Council for Civil Liberties and its Canadian counterpart, the Canadian Civil Liberties Association. Advocates of popular (and sometimes unpopular) liberties can sometimes appear as cranky, relentless in their zealous campaign against public complacency – modern counterparts of William Lyon Mackenzie and Francis Collins; yet they offer an indispensable counterweight to the pressures exerted on officers of state by special interests, and sometimes by public opinion.

'This is not the liberty which we can hope, that no grievance ever should arise in the Commonwealth, that let no man expect; but when complaints are freely heard, deeply considered, and speedily reformed, then is the utmost bound of civil liberty attained that wise men look for.' Thus another great literary libertarian, the poet John Milton, defined the limits of the possible in 1644. In such a commonwealth the watchers will watch in a more generous spirit than Mackenzie and Collins in 1828, and the watched will accept that vigilance more graciously than John Beverley Robinson.

Appendix

John White	1791-1800	
Thomas Scott	1800-6	Chief justice of Upper Canada 1806-16
William Firth	1807-12	
John Macdonell	1812	Acting attorney general 1811-12
D'Arcy Boulton	1814-18	Solicitor general 1805-14; justice of King's Bench 1816-25
John Beverley Robinson	1818-29	Acting attorney general 1812-14; solicitor general 1814-18; chief justice of Upper Canada 1829-62; president, Court of Error and Appeal 1862-3
Henry John Boulton	1829-33	Acting solicitor general 1818-20; solicitor general 1820-9; chief justice of Newfoundland 1833-8
Robert Sympson Jameson	1833-7	Vice-chancellor of Upper Canada 1837-50
Christopher Hagerman	1837-40	Solicitor general 1829-37; justice of Queen's Bench 1840-7
William Henry Draper	1840-2	Solicitor general 1837-40; justice of Queen's Bench 1847-56; chief justice of Common Pleas 1856-63; chief justice of Upper Canada 1863-9; president, Court of Error and Appeal 1869-77

Robert Baldwin	1842-3	Solicitor general 1840-1
William Henry Draper	1844-7	
Henry Sherwood	1847-8	Solicitor general 1842, 1844-6
Robert Baldwin	1848-51	
William Buell Richards	1851-3	Justice of Common Pleas 1853-63; chief justice of Common Pleas 1863-8; chief justice of Ontario 1868-75; chief justice of Supreme Court of Canada 1875-9
John Ross	1853-4	Solicitor general 1851-3; receiver general 1858; president of Executive Council and minister of agriculture 1858-62
John A. Macdonald	1854-62*	Receiver general 1847; commissioner of Crown lands 1847-8; minister of militia affairs 1862, 1865-7; prime minister of Canada 1867-73, 1878-1891; minister of justice and attorney general of Canada, 1867-73
John Sandfield Macdonald*	1862-4	Solicitor general 1849-51; minister of militia affairs 1862-4
John A. Macdonald	1864-7	
J. Sandfield Macdonald	1867-71	
Adam Crooks	1871-2	Treasurer 1872-7; minister of education 1876-83
Oliver Mowat	1872-96	Provincial secretary 1858 (2-6 August); postmaster general 1863-4; vice-chancellor of Ontario 1864-72; minister of justice and attorney general of Canada 1896
Arthur S. Hardy	1896-9	Provincial secretary 1876-89; commissioner of Crown lands 1889-96

SOLICITORS GENERAL OF UPPER CANADA, 1795-1867

Robert Gray	1795-1804	
D'Arcy Boulton	1805-14	(See AGS)
John Beverley Robinson	1814-18	(See AGS)
Henry John Boulton	1820-9	(See AGS)

* Sandfield Macdonald was attorney general from 2 to 6 August 1858.

Christopher Hagerman	1829-37	(See AGS)
William Henry Draper	1837-40	(See AGS)
Robert Baldwin	1840-1	(See AGS)
Henry Sherwood	1842	(See AGS)
James E. Small	1842-3	County judge of Middlesex 1849-69
Henry Sherwood	1844-6	
John Hillyard Cameron	1846-8	
William Hume Blake	1848-9	Chancellor of Upper Canada 1850-62
J. Sandfield Macdonald	1849-51	(See AGS)
John Ross	1851-3	(See AGS)
Joseph Curran Morrison	1853-4	Receiver general 1856-8; justice of Common Pleas 1862-3; justice of Queen's Bench 1863-7; justice of Court of Appeal 1877-85
Henry Smith	1854-8	
G. Skeffington Connor	1858*	Justice of Queen's Bench 1863
Joseph Curran Morrison	1860-2	
James Patton	1862	
Adam Wilson	1862-3	Justice of Common Pleas 1863-8, justice of Queen's Bench 1868-78; chief justice of Common Pleas 1878-84; chief justice of Queen's Bench 1884-7
Lewis Wallbridge	1863	Chief justice of Manitoba 1882-7
Albert Norton Richards	1863-4	
James Cockburn	1864-7	

* 2 to 6 August only

Bibliographical Note

This book is based chiefly on standard sources for the political, constitutional, and administrative history of Upper Canada and Ontario in the nineteenth century: statutes, parliamentary records, executive archives. What follows is not a survey of historical sources for the administration of justice. No special mention is made of the collections of law reports cited herein.

The essential starting-point for study of the office of attorney general in the British empire and Commonwealth is John Ll.J. Edwards *The Law Officers of the Crown* (London 1964). See also his *The Attorney-General, Politics and the Public Interest* (London 1984) and (of particular relevance to Canada) *Ministerial Responsibility for National Security as It Relates to the Offices of Prime Minister, Attorney General and Solicitor General of Canada* (Ottawa 1980); the latter was written for the Commission of Inquiry Concerning Activities of the Royal Canadian Mounted Police (the McDonald Commission). Two books by James W. Norton-Kyshe are useful: *The Law and Privileges Relating to the Attorney-General and Solicitor-General of England* (London 1897) and (less so) *The Law and Privileges Relating to the Colonial Attorneys-General* (London 1900).

My chief sources for the period 1791-1841 are government records. The British Colonial Office records relating to Upper Canada, especially CO42 (PRO; microfilm copies at PAC and AO), are a source of unexpected illumination on the administration of justice, as on many other aspects of provincial history, but one must beware of being unduly influenced by the official viewpoint on events and individuals. The same holds for the main general series of provincial government records (PAC RG5 A1, the 'Upper Canada Sundries') and the state papers of the Executive

Council (PAC RG1 E3). Other major sources include the printed Journals of the House of Assembly of Upper Canada, especially the appendices, from 1825 on; the government financial accounts printed therein are a valuable source for the administration of justice in general, as are the Colonial Office statistical Blue Books (CO47, microfilm at PAC). The journals of the Assembly from 1791 to 1824 are printed in the annual *Report* of the Ontario Bureau of Archives for 1910-14. Newspaper reports of the parliamentary debates usefully amplify the *Journals*, just as their reporting and commentary on public affairs in general amplify the government archives, but the coverage in both cases is less complete than is at first apparent. A valuable collection of printed primary sources relevant to topics treated in this book is *Documents Relating to the Constitutional History of Canada* (I: 1759-91, II: 1791-1818, III: 1818-28; Ottawa 1914-35), published under the auspices of PAC.

For the politics surrounding the attorneyship in the Union period (1841-67) CO42 was again consulted, but the chief sources are the manuscript journals of the Executive Council of Canada (now functioning as a cabinet) and the printed *Journals* and appendices of the Legislative Assembly of Canada. The compilation from newspaper accounts of the *Debates of the Legislative Assembly of United Canada* (vols I-, Elizabeth Nish, ed., Quebec 1970-) is an invaluable complement to these; it has reached 1854-5. The Canadian Library Association collecton of *Parliamentary Debates* on microfilm is not as good, but goes up to 1866. A valuable professional perspective is available from 1855 on in the *Upper Canada Law Journal* (later the *Canada Law Journal*); one must remember, as to political bias, that it emerged from a coterie surrounding John A. Macdonald. For the post-Confederation period one must use the printed records of both the dominion and the provincial legislatures. The *Journals* and *Debates* of both houses of Parliament are in print, but only the *Journals* of the Legislative Assembly; for what was said there one must rely on newspapers.

The archives of the Ministry of the Attorney General itself (AO RG4) are of course essential to any definitive study of the office, especially in the twentieth century. If they were very selectively used in this study, one reason is that the great bulk pertains to the twentieth century; another is the condition of the nineteenth-century records. The only major body of material is the deputy attorney general's letterbooks from 1869 on, which have no subject index and consist of semi-legible blotting-paper copies which make skimming impossible. The Central Registry Files from 1870 on are a treasure, but unfortunately the nineteenth-century material at least was heavily culled by the ministry before being passed to AO. The pre-Confederation records, though slender, are far from negligible and include the originals of John Beverley Robinson's draft correspondence concerning the treason trial of 1814 (these are also on the microfilm of 'John Beverley Robinson

Papers' mentioned below). Particularly useful to me was the letterbook of 1843-51, which documents Robert Baldwin's handling of the administrative routine of the office. It should be noted that some of the attorney general's pre-Confederation records seem to have accompanied John A. Macdonald in his transition from attorney general, Canada West to attorney general, Dominion of Canada in 1867; these have landed in the archives of the Department of Justice (PAC RG13; the relevant subgroup is B1).

Private papers were not much used for this study. There are two major collections of attorneys general's papers from the nineteenth century: the Robert Baldwin Papers at MTL and the John A. Macdonald Papers at PAC. Also useful are the John Beverley Robinson Papers at AO and the John White Papers at PAC. The papers of Solicitor General John Hillyard Cameron are at MTL. Other major collections pertinent to the administration of justice in nineteenth-century Ontario are the Blake Papers at AO and the James R. Gowan Papers at PAC. The papers of a deputy attorney general, John R. Cartwright, are among the Cartwright Family Papers in the archives of Trinity College of the University of Toronto.

As befits the major political figures they were, several nineteenth-century attorneys general are the subject of biographical studies, but nearly all of these are traditional political biographies and pay little attention to their subjects' execution of the office. The classic study of John A. Macdonald is Donald Creighton's two-volume eponymous biography; Macdonald's pre-Confederation career is also treated in J.M.S. Careless, ed. *The Pre-Confederation Premiers: Ontario Government Leaders, 1841-1867* (Toronto 1984) as are W.H. Draper, Robert Baldwin, and Sandfield Macdonald. Patrick Brode's *John Beverley Robinson: Bone and Sinew of the Compact* (Toronto 1984) pays more attention to its subject's professional career than most studies, as does another book by a lawyer, C.R.W. Biggar's *Sir Oliver Mowat: A Biographical Sketch* (2 vols, Toronto 1905). Biggar was Mowat's son-in-law, but a modern and perhaps more critical biography of Mowat is forthcoming in the Ontario Historical Studies series from A. Margaret Evans. The two Boultons are principal subjects of John Lownsbrough *The Privileged Few: The Grange and its People in Nineteenth Century Toronto* (Toronto 1980): 'popular history' but well-researched, delightfully perceptive, and charmingly written. A full-scale scholarly study of Robert Baldwin is badly wanted, but there is a major article in the *Dictionary of Canadian Biography*, which will soon have treated, more or less substantially, all the nineteenth-century attorneys general but Mowat and Hardy.

The general historiography of the administration of justice in nineteenth-century Ontario is in its infancy, but two works of special value for this study were William N.T. Wylie 'Instruments of Commerce and Authority: The Civil Courts in Upper Canada, 1789-1812' and Margaret A. Banks 'The Evolution of the Ontario

Courts, 1788-1981,' both published in David H. Flaherty, ed. *Essays in the History of Canadian Law* II (Toronto 1983). Other essays in this and Flaherty's first volume (Toronto 1981) are cited herein, as is J.M. Beattie *Attitudes Towards Crime and Punishment in Upper Canada, 1830-1850: A Documentary Study* (Toronto 1977). There are only two areas in which the history of the attorneyship in nineteenth-century Ontario runs up against a substantial body of scholarship. The whole subject of the administration of justice, both criminal and civil, was so controversial in the 1820s and 1830s that it is noticed in political studies of the period, but always in passing as one more political grievance – never in its own right as a topic in legal history. The second area is the construction of the BNA Act in the Mowat era, but no one has ever studied this from the perspective of Mowat as attorney general (as distinct from premier).

Notes

Archival Repositories

AO	Archives of Ontario, Toronto
MTL	Metropolitan Toronto Library
PAC	Public Archives of Canada, Ottawa
PRO	Public Record Office, London, England

Jurisdictions

Can.	Dominion of Canada
Ont.	Ontario
P. Can.	Province of Canada
UC	Upper Canada
UK	United Kingdom

Law Reports

AC	Appeal Cases (Privy Council), second series
App. Cas.	Appeal Cases (Privy Council), first series
CCC	Canadian Criminal Cases
CRNS	Criminal Reports, new series
Grant	Grant's Chancery Reports (Upper Canada)
OAR	Ontario Appeal Reports
OLR	Ontario Law Reports

Olm.	Richard A. Olmsted, comp. *Decisions Relating to the British North America Act, 1867, and the Canadian Constitution, 1867-1854* 3 vols (Ottawa 1954)
SCR	Supreme Court Reports (Canada)
Taylor KBR	Taylor's King's Bench Reports (Upper Canada)
UCQBR	Upper Canada Queen's Bench Reports
U.S.	United States (Supreme Court) Reports

Texts and Documents

Brit. Parl. Papers	Great Britain. Parliament, Sessional Papers
Brit. Parl. Debates	Great Britain. Parliament, Debates
Can. Sess. Papers	Canada (Dominion). Parliament, Sessional Papers
CSC	Consolidated Statutes of Canada (Province)
CSUC	Consolidated Statutes of Upper Canada
DCB	*Dictionary of Canadian Biography*
DNB	*Dictionary of National Biography*
Debates LA	Elizabeth Nish, ed. *Debates of the Legislative Assembly of United Canada* vols I- (Quebec 1970-)
Docs. Const. Hist. Can.	Canada. Public Archives *Documents Relating to the Constitutional History of Canada* 3 vols (Ottawa 1914-35)
HC Debates	Canada (Dominion). House of Commons, Debates
JHA	Upper Canada. House of Assembly, Journal
JLA	Canada (Province). Legislative Assembly, Journal
ML Papers	AO, Mackenzie-Lindsey Papers
Macm. Dict.	W. Stewart Wallace, ed. *The Macmillan Dictionary of Canadian Biography*, 4th ed. (Toronto 1978)
Morgan *Can. Men*	Henry James Morgan, ed. *The Canadian Men and Women of the Time* (Toronto 1898)
Ont. Sess. Papers	Ontario. Legislature, Sessional Papers
RSC	Revised Statutes of Canada
RSO	Revised Statutes of Ontario
Russell Corr.	E.A. Cruikshank and A.F. Hunter, eds. *The Correspondence of the Honourable Peter Russell* 3 vols (Toronto 1932-6)
Senate Debates	Canada (Dominion). Senate, Debates
Simcoe Corr.	E.A. Cruikshank, ed. *The Correspondence of Lieut.-Governor John Graves Simcoe* 5 vols (Toronto 1923-31)

INTRODUCTION

1 Gerald M. Craig *Upper Canada: The Formative Years, 1784-1841* (Toronto 1963) 1-19; 31 Geo. III (1791) c. 31 (UK)

2 *Docs. Const. Hist. Can.* II 34-5
3 The history of the Ontario court system is summarized in Margaret A. Banks 'The Evolution of the Ontario Courts, 1788-1981' in David H. Flaherty, ed. *Essays in the History of Canadian Law* 2 vols (Toronto 1981-3) II 492-572. See also William Renwick Riddell *The Courts of the Province of Upper Canada or Ontario* (Toronto 1928), and Thomas Mulvey 'The Judicial System' in Adam Shortt and Arthur G. Doughty, eds. *Canada and Its Provinces* XVIII *Ontario* (Toronto 1914) 513-48.
4 RSO 1980, c. 271
5 The ministry's annual report, published since 1974-5, lists acts currently administered by it.
6 Section 5(d)
7 Ontario, Royal Commission of Inquiry into Civil Rights (hereinafter McRuer Commission) *Report No. 1* (Toronto 1968) 931-56

CHAPTER 1

1 John Ll.J. Edwards *The Law Officers of the Crown: A Study of the Offices of Attorney-General and Solicitor-General of England with an Account of the Office of Director of Public Prosecutions of England* (London 1964)
2 14 Geo. III (1774) c. 83 (UK); 32 Geo. III (1792) c. 1 (UC)
3 See below at 126-36 passim, 147.
4 PAC RG68, Upper Canada, Register of Commissions, Liber A 163
5 Ibid. Liber A 16. For other mandamuses and commissions, see Liber B 428 (Thomas Scott), Liber D 9 and 10 (William Firth), Liber D 269 (John Macdonell), Liber D 325 (J.B. Robinson), Liber E 71 (D'Arcy Boulton), Liber F 204 (J.B. Robinson).
6 CO42/349/192; ibid. 359/226; CO47/141/41-2 (Statistical Blue Book, Upper Canada, 1821 9-10); PAC *Report on Canadian Archives, 1899* (Ottawa 1900) 70
7 PAC MG23 HI5 (hereinafter White Papers). The diary, covering 1792-4, is published in *Ontario History* 47 (1955) 147-70. See also DCB IV 766-7, and William Renwick Riddell 'The First Attorney-General of Upper Canada: John White (1792-1800)' Ontario Historical Society *Papers and Records* 23 (1926)
8 *Simcoe Corr.* II 40, IV 192-3; *Russell Corr.* II 22-33, 238-45; PAC RG1 E1, Upper Canada State Book B 84-5. For Gray, see DCB V 388-9, and William Renwick Riddell 'Robert Isaac Dey Gray, the First Solicitor General of Upper Canada, 1797-1804' in Riddell *Upper Canada Sketches* (Toronto 1922).
9 CO42/385/144 (J.B. Robinson to G. Hillier, 17 June 1828); William Renwick Riddell 'William Osgoode: First Chief Justice of Upper Canada, 1792-1794' in Riddell *Upper Canada Sketches; Proceedings of the Legislative Council of*

Upper Canada on the Bill sent up from the House of Assembly entitled An Act to amend the Jury Laws of this Province (Toronto 1836) 6 (copy in CO42/430/199-228)

10 *Simcoe Corr.* I 263, II 55; IV 146, 166
11 Ibid. I 347; Riddell 'First Attorney-General.' For Shepherd, see DNB.
12 White Papers, White to Shepherd, 25 Feb. 1793
13 Ibid. White to Shepherd, 16 Sept. (1795?)
14 Lillian F. Gates 'The Heir and Devisee Commission of Upper Canada, 1797-1805' *Canadian Historical Review* 38 (1957)
15 DCB v 167-72, 402-6; William N.T. Wylie 'Instruments of Commerce and Authority: The Civil Courts in Upper Canada, 1789-1812' in Flaherty, ed. *Essays in the History of Canadian Law* II 3-12. For Cartwright, see also Conway E. Cartwright, ed. *Life and Letters of the Late Honourable Richard Cartwright* (Toronto 1876) and Donald C. MacDonald 'The Honourable Richard Cartwright, 1759-1812' in *Three History Theses* (Toronto: Ontario Department of Records and Archives 1961); for Hamilton, see above all Bruce G. Wilson *The Enterprises of Robert Hamilton: A Study of Wealth and Influence in Early Upper Canada, 1776-1812* (Ottawa 1983).
16 White Papers, White to Shepherd, 25 Feb. 1793; Wilson *Enterprises of Robert Hamilton* 103-18
17 34 Geo. III (1794) c. 2 and 3 (UC); White Papers, White to Shepherd, 20 Sept. 1796; Wilson *Enterprises of Robert Hamilton* 53-5, 116-18
18 *Simcoe Corr.* I 238-9; II 264-5, 268-71; III 109-11, 240-1
19 Ibid. III 111, 2-3
20 White Papers, White to Shepherd, 20 Sept. 1796; Wilson *Enterprises of Robert Hamilton* 121-3
21 *Simcoe Corr.* IV 47-9; Wilson *Enterprises of Robert Hamilton* 55-7; Gates 'Heir and Devisee Commission' 23; and see below at 70.
22 *Simcoe Corr.* IV 141-3, 162-3. For Grant, see DNB. Grant's opinion turned on a secondary question, which is discussed in Gates 'Heir and Devisee Commission' 21-6.
23 *Simcoe Corr.* IV 150-2
24 Ibid. 146-50, 165-7
25 Ibid. 248; White Papers, White to Shepherd, 20 Sept. 1796; Gates 'Heir and Devisee Commission' 28
26 *Russell Corr.* II 24-5; Gates 'Heir and Devisee Commission' 29
27 37 Geo. III (1797) c. 3 (UC). For Elmsley, see DCB v 303-4.
28 *Russell Corr.* II 23-6 (quotation at 26). At the same session Elmsley procured an act for the more easy barring of dower (37 Geo. III [1797] c. 7 [UC]): ibid. 26-8.

29 Also see below at 76-8.
30 William Renwick Riddell *The Life of William Dummer Powell, First Judge at Detroit and Fifth Chief Justice of Upper Canada* (Lansing, Mich. 1924) 14, 82-4, and passim; *Simcoe Corr.* IV 162-3, 165-7, 204-5
31 *Simcoe Corr.* V 147; ibid. 204-5, CO42/320/380 (Powell to Simcoe, 17 May 1796); Gates 'Heir and Devisee Commission' 22-3
32 CO42/320/369-70 (Powell to Portland, 21 July 1796); ibid. 380-93 ('Summary of the Rise, Progress and Actual Situation of the Settlement in Upper Canada')
33 *Russell Corr.* II 18-19
34 42 Geo. III (1802) c. 1 (UC); Gates 'Heir and Devisee Commission' 32-4. For Allcock, see DCB V 17-19; for Askin, see ibid. 37-9, and Milo M. Quaife, ed. *The John Askin Papers*, 2 vols (Detroit 1928-31).
35 S.R. Mealing 'The Enthusiasms of John Graves Simcoe' in Canadian Historical Association *Annual Report* (1958) reprinted in J.K. Johnson, ed. *Historical Essays on Upper Canada* (Toronto 1975); DCB V 754-9
36 *Russell Corr.* II 45. For Russell, see also DCB V 729-32, and Edith G. Firth 'The Administration of Peter Russell, 1796-1799' *Ontario History* 48 (1956).
37 DCB V 439-43
38 CO42/328/3-27 (Allcock to Hunter, 12 June 1801; Elmsley to Hunter, 11 June 1801; T. Scott to Hunter, 4 Aug. 1801). The sheriff's bill became law as 43 Geo. III (1803) c. 1. The married women's property bill seems to have been re-enacted in 1803, becoming law as 43 Geo. III c. 5. This was probably necessary because two years had elapsed before the imperial government decided in its favour, causing it to lapse automatically.
39 For background, see Charles M. Johnston 'Joseph Brant, The Grand River Lands and the Northwest Crisis' *Ontario History* 55 (1963); Barbara Graymont 'Thayendanegea' in DCB V 803-12, and Wilson *Enterprises of Robert Hamilton* 99-100.
40 *Simcoe Corr.* IV 43, 87-8, 125-6, 182-4, 277
41 AO RG4 A-I-1, Simcoe to the attorney general, 5 Mar. 1796; same to same, 19 Mar. 1796
42 *Russell Corr.* I 40, 46-9
43 Ibid. 75-228 passim; Charles M. Johnston 'An Outline of Early Settlement in the Grand River Valley' *Ontario History* 54 (1962), reprinted in Johnson, ed. *Historical Essays on Upper Canada* 10-11; Malcolm Montgomery 'The Legal Status of the Six Nations Indians in Canada' *Ontario History* 55 (1963)
44 *Russell Corr.* II 4-5, III 2-15 (quotation at 14). Compare the opinion of Edmund Randolph, attorney general of the United States, on Alexander Hamilton's bank bill in 1791: John J. Reardon, *Edmund Randolph: A Biography* (New York 1974) 197.

45 *Russell Corr.* I 278-9, 137-8, 144-5, 151-2; II 32
46 Ibid. I 206
47 CO42/319/293-4 (White to Simcoe, 6 Aug. 1795); and see below at 38-40.

CHAPTER 2

1 William Blackstone *Commentaries on the Laws of England* 4 vols (Oxford 1765-9) II 36-7
2 See above at 17.
3 The number of the grand jury was usually twenty-three, since twelve had to concur in order to return an indictment and it was desirable that this constitute a majority; but see below at 295.
4 White Papers, White to Shepherd, 9 Sept. 1793
5 CO42/351/93-4 ('Abstract of Contingent Account for Conducting Criminal Prosecutions at the Assizes, 1792-1811')
6 White Papers, White to Sir John Scott, 17 Feb. 1799; *R. v Wilkes* (1768) 97 English Reports 123; 38 Geo. III (1798) c. 5 (UC)
7 White Papers, White to Shepherd, 6 Mar. 1798; CO42/324/361-2 (White to J. King, 15 Nov. 1798); DCB IV 767
8 DCB V 452-3
9 White Papers, White to Shepherd, 16 Sept. (1795?); CO42/319/287-9 (White to Simcoe, n.d. [1795])
10 CO42/319/291-4 (Jarvis to Simcoe, n.d. [1795]; White to Simcoe, 6 Aug. 1795); and see above at 35.
11 *Simcoe Corr.* IV 74-5; White Papers, White to Shepherd, 21 Aug. 1794, same to same, 20 Sept. 1796, same to same, 6 Mar. 1798, same to same, 15 Nov. 1798; DCB V 453. For the background to the adoption of an official table of fees, see Theodore D. Regehr 'Land Ownership in Upper Canada, 1783-1796: A Background to the First Table of Fees' *Ontario History* 55 (1963).
12 PAC RG1 E3/1/23-4 (Scott to Hunter, 21 Dec. 1802); ibid. 25/15-22 (Sewell to Scott, 5 July 1803); White Papers, P. Russell to Shepherd, 22 Feb. 1800; MTL Powell Papers, B89/125-30; DCB V 440-1, 453; and White Papers, White to Shepherd, 9 Sept. 1793
13 See above at 29.
14 William Renwick Riddell 'Thomas Scott, the Second Attorney-General of Upper Canada' Ontario Historical Society *Papers and Records* 20 (1923); Riddell 'Mr. Justice Thorpe: Leader of the First Opposition in Upper Canada' in Riddell *Upper Canada Sketches*; DCB V 443
15 William Renwick Riddell 'William Firth: The Third Attorney-General of Upper Canada, 1807-11' *Canadian Bar Review* 1 (1923)

16 CO/348/224-5 (Firth to E. Cooke, 6 Feb. 1808); ibid. 348/195-8 (memorial of D'Arcy Boulton, 2 Dec. 1808; draft, Castlereagh to Gore, 8 Apr. 1809)

17 Ibid. 355/219-20 (Firth to Gore, 11 Aug. 1808). In these and later quotations from Firth I have retained the antique forms, which, like the man himself, were old-fashioned even at the time.

18 Ibid. 355/182-6 (J. McGill, W.D. Powell, and P. Selby to I. Brock, 27 Sept. 1812)

19 Powell Papers, B89/95-101; CO42/350/339-46 (Firth to Liverpool, 10 Apr. 1810)

20 Papers relating to this routine administrative business from 1800 on are to be found in AO RG4 A-1, box 9.

21 CO42/350/179-201 (Gore to Liverpool, 4 May 1810, disp. 3, and encs.); Powell Papers, B89/95-101, 125-30; ibid. 102-3 (Powell to Bathurst, 14 June 1815)

22 H.H. Guest 'Upper Canada's First Political Party' *Ontario History* 54 (1962). For Weekes and Willcocks, see DCB V 844-5, 854-9. The crisis of 1806 is extensively documented in PAC *Report on Canadian Archives, 1892* (Ottawa 1893) 32-135, which reproduces material from CO42.

23 CO42/349/169-80 (Gore to Castlereagh, 6 Oct. 1809, disp. 41 and encs.); Powell Papers, B89/95-101, 125-30

24 Riddell *William Dummer Powell* 93-4, 111-12; CO42/350/327 (Law Officers' report on the Rogers case); ibid. 350/343 (Firth to Liverpool, 10 Apr. 1810); ibid. 353/10-16 (same to same, 18 Jan. 1812); *Report on Canadian Archives, 1892* 36-7

25 CO42/369/166-8 (Powell to Gore, 3 Oct. 1809)

26 50 Geo. III (1810) c. 9 (UC)

27 CO42/350/351-3; see also ibid. 350/343 (Firth to Liverpool, 10 Apr. 1810).

28 For this episode, see Wylie 'Instruments of Commerce and Authority' 33-5, and CO42/348/224-5 (Firth to E. Cooke, 6 Feb. 1808).

29 CO42/350/293 (Gore to Liverpool, 23 Aug. 1810, disp. 5)

30 Ibid. 355/221-2 (Firth to Gore, 16 Aug. 1810)

31 Ibid. 351/58-61 (Firth to W. Halton, 7 Mar. 1811; same to same, 8 Mar. 1811). See above at 39.

32 Ibid. 351/63-6 (Report of the Executive Council, 4 Apr. 1811); ibid. 351/81-6 (Halton to Firth, 8 Apr. 1811; Firth to Halton, 6 July 1811; Halton to Firth, 7 July 1811)

33 Ibid. 351/87-8 (Firth to Halton, 8 July 1811); and see above at 17.

34 Ibid. 351/89-92 (report of the Executive Council, 11 July 1811; Halton to Firth, 13 July 1811); ibid. 351/95-102 (Gore to Liverpool, 29 July 1811, disp. 16, and encs.); ibid. 351/205-6 (Firth to Liverpool, 15 Sept. 1811); ibid. 351/113-14 (Gore to Liverpool, 30 Sept. 1811, disp. 20)

35 Ibid. 353/10-16 (Firth to Liverpool, 18 Jan. 1812)

36 Ibid.
37 John Mills Jackson *A View of the Political Situation of the Province of Upper Canada* (London 1809)
38 *Report on Canadian Archives, 1892* 32-135 passim
39 Riddell 'William Firth' 3-4; co42/349/192
40 PAC RG68, Register of Commissions, Upper Canada, Liber D 9-10; co42/350/339-46 (Firth to Liverpool, 10 Apr. 1810)
41 John Lownsbrough *The Privileged Few: The Grange and Its People in Nineteenth-Century Toronto* (Toronto 1980) 20-40
42 *Report on Canadian Archives, 1892* 100-2; co42/348/4 (Gore to Cooke, 14 Jan. 1808); ibid. 350/123 (Boulton to Halton, 1 July 1807); AO RG22, series 134, Court of King's Bench, Assize Minute Books, 3/255-6
43 co42/355/313-23 (Gore to H. Goulburn, 4 Apr. 1814; memorial of John R. Small, n.d.); ibid. 355/383-4 (J.R. Small to Goulburn, 4 July 1814)
44 Ibid. 369/364-5 (John Small to Bathurst, 25 Nov. 1822); ibid. 371/244-9; ibid. 378/82-122 (Sir P. Maitland to Bathurst, 2 Sept. 1826, disp. 36, and encs.)
45 Ibid. 378/99-108
46 Ibid. 109-22; ibid. 379/101-2 (Stephen to R. Wilmot Horton, 2 Dec. 1826)
47 Ibid. 103-4
48 Ibid. 355/193-4; ibid. 351/107-8
49 Ibid. 378/107
50 Edwards *Law Officers of the Crown* 128-30, 309-34
51 co42/324/377 (White to Simcoe, 15 Nov. 1798); ibid. 353/111-12 (draft [?] to Gore, 13 Apr. 1812)
52 Ibid. 351/113-14 (Gore to Liverpool, 30 Sept. 1811, disp. 20); ibid. 352/140-1 (Brock to Liverpool, 31 Aug. 1812); ibid. 352/144-5 (draft [?] to Brock, 16 Nov. 1812, disp. 6); DCB V 520-3
53 Gerald M. Craig *Upper Canada* 214-15; DCB VIII 426-7 (Jameson); and see below at 155, 167.
54 co42/325/102-7 (Hunter to [?], 10 Feb. 1800; Hunter to Portland, 10 Feb. 1800); DCB V 388-9; Riddell 'Robert Isaac Dey Gray'
55 Lownsbrough *Privileged Few* 32-5; co42/350/361 (Powell to A. Gordon, 1 Sept. 1810); ibid. 350/306 (Gore to Liverpool, 25 Sept. 1810)
56 For Robinson, see DCB IX 668-79; see also Patrick Brode *Sir John Beverley Robinson: Bone and Sinew of the Compact* (Toronto 1984).
57 co42/352/168-9, 172-3; DCB IX 74-5
58 PAC RG5 A1/18/7588-93 (Baron de Rottenburg to Sir G. Prevost, 25 Sept. 1813, and encs.); co42/356/282-3 (Robinson to Bathurst, 19 Oct. 1815); ibid. 357/46-7 (Gore to Bathurst, 24 Feb. 1816, disp. 7); ibid. 358/37-40, 127-8 (Robinson to Bathurst, 12 Mar. 1816; same to same, 5 Oct. 1816); ibid.

356/288-9, 292-3 (H.J. Boulton to Bathurst, 30 Oct. 1815; Robinson to Bathurst, 4 Nov. 1815); Lownsbrough *Privileged Few* 36

59 CO42/357/360-1 (Gore to Bathurst, 25 Nov. 1816)

60 Ibid. 354/179-80 (H.J. Boulton to Bathurst, 8 Mar. 1813); ibid. 357/360-5 (Gore to Bathurst, 25 Nov. 1816; same to same, 25 Nov. 1816 [separate]; D'Arcy Boulton to Gore, 21 Nov. 1816); ibid. 359/191-4 (S. Smith to Bathurst, 7 July 1817, disp. 4; D'Arcy Boulton to Smith, 30 June 1817); ibid. 380/50-1 (Boulton to Wilmot Horton, 12 Apr. 1826); ibid. 384/197-8 (Maitland to Murray, 27 Oct. 1828, disp. 5); Lownsbrough *Privileged Few* 50-1

61 CO42/389/61-5 (Colborne to Murray, 19 Aug. 1829); ibid. 126-31 (Hagerman to Colborne, 27 June 1829); S.F. Wise 'The Rise of Christopher Hagerman' *Historic Kingston* 12 (1965); Wise 'Tory Factionalism: Kingston Elections and Upper Canadian Politics, 1820-1836' *Ontario History* 57 (1965)

62 CO42/348/232-4 (Firth to Castlereagh, 4 Apr. 1808)

63 Ibid. 340/139 (Scott to Camden, 20 Sept. 1805); ibid. 348/31 (Scott to Gore, 26 Mar. 1808)

64 CO42/375/78-80 (memorial of H.J. Boulton, 24 Dec. 1824)

65 Ibid. 76-7 (Maitland to Bathurst, 1 Mar. 1825, disp. 176)

66 Ibid. 389/62 (Colborne to Murray, 19 Aug. 1829)

67 Robert Baldwin, Henry Sherwood and John Sandfield Macdonald were the other solicitors general to become attorney general; William Hume Blake, Joseph Curran Morrison, and Adam Wilson left the office for the bench. J.M.S. Careless 'Robert Baldwin' in Careless, ed. *The Pre-Confederation Premiers: Ontario Government Leaders, 1841-1867* (Toronto 1980); Bruce W. Hodgins 'John Sandfield Macdonald' ibid; Hodgins *John Sandfield Macdonald, 1812-1872* (Toronto 1971); DCB VIII 796-801 (Sherwood); DCB IX 55-60 (Blake); DCB XI 617-19 (Morrison); *Macm. Dict.* (Wilson)

68 MTL J.H. Cameron Papers, Cameron to D. Daly, 22 May 1847; Foster Griezic 'John Hillyard Cameron and the Question of Conservative Leadership in Canada West, 1854-1856' *Ontario History* 66 (1974)

69 Debates LA X 773; and see below at 194.

70 Paul Knaplund, ed. *Letters from Lord Sydenham to Lord John Russell* (London 1931) 37, 47, 48; George Metcalf 'William Henry Draper' in Careless, ed. *Pre-Confederation Premiers*

71 C.R.W. Biggar *Sir Oliver Mowat: A Biographical Sketch* 2 vols. (Toronto 1905); DCB XI 730-1 (Richards); DCB VIII 796-801 (Sherwood)

CHAPTER 3

1 31 Geo. III (1791) c. 31, ss. 36-42 (UK); 33 Geo. III (1793) c. 5 (UC), amended by 38 Geo. III (1798) c. 4

2 Craig *Upper Canada* 191-2
3 John Charles Dent *The Story of the Upper Canadian Rebellion* 2 vols (Toronto 1885)
4 *The Debates and Proceedings in the Congress of the United States: Fourth Congress, 1st Session* (Washington 1849) cols 165-244 passim; Quaife, ed. *John Askin Papers* I 568-72
5 CO42/373/57-8, 62-4 (Lease to Canby and McGill, 10 Nov. 1794; Memorial of Robert Randal, 21 Apr. 1800). For Robertson, see DCB V 718-9. Most of the other partners were kinsmen of Askin and Robertson.
6 CO42/373/26-65 (Maitland to Bathurst, 26 July 1824, disp. 148, and encs.); ibid. 375/144-86 (same to same, 4 May 1825, and encs.); ML Papers A-4-1, 1798-1802 passim; PAC MG24 B18 (William Lyon Mackenzie Papers) 14/2492-3 (warrant of arrest, *Durand v Randal*, 21 July 1802). For Hamilton's links with Robertson and Askin, see Wilson *Enterprises of Robert Hamilton.*
7 ML Papers A-4-1, 1806-15 passim; MG24 B18/13/2319-21 (W. McLean to Randal, 23 Oct. 1815)
8 ML Papers A-4-1, 1803-6 passim; CO42/375/185-6 (statement of Clark, 30 Nov. 1816); ibid. 373/56-7 (statement of Clark, 1 Mar. 1817); John Weaver 'An Adventurous Englishman on the Upper Canadian Frontier: James Durand's Eventful Career, 1802-1834' Head-of-the-Lake Historical Society Paper (Hamilton February 1979)
9 ML Papers, A-4-1, note on a receipt dated Montreal, 22 Aug. 1808; Randal to T. Ridout, 2 Apr. 1813; A. Jarrett to Randal, 28 July 1812; record of judgment, *Clark v Randal*, Court of King's Bench, Montreal, 20 June 1812; MG24 B18/13/2341-2, 2345-52 (Randal to H.J. Boulton, 20 May 1819, Randal to S. Sherwood, 2 Sept. 1819); ibid. 14/2609-14 (petition of Randal, 7 July 1821); CO42/373/58-60 (Clark to Gore, 20 July 1814; Bathurst to Drummond, 28 Aug. 1814; Drummond to F.P. Robinson, 14 July 1815); ibid. 376/401-8 (Randal to Canning, 23 May 1825); JLA 1852-3, app. ssss, item 17; *Colonial Advocate* (Toronto) 16 June 1825; *Correspondent and Advocate* (Toronto) 15 Oct. 1835; *Examiner* (Toronto) 21 Aug. 1850; *Mackenzie's Weekly Message* (Toronto) 18 May 1854
10 The following narrative is based on ML Papers A-4-1, 1816-19 passim; MG24 B18/13/2330-1, 2345-52 (D'Arcy Boulton to Randal, 8 Apr. 1816; Randal to S. Sherwood, 2 Sept. 1819); ibid. 2371-5 (Randal to W. Rayen, 22 Nov. 1822); CO42/375/144-86 (Maitland to Bathurst, 4 May 1825, and encs.); JHA appendix, Report of the Select Committee on the Petition of Robert Randal (hereinafter Randal petition report); JLA 1852-3 app. ssss; H.P. Hill *Robert Randall and the Le Breton Flats* (Ottawa 1919); *Colonial Advocate* 7 Feb. 1828; and the newspapers cited above, note 9.

11 ML Papers A-4-1, Randal to [?], 1 Dec. 1819; Sir William Holdsworth *A History of English Law* 6th rev. ed. (London 1938-72) I 336-42; Riddell 'First Attorney General of Upper Canada' 418-19, 428 note 32; Blackstone *Commentaries* III 402-5

12 MG24 B18/13/2353-60 (Bidwell to Randal, 20 Sept. 1819); ibid. 14/2677-85 (Opinion of J. Florance); ibid. 2708-16 (anonymous opinion, 27 July 1844)

13 ML Papers A-4-1, Randal to [?], 1 Dec. 1819

14 Blackstone *Commentaries* III 387. MG24 B18/14/2654-5 is an undated note of Blackstone's dictum in Randal's hand.

15 Wilson *Enterprises of Robert Hamilton* 60-5 and passim

16 Thomas Andrew Green *Verdict According to Conscience: Perspectives on the English Criminal Trial Jury, 1200-1800* (Chicago 1985) 3-27

17 MG24 B18/14/2519-31 (indenture of mortgage, J. Durand with Caldcleugh, Boyd, and Reid, 10 July 1804)

18 See below at 96.

19 *Correspondent and Advocate* 24 Sept. 1835. The progress of Clark and Street's plot against Pell is documented in AO Samuel Street Papers.

20 Johnston 'Early Settlement in the Grand River Valley' 27 note 57, and see below at 121.

21 Randal petition report; *Colonial Advocate* 16 June 1825

22 *Colonial Advocate* 16 June 1825

23 34 Geo. III (1794), c. 2 (UC); John D. Blackwell 'William Hume Blake and the Judicature Acts of 1849: The Process of Legal Reform at Mid-century in Upper Canada' in Flaherty, ed. *Essays in the History of Canadian Law* I 133-4; and see above at 26.

24 *Russell Corr.* III 186-7; CO42/327/77-106 (Hunter to Portland, 1 Aug. 1801, disp. 3, and encs.); ibid. 329/18-20 (Hobart to Hunter, 8 Apr. 1802, disp. 6); ibid. 342/132-4, 138 (Allcock to G. Shee, 14 Mar. 1806; Harrison to Shee, 1 Apr. 1806); ibid. 347/32 (memo of W.D. Powell, 15 Jan. 1807); ibid. 369/309-16 (J.B. Robinson to Bathurst, 18 July 1822); *Report on Canadian Archives, 1892* 44; William Renwick Riddell 'Early Proposals for a Court of Chancery, Upper Canada' in Riddell *Upper Canada Sketches* 146-56

25 William Renwick Riddell 'The "Ordinary" Court of Chancery in Upper Canada' Ontario Historical Society *Papers and Records* 22 (1925) 222-38

26 JLA 1852-3, app. ssss no. 48, 57-8; *Colonial Advocate* 18 Feb. 1830

27 Wylie 'Instruments of Commerce and Authority' 25-8; and see above at 29. For a contemporary perception of the need for a court of equity, see the letter of Singleton Gardiner in the *Colonial Advocate* 14 Apr. 1825.

28 CO42/328/7-10 (Allcock to Hunter, 12 June 1801)

29 ML Papers A-4-1, Randal to A. Cuvillier, 7 Mar. 1808

30 Randal petition report
31 Ibid.; *Colonial Advocate* 16 June 1825
32 ML Papers A-4-1, Randal to [?], 1 Dec. 1819. The most complete statement of
    Randal's side of the case is in his petition to the House of Assembly in
    1828, published in *Colonial Advocate* 7 Feb. 1828
33 Francis Collins *A Faithful Report of the Trial and Acquittal of Robert Randall,
    Esq., a Member of the Commons House of Assembly in Upper Canada, accused of
    Perjury, and tried at Niagara, on Wednesday the 7th of September, 1825* (York, UC
    1825) 22-3; *Colonial Advocate* 2 Nov. 1827
34 Randal petition report
35 ML Papers A-4-1, Address to the Voters of the 4th Riding of Lincoln, 10 July 1820
36 See below at 85-7.
37 ML Papers A-4-1, Randal to Rolph, 7 July 1823; ibid. 22 July 1823; ibid. 1823-4
    passim; MG24 B18/14/2677-85 (Opinion of J. Florance, 7 Aug. 1827); PAC
    RG1 E3/16/58-66; ibid. 100/8-12
38 CO42/374/57-82 (Stephen to Wilmot Horton, 21 Dec. 1824); ibid. 376/33-5
    (same to same, 20 Aug. 1825); ibid. 401-8 (Randal to Canning, 23 May
    1825, and enc.)
39 *Colonial Advocate* 7 Feb. 1828; *Randal v Boulton* (1825) Taylor KBR 127
40 Hill *Robert Randall and the Le Breton Flats* 28-39, 49-53
41 Collins *Trial of Robert Randall* (quotation at 20-1); *Examiner* 21 Aug. 1850; see
    also *Colonial Advocate* 5 Aug. 1824, and ibid. 14 Mar., 27 Mar., 7 Apr. 1825
42 Collins *Trial of Robert Randall* 28; Edwards *Law Officers of the Crown* 271-6; and
    see below at 209-13.
43 William Renwick Riddell 'The Ancaster "Bloody Assize" of 1814' Ontario
    Historical Society *Papers and Records* 20 (1923) 107-25; and see below at
    161.
44 PAC RG7 G5/4/1-4 (Bathurst to Drummond, 10 Jan. 1815)
45 *Docs. Const. Hist. Can.* III 1-5
46 13 Geo. II, c. 7; 30 Geo. III, c. 27
47 *Docs. Const. Hist. Can.* III 5-6; CO42/360/22-3 (Shepherd, attorney general,
    and Gifford, solicitor general, to Bathurst, 15 Nov. 1817)
48 CO42/361/71-2 (Smith to Bathurst, 20 Apr. 1818, disp. 15); ibid. 368/92-7
    (Robinson to Smith, n.d. [1818]); *Docs. Const. Hist. Can.* III 6-9
49 S.F. Wise 'Gourlay, Robert' in DCB v 330-6
50 Ibid. 332
51 Craig *Upper Canada* 92-3
52 *Docs. Const. Hist. Can.* III 10-13
53 CO42/368/161-7 (unsigned report on Gourlay affair in Robinson's handwrit-
    ing, n.d.)

54 Ibid.; co42/362/225-8 (Maitland to Bathurst, 25 June 1819, disp. 40); co42/365/98-101 (same to same, 19 Mar. 1820); E.A. Cruikshank 'The Government of Upper Canada and Robert Gourlay' Ontario Historical Society *Papers and Records* 23 (1926) 90-103. Cruikshank gives a valuable account of the Gourlay affair with many original documents: ibid. 65-179.

55 44 Geo. III, c. 1; *Docs. Const. Hist. Can.* III 14-18; co42/368/153-9 (unsigned report in Robinson's handwriting on the Sedition Act and its application to Gourlay, n.d.)

56 Ibid. 368/135-48 (Memorial of Gourlay, 10 Aug. 1822, and encs.)

57 *Docs. Const. Hist. Can.* III 9

58 J.E. Rea 'Barnabas Bidwell, a Note on the American Years' *Ontario History* 60 (1968) 31-7

59 AO Macaulay Papers, Robinson to Macaulay, 18 Nov. 1821

60 Ibid. Robinson to Macaulay, 13 Dec. 1821; *Docs. Const. Hist. Can.* III 82-5. The debates and proceedings of the Assembly are fully reported in *Kingston Chronicle* 14 Dec. 1821, 1 Feb.-4 Mar. 1822 passim.

61 *Docs. Const. Hist. Can.* III 155-7 (my italics)

62 Ibid. 157-8. Baldwin did not think that Barnabas Bidwell was an alien, though he did think Marshall Bidwell was: *Kingston Chronicle* 8 Feb., 15 Feb., 22 Feb. 1822; 18 Apr., 25 Apr. 1823.

63 *Docs. Const. Hist. Can.* III 158-9. The debates and proceedings in the case of M.S. Bidwell are reported in *Kingston Chronicle* 18 Apr.-9 May 1823 passim.

64 co42/368/88-91 (Maitland to Bathurst, 15 Apr. 1822, disp. 60)

65 PAC RG5 A1/57/30270-9 (Robinson to Hillier, 11 Nov. 1822); Matthew L. Davis, ed. *The Private Journal of Aaron Burr* 2 vols (New York 1838) I 90, 93, 189-200

66 RG5 A1/57/29619-26 (Robinson to Hillier, 23 Aug. 1822); co42/374/370-7 (Robinson to Bathurst, 30 Oct. 1822, and encs., misfiled in papers for 1824)

67 *Docs. Const. Hist. Can.* III 234-5

68 Strictly speaking, the proper style of cause is *Doe ex dem. Thomas* v *Acklam* (1824) 107 English Reports 572. See also the discussion in Holdsworth *History of English Law* IX 86-7.

69 co42/375/9-10 (memorandum in Maitland to Bathurst, 22 Apr. 1825)

70 RG5 A1/73/38834-9 (Robinson to Hillier, 7 July 1825)

71 *Docs. Const. Hist. Can.* III 272-4; co42/376/390-1 (untitled memorandum in Robinson's handwriting of Bathurst's views on different subjects)

72 *Colonial Advocate* 15 Dec. 1825

73 Ibid.; *Upper Canada Herald* (Kingston) 29 Nov. 1825; *Canadian Freeman* (Toronto) 8 Dec. 1825 (in co42/377/110)

74 CO42/377/85

75 Ibid. 380/283-90 (Rolph to Wilmot Horton, n.d.)

76 John Beverley Robinson *Speech in Committee on the Bill for conferring Civil Rights on certain Inhabitants of this Province* (n.p., n.d.). There is a copy at MTL.

77 Ibid. 4-8

78 Ibid. 9-36

79 Ibid. 44

80 Ibid. 46-52

81 *Docs. Const. Hist. Can.* III 294-300 (quotations at 296-7); *Colonial Advocate* 15 Dec. 1825

82 7 Geo. IV c. 68; and see below at 99-100.

83 *Docs. Const. Hist. Can.* III 305-8, 351-62

84 ML Papers A-4-1, CO42/382/255-6 (J. Ketchum et al. to Randal, 11 Apr. 1827)

85 Macaulay Papers, Stanton to Macaulay, 29 Jan. 1826

86 *Docs. Const. Hist. Can.* III 362-3

87 RG5 A1/84/46004-7 (Strachan to Hillier, 22 June 1827)

88 *Colonial Advocate* 6 Sept., 20 Sept. 1827

89 PRO CO324/97/101-6 (Wilmot Horton to P. Robinson, 23 Nov. 1827)

90 9 Geo. IV, c. 21; *Docs. Const. Hist. Can.* III 422-31; CO42/383/172-87 (Robinson to Hillier, 6 Mar. 1828)

91 See above at 89, 90.

92 *Upper Canada Herald* 29 Nov. 1825

93 RG5 A1/80/42970-4 (Boulton to Hillier, 4 Nov. 1826); CO42/380/46-7 (Boulton to Wilmot Horton, 7 Mar. 1826)

94 CO42/380/34-41 (Boulton to Wilmot Horton, 8 Mar. 1826, wrongly dated Feb.)

95 Ibid. 379/93-4 (Stephen to Wilmot Horton, 3 May 1826); ibid. 380/56-61 (Boulton to Wilmot Horton, n.d.); ibid. 358-69 (Rolph to Wilmot Horton, 18 May 1826)

96 CO324/96/58-61 (Wilmot Horton to Robinson, 10 Apr. 1826)

97 AO Robinson Papers, Robinson to Wilmot Horton, 6 Mar. 1827

98 See above at 93-4.

99 CO42/377/178-215 (Maitland to Bathurst, 6 Apr. 1826, disp. 16); ibid. 381/44-55 (same to same, 3 Mar. 1827, disp. 5); ibid. 333-46 (Maitland to Goderich, 28 Aug. 1827); ibid. 383/2-6 (Maitland to Huskisson, 3 Jan. 1828); ibid. 125-34 (Maitland to Wilmot Horton, 4 Feb. 1828)

100 Ibid. 383/235-8

101 Great Britain, Imperial Blue Book 543 (1833) 26

102 Craig *Upper Canada* 111-14, 120; Dent *Story of the Upper Canadian Rebellion* I 122-50. See also the article on Matthews in DCB VI, forthcoming.

103 Craig *Upper Canada* 99
104 Graeme H. Patterson 'Studies in Elections and Public Opinion in Upper Canada' PHD thesis, University of Toronto (1969) 21-39; Fred Coyne Hamil *Lake Erie Baron* (Toronto 1955)
105 Ibid. 40-6; *Gardiner* v *Burwell* (1824) Taylor KBR 189; RG5 A1/61/32234-9 (Powell to Hillier, 10 July 1823; Hillier to Robinson, 11 July 1823); ibid. 139/76219-20 (Gardiner to Rowan, 29 Mar. 1834)
106 MTL W.W. Baldwin Papers, Baldwin to J.B. Robinson, 31 May 1828
107 (1824) Taylor KBR 189-97; *Colonial Advocate* 14 Apr. 1825
108 Paul Romney 'The Spanish Freeholder Imbroglio of 1824: Inter-Elite and Intra-Elite Rivalry in Upper Canada' *Ontario History* 76 (1984)
109 RG5 A1/80/43059-61 (G. Rolph to Hillier, 16 Nov. 1826); ibid. 43076-80 (same to same, 17 Nov. 1826; affidavit of Joseph Sears, 10 Oct. 1826); ibid. 43341-6 (J.B. Robinson to Hillier, 1 Dec. 1826; same to same, 2 Dec. 1826); Josephine Phelan 'The Tar and Feather Case, Gore Assizes, September 1827' *Ontario History* 68 (1976). James Hamilton was no relation to Robert Hamilton: *Dictionary of Hamilton Biography* I (Hamilton 1981) 93.
110 *Gore Gazette* (Ancaster) 25 Aug. 1827; RG5 A1/86/47269-71 (Macaulay's report, 28 Nov. 1827); PAC RG7 G16/18/5 (Hillier to Simons and Hamilton, 24 Nov. 1827). 'Criminal conversation' (crim. con. for short) was adultery.
111 RG5 A1/87/47652-6 (Simons to Hillier, 10 Jan. 1828, and enc.); ibid. 88/48347-50 (same to same, 12 Mar. 1828, and enc.)
112 *Gore Gazette* 25 Aug. 1827; *Canadian Freeman* 15 May, 22 May, 29 May 1828 (this date is in CO42/385/22), 5 June 1828
113 *Gore Gazette* 19 Apr. 1828
114 RG5 A1/88/48678-9
115 *Gore Gazette* 19 Apr. 1828
116 Ibid.; RG5 A1/88/48680-1 (G. Rolph's answers, 14 Apr. 1828); ibid. 48754-7 (affidavit of E. Lesslie, 21 Apr. 1828); ibid. 48807-12 (affidavit of J. Lesslie, 26 Apr. 1828); ibid. 48813-20 (affidavit of J. Ker, 26 Apr. 1828; affidavit of D. Oliphant, 26 Apr. 1828)
117 Ibid. 88/48833-6 (G. Rolph to Hillier, 28 Apr. 1828); ibid. 89/48971-3 (representation of the magistrates of the Gore District, 10 May 1828); ibid. 49299-300 (affidavit of J. Henry and H. Pennebaker, 23 June 1828); ibid. 49360-1 (representation of the late grand jurors of the Gore District quarter sessions, June 1828); ibid. 90/49930-7 (G. Rolph to Hillier, 15 Sept. 1828, and encs.); ibid. 49961-76 (same to same, 19 Sept. 1828, and encs.); ibid. 49988-5003 (same to same, 23 Sept. 1828, and encs.); ibid. 50119-20 (same to same, 10 Oct. 1828, and enc.); ibid. 93/52003-6 (Z. Mudge to G. Rolph, 18 Apr. 1829); ibid. 52086-8 (Rolph to Mudge, 28 Apr. 1829); JHA

1830, appendix, report of the Select Committee on the petition of George Rolph

118 *Gore Gazette* 19 Apr. 1828
119 W.W. Baldwin Papers, unbound misc. papers, file: 'miscellaneous,' G. Rolph to Baldwin, n.d.; MTL Robert Baldwin Papers, A67, 4 (G. Rolph to R. Baldwin, 22 Aug. 1828)
120 *Gore Gazette* 25 Aug. 1827
121 RG5 A1/94/52174-88 (address of the inhabitants of the District of Gore, 9 May 1829)
122 Bryan D. Palmer 'Discordant Music: Charivaris and Whitecapping in Nineteenth-Century North America' *Labour/Le Travailleur* 3 (1978) 5-62
123 *Gore Gazette* 25 Aug. 1827
124 Dent *Story of the Upper Canadian Rebellion* I 151-61; Aileen Dunham *Political Unrest in Upper Canada, 1815-1836* (1927; reprinted Toronto 1963) 109-10
125 AO Robinson Papers, petition of William Forsyth to the House of Assembly, 28 Jan. 1828 (wrongly microfilmed among the papers for 1823-4). It is reprinted in *Colonial Advocate* 28 Feb., 6 Mar. 1828.
126 JHA 1828, appendix, report of the Select Committee on the first petition of William Forsyth
127 CO42/387/65-76 (Stephen to Hay, 15 Oct. 1828)
128 Imperial Blue Book 543 (1833) 24
129 The most complete documentation of the affair, including the Blue Book and other material cited above, is in JHA 1835, appendix, report of the Select Committee on the petition of William Forsyth, which itself forms an appendix to the seventh report of the Select Committee on Grievances.
130 Imperial Blue Book 543 (1833) 2-6
131 Report on the petition of William Forsyth (1835)
132 PAC RG1 E3/73/245-8 (Robinson to McMahon, 21 May 1832)
133 RG5 A1/86/47190-3 (Robinson to Hillier, 22 Nov. 1827)
134 Imperial Blue Book 543 (1833) 4
135 Dent *Story of the Upper Canadian Rebellion* I 157n
136 48 Geo. III (1808) c. 13 (UC)
137 RG1 E3/27/1-3 (Petition of Forsyth, 30 Oct. 1820)
138 PAC RG1 E1, Upper Canada State Book H 18, 34; RG5 A1/84/45834-7 (Clark to Hillier, 30 May 1827); *Colonial Advocate* 8 Mar. 1827 (reprinted from *Black Rock* [NY] *Gazette*)
139 RG5 A1/84/45942-4 (Robinson to Hillier, 14 June 1827); ibid. 45981-2 (Clark to Hillier, 18 June 1827); and citations above, notes 125, 126. See also *Colonial Advocate* 14 June, 21 June 1827
140 RG5 A1/84/45834-7 (Clark to Hillier, 30 May 1827)

141 Imperial Blue Book 543 (1833) 3
142 RG1 E3/31/72-82 (report on petition of William Forsyth, 10 Jan. 1839); and citation above, note 132
143 RG5 A1/67/35433-5 (petition of F. Ellesworth, 25 June 1824)
144 *Colonial Advocate* 31 May, 7 June 1827; ibid. 21 Feb. 1828; Dent *Story of the Upper Canadian Rebellion* I 133
145 *Colonial Advocate* 13 Dec. 1827, 15 May 1828
146 Report on the first petition of William Forsyth
147 CO42/351/73-5 (Gore to Liverpool, 18 July 1811, disp. 15); ibid. 355/182-6 (McGill, Powell and Selby to Brock, 27 Sept. 1812); and see above at 47-8.
148 John Morgan Gray *Lord Selkirk of Red River* (Toronto 1963); DCB V 264-9
149 See below at 138.
150 JHA 1823 and 1823-4 (Ontario Bureau of Archives *Eleventh Report, 1914* [Toronto 1915] 309-10, 404-5, 419, 477); W.W. Baldwin Papers, unbound papers miscellaneous, file: 'House of Assembly – Miscellaneous I'
151 JHA 1823 (*Eleventh Report, 1914* 364, 386, 388, 392, 393, 420)
152 CO42/353/104-5 (unsigned, unaddressed memo, W.D. Powell to Peter Hunter, n.d.)
153 Ibid. 102-3 (Powell to Gore, 6 Apr. 1811)
154 *Upper Canada Herald* 13 Jan. 1824
155 JHA 1828, appendix, report of the Select Committee on the second petition of William Forsyth
156 *R.* v *Elrod* (1824) Taylor KBR 120
157 CO42/378/99-108 (Boulton to Hillier, 16 June 1825); and see above at 52-4.
158 Ibid. 109-22 (Robinson to Hillier, 21 July 1826)
159 Cited above, note 155. For the information ex officio, see above at 15. Like this proceeding, an information exhibited by the master of the Crown Office was a means of bringing prosecutions for serious misdemeanours in the Court of King's Bench without recourse to a grand jury. It was undertaken at the instance of a private citizen, but only with leave of the court, differing in this from the information ex officio, which was exhibited only by the attorney general and at his sole discretion: Edwards *Law Officers of the Crown* 262-7; Holdsworth *History of English Law* IX 241-5.
160 Cited above, note 155
161 Ibid.
162 Dent *Story of the Upper Canadian Rebellion* I 162-71; Robert Hett 'Judge Willis and the Court of King's Bench in Upper Canada' *Ontario History* 65 (1973); *Papers relating to the Removal of the Honourable John Walpole Willis from the Office of one of His Majesty's Judges of the Court of King's Bench of Upper Canada* (1829) (hereinafter *Papers*), in CO42/386/346 et seq.

163 A copy of each pamphlet is in c042/386/136-55.

164 Ibid. 388/154-7 (J.B. Robinson's report on events connected with the indictment and trial of Collins)

165 *Canadian Freeman* 17 Apr. 1828; *Papers* 23-33.

166 The following paragraphs are based on *Canadian Freeman* 17 Apr. 1828 and *Papers* 16-33

167 On the nolle prosequi, see Edwards *Law Officers of the Crown* 227-37. To institute criminal proceedings against an individual for an offence in respect of which punitive damages had been awarded against him was to put him in jeopardy a second time for the same offence.

168 See citations above, note 112

169 *Canadian Freeman* 5 June 1828; *Papers* 179-80

170 W.W. Baldwin Papers, Baldwin to Robinson, 31 May 1828 (draft). Baldwin had just finished his second spell as treasurer and was to serve again from 1832 to 1836.

171 *Report from the Select Committee on Public Prosecutors* (Brit. Parl. Papers [1856] VII 358); see also Edwards *Law Officers of the Crown* 13.

172 *Papers* 209

173 JHA 1823 (Ontario Bureau of Archives *Eleventh Report* 310)

174 *Observer* (Toronto) 12 May 1828 (reprinted in *Papers* 292-304)

175 Mackenzie *History of the Destruction of the Colonial Advocate Press* 18-19

176 c042/362/3-67 (Maitland to Bathurst, 6 Jan. 1819, disp. 15, and encs.); quotations at 15-16, 33-4

177 Edwards *Law Officers of the Crown* 177-225

178 Scott, quoted ibid. 179; Holdsworth *History of English Law* XII 304-5

179 Colin Read and Ronald J. Stagg, eds *The Rebellion of 1837 in Upper Canada: A Collection of Documents* (Toronto 1985) 395

180 *Canadian Freeman* 3 July 1828; ibid. 19 June 1828; JHA 1828, appendix, report of Select Committee on the petition of James G. Strowbridge; 9 Geo. IV (1828) c. 12 (UC); and see above at 81.

181 *Canadian Freeman* 16 Oct. 1828; Dent *Story of the Upper Canadian Rebellion* I 201-2; and see citation above, note 166.

182 JHA 1829, appendix, report of the Select Committee on the petition of Francis Collins

183 c042/390/49-50 (Scarlett, attorney general, and Sugden, solicitor general, to Murray, 30 June 1829)

184 Ibid. 382/329-32 (Willis to Goderich, 8 June 1827; same to same, 29 June 1827)

185 *Papers* 140-4; see ibid. 144-8 for the reports of Robinson and Boulton.

186 Ibid. 273-88, 16

187 Ibid. 5-7, 128-35, 273, 275

188 RG5 A1/81/44270-3 (J. By to Hillier, 16 Jan. 1827; ML Papers A-4-1, Randal to
     Messrs. Berry and Firth, 2 Aug. 1828; Hill *Robert Randall and the Le
     Breton Flats* 48-52

189 RG5 A1/88/48242-5 (Willis to Hillier, 1 Mar. 1828; Willis to L.P. Sherwood, 1
     Mar. 1828); *Papers* 189-91, 200-1, 274, 281, 285-6

190 *Papers* 267-72

191 Ibid.; *Papers* 128-39, 171-4; CO42/384/30-1 (Willis to the colonial secretary, 8
     May 1828)

192 Macaulay Papers, Stanton to John Macaulay, 8 July 1827; but see CO42/
     388/55-9 (J.B. Macaulay to Colborne, 25 Feb. 1829)

193 *Papers* 7-8; 34 Geo. III (1794) c. 2, s. 1 (UC)

194 *Papers* 5-7, 9

195 Ibid. 67-74; *Canadian Freeman* 26 June 1828; 22 Geo. III (1782) c. 75 (UK); 54
     Geo. III (1814) c. 61 (UK). Willis's statement is also printed in JHA 1829,
     appendix, report of the Select Committee on the case of Judge Willis and the
     administration of justice (hereinafter Willis Report) and *Canadian Freeman*
     19 July 1828.

196 *Papers* 84-105, 118-28

197 Ibid. 80

198 Ibid. 75-83

199 CO42/386/94-7 (statement of W.W. Baldwin, John Rolph, and Robert
     Baldwin, 23 June 1828); *Papers* 128-35; *Canadian Freeman* 3 July 1828

200 *Canadian Freeman* 10 July 1828

201 W.L. Morton 'The Local Executive in the British Empire, 1763-1828' *English
     Historical Review* 78 (1963); Elwood Jones 'Willcocks, Joseph' in DCB v 855;
     Fernand Ouellet *Lower Canada 1791-1840: Social Change and Nationalism*
     (Toronto 1983) 88-90; Paul Romney 'A Man Out of Place: The Life of Charles
     Fothergill, Naturalist, Businessman, Journalist, Politician, 1782-1840' PHD
     thesis, University of Toronto (1981) 418-27; Macaulay Papers, Stanton to
     Macaulay, 16 Aug. 1828. For a dissentient view as regards Lower Canada,
     see John L. Finlay 'The State of a Reputation: Bédard as Constitutionalist'
     Journal of Canadian Studies 20 (1985).

202 Dent *Story of the Upper Canadian Rebellion* 1 162-94

203 *Papers* 75-105, 118-28. The text of Willis's commission is printed in Willis
     Report.

204 CO42/386/248-53 (Willis to the colonial secretary, 23 Sept. 1828); *Colonial Ad-
     vocate* 19 June 1828; CO42/386/94-7 (statement of Rolph and the Baldwins,
     23 June 1828)

205 CO42/386/248-53 (Willis to the colonial secretary, 23 Sept. 1828, printed in
     Willis Report)

206 Ibid.; *Colonial Advocate* 10 Dec. 1829; see also *Canadian Freeman* 26 June 1828.
207 Cited above, note 199
208 Cited above, note 205
209 JHA 1829, 60-1
210 CO42/391/299-303 (Robinson to Colborne, 10 Sept. 1830)
211 Dunham *Political Unrest in Upper Canada* 122-3; 4 William IV c. 2
212 Craig *Upper Canada* 194, 202-3; Paul Romney 'A Conservative Reformer in Upper Canada: Charles Fothergill, Responsible Government and the "British Party," 1824-40' in Canadian Historical Association *Historical Papers* (1984)
213 W.W. Baldwin Papers, Bidwell to Baldwin, 28 May 1828; same to same, 8 Sept. 1828
214 CO42/386/314-17 (Stephen to Wilmot Horton, 5 June 1828)
215 W.W. Baldwin Papers, unbound misc. papers, file: 'miscellaneous,' G. Rolph to Baldwin, n.d.
216 *Papers* 188-9
217 W.W. Baldwin Papers, J. Rolph to Baldwin, 5 May 1829; *Colonial Advocate* 7 May 1829
218 Romney 'A Conservative Reformer in Upper Canada'; S.F. Wise 'John Macaulay: Tory for All Seasons' in Gerald Tulchinsky, ed. *To Preserve and Defend: Essays on Kingston in the Nineteenth Century* (Montreal 1976) 190-1; DCB IX 740-1
219 JHA 1829, 55
220 *Papers* 153-69
221 Paul Romney 'A Struggle for Authority: Toronto Society and Politics in 1834' in Victor L. Russell, ed. *Forging a Consensus: Historical Essays on Toronto* (Toronto 1984) 30-2
222 *Correspondent and Advocate* 11 Apr., 14 Apr., 4 May 1835; *Constitution* (Toronto) 11 Oct.-1 Nov. 1837 passim. Mackenzie reverts to this topic in the *Examiner* of 21 Aug. 1850. His anger in the weeks preceding the rebellion of 1837 was intensified by George Gurnett's appointment as clerk of the peace of the Home District.
223 Dent *Story of the Upper Canadian Rebellion* I 235-52; and see below at 167.
224 Craig *Upper Canada* 214-15
225 Charles Lindsey *The Life and Times of Wm. Lyon Mackenzie* 2 vols (Toronto 1862) I 246-9; F.H. Armstrong 'The York Riots of March 23, 1832' *Ontario History* 55 (1963)
226 Patterson 'Studies in Elections and Public Opinion' 207-87 passim, esp. at 246-57
227 *Upper Canada Herald* 17 June 1823

228 Craig *Upper Canada* 232-40

CHAPTER 4

1 CO42/335/1 (Hunter to Hobart, 16 May 1804, disp. 50); ibid. 337/155 (Hunter to Camden, 10 Apr. 1805, disp. 12)
2 *Report on Canadian Archives, 1892* 103-5; ibid. 36-7; CO42/356/107-10 (Gore to Bathurst, 22 May 1815, disp. 13); ibid. 357/193-4 (same to same, 29 Apr. 1816)
3 54 Geo. III, c. 11
4 AO RG4 A-1, box 1, Robinson to Loring, 11 May 1814; ibid., Robinson to Drummond, 25 Mar. 1814
5 CO42/360/102-3 (Drummond to Bathurst, 26 Mar. 1817); Riddell 'Ancaster "Bloody Assizes" of 1814'
6 54 Geo. III, c.9
7 CO42/357/360-1 (Gore to Bathurst, 25 Nov. 1816)
8 PAC RG5 A1/81/44681-4 (Robinson to Hillier, 17 Feb. 1827); CO42/383/135-45 (Maitland to Huskisson, 6 Feb. 1828, disp. 7); ibid. 384/60-4 (Robinson's report on Assessment Law Amendment Act, n.d.)
9 *Russell Corr.* III 217
10 Lownsbrough *Privileged Few* 31
11 *Simcoe Corr.* I 249
12 *Russell Corr.* III 217; PAC MG23 HI3 (Jarvis Papers) Hannah Jarvis to the Reverend S. Peters, 25 Sept. 1793
13 PAC White Papers, White to Shepherd, 4 Aug. 1793; ibid., same to same, 12 Nov. 1799
14 Edith G. Firth, ed. *The Town of York, 1815-1834: A Further Collection of Documents of Early Toronto* (Toronto 1966) 90
15 Brode *John Beverley Robinson* 61, 66-7
16 British Library, Loan 57 (Bathurst Papers) 16/1984 (Wilmot Horton to Bathurst, 22 Nov. 1825); and see above at 59.
17 AO Macaulay Papers, Stanton to Macaulay, 6 Mar. 1831
18 Alan Wilson *The Clergy Reserves of Upper Canada: A Canadian Mortmain* (Toronto 1968) 67-70
19 PAC RG1 E3/9/26-9 (Goderich to Colborne, 6 Mar. 1833, disp. 118)
20 Firth *Town of York, 1815-1834* 91-117
21 *Canadian Freeman* 8 Dec. 1825 (in CO42/377/110); ibid. 19 June 1828
22 CO42/391/299-303 (Robinson to Colborne, 10 Sept. 1830)
23 Debates LA V 1480, IX 292
24 Ibid. IX 292, 294

25 JLA 1850, app. BB, question 105
26 The authoritative studies are J.M.S. Careless *The Union of the Canadas: The Growth of Canadian Institutions, 1841-1857* (Toronto 1967) and Jacques Monet *The Last Cannon-Shot: A Study of French-Canadian Nationalism, 1837-1850* (Toronto 1976).
27 AO RG4 A-1, box 4, 24-8
28 Ibid. 2-3
29 Ibid. 10
30 Ibid. 48, 49, 57, 76; ibid., box 3, T.S. Campbell to attorney general, Canada West, 9 June 1847; ibid., box 9; PAC RG13 B1/796, T.H. Stayner to R. Baldwin, 15 Mar. 1848
31 RG4 A-1, box 4, 76-7, 84-5; Debates LA V 1481. Relator actions are discussed in Edwards *Law Officers of the Crown* 286-95.
32 The authoritative account of local government in this period, in both its administrative and its judicial aspects, is J.H. Aitchison 'The Development of Local Government in Upper Canada, 1783-1850' PHD thesis, University of Toronto (1953). See also Aitchison 'The Municipal Corporations Act of 1849' *Canadian Historical Review* 30 (1949).
33 *Patriot* (Toronto) 21 Nov. 1834
34 RG1 E3/3/210-225a (report of Executive Council, 16 July 1840, and encs.)
35 PAC RG1 E1, Canada State Book A 276-7, 353
36 MTL Robert Baldwin Papers, A39/45-6 (S. Cody to Baldwin, 22 Nov. 1842)
37 RG4 A-1, box 4, 4-5
38 Canada State Book A 181-2
39 8 Vict., c. 14; and see below at 180-1.
40 Blackwell 'William Hume Blake and the Judicature Acts'; PAC MG24 B30 (John Sandfield Macdonald Papers) 1/202-5 (G. Macdonell to Macdonald, 6 June 1850)
41 PAC MG26A (John A. Macdonald Papers) 209/89166-9 (Draper to Macdonald, 30 Apr. 1860); ibid. 89187-93 (same to same, 26 Dec. 1864)
42 29 Vict., c. 28; Biggar *Sir Oliver Mowat* I 124-5
43 RG4 A-1, box 4, 47, 61-2, 67-73; PAC RG13 B1/798 passim; MG26A/507/430 (J.A. Macdonald to S.B. Freeman, 18 Oct. 1860); RG1 E1, Canada State Book AB 306. Robert Baldwin Papers A72/63-117 consists of letters from Smith on various government litigation in 1843.
44 RG1 E1, Canada State Book M 640-1
45 RG13 B1/799, Harrison to H. Bernard, 28 Sept. 1859
46 PRO CO47/194/19 (Canada, Statistical Blue Book 1866)
47 JHA 1830, appendix, 49-59
48 Ibid. 53-5

49 *Upper Canada Herald* (Kingston) 13 Jan. 1824; Debates LA X 1222
50 JHA 1821-2 (Ontario Bureau of Archives *11th Report, 1914* 117, 149, 154); Lownsbrough *Privileged Few* 67; J.Ll.J. Edwards *Ministerial Responsibility as It Relates to the Offices of Prime Minister, Attorney General and Solicitor General of Canada* (Ottawa 1980) 36
51 3William IV c. 49, s. 2; RG4 A-1, box 4, 3-4
52 Debates LA III 305-6
53 RG1 E1, appendix to Canada State Books B-D 285-6; ibid., Canada State Book C 563-9
54 7 William IV (1837) c. 1; and see above at 124-5.
55 JHA 1823 (Ontario Bureau of Archives *11th Report* 431); JHA 1836-7, app. 14; *Upper Canada Herald* 13 Jan. 1824; 8 Vict. (1845) c. 14; Debates LA IV 1031, 1301-4
56 Debates LA IX 292
57 RG1 E1, Canada State Book E 96-7
58 Ibid. 86-100
59 Ibid. 90-6; RG4 A-1, box 4, 30-4
60 Debates LA V 1479-80
61 Ibid. VIII 2337
62 Edwards *Law Officers of the Crown* 177-225, esp. at 189-90, 223
63 Debates LA IX 290-4. The evidence taken by the committee is in JLA 1850, app. BB.
64 App. BB (app. H)
65 Debates LA IX 293
66 Ibid. V 1481
67 Ibid.; JLA 1850, app. BB, question 69
68 JLA 1850, app. BB, question 105; and see above at 169.
69 Ibid. app. BB, questions 40, 107, 108
70 Ibid.; and question 118
71 Debates LA VIII 1793
72 JLA 1850, app. BB, question 108
73 PAC RG1 E7/59a/33-4
74 16 Vict. (1852-3) c. 22 (P. Can.); PAC RG13 B1/798
75 14 and 15 Vict. (1851) c. 13 (P. Can.); RG1 E1 Canada State Book R 71-2; Banks 'Evolution of the Ontario Courts' 514
76 JLA 1850, app. BB, question 118
77 Ibid. questions 12, 16-18; *Macm. Dict.*; G. Maclean Rose, ed. *A Cyclopaedia of National Biography*, 2 vols (Toronto 1886) I 202-3; Morgan *Can. Men*
78 Debates LA XI 3321-2; RG1 E1, Canada State Books A 207, B 336, C 291, D 305, E 546, G 461, K 3, 416, L 250, M 490-1, N 262, 334, O 212, P 382-3; *Quebec*

Mercury 16 Oct. 1856, reproduced in *Bulletin des Recherches historiques* 44 (1938) 9-12

79 Canada State Book M 605-6, 640-1

80 CO47/164/99 (Canada, Statistical Blue Book 1849); JLA 1850, app. vv

81 Debates LA IX 72-3, X 892-3; 14 and 15 Vict. (1851) c. 118

82 See above at 80. The best work on this use of patronage in Upper Canada is S.F. Wise 'The Conservative Tradition in Upper Canada' in Edith G. Firth, ed. *Profiles of a Province: Studies in the History of Ontario* (Toronto 1967).

83 Debates LA IX 324; William Renwick Riddell *The Bar of the Province of Upper Canada, or Ontario* (Toronto 1928) 96; Paul Romney 'Widmer, Christopher' in DCB VIII 934

84 Debates LA VIII 68-9, 96; ibid. IX 293, X 388-92, XI 2406-11, 3232-3

85 R. Alan Douglas, ed. *John Prince: A Collection of Documents* (Toronto 1980); Donald Swainson 'Sir Henry Smith and the Politics of the Union' *Ontario History* 65 (1974); Careless *Union of the Canadas* 104. For MacNab's whining, see also PAC RG7 G14/66, memorial of Sir A. MacNab, 4 Mar. 1844.

86 Debates LA X 392

87 MG24 B30/1/96-9 (Draper to J.S. Macdonald, 7 June 1849); Blackwell 'Blake and the Judicature Acts' 161-4

88 MTL Baldwin-Ross Correspondence, Baldwin to Ross, 28 June 1851

89 Ibid.; Debates LA X 603-7, 612-13

90 Debates LA X 773; A.G Doughty, ed. *The Grey-Elgin Papers, 1846-52*, 4 vols (Ottawa 1937) II 891; MG24 B30/1/392-5 (J.S. Macdonald to E.J. Barker, 27 Dec. 1851); Francis Hincks *Reminiscences of His Public Life* (Montreal 1884) 251-7

91 Debates LA X 769-73

92 3 and 4 Vict. (1840) c. 35, s. 37, s. 42 (UK)

93 CO42/559/169-93 (Elgin to Grey, 22 June 1849, disp. 78)

94 Debates LA IX 68-70

95 14 and 15 Vict. (1851) c. 73, c. 143, c. 146 (Can.)

96 JLA 1852-3, app. XX; Oscar Douglas Skelton *The Life and Times of Sir Alexander Tilloch Galt* (Toronto 1920) 75-6; A.W. Currie *The Grand Trunk Railway of Canada* (Toronto 1957) 10-11; G.R. Stevens *Canadian National Railways* 2 vols (Toronto 1960) I 68-82

97 Debates LA XI 774-80

98 MG26A/507/463-4 (Bernard to J.C. Morrison, 17 Dec. 1860)

99 Edwards *Law Officers of the Crown* 175-6; 30 and 31 Vict. (1867), c. 3, s. 63

100 *Paterson* v *Bowes* [1853] 4 Grant 170 (later *Toronto* v *Bowes*); Paul Romney '"The Ten Thousand Pound Job": Political Corruption, Equitable Jurisdiction, and the Public Interest in Upper Canada, 1854-6' in Flaherty, ed. *Essays*

in the History of Canadian Law II. See also *Thorson* v *A.G. of Canada* [1975] 1
SCR 138 at 154, and John Ll. Edwards *The Attorney General, Politics, and the
Public Interest* (London 1984) 142, note 17.
101 Brit. Parl. Papers (1854-5) XII 14-15, 22-3, 198, 201; Edwards *Law Officers of
the Crown* 98-101, 141-9; and see below at 214-31.
102 See below at 228-9.
103 Edwards *Law Officers of the Crown* 167-8
104 Grey-Elgin Papers II 851; R. MacGregor Dawson *The Government of Canada,*
4th ed., rev. Norman Ward (Toronto 1963) 182-4; DCB VIII 844 (Stuart)
105 *Political Appointments and Elections in the Province of Canada from 1841 to 1865,*
comp. Joseph-Olivier Côté (Ottawa 1866); Debates LA V 1482
106 MTL J.H. Cameron Papers, Draper to Cameron, 22 June 1846; ibid., same to
same, 20 Nov. 1846; AO Henry Smith Papers, J.A. Macdonald to Smith, 3
Sept. 1855; JLA 1850, app. BB, questions 106, 108; PAC RG1 E7/59a/35-6
107 See above at 193.

CHAPTER 5

1 6 Wm. IV, c. 44
2 Holdsworth *History of English Law* V 192-3, IX 223-36, XI 555; James
Fitzjames Stephen *A History of the Criminal Law of England,* 3 vols. (London
1883) I 424-5. The nature of the criminal trial at assize in London and its
environs is discussed in J.M. Beattie 'Crime and the Courts in Surrey 1736-
1753' in J.S. Cockburn, ed. *Crime in England 1550-1800* (Princeton 1977) and
in John H. Langbein 'The Criminal Trial before the Lawyers' *University of
Chicago Law Review* 45 (1978).
3 14 Geo. III (1774) c. 83, s. 11 (UK); 31 Geo. III (1791) c. 31, s. 33 (UK); 40 Geo.
III (1800) c. 1 (UC)
4 Bernard Schwartz *The Great Rights of Mankind: A History of the American Bill of
Rights* (New York 1977) 37, 48-50, 196, 199; *Second Report of His Majesty's
Commissioners on Criminal Law* Brit. Parl. Papers (1836) XXXVI 254
5 Leon Radzinowicz *A History of the English Criminal Law and Its Administration
from 1750* 4 vols (London 1948-67) I 3-35
6 Ibid. 25-8, 31-2, 93-7; Douglas Hay 'Property, Authority and the Criminal
Law' in *Albion's Fatal Tree: Crime and Society in Eighteenth-Century England*
(New York 1975)
7 9 Geo. I (1723) c. 22 (UK); E.P. Thompson *Whigs and Hunters: The Origin of the
Black Act* (New York 1975)
8 MTL W.W. Baldwin Papers, notebook of session of 1823-4; *Upper Canada
Herald* 9 Dec., 16 Dec. 1823; Riddell *Upper Canada Sketches* 37

9 7 Geo. IV (1826) c. 3 (UC); CO42/375/111-12 (memorandum in Maitland to
Bathurst, 22 Apr. 1825); J.M. Beattie *Attitudes towards Crime and Punishment in Upper Canada, 1830-1850: A Documentary Study* (Toronto 1977) 8-18

10 Norman Gash *Mr. Secretary Peel: The Life of Sir Robert Peel to 1830* (London
1961) 326-30; Radzinowicz *History of the English Criminal Law* I 562-607

11 *Upper Canada Herald* 20 Jan., 27 Jan. 1824; *Papers* (CO42/386/46) 21

12 JHA 1825 22, 82; ibid. 1825-6 6, 14; ibid. 1826-7 6, 13; ibid. 1828 10, 18; ibid.
1830 21, 27; ibid. 1831 8, 18; ibid. 1831-2 20, 96

13 *Upper Canada Herald* 4 Feb. 1824; *Upper Canada Gazette and United Empire
Loyalist* (Toronto) 23 Dec. 1826; see also the *Gazette* for 17 Feb. 1827.

14 *Upper Canada Herald* 4 Feb. 1824, 22 Nov. 1825

15 Brit. Parl. Papers (1836) XXXVI 183-204

16 *Gazette and Loyalist* 17 Feb. 1827; Blackstone *Commentaries* 16th ed., with
notes by John Taylor Coleridge, 4 vols (London 1825) IV 355 note 10.
Stanton described the source as 'a late edition of [the] Commentaries which
has only just been received in Upper Canada.' One wonders if it appeared early enough in 1825 for Robinson to bring back a copy.

17 *Canadian Freeman* 2 Oct. 1828; 11 Sept., 18 Sept. 1828; *Gore Gazette* 6 Sept.
1828; *Dictionary of Hamilton Biography* 203-6. I am grateful to Dr Robert
Fraser for drawing this case to my attention.

18 *Correspondent and Advocate* 1 Feb. 1836

19 Brit. Parl. Papers (1836) XXXVI 262; ibid. IV 694-8

20 *Canada Law Journal* 4 (1869) 218

21 Brit. Parl. Debates, 3d series CLIX (1860) 746; Ont. Sess. Papers (1895) 32
(*Report of the Commissioners Appointed to Inquire Concerning the Mode of
Appointing and Remunerating Certain Provincial Officials Now Paid by Fees*) 600;
14 and 15 Eliz. II (1966) c. 80 (Ont.)

22 *Gideon v Wainright* 372 U.S. 335 (1963). In Ontario, by contrast, the right to
legal aid was not entrenched in the constitution: A. Kenneth Pye 'The
Rights of Persons Accused of Crime under the Canadian Constitution: A
Comparative Perspective' in Paul Davenport and Richard H. Leech, eds
Reshaping Confederation: The 1982 Reform of the Canadian Constitution (Durham,
NC 1984) 232-3.

23 Brit. Parl. Debates, 3d series XXXV (1836) 177-86 passim; Brit. Parl. Papers
(1836) XXXVI 202-3, 260-2; IV 694-702

24 Edwards *Law Officers of the Crown* 271-6

25 *Upper Canada Herald* 27 Jan. 1824; *Correspondent and Advocate* 1 Feb. 1836

26 *Upper Canada Herald* 4 Feb. 1824

27 See above at 82.

28 *Upper Canada Law Journal* 9 (1863) 75-6 (*R. v McLellan*)

29 *R.* v *Marsden* (1829), *R.* v *Bell* (1829), *R.* v *Gardner* (1845), *R.* v *Blackburn* (1853), *R.* v *Christie* (1858), *R.* v *Taylor* (1859), cited ibid.

30 17 and 18 Vict. c. 125; Brit. Parl. Debates, 3d series CLIX (1860) 744-8; CLX (1860) 86-8, 180-1; CLXXVII (1865) 576-9, 1725-8

31 28 and 29 Vict. c. 18

32 19 Vict. c. 43

33 29 and 30 Vict. c. 41

34 James William Norton-Kyshe *The Law and Privileges Relating to the Attorney-General and Solicitor-General of England* (London 1897) 143-7, and generally 119-66; Edwards *Law Officers of the Crown* 274; 32 and 33 Vict. (1869) c. 29, s. 45(2) (Can.)

35 Morgan *Can. Men*

36 HC Debates (1880) 113-14, 356-7

37 Ibid. 358-9

38 *R.* v *Le Blanc* (1893) 6 CCC 348; *R.* v *Martin* (1905) 9 OLR 218

39 Lita-Rose Betcherman *The Little Band: The Clashes between the Communists and the Political and Legal Establishment in Canada, 1928-1932* (Ottawa n.d.) 37; 2 and 3 Eliz. II (1953-4), c. 51, s. 558 (Can.); 17 and 18 Eliz. II (1968-9), c. 38, s. 52 (Can.)

40 Radzinowicz *History of the English Criminal Law* I 99-100; J.H. Baker 'The Refinement of English Criminal Jurisprudence 1500-1848' in Louis A. Knafla, ed. *Crime and Criminal Justice in Europe and Canada* (Waterloo, Ont. 1981) 19-24

41 CO42/349/166-8 (Powell to Gore, 3 Oct. 1809)

42 Ibid. 353/102-5 (same to same, 6 Apr. 1811; unsigned, unaddressed copy of memo, n.d. [Powell to Hunter, circa 1800-5])

43 *Papers* 18; *Gore Gazette* 17 May 1828 (reprinted in *Papers* 304-8); Brit. Parl. Debates, 2d series XIV (1826) 1232

44 See above at 154.

45 *Report from the Select Committee on Public Prosecutors* Brit. Parl. Papers (1854-5) XII 193-4 (evidence of Campbell, LCJ); *Upper Canada Law Journal* 5 (1859) 51-2

46 PAC RG13 B1/1391, Small to Baldwin, 19 May 1848; ibid. B1/798, R. Cooper to J.A. Macdonald, 4 Nov. 1856

47 Cited above, note 41; and see above at 125.

48 AO RG4 A-1/4/47, 67, 73-5, 82-3

49 Ibid. 20-3

50 *Upper Canada Law Journal* 1 (1855) 31-4; see also 3 (1857) 57. RG13 B1/798, Patton to J.A. Macdonald, 3 Apr. 1855, proves that Patton wrote the editorial of 1855.

51 See below at 229.

52 4 and 5 Vict. c. 25 (P. Can.); Debates LA v 1482 (O.R. Gowan)
53 *Eighth Report of Her Majesty's Commissioners on Criminal Law* Brit. Parl. Papers (1845) XIV 161 et seq., quotation at 371; Radzinowicz *History of the English Criminal Law* III 258-9, 308, 358n, 445
54 *Report from the Select Committee on Public Prosecutors* Brit. Parl. Papers (1854-5) XII 193-4; *Report from the Select Committee on Public Prosecutors* Brit. Parl. Papers (1856) VII 347 et seq.; Radzinowicz *History of the Criminal Law* II 224-5; Edwards *Law Officers of the Crown* 340-9; Douglas Hay 'Controlling the English Prosecutor' *Osgoode Hall Law Journal* 21 (1983)
55 *Upper Canada Law Journal* 2 (1856) 12-15; Edwards *Law Officers of the Crown* 348
56 Debates LA v 1482
57 JLA 1850, app. BB, proposal of W.H. Merritt and questions 107, 118
58 See above at 192.
59 Debates LA x 388-92; ibid. 1403-5
60 *Globe* 10 Mar. 1857
61 Ibid. 4 Mar., 11 Mar. 1857; *The Leader* (Toronto) 11 Mar. 1857; Canadian Library Association Microfilming Project *Parliamentary Debates* (hereinafter CLA Parl. Debates) 10 Mar. 1857
62 20 Vict. (1857) c. 59 (P. Can.)
63 Blackwell 'Judicature Acts of 1849'; 14 and 15 Vict. (1851) c. 13; 19 Vict. (1856) c. 43; 20 Vict. (1857) c. 61
64 *Upper Canada Law Journal* 4 (1858) 77
65 Ont. Sess. Papers (1895) no. 32, 600
66 Edwards *Law Officers of the Crown* 349-66; Hay 'Controlling the English Prosecutor' 174-80
67 Edwards *Law Officers of the Crown* 238, 367-401; Hay 'Controlling the English Prosecutor' 165-6, 181
68 Frank Armstrong and Kenneth L. Chasse 'The Right to an Independent Prosecutor' 28 CRNS 162. See also Chasse 'The Role of the Prosecutor' in Sandra Oxner, ed. *Criminal Justice* (Toronto 1982), and Chasse 'The Attorney General and the Traditional Crown Prosecutor – An Alternative View of Prosecutorial Powers' *Crown's Newsletter* (Ontario Crown Attorneys' Association) April 1984.
69 See above at 179-88.
70 *Globe* 10 Mar. 1857
71 L.K. Graburn 'The Relationship of the Crown Attorney to the Attorney General' 35 CRNS 259
72 Compare CLA Parl. Debates 10 Mar. 1857, and Leader 11 Mar. 1857 with *Globe* 11 Mar. 1857
73 Ont. Sess. Papers (1895) no. 32, 599

74 *Perth Courier* 23 Oct. 1863
75 *Upper Canada Law Journal* 3 (1857) 195; and see above, note 61
76 PAC RG1 E1, Canada State Book Y 608-9; Z 28, 404, 529-30; AA 499-500; *Perth Courier* 24 Mar. 1865, 23 June 1865
77 *Upper Canada Law Journal* 5 (1859) 49-50; RG13 B1/799, J.J. Burrows to J.A. Macdonald, 8 Feb. 1859; PAC MG26A/507/249 (H. Bernard to H.G. Hopkins, 18 Oct. 1860); ibid. 508/33, 83 (Bernard to R. Dempsey, 8 Jan. 1861; same to same, 13 Feb. 1861); RG1 E1, Canada State Book W 213-15
78 MG26A/297/136186-7 (Memo of 'MG' on letter of J.F. Davis, county attorney, Lambton, dated 23 May 1861)
79 27 and 28 Vict. (1864), c. 5 (P. Can.); *Upper Canada Law Journal* 10 (1864) 253-6; RG1 E1, Canada State Book AA 304-7; MG26A/509/206-8 (J.A. Macdonald to J.D. Armour, 12 Aug. 1864; Macdonald to P. Low, 12 Aug. 1864); ibid. 510/227-8 (Macdonald to A.T. Galt, 31 Jan. 1865)
80 *Upper Canada Law Journal* 3 (1857) 117-18; 4 (1858) 29; RG13 B1/798, G. Davidson to J.A. Macdonald, 2 June 1857; ibid. B1/799 passim
81 MG26A/209/89187-93 (Draper to Macdonald, 26 Dec. 1864)
82 *Globe* 2 Feb. 1865; *Leader* 2 Feb. 1865
83 *Perth Courier* 10 Feb. 1865
84 MG26A/514/58 (Macdonald to J.C. Spohn, 6 Oct. 1867)
85 W.S. Neidhardt *Fenianism in North America* (University Park, PA 1975); Hereward Senior *The Fenians and Canada* (Toronto 1978) 76-106
86 29 and 30 Vict., c. 1
87 CSC 1859, c. 102, s. 8
88 See *Irish Canadian* (Toronto) June-July 1866, passim, and *Canadian Freeman* (Toronto) June-July 1866 passim
89 *Irish Canadian* 6 July 1866
90 MG26A/512/457-8 (Macdonald to J.G. Moylan, 19 July 1866)
91 Neidhardt *Fenianism in North America* 93-108; Neidhardt 'The Fenian Trials in the Province of Canada, 1866-7: A Case Study of Law and Politics in Action' *Ontario History* 66 (1974)
92 PAC RG13 A4/1381, Harrison to Macdonald, 23 July 1866
93 MG26A/513/188-9 (Macdonald to R. Macdonald, 29 Sept. 1866)
94 AO Blake Papers, Mowat to Blake, 25 Mar. 1876; and see below at 251.
95 *Canada Law Journal* 27 (1891) 195-9
96 Radzinowicz *History of the English Criminal Law* II 181-6
97 33 Geo. III (1793) c. 2 (UC); W.C. Keele *A Brief View of the Township Laws ... with a Treatise on the Law and Office of Constable* (Toronto 1835) 15-22; Nicholas Rogers 'Serving Toronto the Good: The Development of the City Police Force, 1834-84' in Russell, ed. *Forging a Consensus* 116-17

98 *Mirror* (Toronto) 18 Oct. 1839; *Examiner* 23 Oct. 1839; JLA 1841 635-7; Rogers
    'Serving Toronto the Good' 117-20; Gregory S. Kealey 'Orangemen and
    the Corporation' in Russell, ed. *Forging a Consensus* 48-50

99 JLA 1841, app. S; *Examiner* 10 Mar., 17 Mar. 1841; *British Colonist* (Toronto) 17
    Mar. 1841; and see above, note 98.

100 RG13 B1/796, J. Aemilius Irving to Baldwin, 12 Mar. 1841

101 Careless *Union of the Canadas* 127-31

102 AO ML Papers A-1-1, Mackenzie to J. Mackenzie, 2 Apr. 1849; MTL Robert
    Baldwin Papers A65/24 (J. Reid to Baldwin, 3 Mar. 1849); Kealey 'Orange-
    men and the Corporation' 56

103 Kealey 'Orangemen and the Corporation' 54

104 Ibid. 67-70; Barrie Dyster 'Captain Bob and the Noble Ward: Neighbour-
    hood and Provincial Politics in Nineteenth-Century Toronto' in Russell,
    ed. *Forging a Consensus*; Ruth Bleasdale 'Class Conflict on the Canals of
    Upper Canada in the 1840s' *Labour/Le Travailleur* 7 (1981)

105 8 Vict. c. 6; 14 and 15 Vict. c. 76; CSC 1859 c. 29; RSO 1877 c. 31; RSO 1887 c. 34;
    RSO 1897 c. 38; RSO 1914 c. 36; 55 Vict. (1892) c. 97, s. 47

106 Michael S. Cross '"The Laws Are Like Cobwebs": Popular Resistance to
    Authority in Mid-Nineteenth-Century British North America' *Dalhousie
    Law Journal* 8 (1983) 103-4, 119-22; *Grey-Elgin Papers* II 450-63

107 14 and 15 Vict. c. 77; Debates LA X 1147-52, 1217-19, 1484-6, 1501-2; *Grey-
    Elgin Papers* I 274, II 600

108 Cross '"The Laws Are Like Cobwebs"' 108-9; Beattie *Attitudes to Crime and
    Punishment* 1, 42-50; AO RG4 A-1/4/53-4 (R. Baldwin to S.B. Harrison, 14
    Aug. 1843); RG13 B1/798, J. Monkman to J.A. Macdonald, 22 Dec. 1855

109 Rogers 'Serving Toronto the Good' 120; Kealey 'Orangemen and the
    Coporation' 67-9; Dyster 'Captain Bob and the Noble Ward' 88-9, 97

110 Radzinowicz *History of the English Criminal Law* IV 158-67; Gash *Mr. Secretary
    Peel* 176-84; 3 Geo. IV (1822) c. 103 (UK)

111 Rogers 'Serving Toronto the Good' 121

112 *Grey-Elgin Papers* II 450-63, III 1141-2, IV 1462

113 RG1 E1, Canada State Book O 415-16

114 JLA 1854-5, app. XX

115 Debates LA X 1147-8, 1484

116 *Globe* 28 Mar. 1855

117 Ibid. 30 Mar. 1855, and April 1855 passim; 18 Vict. (1855) c. 77 (esp. ss 38 and
    39)

118 *Leader* 29 Mar. 1856; *Globe* 31 Mar. 1856; JLA 1856 202, 287, 293, 331, 343, 360,
    402, 490, 572

119 *Globe* 15 Apr. 1856

120 Ibid. 31 Mar. 1856
121 Rogers 'Serving Toronto the Good' 122-6
122 Ibid. 126-9; *In re Prince and Toronto* (1866) 25 UCQBR 175; 29 and 30 Vict. (1866)
    c. 51, s. 400
123 MG26A/297/136188-91 (memo of 'MG,' n.d.)
124 *Globe* 25 Jan., 26 Jan. 1869
125 AO RG4 C-3, 1873, file C1486 (A. MacNabb to J.G. Scott, 15 Nov. 1873)
126 37 Vict. c. 7 (Ont.); 37 Vict. c. 18 (Ont.)
127 Ont. Sess. Papers (1884) no. 91; *Globe* 15 Mar. 1884, 4; 59 Vict. (1896) c. 26
    (Ont.). Other developments in rural police policy during the Mowat era
    are summarized in A.K. McDougall 'Law and Politics: The Case of Police
    Independence in Ontario' (paper presented to the Canadian Political
    Science Association, 1971) 14-16; and see Dahn D. Higley *OPP: The History of
    the Ontario Provincial Police Force* (Toronto 1985) 27-71.
128 Desmond Morton *Ministers and Generals: Politics and the Canadian Militia,
    1868-1904* (Toronto 1970) 40-1; McDougall 'Law and Politics' 16

CHAPTER 6

1 30 Vict. c. 3
2 For example, see Frank H. Underhill 'The Conception of a National Interest'
  Canadian Journal of Economics and Political Science 1 (1935) 400-4.
3 The controversy is reviewed to date in Alan C. Cairns 'The Judicial Committee and Its Critics' *Canadian Journal of Political Science* 4 (1971).
4 Can. Sess. Papers (1873) no. 50; reprinted in part in *Canada Law Journal* 9
  (1873) 178-82
5 Biggar *Sir Oliver Mowat* I 151-3
6 36 Vict. c. 3, c. 4; *Daily Globe* 15 Feb., 27 Feb. 1873
7 18 Vict. c. 92, s. 45
8 *Upper Canada Law Journal* 9 (1863) 113-15
9 *Canada Law Journal* 12 (1876) 103-5; 16 (1880) 286-8; 19 (1883) 239-40; 21 (1885)
  1-2; 26 (1890) 1, 33-4, 49-50; 27 (1891) 386. Volume 21 (1885) 365 uses the word
  'batch'; so does Mowat to Edward Blake, 31 Aug. 1875 (AO Blake Papers).
10 The following summary is based on the sources cited in notes 4, 15, 24, 31,
   and 40. See also HC Debates (1890) 2183-208. For the importance of the
   patronage question, and the Ontario approach to the queen's counsel question in general, see also AO RG4 C-3 (1881) file I1225.
11 Peter Waite *The Life and Times of Confederation* (Toronto 1962); John T. Say-
   well *The Office of Lieutenant-Governor: A Study in Canadian Government
   and Politics* (Toronto 1957) 15; 9-16

12 Biggar *Sir Oliver Mowat* I 132-3; J.C. Morrison 'Oliver Mowat and the Development of Provincial Rights in Ontario: A Study in Dominion-Provincial Relations, 1872-1896' in *Three History Theses* (Toronto: Ontario Department of Records and Archives 1961) 267-8

13 Morrison 'Oliver Mowat' 234-85

14 37 Vict. c. 8

15 W.E. Hodgins, comp. *Correspondence, Reports of the Minister of Justice and Orders in Council upon the Subject of Dominion and Provincial Legislation, 1867-1895* (Ottawa 1896) 110-21

16 *Canada Law Journal* 19 (1893) 130-1, 149-50

17 Hodgins *Dominion and Provincial Legislation* 113

18 Ibid. 110-21

19 Joseph Schull *Edward Blake*, 2 vols (Toronto 1975-6)

20 Hodgins *Dominion and Provincial Legislation* 122

21 See below at 274-5.

22 Hodgins *Dominion and Provincial Legislation* 123-5

23 40 Vict. (1877) c. 3 (Ont.)

24 *Lenoir* v *Ritchie* (1879) 3 SCR 575

25 DCB XI 398-9 (Henry); *Macm. Dict.*; Morgan *Can. Men*

26 *Canada Law Journal* 16 (1880) 286-8; 32 (1896) 642-3

27 Ont. Sess. Papers (1888) no. 37, 12-13

28 Ibid. (1884) no. 40

29 *A.G. for Ontario* v *O'Reilly* (1878) 6 Grant 126, (1880) 6 OAR 576; *Canada Law Journal* 12 (1876) 60-2; W.H. Pearson *Recollections and Records of Toronto of Old* (Toronto 1914) 47

30 DCB XI 529-31 (Loranger); Geo. Maclean Rose, ed. *A Cyclopaedia of Canadian Biography* 2 vols (Toronto 1886) I 680-1 (Bethune); *Macm. Dict.*; Morgan *Can. Men*

31 *Mercer* v *A.G. for Ontario* (1881) 5 SCR 538, at 566

32 Ibid. 567

33 Ibid. 577-8

34 Ibid. 611-12; see also 598.

35 *A.G. of Ontario* v *Mercer* (1883) 8 App. Cas. 767, 1 Olm. 171

36 Christopher Armstrong *The Politics of Federalism: Ontario's Relations with the Federal Government, 1867-1942* (Toronto 1981) 14-22; Morrison 'Oliver Mowat' 95-176

37 Jamie Benedickson 'Private Rights and Public Purposes in the Lakes, Rivers, and Streams of Ontario, 1870-1930' in Flaherty, ed. *Essays in the History of Canadian Law* II 371-4; G.V. La Forest *Disallowance and Reservation of Provincial Legislation* (Ottawa 1955) 53-6; Morrison 'Oliver Mowat' 206-15

38 A. Margaret Evans 'Oliver Mowat and Ontario, 1872-1896: A Study in Political Success' PHD thesis, University of Toronto (1969) 302-21
39 *Hodge* v *The Queen* (1883) 9 App. Cas. 117 at 132-3, 1 Olm. 184 at 198-9
40 Ont. Sess. Papers (1888) no. 37
41 Armstrong *Politics of Federalism* 27-30; Morrison 'Oliver Mowat' 234-85
42 51 Vict. c. 5
43 Hodgins *Dominion and Provincial Legislation* 206-10; Morrison 'Oliver Mowat' 88-91
44 *St Catharine's Milling and Lumber Co.* v *The Queen* (1888) 14 App. Cas. 46, 1 Olm. 236; Edward Blake *The St Catharine's Milling and Lumber Company v. The Queen: Argument of Mr. Blake, of Counsel for Ontario* (Toronto 1888) 5-8
45 *A.G. for Canada* v *A.G. of Ontario* (1891-2) 19 OAR 31; *The Executive Power Case: The Attorney-General of Canada vs. The Attorney-General of Ontario* (Toronto 1892)
46 *The Liquidators of the Maritime Bank of Canada v The Receiver-General of New Brunswick* [1892] AC 437 at 442, 1 Olm. 263 at 268
47 *A.G. for Canada* v *A.G. of Ontario* (1893-4) 23 SCR 458
48 *A.G. for Canada* v *A.G. for Ontario* [1898] AC 247, 1 Olm. 409
49 39 Vict. (1876) c. 24; 43 Vict. (1880) c. 10; 48 Vict. (1885) c. 26: ; Biggar *Sir Oliver Mowat* I 283-4, 322-4, II 463-5
50 39 Vict. (1875-6) c. 26 (Ont.); Evans 'Oliver Mowat and Ontario' 303-12
51 27 and 28 Vict. (1864) c. 18 (P. Can.)
52 41 Vict. (1878) c. 16 (Can.)
53 *Russell* v *The Queen* (1882) 7 App. Cas. 829, 1 Olm. 145
54 7 App. Cas. 96, 1 Olm. 94
55 7 App. Cas. at 109, 1 Olm. at 107
56 Above, note 53
57 *The City of Fredericton* v *The Queen* (1880) 3 SCR 505
58 46 Vict. (1883) c. 30 (Can.)
59 *Hodge* v *The Queen* (1883) 9 App. Cas. 117 at 131, 1 Olm. 184 at 197
60 Supreme Court of Canada Library 'Report of the Proceedings before the Judicial Committee of the Privy Council on the hearing of the petition of the Governor-General of Canada in relation to the Dominion License Acts of 1883 and 1884' (typescript) (hereinafter McCarthy Act Reference Hearing); *Globe* 19 Jan. 1885; *Toronto Daily Mail* 21 Jan., 22 Jan., 24 Jan. 1885; Hodgins *Dominion and Provincial Legislation* 210; Evans 'Oliver Mowat and Ontario' 312-21. Mowat's tax on McCarthy Act licences was enacted by 47 Vict. (1884) c. 35.
61 Evans 'Oliver Mowat and Ontario' 321-4; 53 Vict. (1890) c. 56, s. 18

62 53 Vict. (1890) c. 13, 54 Vict. (1891) c. 46, ss. 2, 3; *In re Local Option Act* (1891) 18 OAR 573

63 Evans 'Oliver Mowat and Ontario' 325-39; 54 and 55 Vict. c. 25, s. 4

64 *Huson v Township of South Norwich* (1895) 24 SCR 145; *In re Provincial Jurisdiction to Pass Prohibitory Liquor Laws* (1895) 24 SCR 170

65 AO RG4 C-3 (1881) file 1689, Ont. Sess. Papers (1882) no. 31

66 24 SCR at 150; see also ibid. at 187-8.

67 *A.G. of Ontario v A.G. for Canada* [1894] AC 189; 1 Olm. 304

68 See above at 197. That the commitment of Mowat and Gwynne in *Toronto v Bowes* was more than just professional is suggested by their voting in the Toronto parliamentary election of 1854, in which Bowes was a candidate. Mowat voted the anti-Bowes ticket; Gwynne 'plumped' for Bowes, voiding his second vote: *Daily Globe* 2 Aug. 1854.

69 Morgan *Can. Men*; *Macm. Dict.*; Nicholas Flood Davin *The Irishman in Canada* (London and Toronto 1877) 303, 604-5

70 24 Can. SCR at 218

71 7 App. Cas. at 110-13, 1 Olm. at 108-11

72 24 SCR at 216-19 (per Gwynne J), and 231-9 (per Sedgwick J)

73 Ibid. 210, 219-23

74 Ibid. 229

75 *A.G. for Ontario v A.G. for Canada* [1896] AC 348 at 362, 1 Olm. 343 at 357

76 Canada, Senate *Report ... by the Parliamentary Counsel, relating to the Enactment of the British North America Act, 1867, any lack of consonance between its terms and judicial construction of them, and cognate matters* (Ottawa 1939) (hereinafter O'Connor Report); Bora Laskin ' "Peace, Order and Good Government" Re-examined' in W.R. Lederman, ed. *The Courts and the Canadian Constitution* (Toronto 1964) 76-9 (reprinted from *Canadian Bar Review* 25 [1947]); Laskin 'The Supreme Court of Canada: A Final Court of Appeal for Canadians' ibid. 130-8 (reprinted from *Canadian Bar Review* 29 [1951]); and generally Cairns 'Judicial Committee and Its Critics.' On the other side, see the equally schematic G.P. Browne *The Judicial Committee and the British North America Act: An Analysis of the Interpretative Scheme for the Distribution of Legislative Powers* (Toronto 1967) and also K. Lysyk 'Constitutional Reform and the Introductory Clause of Section 91: Residual and Emergency Law-Making Authority' *Canadian Bar Review* 57 (1979).

77 McCarthy Act Reference Hearing 189

78 *Russell v The Queen* (1882) 7 App. Cas. 829 at 841-2; 1 Olm. 34 145 at 157-8

79 AO RG4 C-3 (1881) file 1689

80 *A.G. for Ontario v A.G. for Canada* [1896] AC 348 at 360-2, 1 Olm. 343 at 355-7

81 Ibid. at 359-60, 354-5; O'Connor Report Annex 1 41-5; F. Murray Greenwood

'Lord Watson, Institutional Self-Interest, and the Decentralization of Canadian Federalism in the 1890s' *University of British Columbia Law Review* 9 (1974) 253-4

82 Laskin ' "Peace, Order and Good Government" Re-Examined' 78, O'Connor Report Annex 1 39-50, 63-7; Greenwood 'Lord Watson' 252-5; Lysyk 'Constitutional Reform and the Introductory Clause of Section 91' 541

83 Louis-Philippe Pigeon 'The Meaning of Provincial Autonomy' in Lederman, ed. *The Courts and the Canadian Constitution* 37 (reprinted from *Canadian Bar Review* 29 [1951]); and see above at 266-7. Compare Stephen Wexler 'The Urge to Idealize: Viscount Haldane and the Constitution of Canada' *McGill Law Journal* 29 (1984) 633-4, 641, 644-5.

84 Hodgins *Dominion and Provincial Legislation* 210

85 RSO 1887 c. 44, s. 52(2); 53 Vict. (1890) c. 13; and see above at 252.

86 Hodgins *Dominion and Provincial Legislation* 210

87 54 and 55 Vict. (1891) c. 25 (Can.)

88 AO RG4 C-3 (1891) file 576

89 Ibid., and see above at 250.

90 *Citizens' Insurance Co.* v *Parsons, The Queen Insurance Co.* v *Parsons, The Western Insurance Co.* v *Johnston* (1879-80), 4 SCR 215 at 349; and see above at 262.

91 RG4 C-3 (1881) file 1689; Ont. Sess. Papers (1882) no. 31

92 RG4 C-3 (1893) file 1052, Freshfields and Williams to J.R. Cartwright, 19 Aug. 1893, same to same, 13 Oct. 1893; Greenwood 'Lord Watson' 262

93 Morrison 'Oliver Mowat' 92-3 and passim; Greenwood 'Lord Watson' 244-55; O'Connor Report, annex 1, 25, 46. The prohibition reference has received the greater amount of critical attention because it concerned the relation of sections 91 and 92 – a perennial subject of controversy; but my contention here is that resolution of the sovereignty question had an important influence on the subsequent resolution of the distribution-of-powers question. The lingering influence of centralist legalism in commentary on the sovereignty question appears in Greenwood 'Lord Watson' 248, Greenwood 'David Mills and Co-ordinate Federalism, 1867-1903' *University of Western Ontario Law Review* 16 (1977) 101-2, 110-11, and Wexler 'The Urge to Idealize' 610, 639-41.

94 *Daily Globe* 12 June, 24 Nov. 1869; Morrison 'Oliver Mowat' 250-5; G.F.G. Stanley 'Act or Pact? Another Look at Confederation' in Canadian Historical Association Report (1956); Stanley *A Short History of the Canadian Constitution* (Toronto 1969) 90-8. Greenwood 'David Mills' is a useful summary of provincialist ideas as expounded by one man; most of Mills's quoted views seem traceable to earlier statements by Blake or Mowat. The

suggestion (at 97-8) that, in the 1890s, Mowat accepted that prohibition came within the dominion sphere, and that therefore he deliberately 'invited defeat' in the prohibition reference, seems implausible, though there is evidence that he held that view of prohibition in the mid-1870s: see below at 285-6.

95 *Mercer* v *A.G. for Ontario* (1881) 5 SCR 538 at 566; Greenwood 'Lord Watson' 248

96 G.P. Browne, ed. *Documents on the Confederation of British North America* (Toronto 1969) xxii-xxviii; Morrison 'Oliver Mowat' 11-16

97 See above at 243, 249, 257.

98 Greenwood 'Lord Watson' 252-5; *In re Prohibitory Liquor Laws* (1895) 24 SCR 170, at 212-13; and see above at 266-7.

99 *Canada Law Journal* 32 (1896) 642-3

CHAPTER 7

1 16 Vict. (1852-3) c. 119 (P. Can.); 20 Vict. (1857) c. 58; Margaret A. Banks 'The Evolution of the Ontario Courts, 1788-1981' in Flaherty, ed. *Essays in the History of Canadian Law* II 516

2 *Daily Globe* 2 Dec., 9 Dec., 19 Dec. 1868; *Canada Law Journal* 5 (1869) 3-4

3 Banks 'Evolution of the Ontario Courts' 520-2

4 CSC 1859 c. 105, 13 and 14 Vict. (1850) c. 54

5 *Daily Globe* 24 Nov. 1868; HC Debates (1869) 419-21; *Canada Law Journal* 9 (1873) 140-2

6 32 and 33 Vict. (1869) c. 32 (Can.); 32 Vict. (1868-9) c. 6, c. 22, c. 26 (Ont.)

7 Ont. Sess. Papers (1869) no. 16; 33 Vict. (1869) c. 12 (Ont.)

8 Ont. Sess. Papers (1869) no. 16. The relevant section is section 100.

9 AO Blake Papers, Mowat to Blake, 20 Oct. 1875; same to same, 28 Dec. 1875

10 Ibid. Mowat to Blake, 6 Nov. 1875; same to same, 24 Apr. 1876; ibid. memo of Bernard, 28 Apr. 1876

11 Biggar *Sir Oliver Mowat* I 248-51, 289-92; Ont. Sess. Papers (1874) no. 26, (1875-6) no. 37, (1878) no. 10, *Canada Law Journal* 10 (1874) 155-6, 187-8, 12 (1876) 33-7, 14 (1878) 5-8; Hodgins *Dominion and Provincial Legislation* 152-3; and see below at 301-2.

12 *Upper Canada Law Journal* 5 (1859) 123-7

13 DCB XI 621 (Moss); Morgan *Can. Men*; *Macm. Dict.*

14 Blake Papers, Mowat to Blake, 30 Dec. 1876

15 *A.G. for Ontario* v *A.G. for Canada* [1896] AC 348 at 361-2, 1 Olm. 343 at 366-7. It is ironic that Blake, to whom Mowat confessed this, was counsel for the Dominion Distillers' and Brewers' Association in the prohibition reference.

16 36 Vict. c. 48; Biggar *Sir Oliver Mowat* I 185-7

17 Holdsworth *History of English Law* I 445-76

18 A.H. Manchester *A Modern Legal History of England and Wales, 1750-1950* (London 1980) 125-43; Blackwell 'William Hume Blake and the Judicature Acts of 1849'; 12 Vict. (1849) c. 64 (P. Can.); 19 Vict. (1856) c. 43 (P. Can.)

19 Lawrence M. Friedman *A History of American Law* (New York 1973) 341-7

20 Holdsworth *History of English Law* I 643-8, xv 104-25; Manchester *Modern Legal History* 144-50; Brit. Parl. Papers (1868-9) xxv; *Canada Law Journal* 7 (1871) 67-83

21 Ont. Sess. Papers (1873) no. 26

22 Ibid.

23 *Canada Law Journal* 10 (1874) 4-5; Manchester *Modern Legal History* 131-4; Holdsworth *History of English Law* IX passim

24 *Canada Law Journal* 10 (1874) 4-5

25 36 and 37 Vict. c. 66 (UK); 36 Vict. c. 8 (Ont.)

26 *Canada Law Journal* 13 (1877) 330-4, 14 (1878) 33-8, 131-6

27 Ibid. 9 (1873) 335-8, 10 (1874) 4-5; Biggar *Sir Oliver Mowat* I 197-9

28 *Canada Law Journal* 7 (1871) 233, 10 (1874) 4-5; Biggar *Sir Oliver Mowat* I 218, 225-9, 337-8

29 44 Vict. c. 5

30 Sections 66, 67, and 70-2. The old Chancery orders concerning the guardian ad litem, as he was called, are printed in James Maclennan *The Ontario Judicature Act, 1881* (Toronto 1881) 65-8.

31 31 Geo. III c. 2; and see above at 21.

32 *Proceedings of the Legislative Council of Upper Canada on the Bill sent up from the House of Assembly entitled an Act to amend the Jury Laws of this Province* (Toronto 1836) 6 (copy in CO42/430/199-228); 34 Geo. III c. 1 (UC)

33 *Colonial Advocate* 17 Oct. 1833; Elwood Jones 'Willcocks, Joseph' in DCB V 854-9; R.C. Muir 'Burford's First Settler, Politician and Military Man: Benajah Mallory' Ontario Historical Society *Papers and Records* 26 (1930); William Renwick Riddell 'Benajah Mallory, Traitor' ibid.

34 Green *Verdict According to Conscience* 200-49. For an unsentimental account of *Bushell's Case* and its importance, see Langbein 'The Criminal Trial before the Lawyers' 297-300.

35 Green *Verdict According to Conscience* 236-49, 253-60, 321-2

36 Ibid. 267-355

37 *Colonial Advocate* 1 June 1826; and see above at 74, 78.

38 The story takes on a special interest in the light of Langbein's account of relations between judge and jury at the Old Bailey a century earlier: 'The Criminal Trial before the Lawyers' 284-300, 314.

39 *The Canadian's Right the Same as the Englishman's* (York, UC 1823); Paul Romney 'A Man Out of Place' 313-16

40 *Upper Canada Herald* 29 Nov. 1825; *Observer* 5 Dec. 1825; *Canadian Freeman* 8 Dec. 1825 (in CO42/377/110)

41 AO Robinson Papers, Robinson to Wilmot Horton, 24 Dec. 1828

42 PAC RG5 A1/94/51285-6; and see above at 107-14.

43 Above, note 32, quotations at 6 and 31

44 See above at 154-5.

45 13 and 14 Vict. c. 55, ss. 4, 11 (P. Can.)

46 *Upper Canada Law Journal* 2 (1856) 174-5, 3 (1857) 96-9, 4 (1858) 75

47 3 William IV (1833) c. 1 (UC); 7 William IV (1837) c. 12; 4 and 5 Vict. (1841) c. 3 (P. Can.); 8 Vict. (1845) c. 37; 13 and 14 Vict. (1850) c. 53; 16 Vict. (1853) c. 177; J.H. Aitchison 'The Court of Requests in Upper Canada' *Ontario History* 41 (1949)

48 *Upper Canada Law Journal* 2 (1856) 173-5, 3 (1857) 96-9; 4 (1858) 75-8

49 *Upper Canada Law Journal* 4 (1858) 148; 22 Vict. (1858) c. 100, ss 2, 6

50 32 Vict. c. 6, s. 18 (1); 36 Vict. c. 8, ss 17, 18

51 *Upper Canada Law Journal* 5 (1859) 52, 7 (1861) 87

52 *Daily Globe* 18 Jan. 1876; Biggar *Sir Oliver Mowat* I 301-4

53 Holdsworth *History of English Law* I 321-3; Hay 'Property, Authority and the Criminal Law' 31; David Philips *Crime and Authority in Victorian England: The Black Country, 1835-1860* (London 1977) 106

54 Brit. Parl. Papers (1845) XIV 161, (1854-5) XII 1; Radzinowicz *History of the English Criminal Law*

55 Debates LA IX 1253-5

56 See above at 215.

57 *Upper Canada Law Journal* 5 (1859) 51-2

58 22 and 23 Vict. (1859) c. 17 (UK); 24 Vict. (1861) c. 10 (P. Can.). For Lower Canada see also 24 Vict. c. 26, s. 36.

59 *Upper Canada Law Journal* 6 (1860) 274-5

60 John Alexander Kains *How Say You? A Review of the Movement for Abolishing the Grand Jury System in Canada* (St Thomas, Ont. 1893) 11; *Daily Globe* 27 Jan. 1876; *Canada Law Journal* 12 (1876) 50-1

61 Ont. Sess. Papers (1884) no. 40; 42 Vict. (1879) c. 13; *Canada Law Journal* 16 (1880) 188-91

62 Senate Debates (1889) 52-70; *Canada Law Journal* 25 (1889) 133-7; ibid. 26 (1890) 579-82, ibid. 27 (1891) 4-9; Graham Parker 'The Origins of the Canadian Criminal Code' in Flaherty, ed. *Essays in the History of Canadian Law* I

63 Can. Sess. Papers (1891) no. 66

64 *Canada Law Journal* 27 (1891) 388-90, 28 (1892) 5-11
65 Can. Sess. Papers (1891) no. 66, 11; *Canada Law Journal* 27 (1891) 389
66 Hay 'Property, Authority and the Criminal Law'
67 Ibid.; Baker 'The Refinement of English Criminal Jurisprudence' 19-24
68 Can. Sess. Papers (1891) no. 66, 7-8, 24, 26. For biographies of the judges mentioned, see Morgan *Can. Men* and *Macm. Dict.*
69 Can. Sess. Papers (1891) no. 66, 7-8, 12-13, 22. Burton's reply to the questionnaire is placed among those of the county judges, but there was no county judge of that name. For contemporary derision of JPS, see also Parker 'Origins of the Canadian Criminal Code' 267.
70 Ibid. 11-12, 15, 17, 18
71 Ibid. 18, 22
72 Ibid. 21
73 See above at 298.
74 Blackstone *Commentaries* IV 361
75 Canada, Criminal Law Bill 1891 (Ottawa 1891) ss 739-43
76 HC Debates (1892) 4267
77 55 Vict. (1892) c. 29, ss 743-6 (Can.); Vincent M. Del Buono 'The Right to Appeal in Indictable Cases: A Legislative History' *Alberta Law Review* 16 (1978) 452-4. From the clause that became section 743(5) of the act, Thompson omitted an initial sentence that said: 'If the result is acquittal, the accused shall be discharged subject to being arrested again if the Court of Appeal orders a new trial.' The clause that became section 746(e) had originally provided that under certain circumstances the Court of Appeal might, 'in any case, whether the appeal is on behalf of the prosecutor or of the accused, direct a new trial.' Only the last four words of the quoted phrase were retained. Criminal Law Bill 1891 ss 740, 743.
78 R.C. MacLeod 'The Shaping of Canadian Criminal Law, 1892 to 1902' in Canadian Historical Association *Historical Papers* (1978) 64-6; Parker 'Origins of the Canadian Criminal Code' 249-53, 260-4, 271; Martin L. Friedland *Double Jeopardy* (Oxford 1969) 294; HC Debates (1892) 1314
79 Del Buono 'Right to Appeal' 459, 460-2; HC Debates (1930) 388-400, 408-12; Friedland *Double Jeopardy* 295. The Court of Appeal was again restricted to ordering a new trial in 1975: 23-4-5 Eliz. II (1974-5-6) c. 93, s. 75 (Can.)

CONCLUSION

1 S.E.D. Shortt 'Social Change and Political Crisis in Rural Ontario: The Patrons of Industry, 1889-1896' in Donald Swainson, ed. *Oliver Mowat's Ontario* (Toronto 1972)

2 J. Murray Beck 'Rise and Fall of Nova Scotia's Attorney General: 1749-1983' *Dalhousie Law Journal* 8 (1983) 132-3; and see above at 80.

3 *Orpen v A.G. for Ontario* (1924) 56 OLR 327 at 337. On this aspect of the attorney general's duty, see the interesting comment of F. Murray Greenwood 'The Liability of Crown Officers for Advising Refusal of the Fiat' *McGill Law Journal* 8 (1961).

4 Quoted in Donald Creighton *John A. Macdonald: The Old Chieftain* (Toronto 1955) 171

5 Peter Oliver *G. Howard Ferguson: Ontario Tory* (Toronto 1977) 231

6 McRuer Commission *Report No. 1* 955

7 The Constitution Act, 1982, schedule B, part 1. Since its passage, lawyers and political scientists have taken to calling the original dominion charter 'The Constitution Act, 1867.' Historians will not do so any more than they will rename John A. Macdonald. The safeguards in the Charter of Rights are somewhat limited by the power of provincial legislatures to exempt legislation from the Charter: Pye 'Rights of Persons Accused of Crime' 224.

8 56 OLR at 335

9 Romney 'Conservative Reformer in Upper Canada' 54-7

10 Ibid.; Graeme Patterson 'Whiggery, Nationality, and the Upper Canadian Reform Tradition' *Canadian Historical Review* 56 (1975) 34

11 Frank Armstrong 'Guilty in Law – Guilty in Fact' 30 CRNS 287-90 (annotation to *Morgentaler v R.* [1975], ibid. 209). See also the annotation of Graham Parker, ibid. 269.

12 See above at 296, 301.

13 McRuer Commission *Report No. 1* 934, 942-7; RSO 1980 c. 271, s. 5(b)

14 A shift, it might be argued, towards a philistine utilitarian pragmatism; so Frank Underhill averred in 'Some Reflections on the Liberal Tradition in Canada' (in Underhill *In Search of Canadian Liberalism*). What follows can be read as an elaboration of Underhill's argument.

15 E.P. Thompson *Writing By Candlelight* (London 1980) 99-111, 224-36; 'Leave the Jury System Alone' *Manchester Guardian Weekly* 17 Nov. 1985

16 Blackstone *Commentaries* I 155

17 Green *Verdict According to Conscience* 153-99; Donald Veall *The Popular Movement for Law Reform 1640-1660* (Oxford 1970) 97-109; Christopher Hill *The World Turned Upside Down: Radical Ideas during the English Revolution* (Harmondsworth 1975) 271-3

18 *Correspondent and Advocate* 23 July 1835, quoted in Lillian F. Gates 'The Decided Policy of William Lyon Mackenzie' *Canadian Historical Review* 40 (1959) 196

19 MTL Robert Baldwin papers A73:65 (R.B. Sullivan to R. Baldwin [1828]);

ibid. W.W. Baldwin Papers L11 B104, Beardsley to W.W. Baldwin, 1 Aug. 1828; Dent *Story of the Upper Canadian Rebellion* I 216-19

20 *The Oxford English Dictionary* cites, inter alia, Goldwin Smith *Lectures on Modern History* (Oxford 1861) 24, which illustrates the priority of the physiological meaning and its application to social analysis.

21 *Upper Canada Law Journal* 6 (1860) 274; and see above at 300-1.

22 Howard Nenner *By Colour of Law: Legal Culture and Constitutional Politics in England, 1660-1689* (Chicago 1977) 173-96. Nenner captures something of the tone of the Whig constitution and of its democratic successor in the remark (at 173) that 'if any moral emerged [from the revolution], it may well have been that constitutionalism could be preserved as long as it was thought to have been preserved.'

23 See above at 318. The Crown's right of appeal against acquittal was protected by the Constitution Act of 1982: Pye 'Rights of Persons Accused of Crime' 239-40.

24 9 and 10 George V (1919) c. 26 (Can.), c. 46, s. 1 (Can.); Frank R. Scott 'Freedom of Speech in Canada' Canadian Political Science Association *Papers and Proceedings* (1933); reprinted in Scott *Essays on the Constitution: Aspects of Canadian Law and Politics* (Toronto 1977)

25 Betcherman *Little Band* 44; RSC 1927 c. 36, ss 133-4, 238(f)

26 Betcherman *Little Band* 156; Frank R. Scott 'The Trial of the Toronto Communists' *Queen's Quarterly* 39 (1932); reprinted in Scott *Essays on the Constitution*

27 Betcherman *Little Band* 61-2, 77, 80, 84

28 Edwards *Law Officers of the Crown* 57-8, 60-1; Thompson *Whigs and Hunters* 208, 210, 250-1, 256-7, 268; E.P. Thompson *The Making of the English Working Class*, rev. ed. (Harmondsworth 1968) 19-22, 749-57; Eric Hobsbawm and George Rudé *Captain Swing* (New York 1975)

29 Thompson *Making of the English Working Class* 751-3

30 Brode *Sir John Beverley Robinson* 23-5

31 Ibid. 43-52; CO42/362/366-9 (S. McGillivray to Robinson, 14 Sept. 1818); ibid. 373-5 (Robinson to Maitland, 28 Dec. 1818; minute of Executive Council, 14 Dec. 1818)

32 58 Geo. III (1818) c. 10 (UC); CO42/362/233-40 (Robinson to Maitland, 15 July 1819); ibid. 341-54 (Maitland to Bathurst, 30 Nov. 1819); ibid. vol. 363 passim; *The Spectator* (Niagara) 1 Oct. 1818

33 Peter Oliver 'The New Order: W.E. Raney and the Politics of "Uplift"' in Oliver *Public and Private Persons: The Ontario Political Culture, 1914-1934* (Toronto 1975); Betcherman *Little Band* 34-9, 51-2, 162, 212-16

34 Thompson *Whigs and Hunters* 268; Forster 'Liberty in England' in *Abinger Harvest* (London 1936)

Index

solicitor-general (Lower Canada) 169–
200 passim
sovereignty: locus under BNA Act
242–59; parliamentary 318–26
passim
'speedy trial' 283, 301, 309
Stanton, Robert 154, 166, 167, 207
statute consolidation (1877) 284–6
Stephen, Sir James 81, 103, 116, 144
Stevens, Andrew 111, 122, 134
Strachan, John 73, 85, 96, 108, 123,
153, 154
Street, Samuel Jr 68, 74, 76, 82, 119,
120
Strong, Sir Samuel Henry 250, 254,
267, 274, 287
Stuart, Sir James 199
Sullivan, Robert Baldwin 178–9, 185,
186, 199
Supreme Court of Canada: and BNA Act
250–4, 262–76 passim, 280; erection
of 243; reference to 249–50, 252,
263, 265, 274, 275, 276, 302
Swayze, Isaac 80, 86
Sydenham, first baron 165

Talbot, Thomas 106, 107, 108
tar-and-feather outrage 109–14, 116,
121, 133–7 passim, 144, 147, 155, 233
Taschereau, Sir Henri-Elzéar 251, 254
Taylor, Sir Thomas Wardlaw 213
Thomas v Acklam 90–4, 98, 149
Thompson, Sir John 275, 276, 302, 303,
309–10, 379 n.77
Thorpe, Robert 40, 44, 77, 78, 108, 146
Toronto, City of v Bowes 197, 268
trade and commerce: regulation under
BNA Act 260–71 passim, 277–8, 286
treason trials: 1814 83, 161–2, 329; 1866
198, 229

types riot 105, 106, 114, 115, 116, 121,
130–7 passim, 147, 155

Underhill, Frank R. 380 n.14
Union, Act of (1840, UK) 146, 194, 324
Union Bill (1822, UK) 89, 100, 319
United Empire Loyalists 4–5
United States of America: constitution
325–6 (see also Bill of Rights;
separation of powers)
Upper Canada: reunion with Lower
Canada 158
Upper Canada Law Journal 244

Vaara, Aaro 213, 327
Vaughan, Sir John 292
verdict: special 293, 309; unanimous
297, 298
vice-chancellor of Upper Canada:
political role proposed 185
Vincent, Michael 207

Watson, Lord 259, 278, 280
White, John 10, 17–40 passim, 55–6,
71, 76, 139, 168; as district court
judge 21; death 38, 52, 54; political
career 18, 163, 164
Whitney, Sir James P. 317
Wicksteed, Gustavus 187
Willcocks, Joseph 44, 291
Willis, John Walpole 55, 108, 111, 113,
139, 152; and law officers' monopoly
128–33 passim, 136, 137; dismissal
141–50, 152, 153
Willson, John 109, 204–5, 231
Wilmot Horton, Sir Robert 96, 99, 100,
102–3, 165
Wilson, Sir Adam 176, 287, 349 n.67
women: property rights 24, 25, 29, 344
n.28, 345 n.38